Blue Ribbon Edition

From our kitchen to yours.
Cookbook number three

By Debra Stark

Debra's Natural Gourmet
West Concord, Massachusetts

Acknowledgements

To the staff at Debra's Natural Gourmet, past and present, who are like family. To the customers who walk through our doors and have become more than customers. To the farmers and food purveyors who share their stories and food, thank you.

To Meredith Rutter who offered to proof-read even though she was in the middle of writing her own book. I can't believe she got chapters back to me lickety-split.

To everyone on staff and all the customers who allowed me to include their recipes (their names are below). Hugs especially to Jim Leahy and Amanda Loring, who were particularly generous with their recipes.

To my son, Adam Stark, who loves food as much as I do so that when I'm gone, he'll carry on!

To my brother, Daniel Stark, for allowing me to excerpt memories of our mother and the infamous egg drink and exploding bread from his book, *Silence of the Bunnies*.

To my brother, David Stark, who is my art director, IT professional (he did the store's website, www.DebrasNaturalGourmet.com) and solver of my creative problems. Need a cookbook? Davey can do it. Thank you, David.

To Pop for bringing home the bacon (so to speak) so Mom could feed us all the way she did, which eventually led to Debra's Natural Gourmet.

So, thanks to one and all, and here's to the next 20 years and the next 20 years after that.

*These wonderful people who work at Debra's Natural Gourmet allowed me to use their recipes: Kelly Abroms, Will Banfield, Roxanne Bispham, Daniel Buonaiuto, Jocelyn Clark, Lindsey Collins, Alex Gardner, Kevin Gerstel, Janet Hamilton, Alyssa Held, Denise Johnson, Jennifer Johnston, Mary Kadlik, Aaron Kagan, Kenyon Keily, Piera Landau, Chris Lawson, Jim Leahy, Amanda Loring, Matt Merlino, Debbie McCormack, Ray Mong, Cindy Price, Martha Rounds, Donna Seigel, Mary Sterling, Jan Taylor, Mary Jane Wuensch and Tom Yates

Debra Stark / Publisher

Design and production by David Stark
Cover photograph by Neal Higgins

Debra's Natural Gourmet
98 Commonwealth Ave.
West Concord, MA 01742
978.371.7573
www.DebrasNaturalGourmet.com

ISBN 978-0-9742627-2-7

Rev. 1.27.13

CONTENTS

INTRODUCTION

This book is a combination of wonderful, easy to make recipes together with stories about life and laughter. You get to feel the love!

Who doesn't want to be happy, feel sassy and look great? What, you ask, does a cookbook have to do with that?

Well, feeling healthy and looking good are as much about the foods we eat as they are about all those other primal things in life such as laughter, love, friendship and family.

When we nourish ourselves with real food and fresh foods grown organically, our bodies can function at optimal levels. We feel younger and more energetic. We look terrific. As has been said so many times, we are what we eat. There are simply no ands, ifs or buts about it!

In our 3rd cookbook, you'll find more than 250 recipes for dishes that are down-home and old-fashioned; and you'll find recipes that are simple, but fancy enough for company. Most of the recipes in this book are fast and easy, and leave you time to learn the tango!

Eat Well, Be Happy
Debra Stark

NOTES ABOUT THIS AND THAT

In my first two books, I wrote pages defining ingredients and about how to cook things like beans. Since then, we've grown up together, and I know you know how to cook beans (or prefer to buy Eden canned beans). I also know you're not shy and will feel free to ask any questions. Come into the store, or give me a call at 978-371-7573.

So I'll be moseying on. Here are some notes, not in any particular order…

1. Organic. Simply put, organic is better for us and for the environment. I am certain that food grown without pesticides and herbicides, grown the old-fashioned way, the sustainable way—is higher in nutrient values. And organically-grown food sure is safer for the farmer workers.

Although I've not said "organic" in the ingredient listing, know that whenever possible, we use organic ingredients in the store and in our homes. 90% of the time it is possible!

2. Is organic more expensive? Well, commercially and conventionally-grown food prices (as you've heard me say many times before) don't reflect hidden costs such as federal subsidies to farmers who grow non-organically, pesticide regulation and testing, hazardous waste disposal and cleanup, environmental damage, increased health care costs due to exposure to carcinogens, and the harm done to our farm workers exposed to those chemicals.

I once read that if you add those costs up, a commercially grown head of lettuce today costs each one of us more than $5.

3. Greasing: Use a thin film of half liquid soya lecithin and half vegetable oil or butter. Liquid lecithin alone is too thick to spread easily. Diluting with oil works like magic. I always keep a jar of the lecithin/oil mixture on hand in the cupboard to grease with. To grease, use a pastry brush to spread mixture. Nothing will stick to your pans if you grease this way.

4. Eat all kinds of foods. When you sit down to eat, enjoy looking at your plate. You should have a rainbow of colors, and varied shapes and textures. Your plate should look like a beautiful painting!

5. Don't be afraid of eating foods like good fats, walnuts, and sea salt or coconut sugar, just to name a few. I look at what other countries and cultures eat. I have fun exploring their food traditions. I remind myself that most everything is good, in balance and harmony.

6. We keep learning everyday. Too bad I hadn't started using sprouted flours when I typed the dessert chapter, or even years ago. Mom used to give us Food for Life

Sprouted Breads when she was out of her own bread. The Food for Life Sprouted Breads always made me feel good, and I love them still today. We use their breads for many of the sandwiches we make in our kitchen in the store too. The sprouting of the grains yields "flour" that digests like a vegetable instead of like a starch. Obviously, if you don't have access to sprouted flours, use what you have.

Let me end my notes to you all with part of a column Adam wrote for our store newsletter in October 2009. It expresses how we all feel about the grand adventure of food.

THE TEN HEALTHIEST FOODS

Adam Stark

I've never done a Ten Healthiest Foods list, mostly because I don't believe in them. Well, I guess I'm a hypocrite now!

Here's how this is going to work. I'm not going to limit myself to ten. I'm just going to keep writing until I use up my three pages. I'm going to exclude foods that feel more like supplements (so no spirulina or hawthorn berry); brand-name products (Manna bread), and foods that bear too disturbing a resemblance to the ectoplasm in the movie *Ghost Busters*.

I won't rank foods based on what they *have*, but rather what they *are*, and what they *do*. So much nutritional advice these days is based on the reductionist idea that we can understand a food by quantifying a few dozen nutrients, "adding up" the good ones, and "subtracting" the bad ones. It's mathematical! And yet by this logic, a vat of margarine "fortified with 13 essential vitamins and minerals" might be a healthy snack. Meanwhile, green tea—with no vitamins and minerals worth mentioning—wouldn't even show up on the charts. And then there's this bizarre idea that calories are inherently "bad"...?!

(Debra's note: On this subject, Michael Pollan's *In Defense of Food*, is a great read.)

In the end, I'm not looking for "complete" or "perfect" foods. In fact, nothing on this list will have all the nutrients essential to support life. Some of them won't even have the nutrients essential to support a decent snack. What I'm looking for here are foods that can add a little something special to an already-healthy diet.

Perhaps the most nutritious thing to eat is variety. (In alphabetical, not numerical order....)

1. Cacao (the chocolate bean) is a profound antioxidant. Unfortunately, cacao is usually synonymous with white sugar, white flour and hydrogenated oil. But it doesn't have to be. Cacao has been shown to reduce wrinkles, strengthen the structures of the vascular system, and improve circulation to the brain. Due to caffeine content and other reasons, you don't want to eat *enormous* amounts of this one....

2. Coconut: People just seem to feel good when they eat a lot of coconut. Whole coconut is a very good source of fiber, and potassium. Coconut juice ("coconut water") is an extraordinary source of potassium.

Coconut fats (mostly medium-chain triglycerides) are special fats. They burn quickly and efficiently in the body, so they're both slightly energizing and good for controlling weight. (Adding coconut oil to the diet will not help you lose weight, but *replacing* other oils with coconut will). Meanwhile, because they're so easy to process, MCTs help people keep weight *on* when the liver's ability to process normal fats is compromised.

More about coconut fats: they're some of the most stable for high-heat cooking, and have significant antiviral and antifungal properties as well. I stir-fry crisp veggies in coconut oil; Jim, our store's British manager, breaks from tradition each holiday season when he makes the entire staff Christmas pudding with coconut oil instead of lard.

And now we're seeing coconut sugar in the U.S. Made from the sap of coconut flowers, this is by *far* my favorite sweetener. I mean, maple syrup and raw honey are both wonderful, too, but they taste almost too distinctive to use in a lot of recipes. Coconut sugar, on the other hand, tastes like sugar, crossed with some sort of earthy-yet-heavenly caramel. It can replace cane sugar 1:1 in recipes. And it's got a glycemic index value in the mid-30s, better than just about anything else out there.

3. Dyes... By which I simply mean foods that can stain your clothing. The worse something stains your clothing, generally speaking, the more it protects our cells from damage. So think red wine, grapes, blueberries, turmeric, saffron, beets.... A darker colored version of something is almost always better for you than its lighter cousin. So think black beans versus lima beans, dark cherries versus Rainier cherries. (St. Patrick's Day green beer is an exception to this rule).

4. **Pastured Eggs**: My grandma used to say that the "experts" changed their minds on eggs about once a decade, but she never did. She just kept on eating them.

Pastured eggs come from birds that forage for their own food, all those yummy seeds and grains and worms and bugs. They're much healthier than eggs that are "free range" (a term notorious for meaning as much or as little as people find convenient), or eggs from battery-raised hens. The dark yellow yolks of pastured eggs are rich in the healthy omega-3 fatty acids found in fish oil, and loaded with eye-protecting lutein. With all that, plus their dense phospholipids, pastured eggs are a phenomenal "brain food"—really, a phenomenal food for all of our cell membranes—from infancy through old age.

Eggs also get extra points for being practical. First, for being cheap. Even pastured eggs—and yes, they cost more than regular ones—are a bargain compared to fish, steak or chicken. But practical also means easy and versatile. Dinner, lunch, and breakfast are never more than five minutes away.

(But what about the cholesterol? Well, cholesterol is only a problem when our bodies mismanage it. And eggs are the richest natural source of lecithin, a phospholipid emulsifier that helps us manage it. There have been three solid research trials which have shown that eggs do not raise people's LDL "bad" cholesterol at all).

5. Goji Berries: Some might think this breaks the "no supplements" rule. And it's true: for many people, goji is something they "take" instead of something they "eat," a juice measured by the ounce. But the dried berries are like little raisins. You can munch them, add them to hot cereal, bake them into sweet pilafs, etc.

Goji has immune-building polysaccharides like the ones in medicinal mushrooms, aloe vera, and astragalus root. They're packed with antioxidants of especial value to the eyes, where they strengthen night vision and prevent degeneration. They are a strengthening food in general. Over time they feed the good bacteria in our guts, and reduce LDL cholesterol. Two benefits I've seen only with the juice are greater energy and increased libido in both men and women. (But please note: goji won't do anything "weird" to kids).

6. Green Tea: No other food or beverage has accumulated such impressive research data for preventing just about everything that might kill us. Period.

7. **Fresh Herbs**: No matter what tropical superfruit is crowned by the hype-masters as the next "king" antioxidant, it will pale in comparison to the oregano, basil, thyme, and rosemary growing in our back yards. Look at the USDA ORAC data. It's amazing.

8. Maitake Mushrooms: Most gourmet mushrooms are deeply immune strengthening, but Maitake is king. Yeah, it's weird-looking. Sauté in a little butter or oil—don't worry, it's supposed to break into little pieces—and then add to grain dishes (especially buckwheat and/or barley), sauces, and soups. It tastes a little like chicken.

9. Pomegranate: According to some pretty solid research, pomegranate lowers heart disease risk big-time. It's too early to say, but it might do the same for cancer as well. And a recent study ranking various juices for antioxidant levels put pomegranate at the very top. (2nd place, incidentally, went to our very own Concord grape, followed by blueberry, black cherry, açaí, cranberry, orange, and then apple—see "Dyes.")

10. Seaweed: Our richest source of trace minerals, period; and one of our best detoxifiers for toxic heavy metals. A sprinkle of kelp or dulse adds a pleasant mineral saltiness to savory foods. Go easy on them, though, as it's possible to get too much iodine.

11. Sesame: The only way to explain what makes sesame special is to get deep into the science of the liver, and the pathways of essential fatty acid metabolism. So I won't. Just trust me: sesame improves the way we process fats—especially the healthy essential fatty acids found in fish, flax, nuts and seeds, pastured eggs, borage, and evening primrose—and fatty antioxidants, like the vitamin E tocopherols. This isn't something sesame does *better* than other foods; as far as I've been able to tell, this is something that *only* sesame does.

I love adding a spoonful of tahini (roasted sesame seed butter) to sauces, dressings, pilafs, and soups—especially minestrone and miso. It's one of the most versatile things in my pantry.

12. Stocks: My grandmother always saved the water from steaming vegetables. "Don't pour it down the sink!" she'd say. "That's where all the vitamins are!" (To which I'd ask, if all the vitamins are in the water, then why do I have to eat the vegetables?)

Whether or not we want it to, hot water picks up a lot of nutrition from food. By making a stock, we do this on purpose, salvaging nutrition from parts of the food we otherwise compost or throw away: onion peels and shiitake stems, bones and the pieces of meat that hang on to bones, fish heads and shrimp tails, etc.

I don't believe in recipes for stock. Instead, I collect kitchen scraps in plastic bags in my freezer. I keep a bag each for vegetables, meat, mushrooms and shellfish. When I have enough material, I make stock, mixing and matching, adding a bit of salt or rosemary, or maybe onion or garlic. Each time, it tastes a little different.

Bone broth is extraordinarily good for supporting the bones and tissues of the body. Mushroom broth (in my kitchen, always from shiitake stems) is a wonderful immune strengthener.

13. Turmeric: This curry spice will raise the antioxidant status of the liver and reduce cholesterol levels in the blood. Research also strongly suggests it may prevent age-related cognitive decline including Alzheimer's disease, and cancer. It's a good anti-inflammatory. And it appears to fight herpes as well.

14. Almost Made The Cut: Caviar (or the much cheaper "fish eggs" you get on sushi), beets, burdock root, undenatured whey protein, cold-water fatty fish, high mineral content waters, liver, marrow, flax seeds, and fermented foods. And I've always had a hunch that mulberries and poppy seeds were both tremendously healthy in some magical way. But I've never been able to find any data. Anyone have any, let me know!

Appetizers

I am always in a quandary about appetizers. They're supposed to whet the appetite, but they usually fill us up so we really don't need anything else to eat. We're full before the main meal. Do I really want everyone to feel as if they need to be carted away from the table in a wheelbarrow?

And preparing appetizers is often the straw that breaks the camel's back. It's almost as if a whole second meal needs to be prepared. Even if you enjoy cooking, which I do, you think, oh my gosh, I need appetizers too. You have to start all over again. Am I the only one who feels this way?

Do you need another reason to cast a jaundiced eye on appetizers? Well, they give people an excuse to arrive fashionably late for dinner. Appetizers mean no one dies of hunger while waiting for the last guests to arrive. This is both good and bad because entrées can only stay in the oven so long before they shrivel up!

Hmmm, you're thinking, should I even bother with this chapter? Well, yes, you should. There are some wonderful recipes and wonderful ideas. Just chalk this harangue up to momentary madness.

Recipes That Don't Need Recipes

There are tons of recipes that don't need recipes, and these often make great appetizers. Have you ever stuffed a Medjool date with nut butter or cream cheese? Take Medjool date and cut open, take out seed and put about a teaspoon of almond butter inside cavity and lightly close the date. You can use peanut butter, sunflower butter, cashew nut butter or cream cheese. My favorite is pistachio nut butter. And you can stuff celery the same way instead of using dates. Cut your celery in bite-sized pieces before filling.

Lassis: A drink made with yogurt or kefir. Try mixing some yogurt or kefir with a little water and cinnamon and honey. Serve in pretty little glasses. Tell everyone to sip before a meal because it helps with digestion.

Please do refer to our first two cookbooks for more appetizer recipes like the tried and true hummus!

Alyssa's Salmon Gravlax

Alyssa says, "If you have never tried this you simply must! Try it with crispy potato latkes and a dollop of sour cream, or roll it with avocado for instant 'sushi.' My family's favorite!

"Growing up in New York, we had 'appetizing' every Sunday. It was the Jewish tradition and consisted of fresh bagels, cream cheese and smoked fish—especially 'lox' (smoked salmon). I always loved this, but found the lox too slimy, smoky and salty. Later, in culinary school, I stumbled upon a recipe for gravlax and was amazed at its clean, fresh flavor.

"What is gravlax? Gravlax is salmon that is cooked without heat. Rather, it is cured by salt and other ingredients in the refrigerator. I have tried making gravlax many ways—with different herbs and different alcohols—but the method below is by far the best. It gives the salmon a light and refreshing taste. In my house, if you turn your back on your gravlax, it just may disappear directly into my daughter's mouth!"

Serves 8

SPICE MIX
¼ C sea salt
2 Tbsp black pepper
¼ C coconut sugar
cheesecloth
perforated pan and underpan to
    catch drippings (the set that
    came with your oven works fine)

THE REST
1 2 lb salmon fillet (pinbones
    removed)
½ C lemon juice
3 Tbsp vodka
1 bunch fresh dill
heavy cans or bricks to weigh down
    fish as it cures

In a small bowl combine salt, pepper and sugar and mix well. Lay a very large piece of cheesecloth down in a perforated pan (the one with drain holes). Make sure the cheesecloth is twice the size of the pan. Place salmon skin-side down on the cheesecloth. Cover the salmon well with spice mix. Then pour lemon juice over the filet. Sprinkle filet with vodka. Cover with dill. Cover the whole thing with cheesecloth. Then cover top only with plastic wrap or tin foil. Place weights on top of the package and place in refrigerator with underpan under perforated pan to catch the drippings.

In about 12-16 hours remove weights and plastic wrap or foil, and turn the package over. Replace foil or plastic wrap and weight. Let gravlax cure in the refrigerator for another 12-16 hours. Repeat this process once more (turn only one more time), and let gravlax cure 12 hours more. Remove all dill and scrape off spices. Slice very thinly on the diagonal and enjoy!

BAKED BEETS OR ARTICHOKE HEARTS Á LA ORANGE

Beets *or* artichoke hearts? How can one swing from an earthy root vegetable to the delectable, light artichoke heart? Not to worry. This recipe works with either beets or artichoke hearts, and I bet you could use it with fiddleheads, asparagus, mushrooms, olives or turnips and carrots too.

Serve as part of an antipasto or put out in a pretty bowl. Finger food for good friends!

Makes about 2 cups

2 C sliced beets, or 2 C artichoke
    hearts*
½ C blood orange juice*
¼ tsp fennel seeds

4-6 cloves garlic, sliced
2 Tbsp extra virgin olive oil (EVOO)
1 tsp black pepper (optional)

Preheat oven to 325 degrees.

Combine ingredients and bake uncovered until vegetables are heated through and tender, about 20 minutes. Cool slightly. Serve warm.

*I cannot tell a lie. I sometimes use frozen artichoke hearts. I also use Volcano brand blood orange juice if I can't get fresh blood oranges.

Buckwheat Blinis with Mushroom Caviar by Amanda

This one ran in our December 2008 store newsletter. Amanda says, "Have you ever made blinis? They're yeasted savory pancakes, traditionally served with caviar and crème fraîche. This version with mushroom caviar is fun to make (and gluten-free because buckwheat is not related to wheat and is actually a fruit). Use any mushrooms you like and get creative with seasonings too. Make these for your next party!"

Serves 12

12 oz mushrooms, about ¾ lb
2 tsp sea salt
1 Tbsp lemon juice
2 Tbsp walnut oil
1 tsp fresh thyme leaves
3 Tbsp fresh parsley
1 tsp black pepper

1¼ C milk of any kind
1 tsp baking yeast
2 tsp sea salt
1⅓ C light buckwheat flour
2 eggs, separated
oil for "frying"
1 C sour cream or Greek yogurt
minced red onion or chives (optional)

Make mushroom caviar ahead of time: Wipe mushrooms clean of any visible dirt with a damp cloth or paper towel. Chop fine. Place mushrooms in a bowl and sprinkle with the 2 tsp of sea salt. Cover and leave for 2 hours. Then rinse off salty water and pat dry. Toss with lemon juice, walnut oil, thyme, parsley and black pepper. Taste and see if you want any additional salt because this is your caviar!

Making the blinis is a little tricky, but well worth the effort. Heat milk until barely warm (about 110°). Remove from heat, pour into a bowl, add yeast and dissolve by stirring. Let stand for a few minutes. The yeast will begin to bubble. It's alive! Add the salt, flour and egg yolks and stir. Cover with damp cloth or plastic wrap and put in a warm place to rise for 30 minutes. When you have about 5 minutes left of rising time, beat egg whites until they stand in stiff peaks. Fold egg white into risen batter and get ready to fry!

Heat griddle or large skillet until very hot and lightly oil with a nice high-heat oil like macadamia, grapeseed or coconut. Drop spoonfuls of the batter onto the hot griddle and cook until large bubbles appear. Turn, cook briefly on the other side and flip them onto a waiting plate. Garnish blinis with the sour cream or thick Greek yogurt, a generous dollop of mushroom caviar and some minced red onion or chives (or both). Voila! They're fantastic!

CHUNKY CHICKPEA AND SPINACH APPETIZER WITH ROASTED PEPPERS

Serves 4-6 with crudités

1 can Eden chickpeas, about 2 C
   cooked
2 C roasted sweet bell peppers*, diced
2 Tbsp extra virgin olive oil (EVOO)
4 cloves garlic, pressed
1 tsp cumin powder
1 tsp coriander powder
1 tsp ginger powder

1 tsp chili powder
1 tsp black pepper
2 Tbsp tomato paste
4 C baby spinach
¼ C water
yogurt (optional)
naan, pita bread or chapattis
   (optional)

Mash chickpeas and set aside. Dice roasted peppers and set aside.

In a large skillet, gently warm EVOO. Add garlic and sauté. Add spices and warm them until they are aromatic. When they are (about a minute or two), add tomato paste, baby spinach, water, chickpeas and roasted peppers. Cover skillet and simmer for 5 minutes until spinach is wilted.

This makes a flavorful appetizer spooned into a decorative bowl and served with a dollop of yogurt on top. Or serve with naan, pita bread or chapattis as scoopers.

I buy the jarred roasted peppers. I usually have a jar of red and a jar of yellow roasted peppers in my cupboard for culinary emergencies!

COCONUT OIL POPCORN

This recipe is from *The Maker's Diet* by Jordan S. Rubin, and Garden of Life demo person (beyond compare) Carol McDonough has made it in our store so many times that we feel it must be our recipe! It's not, and here it is for you to make in your home.

Coconut oil has a very high "flash point," which is the point when an oil starts to smoke and becomes a trans-fat (you don't want trans-fats in your diet). And because of its high flash point (over 400 degrees Celsius), coconut oil is a healthy, high heat cooking oil. Butter has a slightly lower flash point, which means you typically want to add butter at the end of cooking. Flax seed oil is damaged by heat, so don't cook with it!

If you don't have access to a garlic-chili flax oil, use plain flax oil and sprinkle on your own garlic and chili powders.

Serves 2-4

3 Tbsp extra virgin coconut oil
½ C popping corn
2 Tbsp butter

2 Tbsp garlic-chili flax oil
Herbamare seasoning to taste
 (start with 1 tsp)

Melt coconut oil in pan over medium heat. Pour popping corn into pan. Cover pan with lid quickly! While popping, melt butter in second pan. When corn is popped, pour into large bowl and add butter, garlic-chili flax seed oil and Herbamare. Mix thoroughly and enjoy every last popped kernel.

Thanks, Garden of Life!

DONNA'S KALE-AVOCADO-DATE ROLL-UP

Donna says, "Adapted by my husband, Gene, from a David Wolfe principle, this is very simple to make and is healthy too. I made this for the recent potluck here at Debra's and everybody really liked it."

Kale is known as the king of calcium, avocado is a great source of healthy fats and has more potassium than a banana, and mineral-rich Medjool dates are a delectable sweet.

Makes 8 roll-ups

4 large lacinato kale leaves
2 large Hass avocados, mashed

4 Medjool dates, sliced lengthwise and pitted

Remove the spine from each lacinato kale leaf so that you have the 2 halves of each leaf ready to roll up.

Spread 1 Tbsp mashed avocado on each ½ kale leaf. Place ½ Medjool date at the tip of the leaf and rollup tightly. Put a toothpick through the roll-up and serve!

Note from Debra: When I made these, I couldn't leave well enough alone and added a pinch of cayenne pepper and a little lemon juice. Another time I used 1 C of sesame tahini in lieu of an avocado. A third time I made these, I first steamed the kale, cooled the leaves and then filled.

Eggplant Cilantro Spread

Serve this savory spread with pita bread wedges. Summertime is a perfect time to make this, and I look forward each year to having a bumper crop of peppers, eggplants and cilantro to harvest. If you don't have a vegetable garden, consider starting one. If you don't like to grow things, then I know you'll support all the local farmers and stores who have fresh, local and organic produce in your area.

One of my favorite websites, www.vegparadise.com, says the following about eggplants: "Though eggplant was little known in the average household of the mid 1800's, it was one of President Andrew Johnson's favorite foods, especially Stuffed Eggplant Spanish Style. Prepared for intimate gatherings, the eggplant was first halved and the flesh chopped. The stuffing was a combination of tomatoes, onions, breadcrumbs and celery, and seasoned with basil butter, salt, pepper and a touch of sugar. Before they were served, the eggplants were garnished with overlapping fresh tomato slices and a strip of broiled bacon.

"With the arrival of Chinese and Italian immigrants to the U.S. during the late 1800's, new cuisines established permanent residence. Many cities, such as Detroit and New York, offered immigrant gardeners the use of vacant lots to grow their familiar vegetables like eggplants, tomatoes and peppers."

Makes 3 cups

1 large eggplant (about 2 lb), cut into ½-inch rounds	½ C chopped cilantro
½ C extra virgin olive oil (EVOO)	3 Tbsp lemon juice
1 yellow pepper, halved and seeded	1 tsp paprika
1 red pepper, halved and seeded	½ tsp ground cumin
1 C red onion, finely chopped	10 cloves garlic, pressed with garlic press

Prepare barbecue. Brush eggplant and toss peppers with EVOO. Grill eggplant and peppers until tender and eggplant is golden and the peppers' edges curled and browned, about 5 minutes per side. Cool both and then chop coarsely. Mix in onions and remaining ingredients. Season to taste with salt and pepper.

Cover and refrigerate. Serve cold or at room temp. A big yum-yum-yum for this appetizer.

GREEK YOGURT WITH ZA'ATAR

An easy, breezy summer appetizer that first appeared in our July 2004 newsletter. Of course you can use it to build an even easier summer meal.

What is Za'atar? Otherwise known as "the holy hyssop," it is a Middle Eastern seasoning mix typically made from hyssop, Israeli sumac (different from American sumac), sesame seeds, thyme, parsley and sea salt. Refrigerate after opening to keep fresh. I fell in love with Za'atar in Israel over 40 years ago.

Greek yogurt is to die for. Like sour cream only better because it's got gut-friendly, probiotic bacteria.

Enough to cover 1 dinner plate

1 C Greek yogurt   **1 Tbsp Za'atar**
3 Tbsp extra virgin olive oil (EVOO) **2 Tbsp pine nuts**

Using a rubber spatula, spoon out Greek yogurt onto a dinner-size plate (I much prefer the yogurt that has fat as opposed to the fat-free versions). Swirl yogurt so plate is covered, leaving ½-inch clear around the sides of the plate. Drizzle with EVOO, sprinkle with Za'atar and pine nuts. Serve with whole-grain pita or veggies.

How to make this a great summer dinner? Put out on table with a plate of sliced red, yellow and orange tomatoes garnished with chopped fresh basil, a bowl of taboulie and a dish of succulent olives. Round that assortment off with a plate of cucumber rounds, and voila!

If you want to make this meal more substantial, grill chicken or shrimp sprinkled with Za'atar. Or toss together a can of organic black beans and 2 C organic corn (fresh or frozen). Season that with Za'atar too!

How else to use Za'atar? Liz, who used to work in our kitchen, liked to drizzle veggies with EVOO, grill them and sprinkle with Za'atar. Liz's favorite way to use Za'atar was to mix a spoonful into Bariani olive oil and use as a dipping oil for bread or crudités.

Tsippi Lasman says to cut pita bread into wedges, brush with olive oil, sprinkle with Za'atar and then toast in a hot oven for 5-10 minutes. Cool and serve nice and crunchy. Nibble on pita wedges or dip in our hummus.

Guacamole with Lots of Garlic

There's been a guacamole recipe in each of our cookbooks because it's one of my favorite appetizers. I always make Mom's Corn Crisps (in the bread chapter) to put out alongside, but simple, organic, store-bought corn chips work too.

I know you know how healthy avocados are. I know you know that the fat in avocados is also good for us. Did you know that avocados even have a fair amount of protein?

Serves 4-8 depending upon what else you serve and how fanatic people are about their guacamole

4 Hass avocados (halved, peeled and pitted)*
juice of 2 lemons or limes, about 1 C
1 tsp sea salt
12 cloves garlic, pressed with garlic press

½ C diced red onion
4 Tbsp chopped fresh cilantro
4 plum tomatoes, diced
pinch cayenne (optional)

In a medium bowl, mash together the avocados, lemon or lime juice and salt. Mix in garlic, onion, cilantro and tomatoes. Stir in cayenne pepper.

Note: Do you have some ripe avocados but no time to make guacamole? Mash avocadoes and add 1 C of your favorite salsa.

*Save pits. If you're not serving immediately, press pits into guacamole and cover with plastic wrap. The pits help prevent the dip from turning brown for a couple of hours.

KELLEY'S BAKED KALE CHIPS

Kelley says, "I was inspired to come up with this recipe because along with Adam, I became a huge fan of the raw kale chips made by Blessings at Alive and Radiant Foods that we sell in the store. My favorite flavors are 'cheesy' and 'ranch.'

"At the moment, I don't have a dehydrator, so I used my oven, which means they're not really raw. My daughter, Josie, can attest to the fact they're still very yummy. Even for those of us who grew up with French fries, these are a hit."

Serves 4   *Bake at 350 degrees*

1 large bunch curly kale   **1 Tbsp sea salt**
1 Tbsp extra virgin olive oil (EVOO)   **1 tsp black pepper**

Preheat oven to 350 degrees.

Strip stems off kale. Rip leaves into bite-sized pieces and put pieces into a bowl. Add EVOO and mix well with your hands. Spread on a baking tray and sprinkle with sea salt and pepper.

Put tray in preheated oven and bake for approximately 15 minutes. Keep an eye on the kale. Light brown is okay, but you don't want it to burn.

Eat while warm and crunchy.

Note from Kelley: I've also added nutritional yeast at the end to make the kale 'cheesy.'

Note from Debra: If you wash your kale, make sure it's dry before you toss with EVOO and sprinkle with salt and pepper. You can spin it pretty dry in a salad spinner. I have to admit that I don't always wash veggies if I know they're organic and if they look bug and dirt-free! If you don't wash the kale, it's dry and you don't have to use a salad spinner.

Marinated Mushrooms with Blue Cheese

I love cheese and mostly use it when entertaining and with appetizers. Here's an easy recipe with mushrooms, which I also love.

Serves a crowd as an appetizer, 8 when tossed in a salad

4 C fresh button mushrooms	2 tsp sea salt
1 C extra virgin olive oil (EVOO)	1 tsp black pepper
¼ C Tbsp lemon juice	1 tsp dried oregano
¼ C apple cider vinegar	1 tsp dried basil
4 cloves garlic, pressed with garlic press	½ C blue cheese, crumbled

Wipe mushrooms with a clean dry cloth to remove any dirt. Cut off stems and save those for soups or to make a vegetable broth.

Put whole mushrooms together with all the remaining ingredients into a large mixing bowl. Toss with your hands so you can feel mushrooms are coated with everything and blue cheese is nicely dispersed.

Cover and refrigerate 4-6 hours before serving. These make a great addition to an antipasto. They are also nice in a pretty bowl with a little spoon served next to a plate of sturdy crackers.

Note: I've used these marinated mushrooms with blue cheese as my salad dressing tossed with romaine or leafy greens.

MARY'S FIG AND GOAT CHEESE APPETIZER

Mary says, "I made this huge salad one night with many, many ingredients, and in the middle of dinner I picked up a slice of fig, topped it with the cheese and said to my husband, Don, 'This is delicious; wouldn't it make a great appetizer?' He tried it and agreed. A recipe was born."

Did you know that figs are actually a flower inverted into itself? Not I, said the fly! What *did* I know about figs? That they are native to the Middle East and one of the first fruits ever to be cultivated. That the state of California grows more figs than any country except Turkey and Greece. Mary says she knew that figs have lots of fiber and more calcium weight-for-weight than whole milk. She knew that the calcium from figs is more easily absorbed than the calcium from milk.

Serves 8 as a light appetizer

8 fresh Calymyrna figs, trimmed and halved lengthwise

4 oz soft goat cheese (at room temperature)

As easy as 1, 2, 3. Trim and halve the figs. Slice each half into 2 or 3 wedges. Top each wedge with the goat cheese (soft goat cheese becomes spreadable at room temperature). Serve with toothpicks. Follow with dental floss, suggests Mary.

Note from Debra: Alternatively, you can trim figs and cut into half lengthwise. You can then press your thumb into the center of each fig, make an indentation and fill cavities with softened goat cheese. Garnish with 2 Tbsp pine nuts. Or you can mix the pine nuts and ½ tsp cumin into your goat cheese, and use that mixture to fill cavities. Some people like to fill figs with goat cheese and garnish with a dollop of jam.

MOM'S STUFFED SHRIMP

When I was growing up in Orlando, Florida, my mom made these only for special occasions. She used a platter we bought in Mexico which was bright with exotic birds, and she put the platter and shrimp on a coffee table my father had made. We were allowed to help ourselves only after the last guest had helped him/herself. The waiting was torture, and I could never understand why she didn't make these at least once a week! Now I know they are a culinary indulgence and that we need to concentrate on eating plant foods, both for our own health and for the health of our planet.

Serves 8 people three shrimp each

6 C water
24 fresh jumbo shrimp, unpeeled
¼ C green onion, finely chopped

3 oz cream cheese, softened
3 oz blue cheese, crumbled
½ tsp black pepper

Bring the water to a boil and add shrimp. Cook 3 to 5 minutes. Drain well and rinse with cold water. Chill in the refrigerator (at least 30 minutes). Peel, devein and butterfly shrimp. How? Cut along the curved back almost through to the other side of the shrimp. Open each like a book and remove intestinal vein.

Combine remaining ingredients and stuff each shrimp with about 1 tsp of the cheese mixture. Put stuffed shrimp on serving platter. Cover and chill at least 1 hour.

Put these out about an hour before you want to serve as they taste better at room temperature. Keep the kids away or the shrimp will all be gone in a minute!

MY FAVORITE CRUDITÉ PLATTER

A crudité platter can be anything you choose to make it. I like the combination of good old tried-and-true foods together with some surprises. I like some things raw and some things grilled or roasted, and something oil-cured.

I put things helter-skelter on a large oval platter. I don't like concentric designs or carrots all around the perimeter of the plate too-arranged, too-organized. I like carrots *here* in a clump and then olives next to the carrots in their own mound. And so on around the plate. The end result is a wild profusion of different colors and different shapes that stand out, each on their own. And how can you go wrong with the colors and variety provided by Mother Nature?

Serves 12

1 head cauliflower, broken into florets
grilled veggies like eggplant rounds
1 yellow squash, slices or strips
1 zucchini, slices or strips
2 C oil-cured black olives
1 red onion, cut into wedges

1 red, yellow, orange pepper cut
   into strips
2 C sugar snap peas
1 lb bag baby carrots
1 large jicama, peeled and sliced
   thinly

Take out all your fixings. (Do you need all of the above? No. Feel free to use other things like marinated mushrooms or roasted beets. I do. I use what I have in my refrigerator or what's seasonal.)

Steam cauliflower in a pot with 1-2 C of water for a few minutes. (I don't like hard, raw cauliflower.)

To grill or roast veggies. Slice. Toss with some olive oil, salt and pepper and put on a tray into a very hot oven—450 degrees, or put onto a hot grill and cook veggies until they begin to brown and are tooth-tender. Turn halfway through the process.

Plate by breaking with color. And when you come to softer vegetables like eggplant or zucchini or yellow squash, gently overlap slices so they're easy to take and remain intact. Put red onions and peppers on plate so their shiny side is up.

PICKLED VEGETABLES FOR FINGER DIPPING

This one sounds too simple to be good, but good it is! Put this up and keep cold. Pickled veggies keep for several weeks in the refrigerator.

I like these served with hummus, with cheese, with burgers or on their own.

Makes 2-3 cups

MARINADE
½ C rice or umeboshi vinegar
1 Tbsp extra virgin olive oil
2 bay leaves
1 tsp dried basil

VEGETABLES FOR DIPPING
2 C vegetables like diced celery, carrot rounds, sliced beets, onion or cabbage chunks, or halved and sliced cukes, zucchini or yellow squash

Prepare marinade by whisking together in large measuring cup. Set aside.

Bring 3-4 C of water to a boil and drop vegetables into pot. Turn off heat, cover pot and let stand for 2-3 minutes. Drain. Put veggies into glass bowl or large jar. Pour in marinade. Refrigerate.

If your family likes things spicy, add a hot pepper to the mixture. If they like things garlicky, add garlic cloves once your veggies are in the bowl or jars. Like ginger? Add some minced or grated ginger.

Note: I like to use an assortment of vegetables and make sure the mixture is colorful. I also always make way more than this recipe calls for. So I multiply everything by 4 or even 8. I use wide-mouth peanut butter jars that I save and use and reuse.

Pumpkin Seed Tomatillo Dip

This is from our first cookbook, now out of print. Over the years, I've seen our recipes pop up elsewhere as people adapt and make them their own, but I've never seen anyone claim this one. It really makes a terrific party dip with tortilla chips. I've used it as a topping for grains or beans, and for chicken and fish too.

We make this dip to this day in our kitchen because people love it.

Pumpkin seeds were used medicinally by Native Americans for the treatment of digestive problems. From 1863 to 1936, the United States Pharmacopoeia listed pumpkin seeds as a treatment for intestinal parasites, and although we don't know how or why, we do know that pumpkin seeds ease urinary problems. They also exhibit antioxidant activity and anti-inflammatory properties.

Makes 4 cups

2 C tomatillos, husked
1 C pumpkin seeds*, hulled of course!
4 large garlic cloves
½ tsp coriander
¼ C fresh parsley
2 jalapeño peppers, seeded

2½ Tbsp lime juice
½ C water
1 tsp sea salt
1 tsp black pepper
2 Tbsp extra virgin olive oil (EVOO)
minced red onion as garnish

Placed husked tomatillos in a pot with enough water to cover. Bring to a boil, cook for 2 minutes and then drain.

Roast pumpkin seeds in a 350 degree oven on a cookie sheet for 4 minutes, until lightly toasted and fragrant, but still green.* Cool.

Using quick on/off turns of the food processor (use the steel blade), puree tomatillos, pumpkin seeds, garlic, coriander, parsley, jalapeño peppers, lime juice, water, salt and pepper together with EVOO.

Taste and adjust seasoning. You may want more pepper or more salt. Serve in a bowl garnished with chopped red onion.

This recipe is chockablock full of nutrition.

*You can save yourself some time by buying pumpkin seeds that are already roasted. As long as you know they're nice and fresh, there's no reason not to.

SEVICHE BY ALYSSA

"Seviche," says Alyssa, "is a delicious cold fish dish that makes a superb hors d'oeuvre or appetizer. It is very flavorful and very colorful as well. The fish is cooked by marinating it in lime juice. No heat is involved! I like to serve it in toasted corn cups with a garnish of cilantro. It is also fun to serve it as an appetizer for a dinner party in martini glasses with a slice of lime on the rim. Serve this *immediately* as it is best the first day."

Makes about 2 cups

1 lb of any firm, white fish or scallops
juice and zest of 3 limes
1 bunch cilantro, about ½ C of leaves
1 jalapeño, seeds removed, diced
1 C red onion, diced

1 C sweet red pepper, diced
2 Tbsp extra virgin olive oil (EVOO)
1 tsp sea salt
1 tsp black pepper
1 ripe Hass avocado

Dice the fish filets into bite-sized pieces and marinate them in the lime juice, refrigerated, for about 3 hours. You will be able to tell when the fish is fully "cooked" because it will be white when it is done, just as it looks when cooked with heat! Alternatively, marinate scallops the same way.

Add all remaining ingredients except the avocado, and stir to combine. Marinate fish or scallops in the refrigerator another 30 minutes. Then taste and adjust the flavor with salt and pepper. Just before service, dice the avocado and toss very gently with the mixture.

As an hors d'oeuvre: Serve in corn chip cups or on endive leaves. You can also serve these in cucumber cups. To make cucumber cups, take English cucumbers and cut into ¾-inch rounds. Using a melon baller, cut out a small scoop in the center of each piece. Fill with the seviche. Garnish with cilantro.

As an appetizer: Serve by placing the seviche in martini glasses garnished with slices of lime on the rim.

Shiitake Mushrooms with Garlic

In a 1974 study, researchers concluded that shiitakes had "completely nullified" the effect on cholesterol in the participants when they consumed 60 grams of butter daily. Another study reported that women who consumed ⅓ of an ounce of dried shiitake or 3 ounces of fresh every day for 7 days had their total cholesterol levels drop between 7-12%.

Today shiitakes have achieved "star-celebrity" status in the culinary world. You might find them called "Chinese black mushrooms" or "golden oat mushrooms." They are chewy, meaty and have an earthy, smoky flavor.

Serves 6-8 as an appetizer

4 oz dried shiitakes*
¼ C extra virgin olive oil (EVOO)
¼ C garlic, pressed

1 tsp sea salt
1 tsp black pepper
1 Tbsp dill weed (optional)
1 C pesto (optional)

Soak dried shiitakes in 8 C hot water for about 30 minutes. Squeeze out excess liquid (save broth to drink as tea or put into soups).

Gently warm EVOO in skillet and sauté mushrooms with garlic, salt and pepper. Serve alongside the entrée, or as a special appetizer.

Note: Alternatively, you can toss shiitakes with your favorite pesto and then roast in a 350-degree for about 20 minutes.

*If you want to use fresh shiitakes, use about 8 oz. (This is about 4 C fresh.)

String Beans and Eggs by Beatrice

Boy, did I hate this as a child! As an adult, I've come to appreciate and love this greener version of what my mom used to call "faux chopped liver." Leftovers make a wonderful lunch the next day, and I like to add a tomato served on the side for color.

American Indians planted beans around the base of corn plants because all American beans at that time were vines, "bush beans" having come onto the scene in this generation. Cornstalks were a great trellis for the beans, and the beans gave corn much-needed nitrogen.

Serves 4

½ C extra virgin olive oil (EVOO)
1 C mushrooms, finely diced
1 C red onion, finely diced
2 C string beans, steamed

6 hardboiled eggs
2 cloves garlic, pressed
1 tsp Spike seasoning
1 tsp black pepper

Gently warm EVOO in a skillet and sauté mushrooms and onions until the onions are soft and slightly brown, about 5 minutes.

To steam the beans, trim off ends, put the beans into a pot with a cup of water, bring water to a boil, cover pot and steam beans for 3-5 minutes. Pour into colander and cool. Chop beans coarsely. I use a two-blade hand chopper left to me by my Grandma Sarah, but a cleaver or any good chopping knife will do.

Peel eggs and mash in a mixing bowl. Add sautéed mushrooms and onions together with chopped beans and garlic and seasonings. Mix thoroughly.

You can serve right away with crackers or pumpernickel bread, or refrigerate for a few hours or overnight.

Stuffed Eggs with Watercress

I've always loved deviled eggs. This is a more sophisticated version which is also yummy. Of course use fresh, local eggs from chickens that eat well and run around the yard happily.

Serves 4-6

6 hard-boiled eggs
½ C crème fraîche, or sour cream
½ C chopped watercress
¼ C finely minced red onion

1½ tsp sea salt
½ tsp garlic powder
¼ tsp ground nutmeg
½ tsp black pepper
paprika for dusting

Peel the eggs. Halve them lengthwise and remove the yolks. Arrange the whites on a serving dish and set aside. In a bowl, mash the egg yolks together with the crème fraîche or sour cream. Lightly stir in the remaining ingredients. Divide the mixture between the 12 egg-white halves, mounding high. Dust with paprika and serve cold or at room temperature. If you're not serving within the hour, cover the plate of stuffed eggs with plastic wrap.

Note: You could add chopped smoked salmon or caviar to the filling for an extra-special treat.

TOM'S SHIITAKE SUSHI

Tom says, "Many people think that sushi has to include raw fish of some kind, and since they don't like the idea of eating raw fish, they avoid sushi. However, the term sushi refers to rice which has been seasoned with vinegar, salt and sugar, and topped with or rolled up with any number of ingredients. Here's a rolled sushi which contains shiitake mushrooms, scallions and umeboshi pickled plum. Try it, you'll like it!"

Makes 6-8 rolls

2 C short grain brown rice
4 C water
½ lb fresh shiitake mushrooms
1 tsp toasted sesame oil
1 Tbsp canola oil
1 Tbsp tamari (soy sauce)
½ C brown rice vinegar
¼ C agave nectar

1 tsp sea salt
2-oz pkg pickled ginger, minced
6 sheets of nori
½ C umeboshi paste
1 bunch diced scallions
black sesame seeds for garnish
2 Tbsp wasabi (Japanese horseradish) powder
tamari (soy sauce) for dipping

Combine rice and water in small saucepan, cover pot and bring to a boil. Turn down heat and simmer until water is all absorbed, about 25 minutes.

While rice cooks, sauté mushrooms in oils. When mushrooms are soft, add tamari. Sauté 1-2 minutes more. Set aside.

When the rice is done, put it into a large bowl, toss with the vinegar, agave, salt and pickled ginger. Mix well and set aside to cool.

To assemble, place a nori sheet on a rolling mat (available at fine gourmet shops) or use a sheet of plastic wrap. Place about ⅔ C of cooked rice on the nori. Then, using your fingers or a spatula, spread the rice out so it covers the bottom ⅔ of the sheet. Spread about 1 tsp of umeboshi paste in a line across the center of the rice. Do the same with about 2 Tbsp mushrooms. Sprinkle with scallions. Now roll up the whole from the bottom up. Moisten the end with a little water to make it stick.

Slice each roll into 6 or 8 pieces with a very sharp knife. Garnish with black sesame seeds. Mix wasabi powder with a few Tbsp water, just enough so you have a paste. Serve sushi with wasabi and soy sauces for dipping. Yum.

Soups

Random thoughts about soup...You don't have to use bouillon cubes or canned soup broth to make good soup. Chopped onions and garlic make a great base together with vegetables and herbs. You save money, feel virtuous and infuse your soup with the therapeutic properties attributed to onions and garlic.

Save liquid from steaming vegetables in glass jars and store in the refrigerator or freezer to use in soups too. No more pouring this nutrient-rich liquid down the drain!

Cut vegetables into pieces which fit easily onto a spoon and into your mouth.

Add salt or miso or tamari when soup is done. Add seaweed such as kombu (kelp) to soup at the beginning whenever it contains beans because kombu breaks down the part of beans we have difficulty digesting. Add a spoonful of vinegar to soups that have bones so the calcium from the bones gets pulled into the soup.

Save sugar and flour for desserts. Why would any soup (except a dessert soup) need to be sweet? And it's easy to thicken soups with pureed vegetables like potatoes, which work wonderfully.

If you want your soup to taste decadent, sauté onions and garlic in extra virgin olive oil, butter, ghee or coconut oil before adding remaining ingredients to kettle.

Many soups taste better the second day when flavors have had a chance to marry. Feel free to freeze leftover soup in glass jars (leave room at top for expansion). Or use up soup by inviting friends over for a soup party!

For exotic flavors, use tart dried cherries or tamarind concentrate instead of lemon juice. Use Lightlife Fakin' Bacon (smoky tempeh strips) to impart a smoky flavor. Garnish soups with mint, parsley, scallions, red onion, celery leaves, dill, croutons, a dollop of yogurt or cubes of tofu.

Russian soup recipe. "Take what you like. Wash, chop, and put in pot."

Aaron's Peanut Soup

"This recipe was adapted from one by George Washington Carver, who created a similar soup for the dining hall of the Tuskegee Institute. Unlike Carver's recipe, this one doesn't have oysters, cream or sherry. I first had peanut soup as a child on vacation in Colonial Williamsburg and had wanted it again ever since. One day, I realized I could just make it myself!" So sayeth Aaron.

About.com says "Peanuts, actually legumes rather than nuts, are sometimes called groundnuts because of their unusual fruit development. After the flowers are fertilized, they wither to the ground and bury themselves; the pods mature underground. They are usually harvested by uprooting the whole plant to dry the nuts. Another common name for peanuts here in the South is 'goober,' or 'goober-pea,' which comes straight from the African 'nguba.'"

Serves 6

2 Tbsp extra virgin olive oil (EVOO)	2 Tbsp flour (optional)
2 onions, about 4 C, sliced	1 Tbsp sea salt
5 cloves garlic, chopped coarsely	1 Tbsp black pepper
1 C smooth peanut butter	¼ C lemon juice
1 qt chicken stock	1 bunch scallions, chopped

Gently warm EVOO in a soup kettle. Add onions and sauté until they begin to brown. Add the garlic and stir. Sauté. When the garlic begins to brown, add the peanut butter and a small amount of the stock, about 2 C.

If you desire a thicker soup, add the flour.

Whisk the contents of the pot until smooth. Add the remaining stock and salt and pepper.

Heat soup over a medium flame, stirring often, until hot but not boiling. Remove from heat, add the lemon juice and ladle soup into bowls or mugs. Garnish with the (washed!) scallions and a grinding or two of black pepper.

Anasazi Pepita Potato Soup

The Anasazi ("Ancient Ones") lived in the American Southwest between 700 and 2,000 years ago. Mesa Verde National Park in Colorado has many examples of dwellings preserved from the years when this largely nomadic people learned to plant and cultivate corn, beans, pepitas and squash. They invented a water collection system to rival any found anywhere in the world. No one knows for sure why the Anasazi left, but it is thought that years of prolonged drought gave them no choice but to seek greener pastures.

This soup has, like all soups, many possible variations. Use any kind of sausage you choose. Use another bean, or use winter squash instead of sweet potatoes or yams. Feel free, too, to use white potatoes instead of sweet potatoes or squash. Whatever, good soup warms the cockles of one's soul when it's cold outside.

This hearty, satisfying soup provides complete protein. Serve with a green salad. A little wine and thou is nice too.

Serves 8

¼ C extra virgin olive oil (EVOO)
12 oz sausages (your favorite kind*)
1 onion, chopped, about 2 C
8 cloves garlic, minced
1 green bell pepper, chopped
1 red bell pepper, chopped
1 can Eden kidney beans, or 2 C cooked
2 C corn kernels (frozen corn is okay)

3 C ½-inch cubed sweet potatoes or yams
7 C water or vegetable broth
2 bay leaves
1 tsp dried oregano
1 tsp dried thyme
1 tsp sea salt
1 tsp black pepper
1½ C toasted, shelled pepitas**

In a soup kettle, gently warm EVOO. Add sausages, onion, garlic and peppers to kettle. Stir and sauté 5 minutes over medium flame. Add remaining ingredients except salt, pepper and pepitas to pot. Bring soup to gentle boil. Lower flame to lowest and simmer soup, covered, for 15 minutes.

If you didn't buy roasted pepitas, toast yours by stirring in a dry skillet on low for a few minutes—just until aromatic—or by spreading them on a cookie sheet and popping into a 350⁰ oven for 5 minutes.

Using a food processor, coffee grinder/seed mill, or blender, finely grind all pepitas but ½ C. Stir ground pepitas into soup. Taste. Adjust seasoning. When you serve, garnish with reserved pepitas. Ole!

*You can use whatever kind of sausages you like, beef, pork, lamb or veggie. If you're a vegetarian, Field Roast veggie sausages are delish.
**Pepitas are pumpkin seeds, and you can buy them already roasted, which saves a step.

Ayurvedic Gingery Dal

Ayurveda is the medicine of India, which focuses on holistic living and eating the right kind of food. According to Ayurveda, food is energy and where healing starts. This soup uses many foods important in Ayurveda to enhance nutrient absorption and increase health.

Split mung beans are easier to digest than other beans and are said to be healing. Used in soup, they nourish, satisfy and cleanse the body. Ghee, clarified butter, is an important Ayurvedic ingredient which seems to be fine for most folks who are lactose intolerant. Asafoetida, also known as hing, devil's dung, stinking gum and more, has a pungent, unpleasant smell when raw, but once it's in cooked dishes, gives a flavor reminiscent of leeks. Asafoetida is used here in lieu of garlic (so the recipe below is not authentic because I just can't make soup without throwing in garlic!).

Serves 4

2 C yellow or green split mung beans	1 Tbsp brown mustard seeds
12 C water or vegetable broth	1 tsp ground turmeric
6 cloves garlic, minced	1 Tbsp ground coriander
2 Tbsp fresh ginger, minced	1 Tbsp cumin seeds
2 C veggies like chopped kale, green beans, diced carrots or asparagus	½ tsp asafoetida*
	2 tsp sea salt
2 Tbsp ghee	½ tsp black pepper

Rinse dal. Place in soup pot with water or vegetable broth, garlic, ginger and vegetables. If you've chosen asparagus, cut into 2-inch pieces, but reserve. Bring soup to a gentle boil. Then lower heat, cover pot and simmer soup for one hour.

In a small pan (I use a speckled enamel one my grandmother gave me when I was in college) and with a low flame, melt ghee. Add spices and stir just until seeds begin to pop. Stir spiced ghee mixture into cooked dal together with salt and pepper. If using asparagus, add cut pieces now. Cover pot and let soup stand for 2 minutes so flavors meld. Taste. Adjust seasoning. Serve and enjoy.

This measurement is based upon Frontier Herb and Spice brand asafoetida, which is diluted with rice flour.

Butterbean and Green Bean Soup

Butterbeans are a tender, smaller variety of lima beans. I always keep a can of Eden butterbeans at home to throw into soups or stews. They're light, flavorful and so cute! Paired with green beans and peas here, they're perfecto.

Butterbeans, like all legumes, have soluble fiber, which helps the cardiovascular and digestive systems, but also helps stabilize blood sugar levels. Did you know that? So bring back and bring on the beans! They're good for us, easy to grow and good for our planet too.

Serves 4

¼ C extra virgin olive oil (EVOO)
2 onions, about 4 C, chopped
6 cloves garlic, minced
4 C water, or vegetable or chicken
    broth
1 tsp dried thyme
1 tsp dried marjoram leaves
2 tsp sea salt
1 bay leaf

1 tsp black pepper
1 can Eden butterbeans, about
    2 C cooked
6 C fresh green beans, ends trimmed,
    cut into 1-inch pieces
2 C green peas
about 1 C grated parmesan or
    Pecorino romano

Gently warm EVOO in a large soup pot over medium heat. Sauté onions and garlic until onion is translucent, about 5 minutes. Add water or broth together with herbs and butterbeans. Bring soup to a boil, lower heat, cover pot and simmer 15 minutes.

Add string beans and peas to pot. Simmer 5 minutes more. Taste, adjust seasoning and serve with cheese sprinkled on top.

Note: Can you add more butterbeans, another kind of bean, greens or sausage (real or veggie)? Yes, yes, yes, yes.

CATALAN TOMATO SOUP

Catalan cuisine is popular in this country, and it's not hard to see why! Recipes combine the flavors of Spain and France from seafaring villages that nestle between the sea and the Pyrenees Mountains.

This ran in our April 2003 newsletter. You could call this a hot gazpacho, rich in the antioxidant lycopene—the pigment that gives vegetables and fruits such as tomatoes, pink grapefruit and watermelon their red color. Several studies suggest that consumption of foods rich in lycopene is associated with a lower risk of prostate cancer and cardiovascular disease. Did you know that red peppers have more vitamin C than oranges do?

This soup is dressy enough for company but works for family at home too. For a complete meal, add some leftover grain and choose a protein like tofu, shrimp, chowder fish, scallops or chicken. Want to mix in a can of organic white beans? Excellent choice too!

Studies show people who eat soups have less difficulty controlling weight because no matter how thick a soup and how filling, it's still largely water and vegetables, which are low in calories. And hot soup makes us eat slower, which gives time for the brain to signal that we've had enough.

Serves 8

¼ C extra virgin olive oil (EVOO)
2 onions, about 4 C, finely chopped
2 C roasted red peppers, chopped
  coarsely
6 cloves garlic, crushed
¼ C parsley, dried
6 C diced tomatoes, fresh or canned
6 C tomato juice*

1 tsp dried basil
1 tsp dried oregano
1 tsp dried thyme
dash hot sauce
1 pound tofu, shrimp, etc. (optional)
sea salt and pepper to taste
chopped scallions (optional)

Gently warm EVOO in a soup kettle. Add onions and peppers and stir. Using low heat, simmer mixture 15 minutes, or until onions are translucent. Add garlic, parsley, tomatoes, strained tomatoes or tomato juice, herbs and hot sauce. Simmer on low, uncovered, for 15 minutes, stirring from time to time, until soup has thickened. Add protein if you like. Cover pot and continue to simmer (still on low) for another 10 minutes. Taste and adjust seasoning. Ladle soup into bowls. Garnish with scallions if desired.

If you use tofu, don't worry about dicing, it will break up by itself as you stir. I like to use soft tofu. Shrimp or scallops? Cut them or not, depending upon your taste.

*Bionaturae makes a strained tomato that is like tomato juice and to die for. If you can get this brand, do! It's my all-time favorite.

COLD BEET AND POTATO SOUP WITH LEMON AND CRÈME FRAÎCHE

I've always thought beets were incredibly high in iron, but it seems that's not exactly true. What is true is that the iron they contain is easily utilized by the body. Beets both clean and build blood. They are recommended during pregnancy because they are high in folic acid. Did you know that beets are alkaline and so balance pH? Beets also relieve constipation.

Eat beets because they taste wonderful and make dishes look beautiful!

Serves 6
about 4 C red beets, cut into 2-inch dice
about 4 C potatoes, cut into 2-inch pieces
4 Tbsp extra virgin olive oil (EVOO)
1 Tbsp black pepper
2 Tbsp lemon juice
4 C water or vegetable broth

Roast at 425 degrees
½ C crème fraîche
1 Tbsp sea salt
2-inch piece fresh lemon peel
chopped chives for garnish
chopped eggs for garnish or protein
more crème fraîche for garnish

Preheat oven to 425 degrees.

Prepare beets and potatoes. Place in roasting pan or oven-proof skillet. Toss with EVOO and black pepper so beets and potatoes are well-coated. Roast for 30-40 minutes, or until beets and potatoes are tender (easily pierced with a sharp little knife).

Let cool and transfer to a food processor. Puree in batches with lemon juice, water or vegetable broth, crème fraîche, salt and lemon peel (I drop in the whole piece of lemon that I've squeezed to get the original 2 Tbsp of lemon juice). Soup will never be completely smooth. It will have flecks of beet and potato peel.

Chill soup thoroughly and then serve garnished with chives or chopped eggs. Do use a dollop of crème fraîche. It's worth the calories.

Note: Don't peel beets or potatoes. Simply scrub with a vegetable brush and trim. You want the rustic, peasanty look with flecks of peel because it makes the soup look interesting. And by not peeling, you've saved yourself time, and gotten all the nutrition you can out of those veggies.

Note: Can you steam beets and potatoes instead of roasting them, thereby eliminating the need for EVOO? Yes. Roasting makes the vegetables sweeter. Can you roast an onion along with the beets and potatoes so the soup has that tang? Of course.

GARLICKY MEXICAN CHEESE SOUP

When I was a child, my family took a car trip from our home in Florida to Texas and down into Mexico. We traveled for a number of weeks in Mexico, and one day my father got lost. We found ourselves stranded in a little village where no one spoke English. We were tired, hungry and scared. The village clucked over us and fed us a soup I've never quite been able to re-create. In my mind, I see the rustic wooden table outside, the kind faces and the fragrant, steaming bowls of soup.

Serves 4

½ C extra virgin olive oil (EVOO)
2 C garlic, chopped coarsely
1 poblano or green pepper, 2 C, chopped
8 C water or vegetable stock

4 eggs
1 C Monterey jack cheese, grated, or another soft melting cheese, or lots more cheese if you want

Gently warm EVOO in a soup pot. Add garlic and pepper and sauté over medium heat, stirring occasionally until garlic softens, a few minutes. Add water or vegetable stock. Bring soup to a boil, lower heat, cover pot and simmer for 30 minutes.

To serve, crack an egg into each serving bowl, ladle hot soup over and cover top of soup with grated cheese.

Note: This soup was an adventure. It was like eating a bowl of garlic-flavored melted cheese, which is why I say you can use way more cheese than called for if you want to pretend you're in a village somewhere in Mexico.

Georgian Red Lentil Soup

This lovely lentil soup ran in our January 2008 newsletter. Soups are perfect for those with allergies because they can easily be made without wheat, soy, dairy, eggs, or other foods that are difficult for many folks out there these days. And soups are true comfort food when it's dark outside.

We've become addicted to maitake mushrooms, also called "hen of the woods" or "dancing mushrooms." Not only do maitakes have an amazing taste and firm texture, but they are one of the most revered deep-immune tonics in Chinese medicine. In Japan, doctors use maitakes to lower blood pressure and boost immune systems. As Adam wrote in our March 2006 newsletter, maitakes regulate blood sugar, protect the liver—and taste a little like chicken.

This is not the prettiest soup (don't let that stop you from making and loving every spoonful!). Unlike other soups, it is best eaten the day it's made.

Serves 4

4 Tbsp extra virgin olive oil (EVOO)	8 C hot broth or hot water
⅛ C garlic cloves, sliced	½ C red lentils
several threads saffron	3-4 oz maitake mushrooms
1 tsp ground coriander	4 C baby spinach
1 tsp curry or fenugreek powder	1 can unsweetened coconut milk*
1 tsp red pepper flakes	¼ C lemon juice
1 tsp dried basil	sea salt and pepper to taste
1 tsp dried mint	2½ Tbsp chopped fresh cilantro

Gently warm EVOO in a soup pot. Add garlic and sauté over medium heat, stirring occasionally until garlic softens, a few minutes. Add saffron, coriander, curry or fenugreek powder, red pepper flakes, basil and mint. Stir a minute, and slowly add hot broth and then red lentils.

Bring soup to a boil, lower heat, cover pot and simmer for 30 minutes. Then add mushrooms (torn wildly, with great glee, into bite-sized pieces) and spinach. Simmer an additional 5 minutes. Add coconut milk (or more broth if you prefer) and lemon juice. Turn off heat, and let soup stand for 5 minutes. Taste and add salt and pepper (I like about a tsp of each). Serve garnished with cilantro.

Want to add tofu, tempeh, shrimp or chicken to this soup? But, of course!

*Coconut milk isn't authentic, but I like the way it marries flavors. If you omit, flavors will be a little sharper.

IMMUNE BOOSTING SOUP

This one was featured in *Yankee Magazine* in 2004. I always believe in trying low-tech and natural first, before resorting to big-gun medicines. This version of our immune boosting soup combines ingredients like shiitake mushrooms, burdock (said to be the most strengthening of vegetables), ginger and cayenne (both of which warm and get the circulation going).

Amy Traverso, writing for *Yankee*, said, "*Yankee's* editors found that the soup did indeed help stave off a round of oncoming colds. Debra recommends eating the soup twice daily at the onset of illness, or once daily for two weeks to boost the immune system."

Serves 4

1 Tbsp extra virgin olive oil (EVOO)
1 onion, about 2 C, chopped
6 cloves garlic, chopped
¼ C dried shiitakes, or 1 C fresh
4-inch piece burdock, chopped
½ C dried wakame or kombu (kelp)
½ C cubed tofu
8 C water

2 C vegetables, chopped, like carrots celery, kale, daikon, turnips, parsnips, beet tops or lotus root
1 dropper-full of tincture of astragalus*
1 dropper-full of tincture of reishi*
2 Tbsp miso

Gently warm EVOO in soup kettle. Sauté onion and garlic until onion is translucent, about 5 minutes. Add remaining ingredients except tinctures of astragalus and reishi, and miso.

Bring soup to a boil. Reduce heat, cover pot and simmer 15 minutes. Add astragalus and reishi. Cover pot again and simmer soup on low for another hour.

Whisk miso in now. Taste and adjust seasoning. Enjoy soup hot, or put pot in the refrigerator and heat individual portions during the week as needed.

Note: Want another healing soup to boost your immune system? I found the simple recipe below for koji (Japanese gruel) in my files at home and it reminded me that sometimes the simplest foods are what do a body good. When we're ill, our body needs its energy to heal, not to digest a heavy meal. Koji is easy to digest.

To prepare, put 2 Tbsp brown rice into 1 C water. Cook overnight in a crockpot or simmer in a covered pot on very low heat for 2 hours. Eat. That's all. If you're cold, add ginger and honey and milk (cow, soy, rice, almond or oat). If you're nervous, add 1-2 Tbsp sea vegetables like kelp while cooking. If you have heart problems, incorporate 1-2 Tbsp millet or winter squash to gruel.

*Tinctures can be found in the supplement department of natural product stores. Use them here if you can, but still make and eat this soup even if you don't have them.

GRANDMA'S MUSHROOM BARLEY SOUP

Grandma Sarah, my mom's Mom, came from Russia-Poland, and this was one of her favorite soups, which she made for us whenever she came to visit.

Barley comes to the world from Ethiopia and Southeast Asia, where it was cultivated as early as 8,000 B.C.E. Most of the barley grown today is used either to feed livestock or to make alcoholic beverages. Seems to me we should change that picture since barley packs a double punch, lots of fiber plus selenium. We don't get enough selenium in our diets, even though this trace mineral is so important to our health. Selenium helps ward off the moody blues, it works as an antioxidant and bolsters the immune system to fight off bad bugs too.

Serves 4

3 Tbsp butter or ghee
2 C fresh mushrooms, sliced
1 onion, chopped, about 2 C
2 oz dried mushrooms
8 C water or vegetable broth
½ C barley
about 2 C carrot, diced
about 2 C celery, diced

about 2 C parsnips, diced
about 2 C potato, diced
1 bay leaf
2 tsp black pepper
1 Tbsp sea salt
2 Tbsp dried dill weed
chopped fresh dill for garnish

Gently warm butter or ghee in a soup pot (larger is better). Add fresh mushrooms and onions and sauté until onions soften and mushrooms start to give off liquid, about 10 minutes. Add remaining ingredients, except chopped fresh dill, to soup pot and bring soup to a boil.

Lower heat, cover pot and simmer for about an hour. Barley likes to bubble over, so watch pot carefully. That's why, too, once the soup has come to a boil, I move the pot partially off the burner.

When soup is done and barley is nice and soft, taste and adjust seasoning. Serve garnished with fresh dill. If you don't have fresh dill, simply use more of the dried dill weed.

If you like your soup a little thinner, add more water or broth.

ITALIAN PLUM AND BLUEBERRY SOUP

Fresh Italian plums, aka prune plums, have such a short season. I love them because they are darling, make good eating, terrific pies, cobblers and, here, soup. During the rest of the year, when I can't get them, which is about 50 weeks out of the 52 (!), I use prunes, their dried cousins. There's a brand called St. Dalfour that makes the most succulent and moist pitted prunes you'll ever taste. They come in a little jar, and you want them, believe me! Add blueberries, and wow. Taste explosion. Top nutrition.

Did you know that blueberries were picked by hand until the invention of the blueberry rake by Abijah Tabbutt of Maine in 1822?

Cinnamon warms us inside, and dried orange peel, which is bitter and pungent, is said to invigorate the movement of *chi* and dry dampness. It balances the flavors here perfectly.

Serves 4

2 C Italian prune plums, halved, pitted
2 C blueberries, fresh or frozen
1 qt water
2 C orange juice (I love Volcano blood orange)
1 tsp cinnamon
1 tsp sea salt

1 C lemon juice
½ tsp lemon extract
1 tsp orange extract
1 tsp dried orange peel
2 Tbsp agave, honey or coconut sugar (optional)
garnishes (optional and below)

Unless you have a large blender like a Vitamix, you'll need to make this in two batches and combine them in a clean soup pot or large mixing bowl.

Blend all ingredients on high speed for a couple of minutes, so soup becomes smooth and silky.

Taste. If you want this a little sweeter, add the agave, honey or coconut sugar.

Chill for an hour or two. Ladle into pretty soup bowls.

Garnish, if you like, with a few leaves fresh mint, a dollop of yogurt or sour cream or a little swirl of heavy whipping cream. Another garnish? A few whole blueberries.

Kenyon's Calcium Soup with Beef Bones

This soup is Kenyon Keily's rendition of a classic bone broth. It's hearty with barley and rich in bone-strengthening seaweed and greens. Talk about high calcium content!

Broths made from the bones of animals have been made and eaten throughout history and are a classic folk remedy to nourish anyone who is sick.

Today, most of us buy our broths in a can or aseptic container. With a little planning, you can make your own broths for pennies. You can feel like a character out of an Arthurian legend, with your broth simmering on the stove, while you read the Sunday paper. You can freeze broth in ice cube trays, then save the cubes in a container in your freezer so you always have some on hand.

Serves 6-8

2 C barley
8 C water
3 lb beef soup bones
3½ qt water
1 yellow onion, unpeeled, quartered
10 garlic cloves, unpeeled, crushed
2 dried bay leaves

¼ C vinegar (rice or apple cider)
2 dried mushrooms such as shiitakes
3 C stemmed, chopped kale
3 sheets nori seaweed, crumbled, or
   any other seaweed of choice
¼ C soy sauce
¼ teaspoon freshly ground black
   pepper

In a medium bowl, soak the barley in 8 cups of water for 8 hours, or overnight. Drain and discard water. In a large, heavy, non-aluminum soup pot, add beef bones, water, onion, garlic, bay leaves and vinegar, and bring soup to a boil. Skim foam from the stock the first few minutes, then reduce heat to simmer and cook for 2 hours, uncovered.

Strain soup. Kenyon says to discard or save the stock ingredients, but who would ever just throw food away?!? I'd eat for lunch!

Rinse and wipe pot clean and return stock to it. Place back on low heat to simmer. It is best to keep the fat floating on the top of the stock because calcium must be eaten with fat to be absorbed. Add barley and mushrooms into the simmering stock and cook about 1½ hours, covered. Add the kale, nori seaweed, soy sauce and pepper and simmer 15 minutes more.

Variations: Add to soup mixture 2 sticks of astragalus and/or 1 medium sized piece of reishi mushroom, approximately 3 inches in diameter, cut into smaller pieces. Simmer with other ingredients. When simmering soup with barley and mushrooms, feel free to also add ¼ C goji berries, or 1-2 tsp of crushed Deer Velvet Antler. Feel free to use organic chicken instead of beef bones.

MEDITERRANEAN CANNELLINI AND LENTIL SOUP

Cannellini beans look like white kidney beans. I often mix and match cannellini, great northern, or navy beans, although, for sure, they are different. Great Northern beans look a little like baby lima beans (butterbeans), and navy beans are smaller and rounder than either.

All three work fine in soups and stews. Cannellini beans take a little longer to cook and are a little starchier. I like their larger size here because lentils are small, and the larger bean adds visual interest.

Cannellini beans have a nutty taste and mild earthiness. Like all legumes, they have lots of good carbs and fiber. Indulge mama mia and papa bear.

Serves 4

¾ C dried cannellini beans, or 2 C
   canned
12 C water or vegetable, beef or
   chicken broth
2 tsp dried coriander
¾ C lentils of any kind
⅓ C brown rice
2 onions, about 4 C, chopped

6 cloves garlic, minced
2 Tbsp dried parsley
1 tsp cinnamon
2 tsp sea salt
2 tsp black pepper

Sort beans to check for stones. In a large soup kettle, place cannellini beans and water or broth. Bring soup to a boil and simmer 15 minutes uncovered. Add remaining ingredients and simmer soup, covered, until cannellini are tender, about 45 minutes. Taste and adjust seasoning. (Naturally, if you're using canned cannellini beans, you can have soup ready in 15 minutes.)

Serve with whatever your heart desires. In winter I like a good piece of cheese and a garlicky green salad, or roast chicken and stir-fried greens.

Of course you can make this soup colorful and change the flavor profile too by adding sliced carrots and/or diced parsnips.

MIDDLE EASTERN COLD YOGURT OR KEFIR SOUP

The Middle East combines sweet and savory in ways we don't. I like the way this soup has overtones of Persia, Bulgaria and Russia. It's not smooth, but life should have something to chew on, shouldn't it?

I always end up with overgrown cucumbers in my garden, and this recipe helps me use those up nicely.

Did you know that cucumbers come from the same family as watermelon, zucchini, pumpkin and other types of squash? Cucumbers are mostly water, but their skin contains nutrients like silica, and silica is an essential component of healthy connective tissue (muscles, tendons, ligaments, cartilage and bone). Cucumber juice is often recommended as a source of silica to improve the skin tone and complexion. So enjoy this soup!

Serves 4

½ C raisins or minced dried apricots
4 C plain yogurt or kefir
3 C cucumbers*, unpeeled, grated or
   chopped
2 hard-boiled eggs, chopped
½ C chopped scallions
1 stalk celery or 1 apple, finely
   chopped

1 tsp sea salt
½ tsp black pepper
1 Tbsp fresh dill, chopped
½ C walnuts, chopped,
   or 1 C shelled pistachios
garnishes optional and below

Soak raisins in cold water for 15 minutes, if you're using raisins. If you're using dried apricots (the unsulphured kind, of course), just mince those finely—no need to soak. If using raisins, drain after 15 minutes. (Drink the soaking water!)

In a large bowl, combine all ingredients. Mix well. Refrigerate for about 2 hours.

You can garnish with chopped parsley or mint leaves too. You can stir in a spoonful of pomegranate syrup as well.

I grow and use small pickling cucumbers, which I love. They have a short season, so feel free to substitute the long English cucumbers instead. Neither of these cucumbers is sent to market with a wax coating. Both have smaller seeds inside too.

Moroccan Lentil Vegetable Soup

Ready in 15 minutes, this soup from our January 2009 store newsletter is fast food the natural way!

Lentils are eaten around the world, at least twice a day in "any self-respecting Indian household," says Kavita Mehta, founder of Web-based Indian Foods Co. Lentils are eaten every day in Morocco, but especially during Ramadan. Lentils taste great and give us protein, cholesterol-lowering fiber and more nutrition for their size than almost any other food.

Do they contain iron and B vitamins too? Yes!

These cute little pulses come in all colors and are easy on the pocketbook too. A handful feeds many. This soup, like most soups with legumes and vegetables, helps whittle down your waist.

Serves 6

2 Tbsp extra virgin olive oil (EVOO)
1 large onion, about 2 C, chopped
1 Tbsp ground cumin
1 Tbsp ground ginger
1 tsp paprika
¼ tsp cayenne pepper
1 tsp black pepper
6 cloves garlic, chopped
3 C tomato juice*

4 C water or vegetable broth
¼ C lentils of any kind
1 bunch chard, coarsely chopped
2 zucchini, about 4 C, halved and
**   sliced**
1 tsp sea salt
1 C cilantro leaves, slightly chopped
**   (optional)**
2 Tbsp lemon juice

In a soup kettle or pot, gently warm EVOO. Add onion and stir to coat. Add spices and garlic and stir for a couple of minutes, just so garlic starts to brown and is aromatic. Your kitchen will smell heavenly!

Add tomato juice and water or vegetable broth. Bring soup to a gentle boil. Rinse lentils in a colander in cold water and add to soup pot. Stir, turn flame low, cover pot, and allow soup to simmer while you prepare vegetables (5 minutes, if that).

Add cut vegetables to soup and cover pot again. Simmer 10 minutes more. Stir in salt, cilantro leaves and lemon juice. Taste and adjust seasoning. Serve right away. Lap it up!

Note: If you want this soup thicker, add an additional ¼ C lentils. A nice combo is ¼ C brown lentils and ¼ C red lentils. Or use blue lentils. If you want more veggies, that's fine too. (cont.)

Add chopped carrots, parsnips or whatever you have in your fridge. Mushrooms are wonderful. Soup too thick? Add more water or vegetable broth. This soup, like many soups, tastes even better the second day.

Bionaturae makes a strained tomato that is like tomato juice and to die for. If you can get this brand, do! It's my all-time favorite.

MULLIGATAWNY CHICKEN SOUP WITH COCONUT MILK

I first experimented with this for a party on New Year's Day, and when guests asked for the recipe, I decided to run it in our January 2007 newsletter.

Mulligatawny means "pepper water," and so this soup is rich in flavor. Feel free to add more lemon, cayenne pepper and other spices to make your taste buds happy!

Lentils are most likely indigenous to Asia, and there is evidence they were used in the Bronze Age, and in Greece and Egypt before biblical times. High in protein, lentils are consumed world-wide, especially by the poor, but used more and more in the United States by all of us who know and love them! They're easy to cook, satisfying, rich in fiber, versatile and, as just mentioned, inexpensive. A cup of lentils costs pennies and goes a long way.

Interesting that it's the lentil's shape which gave us the word magnifying "lens."

Lentils are said to have the same anti-inflammatory antioxidants found in tea, fruits, red wine and cocoa beans. They're said to promote healthy collagen and cartilage too.

Serves 8-10

¼ C extra virgin olive oil (EVOO)	2 bay leaves
2 onions, chopped, about 4 C	2 C red lentils
6 cloves garlic, chopped	8 C chicken broth
1½ Tbsp garam masala	2 C diced, cooked chicken*
1½ tsp ground coriander	1-2 cans unsweetened coconut milk
1 tsp turmeric powder	3 Tbsp lemon juice
½ tsp cayenne pepper	1 tsp each sea salt and pepper

Heat EVOO in a heavy, large pot. Sauté onions until golden, stirring frequently, about 15 minutes. Add garlic and sauté 2 more minutes. Add spices and stir another minute until your nose says, "Ahhh." Believe me, it will!

Add lentils and stir to coat. Add chicken broth and bring soup to a gentle boil. Reduce heat to medium, cover pot and simmer until lentils are tender, about 20 minutes. Remove bay leaves.

Working in batches, puree soup until smooth (if you own a bir-mixer or hand blender, just insert into pot and blend all at once). If you have to puree in batches, you'll add what you've pureed to a new pot. When done, stir in chicken, coconut milk and lemon juice. Season to taste with salt and pepper.

* I like and use dark meat chicken. And it has to be organic, of course!

MUSHROOM AND CURRIED QUINOA SOUP

We have wonderful mixed dried mushrooms in the store. I like the mixtures and keep mine at home in the freezer, where they can stay fresh for years. I consider them an essential pantry item because I love throwing them into soups and stews with gay abandon.

Mushrooms appear in mythology because of their seemingly magical ability to appear overnight. They are strong enough to push away stones as they grow upright through the soil. They are revered as well because of their medicinal value.

Serves 6

2 Tbsp extra virgin olive oil (EVOO)
1 onion, about 2 C, chopped
4 cloves garlic, minced
1 green pepper, about 2 C, chopped
   coarsely
1 tsp dried cumin powder
½ tsp dried coriander
½ tsp cinnamon
1 tsp ginger powder

¼ tsp cayenne pepper
½ tsp turmeric powder
2 tsp sea salt
1 tsp black pepper
½ C quinoa
2 C assorted dried mushrooms
5-6 C water or vegetable stock
4 C milk of any kind*

Gently warm EVOO in a large soup kettle. Sauté onion and garlic until onion is translucent, about 5 minutes. Add spices and stir a minute or two until fragrant.

Add quinoa, mushrooms and water or vegetable broth. Bring soup to a boil, turn down heat to lowest, cover pot, and simmer for about 45 minutes. Turn off flame, stir in milk and taste. Adjust salt and pepper if needed.

There's regular cow's milk, goat milk, coconut milk, almond milk, and hemp seed, soy or rice milks. All work and are good.

OH, SO SIMPLE BARLEY BEAN SOUP WITH PESTO

This one is from our December 2003 newsletter. Working long hours? Trying to get too much done before the holidays? Make a pot of soup on the weekend (let it simmer on the stove while you read the paper), and then all you have to do it warm it up during the week.

But I hear you grumbling in the background that beans and barley contain carbs. Please, oh, please, don't go crazy and stop eating good carbohydrates. We need protein, fats and carbohydrates so that we can stay trim and slim. Good, complex carbs don't make you fat. And remember that protein and fats satisfy appetite, and good, unrefined carbohydrates like those in whole grains and beans boost mood by lifting serotonin levels. Complex carbohydrates keep us feeling happy.

Barley is soothing and nourishing. Burdock tastes earthy to me, but I use it sometimes because I hear it's a blood cleanser and boosts the immune system. Why pesto? It's an easy way to make everything taste delish.

Serves 6

12 C water or vegetable stock	**2-inch piece scrubbed burdock, sliced**
1½ C barley-bean soup mix*	**2 bay leaves**
2-inch piece kombu (kelp)	**1-2 C pesto, your favorite****
4 carrots, about 6-7 C, diced	**1 tsp sea salt**
2 parsnips, about 4 C, diced	**1 tsp black pepper**
8 cloves garlic, minced	

Place water and barley bean mixture in a large soup kettle. Toss in kombu. Bring soup to a boil and cook, uncovered, for 5 minutes. Add carrots, parsnips, garlic, burdock and bay leaves. *I know you know **not** to peel carrots....* Cover pot, lower heat, and simmer soup 3 hours. Beans and barley will be nice and meltingly soft.

Turn off heat. Stir in pesto, salt and pepper, and let soup sit for 10 minutes off the stove. Then taste and adjust seasoning. Spoon into bowls and eat, or put away to warm up during the week. This soup actually tastes better a day or two later.

Want to add chopped kale to make this even heartier? Feel free.

Note: Why do we add kombu? It breaks down the indigestible part of the bean which causes gas.

*You can find bean and barley soup mixes everywhere. We have one in our bulk bins.
**Can't do dairy? There are dairy-free pestos that are wonderful. Linabella's makes one, as does Whole in the Wall.

Old-Fashioned Split Pea Soup

This homey soup is another recipe from our first cookbook, now out of print. It's one we still make in our kitchen, and it's hard to believe that so few ingredients can make the whole store, or your home, smell this good, but they can. Make this one to share with family and friends.

What is a split pea? Are there lots of little people with little knives cutting peas in half? Well, it seems that when the pea is ready in the field, the "skin" dries and falls off, revealing that the pea is actually in two pieces and easily separated mechanically. The peas almost split themselves.

One of my favorite websites, www.vegparadise.com, says that during the Middle Ages, dried peas became a staple food of European peasants. In their dried form peas could be easily stored for winter. They were inexpensive and plentiful and made a filling, wholesome meal the poor could afford.

Serves 6-8

4 C green split peas	2 Tbsp dried parsley
12 C water or vegetable stock	A bay leaf
8 cloves garlic, minced	1 tsp sea salt
1 lb carrots*, diced	1 tsp black pepper

Wash peas in colander. Place them together with everything but salt and pepper in a soup kettle. Bring soup to a boil, reduce heat, cover pot and simmer until split peas are tender (and splut!), about 1½ hours. This soup likes to boil over, so watch it carefully until it comes to a boil and you turn the flame down as low as you can.

Add salt and pepper. Taste. Adjust seasoning. I personally like a lot more salt and pepper.

Note: This soup gets very thick overnight in the refrigerator. To re-heat, you'll need to thin with more water. Because it's so thick, you could actually use it as a dip. In that case, stir in some good, exotic oil and spike with a little cayenne pepper.

*I haven't been saying this in every recipe, but just scrub carrots. Don't peel. No need, no time, and you deserve the extra nutrition in the peel. Make this a rule for yourself—don't ever peel your carrots, parsnips, potatoes or any other vegetables you're accustomed to peeling!

Piera's Turkey Meatball Soup with Escarole

Piera said she peels her carrots, but I bet you can skip this step and have soup all the same.

Escarole is a type of endive and is considered the least bitter of that leafy veggie family. Like all greens, escarole has almost no calories and lots of vitamins. It is used right and left in Italian cooking, and is making inroads here too. It makes a great addition to soups and pasta dishes, but it can also be made by simply sautéing with lots of garlic and extra virgin olive oil.

Serves 8

SOUP
2 Tbsp extra virgin olive oil (EVOO)
3 carrots, about 4 C, diced
1 onion, about 2 C, diced
2 stalks celery, about 3 C, diced
1 tsp sea salt
1 tsp black pepper, or to taste
2 garlic cloves, minced
6 C water
6 C chicken stock

MEATBALLS
1 lb ground dark turkey
½ C plain bread crumbs
2 tsp garlic powder
⅓ C chopped fresh parsley
1 egg
1 tsp sea salt
1 tsp black pepper, or to taste
½ C parmesan cheese
1 lb escarole, chopped

To make meatballs: Add all ingredients in a large bowl. Using your hands, mix until well combined. Set aside.

For the soup: Gently warm EVOO in a heavy soup pot over medium heat. Stir in carrots, onion, celery, salt and pepper. Cook 8-10 minutes, stirring occasionally. Add garlic and cook 2 minutes more, making sure garlic does not brown. Add water and chicken stock, bring soup to a boil and then reduce heat to a simmer.

Take reserved meatball mixture and begin forming into small balls about 1-inch each. Drop balls into the simmering soup as you make them. Cook for 5 minutes.

Add chopped escarole and cook 5 minutes more until the meatballs are cooked through. Taste broth and season with salt and pepper if needed. Sopa for the familia!

PIERA'S QUICK HERBED CHICKEN SOUP

Piera's chicken soup is made with orzo, which is a type of pasta that resembles grains of rice. The word "orzo" means "barley" in Italian, but even though it looks like rice and is sometimes used as a substitute, it is not barley, but made from semolina flour. Don't try and figure out this tangled word-web, just enjoy!

Piera says her family, which includes two of the next generation, loves this soup. If your family needs to be gluten-free, pick out a gluten-free pasta that your kids enjoy.

Serves 6-8

2 Tbsp extra virgin olive oil (EVOO)	1 tsp dried oregano
1 small onion, about 1 C, diced	1 tsp dried thyme
3 carrots, about 6 C, diced	1 large chicken breast on the bone
2 stalks celery, about 4 C, diced	1 large chicken thigh on the bone
3 cloves, garlic, crushed	1 qt chicken broth
1 tsp sea salt	1 qt water
1 tsp black pepper	½ C orzo pasta

Gently warm EVOO in a heavy-bottomed pot over medium heat. Add onion, carrots, celery, garlic, sea salt, pepper, oregano and thyme to pot. Sauté until the vegetables begin to soften and the herbs become fragrant, 5 minutes.

Push the vegetables to the side and place the chicken breast and thigh skin side down in the bottom of the pot. Allow the chicken to brown about 5 minutes. Stir the vegetables on the side occasionally so they don't burn (it is fine if they begin to lightly brown). Once chicken is browned, turn pieces over and pour in chicken broth and water. Make sure to scrape up any brown bits from the chicken.

Raise the heat and bring soup to a boil, then reduce heat and simmer gently for 30 minutes.

Remove chicken pieces and allow them to cool for several minutes. Add the orzo and continue to simmer until the orzo is tender, 8-9 minutes. Remove skin from chicken and dice meat into small cubes. Add diced chicken back to the soup and taste for salt and pepper. Ladle soup into bowls and serve.

Pumpkin Soup with Pumpkin seed Oil

Rich, nutty-tasting pumpkin seed oil from Austria is one of the few ingredients that can really change a dish and make it a show-stopper. Chefs are wowed by it.

Because pumpkin seed oil is damaged by high heat, don't cook with it. Do use it as an alternative for butter when eating bread, drizzle over salads (see our recipe for raw kale salad), drizzle over rice, potatoes, mushrooms, poultry or whatever else you choose. It definitely makes this soup different!

Healthy? Absolutely. The Styrian pumpkin was developed in Austria, back in the 17th century. It's nothing like our sugar pumpkin—it's more like the ornamental gourds we use as decorations, and isn't even edible. Early growers discovered that the green seeds of the Styrian pumpkin prevented bladder and prostate problems, and eliminated intestinal parasites (one wonders how they discovered that!). Austrian farmers grew these pumpkins for the seeds and oil from the seeds alone.

Serves 6

¼ C extra virgin olive oil (EVOO)	1 tsp black pepper
1 onion, about 2 C, chopped	4 C water or vegetable broth
6 cloves garlic, minced	1 C cooked black beans (optional)
4 C cooked pumpkin puree*	6-12 Tbsp green pumpkin seed oil
1 Tbsp curry powder	from Austria
1 tsp sea salt	hulled pumpkin seeds for garnish

Gently warm EVOO in a soup kettle. Sauté onion and garlic over medium heat until onion is tender and translucent, about 5 minutes. Stir in pumpkin puree, curry, salt and pepper. Add water or vegetable broth. Cover pot and simmer soup for 10 minutes. Taste, adjust seasoning. (I like more salt and pepper myself.)

Ladle out soup and put a spoonful of cooked black beans (I open a can of Eden black beans) in the middle of each bowl. Drizzle about 2 Tbsp pumpkin seed oil over soup and sprinkle soup with pumpkin seeds.

How to make your own pumpkin puree? Simply steam peeled, seeded chunks of pumpkin in a pot with a few cups of water until tender (easily pierced with a knife). Shouldn't take more than 10 minutes. Alternatively, you can steam a sweet potato or yam (in this case, scrub but don't peel). Puree in food processor.

Today we can buy canned pureed pumpkin, squash or sweet potato. Make sure you buy plain, nothing else added.

SAVORY CHESTNUT AND PARSNIP SOUP

This recipe goes back to our January 2000 store newsletter. Dried sweet chestnuts (native to southern Europe and not to be confused with horse chestnuts, which are inedible) can be found in our store, of course.

Did you know chestnuts, which make this soup sweet and smoky tasting, are high in protein and low in fat?

A root vegetable of the carrot family, the parsnip is one of my favorite vegetables. I use it in soups and stews, roast along with beets, carrots and potatoes, and sometimes use instead of potatoes.

Who started using the parsnip? Well, we know the Romans cultivated it, and that during the Middle Ages varieties were developed whose roots were larger, sweeter and had more meat, so to speak.

Serves 8

1 onion, about 2 C, chopped	½ tsp dried tarragon
2 lb parsnips, scrubbed, diced	½ tsp dried thyme
¾ C dried chestnuts	3 Tbsp miso*
10 C water or vegetable broth	1 tsp sea salt
	1 tsp black pepper

Place onion, parsnips, chestnuts and water or broth in soup pot. Bring to a boil, lower heat and cover pot. Simmer until chestnuts are soft, about 30 minutes. Add remaining ingredients, simmer 10 more minutes.

Puree soup in a blender or food processor (you'll probably need to do this in 2-3 batches). Put each pureed batch into a clean pot. When all the soup is blended and in the new pot, taste, adjust seasoning.

*Can you eliminate the miso? Yes. You will want to use more salt.

Soup of Chickpeas, Chard and Orzo Pasta

An oldie but goodie from the store's January 2003 newsletter. Most of the soup recipes from our newsletter have appeared in January. January is national soup month, and it's cold and dark here in New England. It's a perfect time of year for soups.

This one is hearty, easy, and economical—an ideal way to get back on track after the holidays. And on dark winter nights, soup is heaven to come home to. So invite some friends over to share a bowl of soup and your own excellent company.

Serves 6

1 bunch organic Swiss chard* or kale or collards
2 Tbsp extra virgin olive oil (EVOO)
1 onion, about 2 C, chopped
6 cloves garlic, minced
2 stalks celery, about 3 C, sliced
4 carrots** or parsnips**, about 6 C, diced

1 can Eden chickpeas, or 2 C cooked
2 bay leaves
6-8 C water or vegetable broth
⅔ C orzo pasta
1 C pesto, your favorite
2 Tbsp Spike seasoning

Rinse veggies. Cut stems and center ribs away from chard leaves. Slice stems. Chop leaves coarsely and save for later. (See note if you're using kale or collards.)

In a soup pot or kettle, gently warm EVOO. Add onion, garlic, celery and chard stems. Sauté about 5 minutes, until onion is soft and translucent. Add carrots or parsnips, chickpeas, bay leaves and water or vegetable broth to pot. Bring to boil, turn down heat, cover pot and simmer 10 minutes or until carrots are tender.

Stir in orzo and cook another 10 minutes. Stir in chard leaves.* Add pesto. Add Spike. Simmer 5 minutes so chard wilts, and voila.

If using kale or collards, chop and add altogether with chickpeas to soup. These greens are hearty and can withstand a longer cooking time.

**Don't peel either carrots or parsnips. Most of the vitamins are in the peel. That's good. You want those....*

SOUTH AMERICAN CHICKEN SOPA WITH CORN

Mom's chicken barley soup, which we make just about every day in our kitchen in the store, is chicken soup made in the eastern European tradition. This chicken soup hails from warmer climes south of us. (You can find the recipe for Mom's Chicken Barley soup, by the way, in our second cookbook called *Debra's Natural Gourmet: Eat Well, Be Happy, A Second Bite*. Don't have a copy of our second cookbook yet? Never fear, you can buy in the store or on line.)

According to food historians, chicken soup was made here, there and everywhere, and its medicinal use is recorded throughout history. There are written records of chicken soup prescribed as a cure for the common cold in Ancient Egypt. A 10th century Persian physician, Avicenna, wrote the same.

Serves 6-8

⅓ C extra virgin olive oil (EVOO)
2 large onions, 4 C, finely chopped
1 tsp black pepper
3 carrots halved and sliced, about 6 C
2 C corn kernels (frozen okay)
2 C water or chicken broth
6 C tomato juice (Bionaturae preferred)
2 tsp dried oregano

1 tsp sea salt
1 lb boneless skinless chicken*, diced
4 Tbsp minced fresh cilantro
2 C chopped spinach, chard or kale**
more chopped cilantro as garnish
2 Tbsp capers as garnish (optional)
baked potatoes, baked yams, or
    4 C cooked rice (optional)

In a large soup kettle, gently warm EVOO. Add onions and sauté about 5 minutes, or until translucent. Add black pepper, carrots, corn kernels, water or chicken broth, strained tomatoes or tomato juice, oregano and salt. Bring soup to a gentle boil. Lower heat as much as you can, stir in chicken, cover pot and simmer soup 15 minutes. Turn off heat. Stir in greens, cover pot and let soup stand another 10 minutes. Greens will wilt but be bright green.

Ladle into bowls and garnish with whatever floats your boat. You can put a long half of a baked potato or yam in the middle of each bowl, or ladle into bowls over steamed rice. This soup then becomes a hearty meal.

I prefer chicken thighs because I think the dark meat has much more flavor, but if you must use breasts, then use breasts!

**You can use the stems (or not) of whichever green you choose. If you decide the stems add too much crunch for your crowd, save them to sauté with other veggies or steam them with your greens the next day.*

Spanish Summer Soup

We keep hearing how healthy the Mediterranean diet is, and the traditional Spanish summer soup gazpacho was the subject of a two-week trial some years back. Subjects who ate two bowls of gazpacho, something like the soup below, every day for two weeks, were found to have more vitamin C in their blood and to show a decrease in key stress markers. The study, reported in the *Journal of Nutrition*, 2004, said: "Consumption of the vegetable soup decreases oxidative stress and biomarkers of inflammation, which indicates that the protective effect of vegetables may extend beyond their antioxidant capacity." So, this is good for you. It tastes great. Yes, treat yourself.

Serves 6

1 cucumber, about 2 C, chopped
2 medium tomatoes, about 3 C, chopped
1 small green pepper, about 1 C, chopped
2 C tomato juice*
¼ C red wine vinegar

2 strands saffron
1 onion, about 2 C, chopped
2 cloves garlic, minced
¼ C extra virgin olive oil (EVOO)
pinches of oregano and basil

Prepare vegetables, and save and set aside about 2 Tbsp of chopped tomato, pepper and onion. Blend everything else in your blender or food processor. Unless you have a large blender like a Vitamix, you will need to blend in a couple of batches. Put each blended batch into a soup pot or tureen. Stir. Refrigerate covered for a couple of hours.

Serve soup in bowls garnished with the reserved chopped tomato, pepper and onion.

You can put cooked scallops or shrimp or seasoned tofu into soup when serving. You can also sprinkle diced Serrano ham or hard boiled egg on top. Serve with crusty bread and more EVOO for dipping. Yumm.

As I've said in several other places, Bionaturae strained tomatoes are the best tomato juice you'll ever taste. You can, of course, blend tomatoes from your garden instead.

Spring Organic Asparagus Soup

This recipe comes from our April 2006 newsletter, and it said, "Since ancient times, harvesting wild asparagus, famous for its medicinal qualities, was a springtime ritual. Asparagus folklore credits the delicious green spears with everything from curing toothaches to being a reproductive tonic. Today we know asparagus is an excellent source of folic acid, vitamin C and carotenoids, strong disease-fighting antioxidants. According to the National Cancer Institute, asparagus tested higher than any other food for glutathione, one of the body's most potent cancer fighters, protector of the liver and lungs. Additionally, asparagus is high in rutin, which strengthens the blood vessels.

Serves 4-6

2 Tbsp extra-virgin olive oil (EVOO), or butter
1 onion, about 2 C sliced
1 lb asparagus
1 C green peas or ½ lb spinach
¼ tsp dried thyme
¾ tsp dried tarragon

4 C water or vegetable stock
¼ C almond meal (optional)
1 tsp sea salt
1 tsp black pepper
1 Tbsp umeboshi vinegar
1 tsp truffle oil (optional)

In a soup kettle, gently warm EVOO or butter. Sauté onion until soft and translucent, about 5 minutes.

Rinse asparagus, snap off and discard the tough stem ends, and slice off and reserve the tips. Cut spears into 1-inch pieces and add to soup pot along with peas or spinach, thyme, tarragon, water or vegetable stock, almond meal, salt and black pepper. Stir, cover pot and simmer about 5 minutes.

Blend soup in food processor or blender, or use a Bir mixer right in the pot (a Bir mixer is an immersible hand-held blender). Put pureed soup back into pot.

Add umeboshi vinegar, truffle oil (if desired) and reserved asparagus tops. Cover pot and let soup stand for 5 minutes so tips soften slightly and flavors meld. Serve to "umms and yumms." This soup is light and lively and you'll be glad you made it!

Note: You might want to serve this soup with wholegrain bread or crackers topped with pumpkin seed butter and a spring salad garnished with watercress.

Summer Minestrone

If you're missing one of the vegetables listed in the ingredients, don't worry. Just use a little more of any vegetable you have in your refrigerator or garden. And if you don't like the vegetables I've chosen, choose your own combination. Remember, it's your soup, dollink.

Don't bother to peel carrots. Scrub and slice. Most of the vitamins are in the peel, so read a good book instead of standing over the sink peeling carrots!

Serves 6

6 C water or vegetable broth
6 cloves garlic, minced
1 onion, chopped, about 2 C
2 carrots, halved & sliced, about 4 C
2 celery stalks, about 3 C, sliced
2 leaves kale, diced
2 tomatoes, diced, about 4 C
½ lb green beans
2 zucchini, about 4 C, halved, sliced

1 can Eden cannellini beans, or 2 C cooked
2 Tbsp fresh parsley, chopped
2 tsp each fresh basil, oregano, minced
2 C spinach leaves, chopped coarsely
1 tsp each salt and black pepper
2 Tbsp extra virgin olive oil (EVOO)
2 Tbsp Pecorino romano

Put water or vegetable broth, garlic, onion, carrots, celery, kale, tomatoes, green beans, zucchini, cannellini beans and herbs into soup kettle. Bring soup to a boil, turn flame down to low, cover pot, and simmer soup for 10 minutes. Turn off heat and stir in spinach. Cover pot again and let soup sit for another few minutes.

Ladle into bowls. Serve drizzled with EVOO and a sprinkle of Pecorino (or you can serve plain, without EVOO and romano).

Can you put this soup in the refrigerator and serve it cold? Yes. It's perfect in the summer when we can take advantage of all the fresh garden veggies. But you can eat it hot anytime of year too.

SZECHWAN CARROT

A carrot soup that delivers protein, beta carotene and phytoestrogens. Wow. Tastes good too. Serve with a tossed green salad and wholegrain bread. Dinner complete.

Is it better to eat carrots raw or cooked? There is some evidence that says cooked carrots are more nutritious. Practitioners of traditional Chinese medicine have always recommended that their patients eat lightly cooked carrots in order to get the best nutritional absorption. Which isn't to say you should stop chomping on a fresh, raw carrot when the mood strikes.

Can you use this recipe and substitute parsnips, squash or yams for carrots? Of course you can!

Serves 6-8

3 onions, about 6 C, chopped
3 ribs celery, about 4-5 C, sliced
1 Tbsp garlic, minced
3 lb carrots, sliced (scrubbed, not peeled)
3 Tbsp fresh ginger, not peeled, chopped
⅓ tsp cayenne pepper

12 C water or vegetable stock
6 Tbsp tamari (soy sauce)
6 Tbsp peanut butter*
1 Tbsp toasted sesame oil
4 C milk, soy or almond or rice milk
Sea salt or black pepper to taste

In a large soup kettle, put onions, celery, garlic, carrots, ginger, cayenne and water or vegetable stock. Bring soup to a boil, turn down heat, and cover pot. Simmer soup about 45 minutes.

In a food processor or blender, puree soup together with tamari, peanut butter and sesame oil. Unless you have a large blender or food processor, you may need to puree in batches. Put each batch of pureed soup into a clean soup pot. Add milk of your choice. Stir soup well. Taste and adjust seasoning. Dot's all there is to this one.

Make sure you use a real peanut butter, one that contains just peanuts. If you use a homogenized peanut butter with ingredients you can't even pronounce, this recipe will not work!

Yellow Potato Corn Chowder

Many people called the store when this ran in our January 2005 newsletter to ask if I really meant to use that much corn. I did and do, but you can use more potatoes and less corn if you prefer. I like, really like, lots and lots of corn! However, using more potatoes and less corn saves mucho dineros.

I don't usually make soups with milk or with bacon, but this one is truly great! Of course there are variations, and you can use rice or soy milk instead of milk-milk, which is lovely too. Don't do bacon? A terrific vegetarian option is one of my favorite products by Lightlife made from tempeh called "Fakin' Bacon smoky tempeh strips." Tempeh is an easy-to-digest, fermented soybean product.

This soup is a snap, and, yes, do use organic everything so you get the most bang for your buck, the most nutritional value, the most vitamins, all without pesticides, herbicides or the other "cides" that don't do a body good.

Serves 4

2 yellow potatoes, about 4 C, diced	6 C whole milk
2 Tbsp butter or ghee (or olive oil)	12 C corn kernels (frozen okay)
1 onion, about 2 C, chopped	6 oz duck bacon or Fakin' Bacon
1 tsp sea salt	2 Tbsp dried parsley flakes
1 Tbsp black pepper	

Start by scrubbing your potatoes... dice but don't peel.

Melt butter or ghee in a soup kettle. Add onion, salt and pepper, and sauté until onion is slightly colored. In a blender, put half the milk and half the corn. With on-off motions of blender, chop the corn kernels.

To soup kettle, add potatoes, remainder of milk, remainder of corn and corn-milk mixture. Heat gently.

While soup is warming, cook bacon over medium heat in a dry pan until crisp. With a slotted spoon, transfer bacon to a plate.

Watch soup carefully so milk doesn't boil over. Just as the soup is about to come to a boil, turn heat to low, cover pot, and simmer 20 minutes or until potatoes are tender. In the meantime, crumble bacon, then add half to soup. When soup is done, taste and adjust seasonings. (I like with extra black pepper.)

Dish out, sprinkle with parsley and remaining bacon bits. My brother David says this is the best soup he's ever eaten. It does satisfy the craving in winter for something fatty and tasty. And the corn color reminds us of summer sunshine, sorely missed in winter.

Velvety Swedish Fruit Soup

A perfect summer recipe which appeared in our August 2005 newsletter. Not only refreshing and cooling, this fruit delight serves as a perfect remedy for people who are stressed from mental pressure or hot weather. Plus it tastes delicious!

Blueberries, one of my favorite fruits, come originally from northern Europe but are grown today mainly in the US (blueberry's smaller European cousin is the bilberry). Blueberries, like cranberries, contain an antibiotic-like compound which prevents recurring urinary tract and bladder infections. Blueberries are said to help with hypoglycemia and tinnitus, and are high in manganese, vitamin A, potassium, silicon and iron, and the blue pigment is said to be liver-protective. As if that's not enough, blueberries contain a class of vitamins called anthocyanins, which are used to treat fragile capillaries and varicose veins.

Studies show anthocyanins are helpful in preventing cataracts and retinal degeneration too.

One of the nicest things about blueberries is that they require no prep before using or eating. Rinse and pop those puppies into your mouth. Of course organic is the best way to go!

Serves 8

1½ qt water	1 C sliced peaches
1 orange, sliced thinly, peel on	1 C pitted cherries
½ C raisins	3 Tbsp lemon juice
¼ C diced, dried pineapple	1 tsp orange extract
2 Tbsp tapioca pearls	1 tsp lemon extract
½ tsp sea salt	¼ tsp cinnamon
1 C blueberries	½ C honey or agave

Combine water through sea salt in a large kettle and simmer for 20 minutes. Remove soup from flame and let cool. Add remaining ingredients, mix thoroughly and refrigerate. Serve very cold.

Of course if you use frozen fruit, the soup takes minutes to prepare because the slicing and dicing has been done for you...

Note: A naturopathic physician I spoke to said frozen blueberries are actually higher in nutrients than the fresh ones. We do carry 5# bags of organic frozen blueberries in our store, which have no label because these are meant for food service. Many of you have already discovered them together with unmarked 5# bags of strawberries and more. Buying them this way is a cost savings for sure. Perfect for smoothies too.

Salads

I love lettuce, and romaine is my favorite. I could happily eat a salad of romaine lettuce everyday if someone else would wash it for me! But there umpteen other varieties of lettuce, some crisp and some soft like butter with edges of scarlet. It's hard to decide which is the more perfect, the more beautiful in the salad bowl. Lettuce is my salad mainstay in spring and early summer, and it's a thrill to see it arrive in our store from local farms, each head like a painting, a work of art.

Then it gets hot. Summer truly arrives, and with it, tomatoes of all kinds and colors, and pickling cucumbers. Cilantro, dill and lots and lots of basil. It's time to switch gears and use less lettuce. I eat along with Mother Nature and her cycles.

That's why I like cabbage salads in the winter, when there are no more local, juicy tomatoes. Not everyone agrees, and I thought a good introduction to this salad chapter would be Adam's article from our July 2009 newsletter, which shows different strokes for different folks.

The Mediterranean Salad: Lettuce-Free Zone

I was in Israel and Turkey recently, and I ate a lot of salad. I wasn't trying to—just every time I sat down to a meal, there it was. So I ate it. And I enjoyed it.

And it got me to thinking: we do salads wrong in this country. Forgive my lack of patriotism, but when I think of the American salad, I think of lettuce, lettuce, and more lettuce, dotted with the occasional "other" vegetable. The only thing that changes night-to-night is the dressing—hopefully enough of it so you don't actually have to see the lettuce.

(We'd never tolerate that monotony from our entrees: "What are we having for dinner every night for the next eight weeks, mom?" "Chicken?" So why do we tolerate the same salad every night?)

Since when have we been so hung-up on lettuce, anyways? It's really not that special. And it's so delicate! It doesn't keep. So eating it off-season is ecologically rough—all that fuel and refrigeration to get it to you fresh. And a salad based on lettuce isn't very filling, either. A bowl of lettuce is mostly a bowl of air. Tomatoes, carrots, cabbage, and cucumbers, on the other hand, are solid.

The trick with solid vegetables is to get them into a fork-able state. So you're going to want a vegetable peeler. Not to take the peel off—lots of nutrients in that peel—but because a peeler turns carrots, radishes, etc., into perfectly toothsome, fork-able ribbons. A decent-sized carrot is reduced to ribbons in 20-30 seconds.

You really don't need a recipe. Nevertheless, here are three.

Adam Stark

PURPLE & ORANGE (THE COLOR, NOT THE FRUIT) SALAD

- **Roughly equal weights carrots and purple cabbage**
- **Extra virgin extra virgin olive oil (EVOO)**
- **Lemon juice, or lemon wedges**
- **Coarsely ground black pepper**
- **Sunflower seeds (optional)**

Use the peeler to shred the carrots, and then use a knife to do the same to the cabbage. Toss with some EVOO, sunflower seeds (optional) and black pepper to taste. You can either toss it with lemon juice, too, or serve each plate with a lemon wedge at the table.

Red*, White, and Green Salad

· **Plenty of lovely ripe tomatoes (may be any color!)**
· **Feta, ricotta salata, or any crumbly white salty cheese**
· **Capers in brine**
· **Extra virgin extra virgin olive oil (EVOO)**

Chunk the tomatoes. Crumble on some cheese. Fork some capers out of the bottle. Don't rinse them—you want that bit of vinegar. Toss it all with EVOO.

Classic Chopped Salad

· **Roughly equal parts tomatoes and cucumbers. (You're going to want plain ol' pickling cukes, not the big "impressive" English ones. Cheaper and tastier).**
· **Chopped red onion to taste.**
· **Extra virgin extra virgin olive oil (EVOO)**
· **Seasoning (I love oregano, but you can use other herbs; or Za'atar seasoning mix, with hyssop, sumac, and sesame seeds).**
· **Optional add-ins include: black or green olives, chopped bell pepper, fresh mozzarella, fresh herbs, summer squash, scallions, leftovers …**

Chop 'em up chunky, or mince 'em down fine. It's up to you. Dress with EVOO and lemon juice (or serve lemon wedges at the table)

It's me (Debra) again.

Enjoy the following recipes in our salad chapter. Yes, use ingredients that you love. Experiment. Change with the seasons. Use organic because you get higher nutrient values with organic produce.

I haven't used the word "organic" when listing ingredients for recipes, but I use only organic at home. I believe I'm investing in the future—no pesticides, no herbicides makes the world we live in safer. By eating organic, my veggies have more antioxidants, more vitamins and minerals, and so I'm helping lower health care costs too. Does organic cost more? Sometimes. Not always. But when I choose to spend my dollars on organically-grown produce, I am supporting famers who grow the healthiest and tastiest vegetables possible, and I am making an investment in my own health. I'm worth it. You're worth it too!

Aaron's Spanky Raw Corn Slaw

"After my car slid off a muddy road near the small town of Lava, Idaho, I realized the rest of my road trip would have to wait until things dried up the next day. Luckily I had slid into a very nice field with soft, even ground, so I pitched my tent and set about making dinner. Having few options, I simply mixed all of my remaining foodstuffs into one raw salad, but the combination proved memorable. I ate it then out of necessity, but I continue to eat it every summer out of sheer love for the marriage of complimentary flavors: the sweetness of the raw corn, the heat of the cayenne, the coolness of the cilantro, and so on. This dish is a celebration of texture, color and seasonality, and it's the perfect summer slaw. There are plenty of similar recipes out there, but this one gets it right."

Serves 4-6

1 heirloom tomato, diced, about 2 C
1 small red onion, diced, about 1 C
1 ripe Hass avocado, halved, peeled, diced
the fresh juice of 1 lime, about 2 Tbsp
2 ears native corn suitable for eating raw

1 can Eden pinto beans, or 2 C cooked
1 bunch cilantro, about 2 C
1 tsp cayenne pepper
1 Tbsp sea salt
2 Tbsp extra virgin olive oil (EVOO)

Place the diced tomato in a strainer to drain. Let the diced onion and avocado sit in the juice of the lime while you prepare the other ingredients. Shuck the ears of corn, break them in half and slice the kernels from the cob. Open, drain and rinse the pintos. Carefully wash and then coarsely chop the cilantro.

Combine all of the ingredients in a mixing bowl, stirring carefully so as not to "smush" the avocado.

Adjust the amount of salt and lime juice to taste (I like lots of both). Serve room temperature or chilled. Serve alone, as a dip for tortilla chips, or a sandwich topping. Don't forget to drink the tomato water. It's great; you just don't want it sloshing around in the slaw.

Note from Debra: I always toss my salads with a rubber spatula, which doesn't mush or smoosh anything.

ALMOND KELP NOODLE SALAD

Amanda adapted this in May 2008 from a recipe on a package of Sea Tangle kelp noodles. Amanda says, "This lively and delicious salad will surprise everyone when you tell them the 'noodles' are actually mineral-packed sea kelp! Jazzed up with toasted sesame oil and lemon, this dish tickles and brightens the palate and satisfies a salt craving without weighing down your system."

Kelp noodles are gluten-free, and very low in carbohydrates and calories. Their texture is chewy, and you can use them anywhere you'd use pasta. They are, for those of you who follow a raw food diet, raw and ready to use right out of the bag. Ingredients? Kelp, water, sodium alginate (from brown seaweed).

The coconut water in the recipe is interesting, in addition to which, you get to drink the rest. Coconut water is refreshing, tastes great, energizes and replaces electrolytes. Much, much better than Gatorade!

What to serve this dish with? Amanda suggests a pairing with simple tofu broiled in a little oil and salt, sprinkled with black sesame seeds. She uses black sesame seeds to garnish the noodle dish too.

Serves 6 as a side dish, 4 as a main dish

12-oz pkg Sea Tangle kelp noodles
1 C carrots, grated
1 C each red and green cabbage,
   shredded
2 C sliced baby bok choy
¼ C shredded daikon or red radish
6 Tbsp almond butter*

2 Tbsp grated ginger
½ C coconut water
1 Tbsp toasted sesame oil
2 Tbsp lemon or lime juice
1½ tsp sea salt
1 Tbsp tamari (soy sauce)
½ tsp cayenne pepper (optional)

Place kelp noodles (these noodles are ready to use, ready to eat—just open the package and put in bowl—what could be easier?) in a salad bowl. Using a food processor or knife, grate carrots, cabbage and radish. Place in a bowl together with bok choy and kelp noodles.

Get out that handy blender and blend the almond butter, ginger, coconut water, sesame oil, lemon juice, sea salt, tamari and cayenne (if you're going spicy). Pour dressing over your vegetables and noodles, toss and let salad sit to marinate for 30 minutes.

*Feel free to substitute another nut butter or soy nut butter for the almond butter. Do what floats your boat and suits your nutrition needs.

Arame Salad with Ginger and Sesame

We all know how healthy seaweed is. There, I've said the "h" word. "Healthy" is a turn-off for most people. But don't be afraid—give sea veggies a try. Virtually calorie-free, high protein, they've been used in other cultures as food and medicine for thousands of years. The Chinese use seaweed to disperse congestion, remove fat, reduce internal heat, suppress coughs and remedy high blood pressure. The Japanese use daikon radishes to help digest rich, starchy food, and daikon radishes, like other sulfur-bearing vegetables, are said to have cancer-preventative properties.

We developed this recipe in our kitchen when customers asked us how to use arame.

Will you know you're eating seaweed? Sure. This is not an ice cream sundae, but remember that variety is the spice of life. So vary what you eat!

Serves 4

1 pkg Eden arame seaweed (about 2 oz)
2 C sliced red radishes
2 C sliced daikon radish
4 C sliced red onions
¼ C brown rice vinegar
4 C carrots, scrubbed, not peeled, diced

½ C tamari (soy sauce)
1 Tbsp ginger powder
½ tsp black pepper
2 tsp umeboshi plum vinegar
¼ C toasted sesame oil
¼ C brown, unhulled sesame seeds*

Soak arame for 1 hour. Drain thoroughly and squeeze. The stuff is hardy and can take that kind of abuse, so squeeze away. Mix all ingredients in a large bowl. Toss using hands or spoon and fork.

Use as a salad or as a condiment. A little dab will do you with a meal. This keeps nicely for a few days.

* Use brown, unhulled sesame seeds because they'll give you 10 times the calcium and magnesium that you get if you use the white, hulled ones. I buy the brown, unhulled sesame seeds from our bulk bin and store at home in my freezer. They cost pennies compared to little packets of sesame seeds you buy in supermarkets.

Arugula and Fennel Salad with Walnuts

Arugula is also known as rocket, roquette, rugula and rucola, and is popular in Italian cuisine. Popular now here too! It's aromatic and can be quite peppery depending upon the time of year it is harvested and how mature the plant is. Like other greens, arugula is low in calories—heck, you can eat a whole cup and it will be only 4 calories. Don't have arugula? Feel free to use watercress for a similar peppery flavor. If you don't like the peppery taste, make this with baby spinach.

Walnuts are one of the best plant sources of protein. And they have significantly higher amounts of omega 3 fatty acids when compared to other nuts. I love their taste and the fact you can see them easily in this salad. Pine nuts, which I also love, would tend to get lost.

Serves 6

8 C arugula, trimmed, torn
1 large fennel bulb, trimmed,
   quartered lengthwise and sliced
   thinly crosswise
1 head Belgium endive
1 red onion, sliced thinly, about 2 C

3 Tbsp extra virgin olive oil (EVOO)
1½ Tbsp lemon juice
4 cloves garlic, crushed
1 tsp each black pepper and sea salt
1½ C walnuts

Prepare all vegetables so the pieces will fit into your mouth easily. There's nothing like trying to eat a salad with a long stem of arugula hanging out of your mouth as you try to chew it delicately. Put all veggies into a large salad bowl and add remaining ingredients except for ½ C of the walnuts. Save those for garnish.

Toss vegetables and dressing until all the greens are well-coated. I like to use my hands. I like to be able to feel the salad. And, yes, I do wash my hands before using them as my tossing tool! Alternatively, use your serving salad fork and spoon to toss.

Divide salad amongst 6 plates and garnish with reserved walnuts.

If instead of walnuts you prefer shredded parmesan cheese, that's nice too!

CURRIED LEMON CHICKEN SALAD WITH KEFIR

The word "kefir" comes from the Turkish and means "good feeling." Kefir is a cultured and microbial-rich food, which means it's rich in probiotics, the good bugs that live in our gut. Kefir helps with digestion and is sometimes fine for people who are lactose intolerant. Folks round the world such as the healthy Hunzas, who live at the extreme northern point of India where the borders of Kashmir, China, India and Afghanistan converge in the Himalayan Mountains, and people in Bulgaria rely on kefir to stimulate the immune system and keep them well. Refreshing, and you'll love the taste!

For those who don't eat chicken, substitute extra-firm tofu (cubed) or diced sweet potatoes or winter squash. Shrimp or scallops in lieu of chicken are also delish. For those who do eat chicken, Eberly's organic chickens are the best!

Serves 8

1 C plain kefir	3 C organic cooked chicken, cut into bite-sized pieces
2 tsp curry powder	
1 tsp dried thyme	2 C apples, cored, with skin on, diced
½ tsp ground coriander	2 C cooked sliced carrots
1 tsp ground cumin	2 C raw zucchini, cut lengthwise into quarters and then thinly sliced
1 tsp black pepper	
1 tsp sea salt	½ C lemon juice
2 Tbsp extra virgin olive oil (EVOO)	½ C roasted cashews (optional)
½ C raisins (optional)	

In a large bowl, whisk kefir with herbs, spices, EVOO and raisins (if you want to use those). Add chicken and toss well. Add apples, carrots, zucchini and lemon juice. Toss well again so everything is coated with dressing. Allow salad to stand at room temperature for about an hour. That gives the spices the time they need to permeate and flavor the salad.

Ready to serve? Serve on a bed of greens, or over a grain like basmati rice or quinoa. Garnish with roasted cashews. Tuck into pita to package and send for lunch.

If any vegetable you cut yields a little more than the recipe calls for, feel free to use it up in the salad. That's why we taste and adjust seasoning at the end!

DEBRA'S NATURAL GOURMET TABOULIE

New and improved, as they say. Our original taboulie recipe appeared in our first cookbook, now out of print, and this juicier version appeared in our May 2004 newsletter. Try eating it wrapped inside a romaine lettuce leaf, or inside a whole wheat pita with tahini sauce.

All you low-carb folks, don't be afraid of whole grains and beans! Yes, whole grains and beans are carbohydrates, but they are complex carbohydrates which stabilize blood sugar levels. If you don't eat good carbs, your body will crave them. Good carbs also contain vitamins, minerals and fiber, as well as some protein.

For those of you who have trouble with beans, this recipe combines beans with olive oil, which makes them easier to digest. And chickpeas, also known as garbanzo beans, are said to be more easily digested than other beans*. Besides, they provide texture and interest to this dish. They taste great too!

Serves 6

1 C coarse red bulgur
1 C boiling water
1 can organic diced tomatoes, 2 C
⅓ C red onion, diced
½ C extra virgin olive oil (EVOO)

4 C fresh parsley, chopped
1 can Eden chickpeas, or 2 C cooked
⅓ C lemon juice
1 tsp sea salt
1 tsp black pepper

Place bulgur in a large bowl and pour boiling water over it. Stir and let stand until water is absorbed, about 30 minutes. After the 30 minutes, fluff grain with a fork from time to time to cool.

Drain tomatoes, gently squeeze excess liquid out (save liquid for soups). When bulgur is cool, add tomatoes together with remaining ingredients. Toss until well mixed. Let stand, covered, for an hour so the flavors marry.

Want a quick dinner? Serve with a dollop of hummus and some stuffed grape leaves. Carrot sticks, kalamata olives and sliced cucumbers add variety and color.

Note: Is this gluten-free? No. Bulgur, the oldest processed food known, is wheat, which is soaked, dried and then milled to remove the outer bran. If you can't eat wheat or gluten, try making this with a grain like sorghum. Sorghum, of course, will need to be cooked, but you can keep some cooked in glass jars in your freezer, can't you?

Eden brand beans are cooked with a piece of seaweed called kombu, which makes beans more digestible. That's one reason Eden beans are my favorite, when I don't cook my own.

Dilled Potato Salad with Green Peas, Chicken and Lentils

I love all the information one can find on the internet! I learned that lentils have been feeding people since prehistoric times, and lentil artifacts have been found at archeological digs dating back 8,000 years. The potato, on the other hand, is thought to have been discovered first by pre-Columbian farmers about 7,000 years ago. Lentils traveled around the world pretty quickly, but Western peoples didn't learn about potatoes until sometime around 1537 when the Conquistadors tramped through Peru. And it was even later, about 1570, that the first potato made its way across the Atlantic to make a start on the continent of Europe.

Don't stint on the olive oil, because you want your food to have pizzazz. This salad is best served at room temperature.

Serves 4

- 1 lb small red or yellow potatoes, scrubbed and cut into bite-sized pieces
- 2-3 C water for cooking lentils
- 1 C black, brown or blue lentils, rinsed
- 1 red or white onion, minced
- 1 C peas
- 4 C large-dice cooked chicken
- ½-1 C extra virgin olive oil (EVOO)
- 1 C marinated sun-dried tomatoes*
- 1 Tbsp dried oregano
- 1 bunch fresh dill, chopped, about 2 C
- 4 cloves garlic, pressed
- 1 tsp sea salt
- 1 tsp black pepper

Steam potatoes in a small pot with a cup or two of water until tender, which means you can easily pierce potato with a small knife. Drain and put into mixing bowl.

Bring 2-3 C water to a boil. Add lentils to boiling water. Cook until tooth-tender, about 15-20 minutes. Drain lentils (there may be a little water that hasn't been absorbed) and add them to potatoes.

Add remaining ingredients and toss with a rubber spatula until salad is well mixed. Be careful not to stir. You want your potatoes and lentils to have definition and shape.

You can drain your sun-dried tomatoes (I'm assuming they're in luscious EVOO) and use that oil as part of the EVOO in the ingredient list above.

FLAMENCO TURTLE BEAN SALAD

This ran in our May 2001 newsletter, and we still make it in the kitchen. Not only does this salad look beautiful and taste great, but umeboshi plum vinegar (I know I've said this several times already, but it's true…) has digestive enzymes. Avocados provide good fat which helps dissolve bad fat, or so they say. But avocados are one of the most perfect foods, and I love them madly and dearly. Don't be afraid to eat them, please.

Black beans, botanicallyknown as *Phaseolus vulgaris*, are native to Central and South America where they're also known as turtle beans, caviar criollo, and frijoles negros. They've been a staple for more than 7,000 years in Central and South America. Aren't we lucky they were brought north to us?

This is an easy salad to make, and even easier if you use organic produce. You can save time because you don't have to peel waxed and sprayed cucumbers.

Serves 4

1 can Eden black beans, or
  2 C cooked
2 ripe Hass avocados, halved, peeled,
  diced
2½ C English cucumbers, diced
½ C red onion, minced
2 C red pepper, diced
2 Tbsp lemon juice

2 Tbsp umeboshi plum vinegar*
¼ C extra virgin olive oil (EVOO)
1 tsp sea salt
1 tsp garlic, minced
¾ tsp dried basil
¾ tsp dried oregano
1 tsp black pepper

Make sure your beans are nicely drained. Place ingredients in a large bowl and toss using a rubber spatula, not a spoon that will mush your avocado. If your cucumber (or any vegetable) yields a little more than the recipe calls for, feel free to use it. Simply taste and adjust seasoning at the end.

Serve right away or chill an hour.

Note: If you want to prepare this the night before, add avocado just before serving instead of when making the salad. At times I add feta, chopped hard-boiled eggs or tofu to make it a whole meal. It all works!

*Or substitute 1 Tbsp umeboshi plum paste

GARLICKY RADISH SALAD

Ben Jonson, a contemporary of Shakespeare, suggested radishes be eaten before tasting wine. I'm not sure how he arrived at that conclusion, but did you know that the radish gets its name from the Greek word for "fast-appearing," because it is quick-growing? Historians tell us that radishes were first cultivated in China, and then popular in Egypt where they were fed to the slaves to keep them strong and healthy.

I didn't know that radishes are a member of the mustard family. I did know they come in reds, purples, whites and blacks, and can grow up to 100 pounds each. Radishes come in different shapes too, and some are as long as 3 feet.

More avocados here. Eating avocado everyday will not make you fat, but it might lower your bad cholesterol. Avocados help your skin look lovely. Psoriasis is said to be relieved by eating half an avocado a day. Avocado is also said to soothe inflammation, and topically, you can mash avocado and smooth over your skin. Instant facial! Just rinse off with warm water before you head out the door.

Serves 4

1 C grated carrot
1 C grated daikon radish
1 C grated red radish
1 ripe Hass avocado, halved, peeled, diced
1 green bell pepper, chopped

¾ C plain yogurt
1 tsp dried dill weed
1 Tbsp extra virgin olive oil (EVOO)
6 cloves garlic, pressed
1½ Tbsp tamari (soy sauce)

Using the coarse shredding disk of your food processor, grate carrots and daikon radish. You can grate red radishes too, but I prefer to slice these.

Put all ingredients in a salad mixing bowl. Toss. Do a little dance while salad chills about an hour. Serve. You done good, honeybunch.

Glowing Salad

I've taken the liberty of repeating in this, our third cookbook, a few of my favorite recipes published in our first cookbook, now out of print, because they are too good to let die.

This is one my mother used to make once a week so our skin would be clear and healthy. She'd serve it on a romaine lettuce leaf with a slice of avocado and a sprig of parsley as edible garnishes. The combination was beautiful. The taste, divine.

Mom used to grate this salad by hand. Nowadays, I use a food processor, and it takes literally minutes to make!

Don't know how to cut a fresh pineapple? Lay the pineapple on its side, with the spiky green end on your right (if you're right-handed, vice versa if you're left-handed). Hold the body of the fruit with you left hand and carefully cut off the top. Turn the fruit around and cut off the base. Cut the fruit into quarters lengthwise. Cut each quarter in half crosswise. Then stand each section on the wider part, and carefully cut the tough rind off the section by sawing gently downwards. Each section of the fruit should now be free of exterior rinds. Now, with each section still standing on its wider end, cut the inner core from the pineapple. Finally, cut each section in half lengthwise, then chop crosswise into bite-size chunks.

Serves 4

1 fresh pineapple, cubed
1-2 large carrots
1 apple, halved and core taken out
1 medium red beet, trimmed and
   halved

1 C juice like orange or mango
1 C raisins (optional)
4 romaine lettuce leaves
4 sprigs of parsley
1 Hass avocado, quartered

Cut pineapple and put in salad mixing bowl. Scrub carrots, apple and beet. Trim but don't peel. You want the vitamins contained in the peel in you and not in the compost pile. Besides, who has the time to peel vegetables?

Using the coarse grating blade of a food processor, grate carrots, apple and beet. Add to pineapple in bowl together with the juice. Using a rubber spatula, mix salad well so you don't have clumps of beet and so the whole salad is rosy, red. Chill, covered, in the refrigerator for about an hour before serving. Can be made the day before too. Spoon onto romaine lettuce leaf and garnish with parsley and avocado.

Note: Beets are high in iron. They not only enrich blood, they cleanse the system. This raw salad does wonders for all of you. Kids love this salad too.

GREEN BEAN AND RED CRANBERRY SALAD

Most kids love green beans, and they are one of the most popular vegetables to grow at home because they are easy to take care of and the plants produce lots. The only problem is that rabbits love them too, and in my garden, the bunnies make a bee-line for my beans. I don't mind sharing, but they always seem to eat more than half, and so I never have quite enough to freeze.

The old English word "bean," which came first from the German, means a legume that is picked when immature. Green beans *are* just the beginnings of a full-grown, adult bean, aren't they?

No need to worry about calories while getting iron, fiber and other nutrients because 2 cups of green beans gives you only about 85 calories.

Serves 6

1 small red onion, minced, about 1 C	4 oz arugula, about 8 C
¼ C extra virgin olive oil (EVOO)	1 C dried cranberries
1 Tbsp umeboshi plum vinegar	3 hard-boiled eggs, peeled, chopped
1 tsp black pepper	coarsely
1 lb young green beans, trimmed	1 can Eden chickpeas, or 2 C cooked

Place first 4 ingredients in a salad bowl. Stir.

Steam green beans in a medium pot with 1 C of water until crisp-tender, about 3 minutes. Pour into colander and run under cold water to cool. Drain well. Transfer to salad bowl and add arugula, cranberries, ½ the eggs and chickpeas (make sure you drain these beans too). Toss everything to coat. Serve topped with rest of chopped eggs.

Note: Can you substitute another green for arugula? Yes. Can you use chopped dried apricots instead of cranberries? Or use pecans? Of course. Do you have to use eggs? No. This becomes your recipe, just as they all do. So do what floats your boat.

Green Potato Salad with Cilantro and Spinach

I love this recipe by Amanda. The website, www.WhatsCookingAmerica.net has wonderful information about potatoes, such as archaeologists working in Peru and Chile found potato remains dating back to 500 B.C.E. The Incas of Peru not only grew and ate potatoes, but buried them with their dead, so revered were they. Potatoes were also dried and carried on journeys to eat on the way or make into stew.

Each year, I look forward to the new crop of yellow potatoes and love the purple ones too!

Why cilantro? Because it tastes great. But did you know that cilantro, used as medicine and food by the Romans, is said to help detox the liver? It's also a good blood cleanser, and I like that cilantro is said to stabilize blood sugar since potatoes have a high glycemic index. This doesn't mean a diabetic is okay eating 5 pounds of potatoes, even with cilantro and with the addition of a good fat like olive oil to help "smooth" things out. So exercise good judgment if you have blood sugar problems!

Serves 8

5 lb yellow potatoes with skins, scrubbed and halved
⅓ C raw apple cider vinegar
1 tsp each sea salt and black pepper
2 Tbsp minced garlic (or to taste)
juice of one lemon, about ½ C

½ C extra virgin olive oil (EVOO)
1 lb baby spinach
1 big bunch cilantro, washed and chopped, including stems, about 2 C
sea salt and pepper to taste

Cover potatoes in water, bring water to a boil and then cook potatoes until soft, about 25 minutes. Drain and place hot potatoes in bowl. Sprinkle with apple cider vinegar, salt and pepper. Toss.

In a measuring cup, squeeze a little lemon over the minced garlic to mellow it out. Whisk in EVOO.

Pour over the warm potatoes and toss to distribute. Stir in the spinach, which will wilt a little bit and cook from the heat. Sprinkle cilantro and give it another good stir. Add salt and pepper to taste and serve!

HIMALAYAN RED RICE SALAD

This recipe from Amanda appeared in our September 2008 newsletter. She says this whole-grain rice tastes great, looks awesome and cooks in only twenty minutes. Himalayan red rice is an ancient short-grain rice grown 8,000 feet up in the Himalayan Kingdom of Bhutan. Irrigated with 1,000-year old glacier water rich in trace minerals, Himalayan red rice has a nutty flavor, soft texture and beautiful red russet color. So sayeth websites that rave about the rice. And, yes, we stock it in our bulk bins. A hand-crafted, heirloom rice, grown without pesticides and herbicides. You'll like it!

Serves 4-6

1 large yam, diced, about 4 C
pinch sea salt
2 C Himalayan red rice
3½ C water
¾ C sliced almonds
1 C celery, chopped
½ C chopped flat parsley

¼ lb Smyrna figs, soaked 10 minutes
  in warm water
1 C chopped red onion
½ C lemon juice
1 tsp sea salt
1 tsp black pepper
1 tsp Chinese five-spice mix
½ C extra virgin olive oil (EVOO)

Amanda says, "Put the diced yam in a pot with a little salt. Cover with water and bring to a boil. Lower to a simmer and cook 15 minutes, until tender but still a little crisp.

Put rice and water in another pot. Bring to a boil, cover pot and turn flame down to a strong simmer. Set timer for 15 minutes. Check rice and add a little extra water if it looks really dry. Cook 5 minutes more. Remove pot from heat. Leave cover on if you prefer a softer rice. Remove cover for al dente.

Put almonds on a baking sheet, set a timer for 10 minutes, and toast at 350 degrees in oven or keep your nose handy; as soon as you can smell those nuts, they're done. Be careful not to burn them!

Chop celery and parsley, slice the presoaked figs and set all aside. Chop red onion and place in a bowl with the lemon juice, salt, pepper and Chinese five-spice mix. Whisk together, and keep whisking as you drizzle in EVOO. Now add yams, cooked rice, celery, figs and parsley. Toss to coat completely (Debra likes to toss using a rubber spatula). Serve warm with toasted almonds on top. Great with a peppery arugula salad!"

IT'S A SUMMER SALAD!

Five minutes is all you need for this dish which appeared in our July 2008 newsletter, and five years before that in another variation. The only ingredient needing advance prep are the spelt berries (or whichever grain you choose to use). I often cook up a pot-full when I'm reading the Sunday paper and then freeze in 2-C portions for future use.

Serves 4 as a main dish, 6-8 as a side dish

- 2 C cooked spelt berries*
- 2 C diced or sliced young zucchini
- 1 C minced red onion or sliced scallions
- 1 jar marinated artichoke hearts, about 1½ C (use marinade from jar too)
- 1 C crumbled organic feta or blue cheese
- 2 Tbsp fresh lemon juice
- 1 tsp fennel seeds or 1 C diced fresh fennel
- 1 Tbsp dried dill weed
- ¼ tsp allspice
- ¼ tsp garlic powder or 1 tsp minced fresh garlic
- ¼ tsp dried oregano
- ¼ tsp dried tarragon
- ¼ C extra virgin olive oil (EVOO)

Combine everything in a large bowl, and toss with a rubber spatula to mix. I find using the marinade from the artichoke hearts is a fine dressing, but have to admit, I do use the extra EVOO because I like olive oil (yes, I have used pumpkin seed oil, hemp oil and flax seed oil too).

Like many recipes, this one lends itself to almost endless variations or additions. Add wax beans, sliced mushrooms, pitted kalamata olives, hard-boiled eggs, cherry tomatoes or leftover chicken.

Spelt berries make this nice and chewy, but you can replace spelt with barley, wheat or rye berries. Alternatively, you can open a couple of cans of chickpeas and use those instead of the grain.

This is a fun dish to bring to a cookout or a potluck.

*How to cook spelt berries? Put 1 C berries together with 3 C water in a large pot that has a tight-fitting lid. Bring water and berries to a boil uncovered. Turn down heat to lowest, cover pot and move slightly off burner. Simmer for about an hour. If there's any water left (there shouldn't be), simply drain. Voila. Feel free to multiply the amount of berries and water if you want to have leftovers.

Jim's Dilled Carrot & Green Bean Estival Festival

Jim says, "This makes a refreshing summer salad. It's simple and flavorful, particularly when the great organically grown produce from our local farmers is right at hand. Fresh carrots, green beans and dill make a wonderful combination with a little balsamic vinegar. The chickpeas add protein and the red pepper and broccoli add color, flavor and texture. What more could you want on a hot summer evening?"

The World Carrot Museum says, "Carrots originated in present day Afghanistan about 5,000 years ago, probably as a purple or yellow root." Years later Dutch growers took carrots under their horticultural wings and developed them to be sweeter and more practical…

Serves 4

2 Tbsp extra virgin olive oil (EVOO)
2 onions, chopped, about 4 C
4 carrots, sliced thinly, about 6 C
1¼ lb green beans, cut into 2-inch pieces
½ C fresh dill, chopped
1 can Eden chickpeas, or 2 C cooked
1 red pepper, sliced

2 C broccoli florets
3 Tbsp tamari (soy sauce)
3 Tbsp water
4 Tbsp balsamic vinegar
sea salt or Herbamare seasoning

Wash and prepare all vegetables. Gently warm EVOO in large sauté pan. Add onions and sauté on medium heat until translucent, about 5 minutes. Add carrots, green beans and dill, stir, cover and leave on low heat for about 4 minutes. Drain beans well and add them with red pepper, broccoli florets, tamari and 3 Tbsp water and steam covered for about another 4 minutes. Add balsamic vinegar and if you wish, season with a little sea salt or Herbamare. Serve warm or at room temperature.

Kale Provençale Salad with Lentils

Mother Earth Magazine lists kale as one of the "Thirty-Three Greatest Foods for Healthy Living." Grown in Europe since 600 B.C.E., kale was the most common green vegetable, and in Scotland, kale in one dialect meant "food," and the expression "to be off one's kail" meant to feel too ill to eat.

This recipe was in our April 2007 newsletter.

Q. Who is the country's largest consumer of kale?
A. Pizza Hut, where it is used for decorating salad bars.

Serves 4-6

2 C cooked lentils (brown, blue or
  black)
4 hard boiled eggs, diced
1 C shredded carrots
2 C shredded green cabbage
1 C pitted oil-cured black olives
 (French herbed or La Medina)
½ C diced celery
2 C finely shredded kale

½ C diced red onion
½ C sliced radishes
1 jar marinated artichoke hearts,*
  about 1½ C
¼ C extra virgin olive oil (EVOO)
1 Tbsp Spike seasoning
1-2 C feta cheese** (optional)
black pepper (optional)

While this seems like a lot of ingredients, you can simplify by omitting some veggies or doubling up on your favorites. If you have healthy vegetable staples on hand together with foods like eggs, olive oil, olives, marinated artichoke hearts and Spike, this is a snap to make. If you work with a food processor, the prep is quick too.

Drain lentils and add to large mixing bowl. Place eggs in a single layer in a saucepan and cover with 1" cold water. Bring to a boil, cover and immediately remove from heat. Let stand 12 minutes. Drain and run the coldest water you've got over those eggs. Let stand for 2 minutes, then crack by gently tapping the egg against a hard surface. Peel under cold running water.

How to shred carrots and cabbage? Use the food processor, which makes life much easier. Chop kale, dice onions and slice radishes by hand. Add everything to salad bowl (including marinade from artichoke hearts, which then becomes part of the dressing). Toss salad. Taste and adjust seasoning.

If you choose to use artichoke hearts in water, then you'll need to add another ¼ cup of EVOO and ¼ cup lemon or apple cider vinegar.

**If you use feta cheese, cut the Spike to a heaping teaspoon instead of a tablespoon.*

Mexican Harvest Salad

Simple, homey ingredients. Almost too easy to make. Just one taste, however, and you'll be in heaven. Trust me. This salad, together with the last of the sliced organic summer tomatoes and basil, fennel and goat cheese on a separate platter, and you've a colorful, flavorful repast! This ran in our September 2004 newsletter.

I'm convinced (even before the scientific proof is in) that organic foods have more antioxidants and more of all the stuff that makes us healthier and happier too! How could they not, when they are grown in soil that is healthier and alive with life-promoting organisms?

Serves 6

3 C carrots, grated,* about 6 C
3 C zucchini or summer squash
8-12 large cloves garlic, peeled and pressed
3 ripe Hass avocados, halved, peeled, diced
1 can Eden black beans, or 2 C cooked

1 red pepper, diced
½ C lime juice
¼ C extra virgin olive oil (EVOO)
1 tsp black pepper
1 tsp sea salt

Rinse carrots and zucchini, but don't peel. (Why? You've better things to do with your time and you want to eat all the vitamins that are just under the skin instead of dumping them in the compost pile!) Grate carrots and zucchini with the coarse grating blade of your food processor.

Drain and rinse black beans. Combine all ingredients, toss and let stand for about ½ hour. Taste, adjust seasoning, toss again and serve.

Note: Can you use other vegetables? Of course. You can make this with only carrots or only squash, or replace either with parsnips, turnips or cabbage.

My machine didn't come with a coarse grating blade, which I ordered. I find I actually use the coarse grating/shredding blade more than any other because it makes terrific instant salads.

MIXED GREENS WITH BLUE CHEESE

So simple. I never get tired of greens with a good, garlicky olive oil dressing and something like blue cheese. Of course you can vary this any way you like.

Serves 8

¼ C Debra's Olive Oil Vinaigrette
   (below)
10 C loosely packed fresh greens*
1 C crumbled blue cheese (reserve
   some for garnish)

pint basket red cherry tomatoes
pint basket yellow tomatoes

Place greens in bowl. Toss with ½ dressing. Add ¾ C blue cheese and toss again. Arrange on plates. Top with red cherry and yellow pear tomatoes. Drizzle remaining dressing over. Sprinkle with reserved blue cheese.

* My mother used to use a whole head of romaine, tear in a bunch of watercress and add some curly endive or chicory. That's the combination I grew up eating and loved.

DEBRA'S OLIVE OIL VINAIGRETTE

You're right that this appeared in our first cookbook, now out of print. It's too good not to repeat here! I always have this dressing in my refrigerator. I store it in recycled glass jars, my favorite kind being the 32-ounce juice jars. Because olive oil gets solid when cold, you have to remove your jar from the fridge and allow dressing to come to room temp, about 15 minutes before you want to use. Shake well, pour, return jar to refrigerator. It keeps for weeks.

Makes 6 cups

4 C extra virgin olive oil (EVOO)
1 C lemon juice
1 C raw apple cider vinegar
10 cloves garlic, pressed in garlic press
1 tsp mustard powder

2 tsp sea salt
2 tsp black pepper
1 tsp dried basil
1 tsp dried oregano
1 tsp dried thyme

Mix everything in a jar, glass bowl or large, 8-cup measuring cup. I like to mix with a fork. Alternatively, make dressing in a blender, in which case you don't need a garlic press. Store in the refrigerator. Your dressing will cloud up and become semi-solid because of the cold. Not to worry.

Napa Cabbage Salad with Blueberries

Napa cabbage, with its long, crisp leaves, is also called Chinese cabbage. It's easy to use in stir fries, soups and Asian dishes like kimchi, but I love it in this salad, too. Napa cabbage seems sweeter and softer than regular green cabbage.

Napa cabbage, like all varieties of cabbage, is a member of the cruciferous vegetable family and has cancer-protective properties.

This recipe ran in our July 2005 newsletter. Yes, you can use frozen organic blueberries, and we've heard that frozen blueberries have more nutrients than their fresh counterparts. True?

Serves 4

12 C shredded Napa cabbage
5 oz baby spinach
2-4 C blueberries (fresh or frozen)
¼ C tamari (soy sauce)
¼ C extra virgin olive oil
    (EVOO)
¼ C lemon juice
4 tsp honey or sweetener of your
    choice

4 cloves garlic
⅛ tsp cayenne pepper
2 tsp chopped ginger root, or
 1 tsp dry powdered ginger
radicchio, carrots, for extra color or as
    garnish

Using a sharp knife, cut cabbage (typically a large head) in half lengthwise and then cut crosswise into ribbons. Put cabbage in salad bowl with spinach and blueberries. To make dressing, put soy sauce, EVOO, lemon juice, sweetener, garlic, pepper and ginger into blender and blend. Pour over cabbage, spinach and blueberries. Toss well. As simple as that!

ORIENTAL BEET SALAD WITH TOASTED SESAME OIL

Toasted sesame oil is made from roasted sesame seeds, which are darker in color and much more intense in flavor. Toasted sesame oil is the primary source of cooking oil in Asia, and once you've tasted it, you'll never want plain old sesame oil again! Whatever you make with toasted sesame oil will become exotic, oriental and just different from the same-old.

In Japan, sesame seeds are toasted and then used to make a condiment called Gomasio (crushed, toasted sesame seeds and salt). Gomasio is found at the table and sprinkled over most dishes. It's yumm.

I read that folk in ancient Greece and Rome used beets to enrich the blood. For many years, it was the greens which were prized, but by the 16th century, beets were cultivated for their roots and widely used as food by the English.

Serves 4

4 small beets, scrubbed, trimmed and grated* (yields about 3 C grated beets)
1 C chopped cilantro
⅓ C chopped onion or sliced green onion
2 Tbsp toasted sesame oil
4 Tbsp lemon juice

½ tsp sea salt
¼ tsp black pepper
¼ tsp ground ginger

1 C pitted oil-cured olives (optional)
2 C fresh mozzarella balls (optional)

Using the coarse grating blade of a food processor, grate beets. Spoon out to salad bowl with a rubber spatula. Add chopped cilantro, onion, toasted sesame oil, lemon juice, salt, pepper and ginger. Toss until everything is mixed well.

Let stand in the fridge for 30 minutes (overnight is fine). Serve onto salad plates and enjoy.

Note: If you're serving this to company and want a salad that is a little more complex, try adding the olives and mozzarella balls.

Honey, don't even think about peeling...

Papaya with Lime and Chile Powder

Papaya has wonderful enzymes, so this salad is all about taste, flavor and digestion!

A ripe papaya feels soft, like a ripe avocado, and its skin has an amber to orange hue. Some say papaya tastes like pineapple or peach, although milder and less tart. I can't compare tastes like that, but it's fun to know that the papaya tree was the first fruit tree to have its genome deciphered!

Like lemons and raw apple cider vinegar, limes balance pH. If you're too acidic, they make you less so. If you're not acidic enough, they increase acid until you're just right. Isn't Mother Nature wonderful?

This recipe was a bonus in our May 2005 newsletter, because I couldn't resist a second recipe. Combination sounds mighty strange, you say? Try it, and you'll like it. The basic concept works with many ingredients besides papayas. It works with firm peaches, pears and apples. I like the dressing with diced jicama, zucchini or shredded cabbage. Really. And it's nice served on a bed of baby greens too.

Serves 4

2 firm Hawaiian papayas, about 4 C　　**1 tsp chili powder**
½ C extra virgin olive oil (EVOO)　　**1 tsp sea salt**
¼ C lime juice　　**1 tsp black pepper**
½ C red onion, minced　　**2 C baby greens (optional)**

Peel papaya. Halve and remove most of black seeds with a spoon. (My Aunt Anna used to eat these because of their nutritional value, and they taste peppery.)

Cut papaya into bite-sized chunks and place in salad bowl. Add EVOO, lime juice, onion, chili powder, salt and pepper. Toss, let stand at room temp for about 30 minutes (this also keeps nicely in the fridge overnight). Serve bedded on baby greens (or not).

PEPITA SUMMER SALAD

Quick to make, which is mandatory in summer! Luscious. How else can one describe a salad that incorporates velvety smooth, emerald-green pumpkin seed oil together with easy-to-digest avocados? This recipe first appeared in our July 2002 newsletter.

Pumpkin seed (aka pepita) oil is made from Austrian pumpkin seeds and comes from a variety of pumpkins whose seeds have no hulls. It's the darkest color oil I've seen. The seeds are dried, crushed, mixed with water and salt (which is said to make them more digestible), then slow-roasted to evaporate the water. Once dried, seeds are pressed to extract the oil.

It takes 5 pounds roasted seeds, or about 35 pumpkins, to produce one liter of oil!

Pumpkin seed oil is heat-sensitive, so don't cook with it.

Serves 6

SALAD
6 C mixed baby salad greens
2 ripe Hass avocados, halved, peeled, diced
1 C pumpkin seeds*
1 C diced celery or fennel
2 C diced small cucumber (skin on is fine)
½ C minced red onion (optional)

VINAIGRETTE DRESSING
2 Tbsp ground cumin
½ C pumpkin seed oil
4 cloves crushed garlic
⅓ C fresh lemon juice
1 tsp sea salt
1 tsp black pepper

Place salad ingredients into a large bowl. Add dressing ingredients and toss merrily. The best tool for tossing a salad is your hands. If you don't want to use hands, I'd mix the dressing ingredients in a little bowl first, then pour over your salad and then toss to heart's content. Taste, adjust seasoning. Serve. Olé.

While this salad needs nothing more, you can add favorites like pitted kalamata olives, feta cheese, scallions, cherry tomatoes, radishes or cubes of seasoned tofu or leftover turkey.

Note: I would rather give up a night on the town than reduce the amount of oil in this salad, but use less if you want. I'm a firm believer that good fats (and nuts and seeds) keep us slim, our skin supple and our hair shiny. The good fats keep us from drying out and wrinkling up.

*Try spicy, roasted pumpkin seeds to give the salad a little kick. Alternatively, the tamari roasted pumpkin seeds are great!

PINEAPPLE MACADAMIA SLAW BY AMANDA

"The earliest European settlers on North America's eastern shores brought cabbage seeds with them, and cabbage was a general favorite throughout the colonies. The Dutch who founded New Netherland (New York State)... grew cabbage extensively along the Hudson River. They served it in their old-country ways, often as koolsla (shredded cabbage salad). This dish became popular throughout the colonies and survives as coleslaw.... By the 1880s, cabbage and its cousins had fallen from favor with the upper class because of the strong sulfurous odors these vegetables give off when cooking. But this sturdy and versatile vegetable never disappeared from middle-class kitchens."

---*Oxford Encyclopedia of Food and Drink in America,* Andrew F. Smith [Oxford University Press: New York]

I was one of the lucky ones who got to attend Amanda's cooking class in September 2008. Every dish was great—creative and gorgeous, as you can see by the following recipe.

Serves 6

½ C umeboshi plum vinegar*
2 Tbsp agave nectar
1 Tbsp crushed red pepper
2 Tbsp ground cumin
¼ C sliced scallions
1 jalapeño, seeded and finely diced
1 tsp black pepper
½ C macadamia nut oil
¼ C toasted sesame oil

5 C thinly sliced red and green cabbage
2 C julienne carrot (1 large carrot)
2 C julienne red bell pepper (1 pepper)
2 C diced fresh pineapple**
¼ C sliced scallions
¼ C chopped cilantro leaves
¾ C toasted, chopped macadamia nuts

Whisk vinegar with agave, crushed red pepper, cumin, scallions, jalapeño and pepper. Slowly whisk in the macadamia and sesame oils. Toss cabbage, carrot, red bell pepper and pineapple with the dressing. Sprinkle scallions and cilantro on top. Toss quickly again. Chill or serve immediately, garnished with macadamia nuts. Your taste buds won't know what hit them except pure delight!

Umeboshi plum vinegar, made from pickled umeboshi plums, is used by Japanese for digestive health. Because it is high in sodium, you don't need salt.

**Don't know how to cut a pineapple? Refer to the recipe "Glowing Salad," earlier in this chapter.*

PRETTY PINK UMEBOSHI PICKLED VEGETABLES

This easy salad or condiment tastes delicious, looks beautiful and keeps for weeks in the fridge. It ran in our November 2002 newsletter. When people actually taste this salad, they fall in love with it. It's fun to toss with scallops, shrimp, tempeh, chicken, tofu or feta.

As a condiment, a forkful on everyone's plate will aid digestion because it's chock-a-block full of enzymes. The trick is to make a batch before the holidays and use a little each day during them to help handle heavy meals and overindulgence. When we overindulge, we're likely to be too acidic, and umeboshi is "the king of alkaline foods." One study showed taking 10 grams of umeboshi plum paste was able to neutralize the acidity created by consuming 100 grams of sugar.

Umeboshi plum vinegar is, however, high in sodium because the plums are pickled with salt, so don't go drinking the bottle of vinegar willy-nilly. If you're on a salt-restricted diet, or if you're prone to water retention or swelling, go easy. No more than a few tablespoons a week.

Serves 12-24 as a side dish

12 C vegetables like cabbage, diced celery, thinly sliced carrot, diced beet, sliced daikon, cucumber spears
12 C boiling water
2 bay leaves
1 tsp dried basil

Marinade
½ C umeboshi plum vinegar
½ C extra virgin olive oil (EVOO)
hot pepper (optional)
garlic (optional)
minced ginger (optional)

Spoon prepared vegetables into the boiling water and stir. Remove pot from heat, cover and let stand 3 minutes, which is just enough to soften veggies but not enough to kill enzymes. Drain. (Save liquid for soups or drink when cold—it's alkalyzing.) Add bay leaves and basil. Pour marinade over vegetables. Mix and store covered in the refrigerator in a glass or ceramic bowl or stainless steel pot.

Note: If your family likes things spicy, add the hot peppers to the mixture. If they like things garlicky, add garlic cloves. Like ginger? Add some minced or grated ginger.

Quinoa Taboulie with Hemp Seeds

Yes, you did see this recipe in our June 2005 newsletter. It's one of my favorites.

Quinoa (KEEN-wah) has been cultivated for more than 5,000 years in the Andes, and was called the "mother grain" by the Incas, who believed eating quinoa gave them superhuman powers. Easy-to-digest and gluten-free, quinoa is a super-grain when you look at its nutritional profile (check out our reference books at the store). Quinoa isn't a grain, however, but the seed of a leafy plant related to spinach. Quinoa sprouts as it cooks, and the World Health Organization says quinoa's protein equals that in milk.

Have you noticed we're using hemp seeds in our kitchen? They, too, are a nutritional powerhouse with lots of fiber, essential fatty acids, vitamin A and vitamin C. And they're an *ecological* powerhouse as well. An acre of hemp produces 4 times more paper per year than an acre of trees. I just learned the oldest printed paper in existence is a 100% hemp Chinese text dated 770 AD, and Thomas Jefferson drafted the Declaration of Independence *and* our Constitution on hemp paper.

How does hemp taste? Like sunflower seeds. Nope, you can't smoke them!

Serves 4

1¾ C boiling water	½ C chopped red onion
1 C yellow quinoa	½ C extra virgin olive oil (EVOO)
⅛ C red quinoa	¼ C lemon juice
½ Tbsp sea salt	½ Tbsp garlic, pressed
1 C diced tomatoes, canned or fresh	½ C shelled hemp seeds
¼ C flat parsley, chopped	

Bring water to a boil. Add quinoa and salt. Stir, cover pot and lower heat. Simmer for 15 minutes. Turn off heat and let quinoa sit covered in pot for another 15 minutes. Water will be absorbed. Dump quinoa from pot into large mixing bowl. Using a rubber spatula*, turn a few times to let heat escape. When quinoa is cool, add remaining ingredients and toss together. Serve and enjoy!

Note: Feel free to make a light and satisfying summer meal with this. Put out on the table with little bowls of oil-cured olives, cucumber slices, strips of red and yellow pepper, roasted eggplant, or anything else your heart desires. Might be more tomatoes, or goat or feta cheese. Voila! Summertime and the living is easy.

Do not mix with a spoon because you'll crush the tender grain. You really do want to toss with a rubber spatula.

Radicchio, Grapefruit and Spinach Salad with Pomegranate Molasses

I just love this salad, which you may have caught in our April 2005 newsletter. It's beautiful and great for family or company.

Spinach is thought to have originated in Persia, and by the 15th century it was cultivated throughout Europe. In China, it has long been popular and is grown on the edges of rice paddies. In India, spinach is called "China Flower." Spinach is grown just about everywhere today.

In literature and legend, fennel is said to be an aphrodisiac. Radicchio, also known as Italian chicory, is red to maroon-colored with white veins, and its slight bitterness is a wonderful spring tonic.

Pomegranates are so high in antioxidants that they are at the top of the chart of foods we should eat to live forever (!), but pomegranate molasses is not molasses, rather a syrup made from concentrated pomegranate juice and sugar. Sugar! For once in my life, I forgot to read the label. Once I tasted and fell in love with this ingredient, I grandfathered it in, because there's nothing that compares with this sweet-tart ingredient. Maybe one day soon someone will make pomegranate syrup with honey or coconut sugar. I'm awaiting and have my eyes peeled.

Serves 4

5 Tbsp pomegranate molasses
½ C extra virgin olive oil (EVOO)
1 tsp sea salt
1 tsp black pepper
2 grapefruits

2 C sliced fennel*
8 oz baby spinach leaves
1 small head radicchio, torn into bite-sized pieces

Combine pomegranate molasses and EVOO in a medium salad bowl. Whisk in salt and pepper. Cut grapefruit horizontally. Using a grapefruit knife (convenient because it's curved and has serrated edges), cut around each half. Then use knife between membranes to release grapefruit sections from skin and from each other. Stir segments into dressing (yes, use the grapefruit juice that comes along with the sections too). Toss in remaining ingredients. Mix so everything is coated. Let salad stand about 15 minutes before serving. Dish out on pretty plates.

Note: You can always compensate and add more of something you like (spinach) for something you might not like (fennel). I serve with a slice of avocado on the side of each plate. Sometimes I'll crumble goat or feta cheese on top of each plate before serving. Depends on what else is being served for dinner.

*To cut fennel, trim off bottom and top of bulb. Cut in half lengthwise, then in half again. Slice thinly. Use feathery fronds in salad, too. If you don't like them here, save for another dish or salad.

Rainbow Chard and Gold Raisin Salad

This appeared in our May 2007 newsletter. May is a transition month because we're ready for summer but, at least in New England, know we're a couple of months away from tomatoes and corn. This easy salad, which can be a meal, suits my fancy in spring.

Did you know that chard came from the Mediterranean and Asia Minor? While it cooks like and looks a little like spinach, it's actually related to beets. Indeed, in Israel, the greens are called "beet leaves." If you eat mesclun, a mix of baby greens, you've already been eating raw chard, so that answers the question, "Can you eat chard raw?"

Chard *is* versatile. It works as a "wrapper" for rice with chickpeas and tomatoes, or a favorite ground beef filling. In Mexico, chard is used to wrap tamale mixtures. Egyptian cooks sauté chard with garlic and coriander, mash it and add it like pesto to stews at the last minute to brighten flavors. One can sauté chard with olive oil and garlic and flavor with cumin or dill or cilantro.

Yes, use organic vegetables for the most nutrition and bang for your buck! Don't you deserve food without pesticides and herbicides?

Serves 4-6

3 C shredded rainbow Swiss chard
3 C torn romaine lettuce
1 C Real Pickles red cabbage sauerkraut*
¼ C extra virgin olive oil (EVOO)
5 garlic cloves, pressed

1 C gold raisins
2 oz feta or fresh goat cheese, crumbled, or gorgonzola
1 tsp sea salt
1 tsp black pepper

Wave chard and romaine leaves under running water and spin or towel dry. Roll chard leaves and slice thinly crosswise, then slice in half lengthwise. (Yes, use stalks and everything. Stalks are the prettiest part of chard, and the crunchiest! We love crunch in potato and corn chips, so why not in our veggies?) Tear romaine leaves into bite-sized pieces.

Put all ingredients in a large salad or mixing bowl. Toss well. Serve this lovely, healthy spring salad at room temperature.

To make a whole meal, serve with wholegrain bread or rice, chickpeas or couscous.

Note: Other mix-ins to try are sliced red onion and 1 C walnuts.

* Real Pickles fermented vegetables contain active cultures and enzymes. Local and good stuff. If you don't live in New England, there must be someone who makes similar lacto-fermented veggies in your neck of the woods.

Raw Kale Salad with Austrian Pumpkin seed Oil

Like most of you, I didn't grow up eating kale. Left to my own devices, I'd probably choose ice cream instead. However, I don't know any other food that is so nutrient-rich and moves things along as nicely so you feel that all is right with the world and working the way nature meant it to.

Let me say, then, that I'm very pleased with this recipe, which I put in the March 2006 newsletter. I experimented with different dressings, but stopped experimenting the day I tried a splash of pumpkin seed oil. And I really love the counterpoint of the red onion and creamy avocado. The lemon or lime adds some zing and provides digestive enzymes too! Remember that lemon and lime normalize pH.

We don't make this salad unless we have organic kale. You really do want those higher nutrient values you get from organic produce, and kale, as all cruciferous vegetables like cabbage, broccoli and Brussels sprouts, are heavily sprayed with chemicals if they're not organically grown. The bugs are smart enough to love cruciferous vegetables. You be smart too.

Serves 4-6

1 bunch kale*
½ C sliced red onion
2 ripe Hass avocados, halved, peeled, cubed

1 C grated carrot (peel on)
¼ C lemon or lime juice
3 Tbsp pumpkin seed oil
¾ tsp Celtic sea salt

Shake kale under water. Shake again to remove as much water as possible. Chiffonade (which means roll up lengthwise and cut across into ribbons). I chop and use the kale stems too, but not everyone likes the stems in this salad because they require even more chewing. It's entirely up to you. I just believe waste not, want not...

Put kale and remaining ingredients in a bowl. Toss well. Marinate for an hour before serving.

* We use mostly Russian red kale in the kitchen because we like the way it looks. Some say green, red and lacinato kale have different flavors. Can't tell by me! Curly, crinkly kale holds the dressing better than the flat leaf varieties.

ROASTED BEETS WITH WALNUTS AND FETA

This one appeared in our October 2004 newsletter and has always been one of my favorites. I was pleased as punch when Ann Fitch told me it rivaled anything she ever ate in Manhattan. That's a compliment if you believe that Manhattan is always the beacon of innovation and good taste.

Beets are rich in iron, dietary fiber, vitamin C, magnesium and potassium, and are a very good source of folate and manganese. During World War II it was found that among all the vegetables dehydrated for military or civilian use, beets were the best.

Did you know that ounce for ounce, walnuts provide the same amount of calcium as any soft cheese?

Serves 8

2 lb beets, red or golden*
1 C halved, sliced organic red onion
⅓ C walnut oil
⅓ C raw apple cider vinegar
2 Tbsp lemon juice
2 Tbsp dried dill weed
2 tsp Spike seasoning
½ tsp allspice

1 tsp garlic powder
1 tsp dried oregano leaf
1 tsp dried basil leaf
1 tsp dried thyme leaf
1 tsp dried tarragon leaf
1 C walnuts (or more!)
¼ lb feta, crumbled

Although I called this salad "roasted beets," you can either steam or roast. How to roast? Wash beets, cut off tops, wrap in foil and put on cookie sheet in a 350 degree oven for about 45 minutes, or until beets are easily pierced with a small sharp knife. How to steam? Wash, trim beets, put into pot with about 2 C of water. Steam about 15-18 minutes, or until tender when poked with a knife. Roasting imparts a richer flavor, but roasting or steaming—the dish works either way.

In a large bowl, place remaining ingredients, except beets, walnuts and feta. Now cut beets into bite-size pieces or wedges (depends upon size of beets) and add them to bowl. Toss until beets and onions are well coated.

How to serve? Lots of ways, but in our kitchen we place some greens on each plate, top with beets, then ¼ C walnuts in one corner and 3 Tbsp feta in another corner.

Alternatively, you can add walnuts and feta to beet mixture and toss all together. Then after dishing out, garnish with a few extra or reserved walnuts.

*Golden beets make this salad very pretty, and they don't discolor other ingredients. I like a combination of red and golden best.

SALAD OF TOSSED GREENS WITH GOAT CHEESE AND PISTACHIOS

A website selling pistachios said that their history reflects their "royalty." Pistachios are said to have been a favorite delicacy of the Queen of Sheba, who confiscated all Assyrian deliveries for herself and for her royal court. Another story goes that lovers used to meet under pistachio trees on moonlit nights. If they could hear the cracking of their pistachios, they were destined to be happy.

Brought from Syria to Italy during the reign of Tiberius at the beginning of the 1st century, they spread (because they are so good.) and were grown in other southern European countries like Greece. Today pistachios are still grown in the Middle East. Where do most of *our* pistachios come from? Mainly from California.

Serves 6

12 C torn salad greens of any kind*
1 C pistachio nuts, shelled**
1 C crumbled goat cheese

4 large cloves garlic, crushed
2 tsp Spike seasoning
¼-½ C extra virgin olive oil (EVOO)
2 Tbsp lemon juice

Wash salad greens and spin dry. (A salad spinner is a great invention, and a must in my kitchen. I remember, growing up, we three kids had to take turns drying lettuce. We'd pat each leaf until dry with a linen towel. Dressing, my mom used to say, doesn't stick to wet greens.)

Put all ingredients in a large wooden salad bowl. Toss well with your hands or salad serving spoon and fork. The choice is yours. Divide salad among 6 plates. Serve to cries of delight.

Note: There are so many greens to choose from. One of my favorite combinations is a head of red leaf lettuce and a head of romaine. Instead of lemon, feel free to use organic raw apple cider vinegar or a splash of umeboshi vinegar (in which case, eliminate Spike).

Don't have time to wash greens? Feel free to use pre-washed organic baby greens like mesclun, spinach or arugula.

We sell shelled pistachios, and I prefer the roasted ones. I'm sure you can find shelled pistachios where you live too.

SAY GOOD-BYE TO WINTER SALAD

This recipe appeared in our April 2009 newsletter. In April in New England, we get one rainy day; one sunny, gorgeous day. Weather is still all over the map, and ripe, summer tomatoes are a few months away. Luckily, it's cool enough to turn on the oven, roast vegetables and dream of summer! (What are you planting in your garden this year? How about cauliflower?)

Cauliflower, the historians say, originated in Asia, and was then brought to Italy where it was available almost exclusively until the 16th century. From there it was introduced to other countries. It wasn't grown in North America until the late 1600s.

Today, cauliflower soups are popular in France. In Italy, cauliflower is popular when made with garlic, olive oil and capers. Think vegetable curries in India!

Serves 6

- 2 C diced yams or butternut squash
- 2 C cauliflower florets (some purple is nice)
- 1 C thickly sliced red onion
- 2 C green cabbage, cut in chunks or thickly sliced
- 4 Tbsp extra virgin olive oil (EVOO)

Roast at 425 degrees

- ½ C pitted kalamata olives
- 2 cloves garlic, pressed
- 2 Tbsp lemon juice
- 2 C baby spinach
- 1 tsp black pepper
- 1 tsp sea salt

Preheat oven to 425 degrees.

Wash yams or squash. Dice yam or squash (use both or one) into 1-inch cubes. (The second time I tried the recipe, I used 1 yam and 1 bag Stahlbush Island Farms diced butternut squash, which made life easy.) Place in mixing bowl together with cauliflower florets, red onion and green cabbage. Toss with EVOO, spoon onto baking pan and roast 30 minutes, stirring halfway through.

In the meantime, using the same mixing bowl, put in olives, garlic and lemon juice.

As soon as yams can be pierced easily with a small knife, remove pan from oven.

Add roasted vegetables to bowl, toss with olives, garlic and lemon juice. Add spinach and black pepper and salt and toss again until spinach is well-coated. (I like to use a rubber spatula so I don't damage the veggies, which are still warm and tender.) Taste, adjust seasoning.

Feta, fennel and watercress are nice additions too.

SHRIMP SALAD WITH BLACK-EYED PEAS AND BASIL

A website called *A2Z of Health, Beauty and Fitness* (www.A2Z.com) says, "David Heber, director of the Center for Human Nutrition at the University of California, Los Angeles, and author of *What Color Is Your Diet?* goes over 15 common myths about nutrition, including the notion that eating shrimp raises cholesterol levels. 'The American Heart Association acknowledged a long time ago that shrimp had been wrongly accused, but lots of people, including some doctors, still believe this myth.'

"A myth indeed. In fact, when researchers from Rockefeller University in New York put volunteers on a diet of 11 ounces of shrimp a day—more than twice the recommended amount of cholesterol—the participants experienced no ill effects on their cholesterol levels and actually saw a 13 percent drop in their triglyceride levels."

I just love shrimp. When I feed them to company, it feels like a party!

Serves 4

1 lb small shrimp, peeled and deveined
1 C pitted oil-cured black olives
1 C roasted red peppers, cut into strips
1 C chopped fresh basil
1 can Eden black-eyed peas, drained, or 2 C cooked
1 Tbsp capers

½ C extra virgin olive oil (EVOO)
¼ C lemon juice
4 cloves garlic, pressed
1 tsp dried marjoram
1 tsp sea salt
1 tsp black pepper
2 C baby greens (optional)

Using a large skillet and 1 C of water, steam shrimp for a few minutes, or just until they turn pink. Remove from pan with a slotted spoon and put right into a salad bowl. Shrimp will cool down quickly, so in about 5 minutes add everything else to salad bowl and toss well. Refrigerate about an hour to give the shrimp and beans the chance to absorb the flavors.

Tastes best at room temperature.

You can serve as is, or extend further by adding 2 C baby greens, snookums.

Smoked Salmon and English Cucumber Salad

Yep, you saw this in July 2003. Remember the piece I wrote on Atlantic (aka "farm-raised") salmon? Since then there've been articles everywhere. Marian Burros, *The New York Times*, wrote that lawsuits accuse the fish farm industry of polluting the ocean, endangering dwindling stocks of wild salmon and failing to tell shoppers that they use artificial colors in fish feed to make the fish red.

Did you know that 80% of salmon sold in the US are farm raised? And did you know that the Department of Agriculture says Atlantic salmon contains more than twice the saturated fat and fewer beneficial omega-3 fatty acids than wild salmon? Atlantic salmon was found to have "consistently higher levels" of toxic contaminants, including 10 times the level of PCB's.

And heavy infestations of sea lice from salmon farms attach themselves to wild pink salmon who swim near the farms, killing them. Alaska has banned fish farms to protect its wild stocks.

So where can you buy wild smoked salmon? Right here in West Concord, in our store. Elsewhere, too, I'm sure.

Serves 2-4

4 oz smoked salmon	1 tsp black pepper
1 C sliced scallions or red onion	1 tsp Spike seasoning or sea salt
1 English cuke or several pickling cucumbers (don't peel!)	1 bunch watercress
	4 C mesclun salad mix
4 Tbsp extra virgin olive (EVOO)	1 ripe Hass avocado, halved, peeled, sliced
2 Tbsp fresh lemon juice	
2 Tbsp chopped garlic	½ t chili powder (optional)

Cut salmon into bite-sized pieces. Place in salad serving bowl. Slice scallions (white and green part) or use minced red onion. Cut cucumbers in half the long way and slice fairly thinly. Add onion and cucumbers to salmon.

Make dressing by combining EVOO, lemon juice, garlic, black pepper and Spike. Pour ½ of dressing over salmon and onions and cucumbers. Cover and chill for an hour.

When ready to serve, add watercress and mesclun salad mix. Pour over remaining dressing and toss gently. Arrange salad on half of each plate. Peel and thinly slice avocado and fan slices on other half of plate. Shake chili powder on avocado. Ain't that purty? Now eat and be happy!

SPANISH POTATO SALAD WITH PURPLE AND YELLOW POTATOES

This recipe appeared in our August 2003 newsletter. It's ideal for fall picnics when the new potatoes are in abundance. You'll note that I never make potato salads with mayo—I just prefer my potatoes dressed with olive oil. And it means that you can also let your salad sit at room temp safely too.

Potatoes are most nourishing when eaten with the skin. According to Paul Pitchford in his book *Healing with Whole Food*, potatoes make us calm. He says we crave potatoes because they help balance the stresses of our high-tech world.

According to Hippocrates, celery calms nerves too. That may be so, but isn't it impressive that you actually burn more calories digesting celery that you get when you eat it? Do use the whole stalk, leaves and all. I remember being horrified when cooks way back when in our kitchen would cut off the leafy tops and throw them away. They didn't know, they exclaimed, that the leaves were edible!

Serves 10-12

2 lb purple potatoes
2 lb yellow potatoes
4 carrots, diced, about 8 C
¼ lb string beans, cut in ½-inch
    pieces
1 C sliced celery or green peas
6 hard-boiled eggs, peeled, diced
1 C zucchini or summer squash, diced
2 C diced apple

1 can Eden chickpeas, or 2 C cooked
1-2 C minced red onion
2 C pitted oil-cured olives
1 C extra virgin olive oil (EVOO)
2 Tbsp sea salt or Spike seasoning
1 Tbsp black pepper
1 tsp dried oregano
¼ C capers (optional)

Scrub potatoes, but don't peel because you've used organic! Cut into bite-sized pieces and place in a pot with water about 2 inches above. Simmer over medium heat until tender, about 10 minutes. Pour into a colander to drain and then into large mixing bowl. Using same pot, add about 2 C water and bring to a boil. Add carrots, cover pot, lower heat and simmer 5 minutes. Add string beans and simmer covered over low another 2 minutes. Drain and add these to potatoes. Let mixture stand so vegetables cool somewhat. You want them still warm.

Add celery or peas, eggs, zucchini or summer squash, diced apple, chickpeas, onion, olives, and EVOO together with herbs and seasoning. Toss gently using a rubber spatula. Serve to cries of rapture.

Note: You can use all one kind potato, and you can leave out some ingredients if you don't have all on hand. Make it your own recipe, my dahling.

SPRING DANDELION AVOCADO SALAD WITH CRISPY TEMPEH

Another creative, delicious recipe from Amanda which originally appeared in our May 2009 newsletter.

We all know dandelion is used as a spring tonic, liver-cleansing. But did you also know that the USDA ranks dandelion in the top 4 green vegetables in overall nutritional value? So eating dandelions in the spring does your bod a world of good!

Amanda uses tempeh, which we love because unlike many other soyfoods, tempeh is made from whole soybeans that are fermented. The fermentation makes tempeh easy to digest, which means no gas. And tempeh is low in sodium. Like fine blue cheese, it contains a natural mold that produces natural, heat-stable antibiotic agents. Indonesians, who eat tempeh as a regular part of their diet, rarely fall victim to the intestinal diseases to which they are constantly exposed. The protein and fiber in tempeh can also help keep blood sugar levels under control. So enjoy!

Serves 4

1 bunch dandelion greens, cut into 2-inch pieces
1-2 ripe Hass avocados, peeled, cubed
juice from one lime
1 ripe, red jalapeño (green okay) (optional)
½ English cuke, quartered lengthwise, chunked
¼ to ½ C fresh mint leaves

1 Tbsp finely minced garlic
1 C fresh dill, chopped
good pinch of sea salt
dollop of honey (optional)
¼ C organic crème fraîche
1 pkg Lightlife Fakin' Bacon. (smoky tasting tempeh)
½ C extra virgin olive oil (EVOO)

Wash 2 two bunches of dandelion greens in cold water to remove all sand. Use a colander and running water, or soak briefly in a large bowl. Drain and pat dry and toss with the rest of your vegetables and remaining ingredients except Lightlife Fakin' Bacon.

In a large skillet, sauté a few strips of Lightlife Fakin' Bacon in hot EVOO until very crisp. It's okay to burn them a teeny bit. Amanda says to give every person about 1.5 strips.

To serve, spoon dressed greens onto plates, divide Fakin' Bacon in strips on top as delightful, delicious garnish. (I used two packages of tempeh because I like it so much in this dish! – Debra)

TAMARIND TOMATO CABBAGE SALAD

Native to tropical Africa, the tamarind tree was brought to India, and from there to Iran where it was called "tamar hindi" (Indian date, from the date-like appearance of the dried pulp), giving rise to both its common and generic names. The fruit was well known to the ancient Egyptians and to the Greeks in the 4th century B.C.E.

So while the tamarind tree has been around for centuries, I didn't know that it was also introduced into Hawaii back in the 1790's. Today, on mainland USA, it's easy to find the concentrate (we have it in our store too, of course), but not the fruit.

Tamarind is sweet-sour, helps digestion and is said to be good for 101 different things, but one use that struck me is its ability to help stabilize blood sugar.

Today we sell tamarind as a supplement called "garcinia cambogia," which is used to keep us slim and trim.

Serves 8

1 tsp cumin seeds	3 C mixed cherry tomatoes
1 tsp fennel seeds	2 C shredded cabbage
2 tsp tamarind concentrate	2 Tbsp extra virgin olive oil (EVOO)
2 Tbsp hot water	sea salt and black pepper to taste

Toast cumin and fennel seeds in a dry, hot skillet by stirring for 1 minute until they pop. Crush with a mortar and pestle or electric coffee/spice grinder. Alternatively, you can use powdered herbs so you don't need to crush. In this case, toast them carefully for 1-2 minutes in a hot skillet.

Whisk tamarind concentrate into hot water until dissolved. Pour into a salad bowl. Halve tomatoes, and then add tomatoes and remaining ingredients to salad bowl. Toss gently so cabbage and tomatoes are well-coated. Let stand 1 hour at room temperature. Taste and adjust seasoning.

TROPICAL BEAN SALAD

This appeared in our May 2006 newsletter. For this salad, choose papayas, pineapple, mango or any combination of all 3 fruits.

The world eats more mangos than any other kind of fruit, and when you get a good one (not always easy to do in this country), you understand why that's true. It is said that Buddha so loved mangos that he was given a mango grove to meditate in!

Papayas, called the "fruit of the angels" by Christopher Columbus, can now be found in our markets throughout the year just like pineapples and mangos. And speaking of pineapples, thank goodness they are being grown in many countries now. I say this because most of Hawaii's pineapple plantations have bitten the dust.

What do all three fruits have in common? All three contain enzymes that digest proteins and inflammation. All 3 fruits are also low in calories and taste darn refreshing.

Eat ripe or unripe? The unripe (green) fruit is prized and said to be richer in enzymes. The green fruit works better in dishes where it is sliced and dipped in chili powder, or sprinkled with soy sauce. You can grate the green fruit and add to any salad or relish, or use as a pickle. When soft and ripe, these work in desserts with coconut cream and sticky rice. You can use either green or ripe fruit with the recipe below.

Serves 4-6

4 C papaya, pineapple and/or mango
2 C watercress or baby greens
1 can Eden black beans, or 2 C cooked
½ C dried goji berries, or dried cranberries

3 Tbsp lemon or lime juice
¼ tsp chili powder (optional)
1 tsp sea salt
1 tsp black pepper

Halve and peel fruit. Cut into bite-sized cubes and put in salad bowl.

If using papaya, remove the black seeds inside using a spoon. If using pineapple, see directions for cutting in *Glowing Salad* earlier in this chapter. Mango? Cut fruit off pit and then peel.

Rinse black beans in a colander. Drain thoroughly.

Combine all ingredients by tossing gently. Feel free to use more of an ingredient or a seasoning you like. Crazy about lime juice? Use as much as you like.

Watercress and Romaine with Sesame Seeds and Mustard Dressing

From a summer cooking class I taught in my home in 2006. Spicy with lots of calcium from the greens and sesame seeds. Lots of fiber and protein too!

Sesame seeds may be the oldest condiment known to man dating back to 1600 B.C.E. They are highly valued for their oil, which is exceptionally resistant to rancidity. "Open sesame," the famous phrase from the *Arabian Nights*, reflects the distinguishing feature of the sesame seed pod, which bursts open when it reaches maturity. Sesame also contains a beneficial fiber called lignans. (Lignans occur in other foods, too, like flax.) Lignans, like other fibers, have a cholesterol-lowering effect and may prevent high blood pressure.

Serves 6

2 C watercress, stemmed
4 C romaine, torn into bite-sized
  pieces
½ C red onion, diced
½ C unhulled brown sesame seeds
2 cloves garlic, pressed

1 Tbsp Dijon mustard
2 Tbsp toasted sesame oil
3 Tbsp apple cider vinegar
1 tsp sea salt
1 tsp black pepper

Combine everything in a large salad bowl. Toss well. Again, hands make great mixing tools, but you can use a salad spoon and fork.

Note: What vegetables might you want to use instead of those listed above? Arugula instead of romaine? Would you like to serve this with whole-grain bread? Also, if you wish, you could use hemp seeds instead of sesame. Both pack a nutritional whallop.

WINTER SALAD WITH ASIAN VINAIGRETTE

I love the colors of this salad that you may have caught in our February 2007 newsletter. It doesn't taste like the tossed salad I make every other night. The toasted sesame oil imparts intense fragrance and robust flavor. If you want a kick because the heat in the house is turned way down and it's snowing outside, add a pinch of cayenne pepper!

Did you know sesame oil contains an antioxidant called "sesamol" which protects the oil from becoming rancid?

How is toasted sesame oil made? Typically by roasting the seeds and then cold-pressing.

Serves 6

2 C broccoli florets
2 C green beans, 3-inch length
2 C sliced fresh shiitake mushrooms
1 C sliced red cabbage
2 C shredded chard or kale
1 C thinly sliced red onion
2 C baby spinach
2¼ C tamari (soy sauce)

3¼ C rice vinegar
4 Tbsp chopped fresh cilantro
¼ C toasted sesame oil
1½ Tbsp minced ginger root, or 1 tsp dry
1½ Tbsp minced garlic, or 1 tsp powder
sea salt and black pepper

In a large skillet, bring 1 C of water to a boil. Add all veggies, except onion and spinach. Lower heat, cover pot and steam for 3-4 minutes, just enough so veggies aren't completely crunchy.

Drain and save steaming water to drink. It's very alkalizing! Let vegetables cool slightly. In a large mixing bowl, whisk together tamari, vinegar, cilantro, toasted sesame oil, ginger, garlic, red onion and baby spinach. Spoon in the still-warm veggies and toss well so everything is nicely coated. Season to taste with salt and black pepper. Add that pinch of cayenne if you like spice.

Note: Of course, I use organic veggies, and I also use organic frozen vegetables when I'm feeling rushed or a little lazy. I love, for instance, the Woodstock frozen sliced organic shiitakes and broccoli florets, which I always have in my freezer. One just never knows when one might need them!

Yams with Black Beans, Avocado and Chile

Another recipe from a summer 2006 cooking class in my home.

Yams have lots of fiber, magnesium and beta carotene. They are crisp when raw and are surprisingly refreshing! The black beans here give you more fiber and protein, as does the avocado. *Bottom Line Health* says one serving of avocado contains 12 grams of fiber—33% more than 1 C of shredded wheat cereal! They also have essential fatty acids to make beautiful skin. *The Journal of Nutrition* published in March 2006 said that avocados allow the body to absorb significantly more of the heart-healthy and cancer-fighting nutrients found in other fruits and vegetables.

Again avocado, you cry? But they are considered to be a nearly perfect food. They have so much nutrition that in some parts of the world babies are given mashed avocados during the weaning process. Anyhow, they are healthy, and I love them.

Serves 6-8

1 lb yams, peeled, cut into
    matchsticks*
1 can Eden black beans, or 2 C
    cooked
2 ripe Hass avocados, halved, peeled,
    cubed

½ C lime juice
1 tsp sea salt
1 tsp chili powder
1 tsp black pepper
2 Tbsp extra virgin olive oil EVOO)

Scrub yams. Since they're not one shape or size, cut them into pieces that you can peel easily. Then cut into matchsticks. Make sure your beans are well drained. Put everything into a large salad bowl. Toss and taste. Adjust seasoning. Serve.

Feel free to substitute jicama for yams. I would imagine you can use this basic recipe, keeping the beans, avocados and dressing, and use whatever vegetable you happen to have on hand. If you decided to use yellow squash or zucchini, your salad would be softer.

ZESTY ZUCCHINI AND SUMMER SQUASH SALAD

When the garden is overflowing with zucchini and summer squash, this recipe is perfect. It's easy and breezy to make. I have to admit that I make it year-round because it is quick, and because I love the taste.

Did you know that zucchini and summer squash are related to melons and cucumbers? There are umpteen varieties, and you can eat the entire vegetable, no matter what kind. There's no waste at all because the skin, flesh and seeds are all edible.

Serves 4

1 zucchini, halved lengthwise and
   sliced thinly
1 yellow squash, sliced the same
½ small red onion, sliced
1 Tbsp capers

1 C pitted kalamata olives
1 C pitted French green olives
¼ C extra virgin olive oil (EVOO)
2 tsp Spike seasoning

Put all the ingredients into a salad bowl, toss, taste, adjust seasoning and serve. Very yummy.

Variation: Add a jar of artichoke hearts.
Variation: Add fresh mozzarella cheese balls.
Variation: Tear in some colorful radicchio.

Vegetables

When we Starks were growing up, vegetables played a starring role at dinner. Mom steamed or sautéed vegetables every night, and the plates that were carried to the table were colorful thanks to all those vegetables. Vegetables shared the plate with a delish protein together with something that was either a grain, a bean or a baked yam or potato.

(This was the second course and followed the first, which was usually a huge green salad. The second course was followed by the third course that was always fresh fruit.)

We ate at lot, but we weren't fat thanks to all those vegetables.

Why did we eat so much? I think Mom wanted us to eat all the foods she believed would make us strong and healthy, but she just couldn't choose from the variety and profusion available. So she fed us a lot, hoping for the best.

Today, like most Americans, I skimp on veggies. I still eat a lot, but I'm not as slim as I'd like to be. Would I slim down if I ate more veggies? I bet I would. So I'd like to propose that we all get back to eating our veggies.

That can be as simple as rinsing a bunch of greens, cutting the bunch into bite-sized pieces, placing those pieces into a pot with no more than 1 C of water and steaming for a few minutes. That's what Mom used to do.

Years ago I was lucky to be a waitress at a restaurant called "Brownies" in New York City. Sam and Edith Brown gave me a copy of their book *Cooking Creatively with Natural Foods*. One of my favorite sentences in that book is, "Mostly the vegetable dies because we do not love it enough."

So let's love them all—from artichokes to zucchini and every vegetable in between!

Adam's Maitake Mushroom Stew

This is Adam's recipe, which I love. He says, "Also known as 'hen of the woods' or 'dancing mushroom,' maitake is one of the most revered deep immune tonics in Chinese medicine. Plus it protects the liver and helps regulate blood sugar—and it tastes a little like chicken!"

Serves 4-6

¼ C extra virgin olive oil (EVOO), or butter

½ lb fresh Maitake mushrooms, about 4 C

1 C chopped onion

anywhere between 1 clove and 1 bulb of garlic, peeled

few pinches dried rosemary

2 each carrots, parsnips, stalks of celery, chopped, about 4 C each

1 can Eden chickpeas, or 2 C cooked

1 stalk of burdock root, sliced (if you can get it)

½ C barley, rice, quinoa, buckwheat groats or other grain, raw

1½ C water*

1 tsp sea salt

1 tsp black pepper

pinch cayenne pepper

In a stew pot, warm EVOO or butter. Sauté mushrooms (the whole ones will break up as you start sautéing) with onion and garlic. When onion is soft, proceed with recipe using the stew pot, or put up recipe in a crock pot and let it simmer all day so it's ready when you come home from work.

Once mushrooms, onions and garlic are sautéed, add rosemary, vegetables, chickpeas, burdock (which we almost always have at the store in our produce department) and the grain you've chosen together with the water.

If you're using the stew pot, simmer stew covered on low about an hour. If using a crock pot, leave it on low all day. Before serving, season to taste with salt, black pepper and cayenne.

Note: You may also want to try crumbled maitakes with seafood seasoning, instead of crabmeat, to make vegan "crab" cakes. Try substituting the same amount of maitakes for crabmeat in your favorite crab cake recipe.

* You can use a little bit of water to make a thick stew; or use a lot for a soup. For a soup, instead of water, you can use chicken, veggie or mushroom broth. The 1½ C above is mostly absorbed by the grain.

ALEX'S ZUCCHINI SUMMER SQUASH CREAM SIDE

"This is a family favorite, going back two generations," says Alex. "It was always a sure-fire way to get us kids to eat our zucchini. Later on, we discovered we could be more indulgent with high-end creamy cheeses."

Serves 2-4 as a side dish

1-3 Tbsp butter
3 cloves garlic, chopped fine or
   pressed
1 large onion (about 2 C), chopped
1 large shallot, chopped
2 medium zucchini, sliced ¼-inch
   thick

1 medium summer squash, sliced
   ¼-inch thick
½ C sour cream or yogurt
1 C flat parsley, chopped
1 pinch cayenne pepper

Gently warm butter in a sauté pan. Add garlic, onion and shallot and sauté until transparent, about 5 minutes.* Add sliced zucchini and summer squash and sauté until desired crispness, about 5 minutes.

Turn off heat. Let veggies cool in pan. Add sour cream. Stir. Just before serving, add parsley and cayenne right into pan.

Note: Alex says this dish can be served with tortellini, angel hair pasta or quinoa.

Alex says this dish tastes better when onions are caramelized, but looks less appealing. To caramelize, sauté longer.

AMANDA'S BROCCOLI WITH PINE NUTS AND RAISINS

We ran this simple and delicious recipe in our February 2009 newsletter. It's beautiful!

Don't you find when you eat veggies and good fats that you feel full but not too full, and that you don't feel thirsty afterward either? It's as if your insides are pampered and hydrated. Amazing how changing what one eats and including more vegetables in one's diet really does change the way you feel.

Can you use Popeye's favorite, spinach, or other leafy greens in this recipe? Sure. You're in charge and you can make whatever floats your boat.

Of course, use organic if you can. Every ingredient below is available organically grown, which means more vitamins for you and better for the whole planet too.

Serves 2-4 as a side dish

4 C broccoli florets, green beans, or
   zucchini, or any combo of these
¼ C pine nuts
3 Tbsp extra virgin olive oil (EVOO)

¼ C raisins
3 Tbsp apple cider vinegar
1 Tbsp chopped garlic
½ tsp sea salt
½ tsp black pepper

Cook your broccoli (or other veggies) so they're bright green and still crisp. There are several ways to do this. "I like blanching in boiling salted water, but steaming is fantastic too," says Amanda. When vegetables are done, place in a colander and run under cold water to stop cooking. Set aside.

Heat a large skillet and toast pine nuts for a couple minutes, stirring with a wooden spoon to prevent burnt bottoms. Add EVOO and toast nuts to a medium brown, another 2 minutes. Add the raisins, cider vinegar and garlic. Stir while cooking yet another 2 minutes. Turn off the heat, taste and then season with salt and pepper (less or more than suggested above). Spoon contents of skillet onto your cooked veggies and toss with gay abandon. Serve immediately. Yum! Fresh and green, sweet and savory, this dish is sure to please any palate!

APPLE AND RED CABBAGE WITH SAUERKRAUT

At times, my mom would give us a hunk of cabbage to munch on as part of dinner. That wasn't my favorite… Here is another way to use cabbage combined with its fermented cousin, raw sauerkraut. Eating live, fermented foods supplies our digestive tracts with living cultures and the enzymes necessary to break down food and assimilate nutrients.

Serves 4 as a side dish

8 C thinly sliced red cabbage
1 apple, diced, skin on
2 C apple juice
½ C raisins
½ C celery, diced

1 Tbsp lemon juice
1 C raw sauerkraut, with juice
1 tsp sea salt (optional)
1 tsp black pepper (optional)
¼ C sliced scallions (optional)

Combine the cabbage, apple, apple juice, raisins and celery in a large covered pot. Simmer over a low flame for about 10 minutes, or until cabbage is tender. Add lemon juice and sauerkraut, then stir and taste. Add salt and pepper if you think the dish needs it.

Spoon out into little glass bowls and garnish with scallions, if you like.

AUTUMN CARROTS AND SQUASH

This appeared in our November 2008 newsletter and is wonderful spooned over lentils, rice, millet or quinoa. Below, I've used black lentils because the contrast is striking, and because I like lentils! All you butternut squash lovers out there, I don't begrudge you the squash, but I have a hard time finding time to peel and cut squash. If I can't buy it already peeled and cubed, I use yams instead, which are just as healthy but a little sweeter. I cannot tell a lie.

Serves 4 as a main dish, 6-8 as a side dish

1 C black lentils
2½ C water
1 tsp sea salt
¼ C extra-virgin olive oil (EVOO)
2 medium onions, chopped, about 4 C
1 lb carrots, sliced (don't peel)
1 lb peeled, seeded butternut squash, cubed
2 tsp cumin seeds

1 tsp paprika
2 tsp tomato paste
6 cloves garlic, peeled but whole
1 tsp sea salt
1 tsp black pepper
2 C water
juice from one juicy lemon
½ C chopped fresh cilantro

Spread lentils on plate and check for stones (or not—I can't remember the last time I checked for stones when using lentils). Place lentils in a colander and rinse. In a medium pot, combine water, lentils and salt. Bring to a boil, lower heat, cover pot and simmer 30 minutes.

In the meantime, in a large skillet, gently warm EVOO. Add onions and sauté, stirring, until onions begin to color, about 5 minutes. Add carrots and squash and sauté another 5 minutes. Then add the remaining ingredients *except* the lemon juice and cilantro. Lower heat and cover pot. Simmer until carrots are tender and the liquid has been absorbed, about 20 minutes.

Coarsely mash carrots and squash right in the pot. I use my mom's old potato masher. Add lemon juice (more if you like things very lemony). Taste and adjust seasoning with more salt or pepper.

Divide lentils between plates and spoon mashed carrot and squash stew on top. Garnish with chopped cilantro. Colors should pop and you'll find this easy autumn meal also hits the spot. I like to garnish with cashews or peanuts, but it also goes well with chicken, hamburger or with a veggie burger. You can drizzle more EVOO on top. It's up to you, mesdames and monsieurs.

BEETS AND GREENS WITH ZING

Beets are cleansing and full of iron. Greens have calcium. The chili powder and lemon juice add zing that you'll love. Feel free to dress this dish up for company with the addition of feta cheese, raisins or pine nuts.

Did you know that chard is a beet that has been chosen for leaf production? Chard contains vitamin K and magnesium, both of which help keep our bones strong.

Serves 4 as a side dish

1 bunch red chard
2 large beets, diced (don't peel!)
2 Tbsp extra virgin olive oil (EVOO)
1 red onion, halved and then sliced
1 tsp sea salt

1 tsp or more red chili powder
¼ C water
½ C lemon juice
crumbled feta, raisins or pine nuts
  (optional)

Rinse greens and chop coarsely so the pieces are bite-sized (a little oversized is fine too). Use the stems as well because they add nice crunch, and waste not, want not.

Scrub beets with a little scrub brush. Dice. Your hands will get pink, but don't worry; color is not permanent and will wash off!

Gently warm EVOO in a large skillet and sauté onion for 5 minutes. Add beets and chard and stir. Sprinkle with salt and chili powder. Add ¼ C water, cover pot, and steam 3-5 minutes, just until greens are tender and a little wilted. Stir in lemon juice. Zing!

If you want to add crumbled feta, raisins or pine nuts, do so now.

Catalonian Eggplant with Pine Nuts

Researchers at the US Agricultural Service have found that eggplants (organic eggplants in particular) are rich in compounds that function as antioxidants. Plants form such compounds to protect themselves against oxidative stress from exposure to the elements, as well as from infection by bacteria, fungi and viruses of all kinds. Commercially grown eggplants are "protected" by pesticides, so the plant itself doesn't have to work at fighting off bad bugs and doesn't develop its own protective compounds, which have the antioxidant properties. That's why organic eggplants are best. And that's why eating "organic" is a guiding principle I live by.

There's a new supplement on the market, described by the manufacturers as "…a fatty acid extracted from pine nuts which can suppress appetite and reduce the amount of food people feel like eating." Why would anyone want to take pine nuts as a supplement when one can have fun by eating them?

Serves 8

1 medium eggplant, about 2 lb
1 can Eden chickpeas, or 2 C cooked
2 C roasted red pepper, sliced
1 C oil-cured, pitted black olives

½ C extra virgin olive oil (EVOO)
½ C pine nuts
1 tsp sea salt
1 tsp black pepper

Peel and slice eggplant. Cook by either of these methods: (1) Roast in a dry skillet over medium heat, turning to brown evenly; remove from skillet when eggplant has become very soft. (2) Or grill dry eggplant by placing it directly on rack for about 10 minutes, turning frequently to brown evenly. Remove when eggplant has become tender.

Slightly cool eggplant and then cut into strips lengthwise. Drain beans. Combine all ingredients and adjust salt and pepper to taste.

Serve as is, or round out this meal with sliced summer tomatoes garnished with chopped fresh basil and goat cheese...

EGGPLANT ROASTED WITH CRUNCHY TOPPING

Eggplants, rich in bioflavonoids, are actually a fruit. Jean Carper says eggplants may lower blood cholesterol (the bad kind) and counteract the negative effects of fatty foods on blood.

Soybeans and soybean granules are a natural source of lecithin, which is a brain food. Chinese manuscripts in 2800 B.C.E. call soybeans the "beef" of China.

My mother used to stir 2 Tbsp soy granules into brown rice once cooked, cover pot and let the mixture stand 5 minutes. The granules absorbed any excess moisture and made the rice "gourmet." They added a nutty-flavored crunch. To this day, I love rice and soy granules.

Serves 4 as a side dish

1 medium eggplant, about 2 lb
¼ C extra virgin olive oil (EVOO)
8 cloves garlic, pressed
1 tsp dried oregano
½ tsp dried basil
1 tsp sea salt

Bake at 375 degrees

1 tsp black pepper
2 more Tbsp EVOO
½ C walnuts, finely chopped
½ C soybean granules (I grew up
  with the Fearn brand)
1 Tbsp fresh parsley, minced

Preheat oven to 375 degrees. Grease shallow baking pan.

Cut unpeeled eggplant into ½-inch thick rounds and place in the pan in a single layer. Combine ¼ C EVOO, garlic, oregano, basil, salt and pepper in a small bowl. Using a pastry brush, brush eggplant slices with herbed oil and put pan in oven. Bake for 15 minutes.

Flip over slices with a metal spatula, brush with remaining herbed oil and bake another 10 minutes.

To the same little mixing bowl, which is pretty empty now, add the last 2 Tbsp EVOO, chopped walnuts, soybean granules and fresh parsley. Spoon on top of eggplant. Bake 5 minutes longer, or broil for 2-3 minutes—just enough to brown.

Note: You might want to add 2 Tbsp grated romano cheese to the soybean granule mixture.

GARDEN GREEN BEANS TOMATO SAUTÉ

I really, really, really love plain steamed green beans. But occasionally everything tastes better a little dressed up. So I make this in the summer when all my green beans and tomatoes are producing like crazy.

Tomatoes contain lycopene, the phytochemical which makes them red but which also has significant antioxidant properties. I used to believe that we got the most bang for our buck, the most lycopene for heart and prostate health, by eating raw tomatoes. Research now shows that cooking tomatoes actually increases their lycopene content.

Serves 4 as a side dish

4 C fresh green beans, cut into 1-inch pieces
1 C water
¼ C extra virgin olive oil (EVOO), or butter
1 C onion, chopped
4 cloves garlic, minced finely

3 tomatoes, chopped, about 4 C
2 Tbsp minced fresh parsley
1 tsp minced fresh oregano (optional)
1 tsp minced fresh thyme (optional)

Steam green beans for 5 minutes in a pot with 1 C water. If your pot doesn't have a tight-fitting lid, you may need to add some more water, but don't drown the beans!

Gently warm EVOO or butter in a large skillet. Sauté onion and garlic until onion is tender, about 5 minutes. Stir in tomatoes and simmer for 10 minutes.

Add in green beans and parsley (and oregano and/or thyme, as you wish). Give a good stir and taste. I don't think you'll need any salt, but if you do, now's your chance.

Note: Want things spicy? Add some cayenne as the tomatoes simmer. Want things lemony? Add a good squeeze of lemon just after you put everything together and taste.

GINGERED PARSNIPS AND CARROTS WITH MISO

According to Paul Pitchford in his book *The Healing Tradition*, parsnips promote perspiration, help clear the liver and are mildly diuretic. While parsnips are also said to help fight colds and flus when you simmer the root and drink the broth, it's miso that is more commonly used for this purpose.

Miso is a fermented soy product, which keeps forever in your fridge. It's the fermentation, creating all those beneficial bacteria, that makes miso so healthy. Mold on top of your miso? Simply stir it back in and don't worry. A little extra penicillin, as they say! Miso is salty and used by some in lieu of salt.

Ah, ginger. I bet everyone knows that ginger gets the circulation going and helps ward off colds and flus too. But did you know that ginger is also used to protect against parasites? True!

Serves 4 as a side dish

2 large parsnips, about 4 C, sliced
2 large carrots, about 4 C, sliced
2 Tbsp honey

2 Tbsp sweet miso
1 Tbsp ginger root, minced
1 C water

Place all ingredients into a pan with a tight-fitting lid. Mix well. Cover and simmer on low for about 10 minutes, or just until parsnips are soft. Remove lid and simmer another 5 minutes to allow most of the liquid to evaporate. Great hot or cold. Great mashed or not.

Greens with Lemon Juice and Olive Oil

Greens like kale, mustard greens, collards and so on all have more absorbable and usable calcium than milk. Combined with lemon juice and olive oil, they are also cleansing and detoxifying.

This combination is great after surgery when constipation is often a problem. You can also use sliced carrots instead of greens anytime constipation is an issue. In our surgery-protocol handout at the store, we suggest carrots, scrubbed, sliced and steamed until very soft. Per 1 C sliced carrots, dress with 1 Tbsp EVOO and 1 Tbsp fresh lemon or lime juice. Eat daily for best results. The whole family can eat this, because it tastes good too.

Serves 4 as a side dish

1 large bunch greens, about 8 C
3 Tbsp fresh lemon juice

3 Tbsp extra virgin olive oil (EVOO)
3 Tbsp garlic, minced (optional)

Rinse and chop greens into bite-sized pieces. Use the stems too, so you don't waste anything, but chop the stems finely.

Put greens into a large pot with 1 C of water. Cover pot and steam greens until tender, about 5 minutes. Drain (sip soup liquor as tea, or save in a jar in the fridge to use in soups or when cooking a grain). Dress greens with olive oil and lemon juice. Add garlic if you like that pungent quality (I do). Serve alongside a simple meal or spoon over a whole grain. Eat and enjoy.

Note: Alternatively, you can gently warm EVOO in a skillet. Add garlic and sauté it briefly. Add greens and stir to coat. Add ½ C water, cover pot and simmer for about 5 minutes. Remove pot from heat. Dress with lemon juice and serve.

GRILLED PORTOBELLAS

This is from our June 2003 newsletter. Portobellas (aka portobellos) are overgrown brown cremini mushrooms. They're gourmet looking, firm and meaty in texture and resemble a burger when grilled.

Because they're drier than most mushrooms, they shrink less. I still brush them with olive oil before grilling or roasting to keep them from shriveling or turning tough.

You can grill lots of these delectable mushrooms so you have leftovers. Use those to slice into salads or to make a sandwich for school or work.

You can store portobellas in a brown paper bag in the fridge for up to 10 days. Clean before using by wiping with a damp cloth or soft brush.

Serves 4

4 large portobella mushrooms, stems trimmed

4 Tbsp extra virgin olive oil (EVOO), 1 Tbsp per mushroom

1 tsp Spike seasoning

4 Food For Life Ezekiel buns* (optional)

1-2 Tbsp sundried tomato spread per bun (or substitute mayo)

2 large bunches arugula or watercress, chopped

1 red onion, sliced

Preheat grill. Brush mushrooms with EVOO—it'll soak right in! Sprinkle each with a little Spike seasoning. Grill until tender, about 5-10 minutes per side. Alternatively, if you want to heat up the kitchen, you can roast mushrooms at 425 degrees for 15 minutes.

Enjoy these mushrooms topped with arugula and watercress and a slice of onion, or you can make a burger. To do that, swirl sundried tomato spread or mayo mixture on buns. Place grilled mushrooms, greens and slice of onion on bun bottoms. Cover with bun tops.

*Ezekiel buns? **Food for Life** *makes these delish buns and their label quotes the Bible, "Take also unto thee WHEAT and BARLEY, and BEANS, and LENTILS, and MILLET, and SPELT and put them in one vessel and make bread of it." These great ingredients are in all their 100% flourless, sprouted-grain breads and buns.*

ROASTED CAULIFLOWER AND BROCCOLI WITH HERBS AND SHIITAKES

Roasting vegetables makes them a little crispy and gives them a smoky flavor. Roasted vegetables can be served hot right from the oven, at room temperature as finger food or chilled and tossed in salads.

We all know that cauliflower and broccoli, which are members of the cruciferous family (together with cabbage, kale, Brussels sprouts, etc.), are said to be cancer protective. The first President Bush wouldn't eat his broccoli, and he's no longer president. Would broccoli have made the difference? I don't know, but do *you* want to take that kind of chance with fate?

As far back as the 14th century, the Chinese described shiitakes as food that activates "Qi," or life force, and protects the immune system. The ancient Chinese used shiitakes to nourish and heal. I like their wonderful chewy texture and woodsy flavor.

Serves 8 as a side dish

6 C cauliflower florets
6 C broccoli florets
2-3 C fresh shiitake mushrooms*
2 tsp garlic powder, or 6 cloves garlic, minced

Roast at 425 degrees

½-1 C extra virgin olive oil (EVOO)
2 tsp Herbes de Provence
2 tsp sea salt
1 tsp black pepper

Preheat oven to 425 degrees.

Toss vegetables with garlic and EVOO in a large bowl. Move vegetables to a shallow roasting pan and put the bowl aside.

Spread vegetables in a single layer in the roasting pan. Roast about 10 minutes. Stir and roast another 10 minutes. Remove pan from oven and return vegetables to the large bowl. Add herbs and seasonings. Toss so everything is well-coated. Taste and add more salt or pepper if desired. Gourmet this is. Healthy it is too!

If you want to use dried shiitake mushrooms, soak 1 C of mushrooms for 20 minutes in hot water. Squeeze and proceed as above. Save liquid for soups, or just drink when the liquid has cooled. The 1 C dried is equivalent to 2-3 C of fresh mushrooms in the recipe.

ROASTED FALL VEGETABLES

This is hearty without being heavy, and parsnips and red potatoes are lower on the glycemic index than yellow or white potatoes. Years ago when my mother was following a diet for arthritics, red potatoes were allowed. Yellow and white potatoes were not because they were classified as "nightshades," which she was supposed to avoid.

Parsnips, beets and sweet potatoes are fine for those with arthritis, but beets and sweet potatoes have a high glycemic count and are not so good for those who are diabetic. Just interesting to know, isn't it?

Serves 6-8 as a side dish

2 parsnips, about 4 C, sliced in 1-inch pieces

2 red potatoes, about 4 C, bite-sized wedges

2 carrots, about 4 C, sliced in 1-inch pieces

2 red beets, about 4 C, bite-sized wedges

2 sweet potatoes, about 4 C, bite-sized wedges

Roast at 425 degrees

½ C macadamia nut or extra virgin olive oil (EVOO)

1 tsp sea salt

1 tsp black pepper

½ tsp ground nutmeg

Preheat oven to 425 degrees.

Prepare veggies (I use only organic) by rinsing and then cutting into bite-sized pieces. Don't bother to peel anything because the vitamins are in the skin and you have better things to do with your time.

In a large shallow baking pan or casserole dish, combine veggies with macadamia nut oil or EVOO and seasonings. Mix with hands. Put pan in oven and roast veggies uncovered for 1 hour. Stir once or twice during the hour. Roasting uncovered allows veggies to brown nicely.

Note: These can be made ahead and reheated. They keep for days in the fridge. If you like, garnish with chopped parsley or watercress. You can also call this dish a simple tzimmes!

SIMPLE FRAGRANT VEGETABLE CURRY

Here's a quick vegetable dish that appeared in our November 2005 newsletter. You can make it during the week or serve at special occasions—even with a Thanksgiving bird for something a little different. Use different vegetables as the mood strikes. Include yams or sweet potatoes because these are rated #2 in terms of overall nutrient content by the Center for Science in the Public Interest!

Turmeric, called poor man's saffron, imparts a lovely yellow color. It's also a terrific antioxidant. People use turmeric not only as a coloring or flavoring agent, but as a supplement to help dispel inflammation.

Serves 4 as a side dish

1 Tbsp toasted sesame oil
4 cloves garlic, minced
1 tsp curry powder
1 tsp turmeric powder
½ tsp ground cumin
¼ tsp cinnamon
½ tsp ground coriander
1 tsp sea salt

4 C veggies like cubed yams, green beans, red onion, sliced cabbage, chopped kale, cauliflower or broccoli florets
1-2 C water
2 C any cooked grain or beans (optional)
handful of pistachios as garnish

Gently warm sesame oil in a large skillet. Add garlic and spices and stir to blend.

These will become aromatic in a flash. Be ready to add vegetables as soon as the aroma builds and then sauté briefly. Add 1 C water, cover pot and simmer mixture until vegetables are tender, about 5-10 minutes. You may need to add more water depending upon how tightly your lid seals.

Feel free to serve over any grain or to mix in any bean. Then garnish with a handful of pistachios.

VEGETABLE MÉLANGE WITH FAKIN' BACON

For the vegetarian and the carnivore. Both will happily eat this…

Everyone knows what an onion and a potato are. But tempeh? Tempeh is a fermented, natural soy product that is high in protein and usable calcium. Traditionally, tempeh is made from whole soybeans fermented with rice or millet wrapped in banana leaves. Made under controlled conditions today, it's still the fermentation which makes tempeh easy to digest. That said, tempeh will never replace chocolate mousse in the popular mind.

Serves 6
2 Tbsp EVOO
2 C red onion wedges
6 oz pkg of Lightlife Fakin' Bacon
4 C potatoes*, bite-sized pieces
4 C carrots, sliced
1 C green peas

Roast at 425 degrees
4 C string beans (mixture of green and purple is dramatic), cut into 2-inch pieces
1 tsp Spike seasoning
1 tsp black pepper
¼ C extra virgin olive oil (EVOO)

Preheat oven to 425 degrees.

Wash and prepare vegetables. Don't bother to peel anything. In an oven-proof dish or shallow roasting-type pan, mix the ¼ C EVOO together with onions, potatoes and carrots. Put pan in oven and roast vegetables for 45 minutes, or until potatoes are just about tender. Pull pan out of oven and stir in green beans. Put roasting pan back into oven for another 20-30 minutes.

In the meantime, gently heat the additional EVOO in a frying pan. When oil is hot, add the tempeh strips and cook a few minutes per side, or until tempeh is golden brown. Turn off flame and set frying pan aside. By the way, it's fine if the tempeh crumbles because that's how you want it anyway. What is important is that the tempeh is nice and crispy.)

Remove vegetables from oven. Gently stir in peas, Spike seasoning and black pepper. Stir in ½ the tempeh crumbles. Use the remainder tempeh pieces as garnish.

*My favorite kind of potatoes for this dish? Buttercream fingerling potatoes! They're a yellow variety of fingerling that is cute and round.

WILD MUSHROOM SAUTÉ WITH SPINACH

This appeared in our September 2007 newsletter. asiago is an Italian company, and we're pleased as punch to carry their mixture of frozen porcini, oyster, shiitake and nameko mushrooms. Adam introduced this product to me, and we both love how easy it is to make dinner by just adding a few other ingredients!

If you want to use fresh mushrooms, do. Three-quarters of a pound of shiitakes, maitakes, oyster or porcinis (or any mixture of those) will do.

I never thought about the fact that because mushrooms lack chlorophyll, they don't produce food for themselves through photosynthesis. Instead, they absorb nutrients from compost, leaves, decaying wood and soil. Wild mushrooms like those asiago includes in its product provide a more intense and exotic flavor. I like to think they also provide more nutrients since that's usually the case with wild foods.

Serves 2 as a main dish or 4 as a side dish

2 Tbsp extra virgin olive oil (EVOO)*
1½ C Asiago brand mixed frozen
  mushrooms
1 Tbsp tomato paste
2 cloves garlic, minced

pinch cayenne
4 C baby spinach**
½ tsp sea salt
½ tsp black pepper

Gently warm EVOO in a large skillet over medium heat. Add Asiago's packaged mushrooms. Yes, use the whole bag. Cook, stirring occasionally, until mushrooms begin to brown, about 5 minutes. Incorporate tomato paste, garlic and cayenne. Stir in spinach and cook just enough to wilt. Taste and season with salt and pepper.

Spoon over just about everything you like—ready-made polenta, pizza crusts, beans, pasta, chicken, fish or tofu—you name it.

You can serve this dish plain, as a side, or as a main dish for 2 of you, and garnished with anything from sunflower seeds to goat cheese or shrimp.

Try coconut butter, ghee or butter instead of EVOO. Try macadamia nut oil. Your choice, toots!
**If you like a chewier mix, chop up kale and stir that in instead of tender spinach. Feel free to use collards or broccoli.*

ZUCCHINI AND POTATO FRITTERS

When zucchinis do well in my garden, I love it, even if it means I have to travel to Manhattan to beg the masses to take and eat my extras. But some years it seems as if every bug on the face of the planet has decided to destroy my plants and I end up hoping organic farmers in my area had better luck than I.

You can make this without potatoes, but I find the mixture very satisfying and it holds me over until Chanukah when I have an excuse to make latkes.

Rinse but don't peel the zucchini or potatoes, because it simply isn't necessary to peel them. You don't want to throw away any nutrients, do you?

Serves 4 as a side dish

2 medium zucchini, about 4 C grated
1 C onion, grated
2 medium potatoes, about 4 C grated
½ C grated romano or parmesan cheese*
2 Tbsp extra virgin olive oil (EVOO)

½ C cornmeal
1 tsp dried basil
1 tsp black pepper
2 eggs (optional)
2 Tbsp more EVOO for frying

Rinse vegetables and coarsely grate the zucchini, onion and potatoes. I use my food processor, which makes this a 1-minute job. Press in a strainer to remove excess liquid.

Put vegetables into a large bowl together with cheese, EVOO (first 2 Tbsp), cornmeal, basil, black pepper and eggs, if using.

Add 2 more Tbsp EVOO to skillet. Gently warm. Shape vegetable mixture into 3-inch fritters or patties and brown on both sides in skillet.

Note: Fritters will hold together better if you choose to use the eggs.

You can use a non-dairy romano or parmesan if you like.

A World of Beans and Whole Grains

Beans and whole grains are the world's staple foods. Grains include wheat, oats, rice, wild rice, buckwheat and corn. Grains are also millet, teff, quinoa, flax, amaranth, barley, rye and spelt. And more grains we are oblivious to in this country, I'm sure. Beans? All kinds, sizes, shapes (such as round or elongated) and colors ranging from black to red to tan.

The cultivation of beans and whole grains goes back tens of thousands of years. These staple foods are central to the lore and history of ancient civilizations. Even today, people in non-industrialized countries revere beans and whole grains as foods which give health and bring wealth.

According to the Glycemic Index, beans and whole grains produce a gradual rise in blood sugar, unlike white breads or pastas, which give us an immediate sugar jolt. And studies say individuals who eat beans and whole-grain cereals have significantly lower rates of heart disease and stroke. The fiber in these foods is said to help prevent many diseases of modern civilization, and they make us feel satisfied too.

Do beans and whole grains make us fat? My own experience is that they do not. When I want to loose a little weight, it's easier to do so if I increase the proportion of beans and whole grains on my plate versus the animal protein and fats. Research done at Harvard, published in the *Journal of Clinical Nutrition*, found that women who eat the most whole grains lose more weight and maintain that weight loss better than women who eat the least amount of whole grains. The same, I'm sure, applies to beans.

Regarding grains—in this country, we eat mainly wheat, rice and corn. In this country, we rarely eat those grains as whole grains. We polish and pearl, removing the part of the grain which can spoil, the part which is nutrient-rich. We sacrifice health for commerce (we want products to be able to sit on the shelves for a long time without spoiling).

The bran we remove from wheat, for instance, not only adds bulk to the digestive system, but helps stabilize blood sugar by regulating absorption of nutrients and sugars in the digestive tract. The bran we remove from grains to make them shelf-stable has been shown to reduce blood cholesterol as effectively as any known cholesterol-lowering drug.

We eat our beans as baked beans with lots of sugar. Or we eat our beans in chili, where they are usually over-powered by fat.

This chapter seeks to take you to a new place, where you can enjoy beans and whole grains for themselves instead of as carriers for the "good stuff."

I challenge you to try cooking beans and whole grains plain and enjoying that taste. I challenge you to have fun dressing them up with a dollop of chutney, marinated sun-dried tomatoes or nuts and seeds with toasted sesame oil and a splash of tamari. Have fun exploring.

ADAM'S FIVE-MINUTE BUTTERBEANS WITH SMOKED OLIVE OIL

Adam wrote this for our April 2009 newsletter. (Whenever it says "I" below, that's Adam.)

I don't normally like smoked foods, but I've been loving that new pine cone, smoked olive oil ever since we got it in a few months ago. But apparently, I'm the only one. Is nobody else buying this but me?

You can use it just about anywhere you'd use a good olive oil. I especially like pairing it with butterbeans, a mild and creamy variety of lima bean. If you're more industrious, you can cook up some beans ahead of time. Otherwise, just crack open a can of Eden butterbeans and let it drain.

If you really want to keep things simple, just drizzle some oil over the cold beans, sprinkle on some Italian herbs and a few spoonfuls of grating cheese. Mash it up with a fork, and you have a simple, but really good, dip. If you want to get fancier (but still not cook anything), add a can of baby shrimp.

But if you can spare 5 minutes, try this: chop up a cup's worth of whatever you have handy (see below), then sauté in about 4 Tbsp of the oil. Then pour the sauté over a can of the drained beans, and mash the whole thing up with a fork. Served over toast, or as a filling for an omelet, or a crude dip, it works like a charm. Or stir it in with plain cooked rice and you'll have instant oh-so-gourmet rice-and-beans.

Whatever you have handy can include:

    minced red onion
    ·chopped celery
    ·maitake or shiitake mushrooms
    ·diced smoked ham
    sardines
    ·hard-boiled egg

AMANDA'S JADE PEARL GREEN COCONUT RICE

From the class on "Light and Lively Grains for Summer," which Amanda and I taught together in 2008. You'll love this dish that is bright green and flavorful. The coconut makes it almost decadent…

Amanda says, "This dish has Ayurvedic roots. I adapted it from Dr. Lad's *Cooking for Self Healing*. Jade Pearl Green Rice is an heirloom rice infused with bamboo. The addition of bamboo results in a rice with more fiber than any other brown rice."

Serves 6

⅓ C coconut oil
1 tsp mustard seed
1 tsp cumin seed
1 tsp cardamom pods
1 tsp cloves
1 cinnamon stick
2 bay leaves
2 C Jade Pearl Green rice
2 Tbsp sea salt
1 C chopped veggies (any!)
4½ C water

SAUCE
½ bunch cilantro
6 Tbsp shredded coconut
2 cloves garlic
thumb-sized knob of fresh ginger
1 tsp sea salt
½ C water
lime wedges
extra cilantro
extra coconut for garnish

Melt coconut oil in a large saucepan with a heavy bottom and add seeds, pods, cloves, cinnamon stick and bay leaves. Sauté until bay leaves turn brown. Add rice and salt to saucepan and stir well to coat rice. Add veggies, give a good stir and then add water. Bring to a boil, turn down flame and cook uncovered at active simmer, stirring occasionally so you don't get the rice stuck to the bottom of the pot and burned. (If you do, don't worry! Just dump the pilaf into a different pot, add a little water and keep going. Never stir a burned crusty bottom into the rest of your lovely dish.)

While the rice is cooking, get the blender out. Put the cilantro, shredded coconut, garlic cloves, ginger, extra tsp of salt and ½ C water in the blender and puree. You'll have a lovely fragrant sauce.

Amanda says, "When the rice is soft and ready to eat, pour the bright green puree in and stir it all up to spread the color. It's dazzling! Serve with lime wedges, extra chopped cilantro and coconut as garnish. So tasty. Yum."

Ayurvedic Black & Yellow Quinoa

Ayurveda is a system of medicine from India that uses food to heal. This recipe has a combination of spices which promote healthy digestion and also make a dish that is scrumptious and easy to eat.

Quinoa is high in protein, and I like the yellow, red and black quinoas. I've found they don't cook the same, however. Red and black quinoas don't absorb as much water as the yellow does. They don't sprout like the yellow when they cook either, and they stay crunchier. That's why I like to use the red and black quinoas as mix-ins, as garnishes, if you will.

Serves 8

4 C boiling water
2 Tbsp ghee (clarified butter)
1 tsp turmeric powder
1 tsp cumin seeds
2 tsp mustard seeds
1 tsp cardamom

1 tsp asafoetida*
2 tsp sea salt
2 tsp black pepper
2 C yellow quinoa
½ C black quinoa
4 C cut-up asparagus, or whole sugar snap peas

Bring water to a boil in a kettle. Using a large skillet and low heat, melt ghee. Add turmeric, cumin and mustard seeds, cardamom, asafoetida, salt and pepper. Stir until mustard seeds begin to pop. *Be careful, they do indeed pop!* Add both quinoas and stir to coat. Add the 4 C of boiling water slowly and carefully. Asafoetida makes everything bubble like the proverbial witches' brew and my stove top invariably gets splattered.

Cover pot, turn heat down to lowest and simmer for 10 minutes. Turn off heat, leave pot covered and let stand for 10 minutes. Now uncover pot and add asparagus or peas. Cover again and let stand another 10 minutes to soften vegetables. Spoon onto plates and serve. If you or your guests love ghee, feel free to add a little more to the top of each plate.

*Asafoetida, related to fennel, is also known as hing or "devil's dung" (because of its smell). Never mind. It's a potent digestive aid and a pinch added to bean dishes is said to reduce gas. So keep some devil's dung in your cupboard. Hey nonny nonny. You'll be surprised. This smelly ingredient brings everything else together into a rapturous whole.

BLACK BARLEY WITH WALNUTS AND GREEN OLIVES

Black (or purple) barley originated in Ethiopia. It's a wild cousin of the barley we know, and its yield is much smaller, which may be one reason it's not widely grown. If you can't get it (we do have it in our store), feel free to use any hulled barley.

Black barley has a great texture, something like that of wild rice. You can serve it plain with just a touch of salt and a generous dollop of butter, if you don't feel like going to the trouble of making the recipe below.

Serves 4

1 C black barley
3 C water
¼ C extra virgin olive oil (EVOO) or butter
1 onion, diced, about 2 C
2 stalks celery, diced, about 2 C
1 sweet bell pepper, diced, about 2 C
4 cloves garlic, minced
2 C fresh mushrooms, sliced (any variety)

1 C walnut pieces
1 tsp dried marjoram
1 tsp dried oregano
1 tsp dill weed
1 tsp black pepper
½ C pitted French green olives (or other great green olive)
1 tsp sea salt
8 C spinach or red chard cut into bite-sized pieces

Place barley and water in a saucepan. Bring water to a boil, reduce flame to lowest, cover pot and simmer barley about 60-90 minutes. Water will be absorbed and barley soft when it's done cooking.

While barley is cooking, gently warm EVOO or butter in a skillet. Sauté onion, celery and pepper for about 5 minutes. Add garlic and mushrooms and continue to sauté another 5 minutes. Add herbs, black pepper, pitted olives and sea salt. Simmer another 10 minutes.

Add the vegetable mixture into the barley and stir well. Cover pot and let it sit on the stove top for about 10 minutes. You can turn flame to lowest if you want to simmer the whole dish. Otherwise, just letting it sit so the barley can absorb the flavors is fine too.

Steam spinach or chard by placing 1 C water in a pot and bringing water to a boil. Add the greens and turn down heat to lowest. Cover pot and steam 1-2 minutes.

Spoon barley mixture onto plates and place steamed greens on the side. Pretty, tasty and satisfying. Good for the heart, waist and planet.

Blue Ribbon Edition

BUCKWHEAT FALAFEL WITH CHICKPEAS

Falafel is a mainstay in the Middle East where its usually served inside pita bread with shredded lettuce, sauerkraut, chopped tomatoes and tahini sauce or hot peppers. You can do the same or serve it as a side to savory lamb dishes, grilled chicken or on their own next to a chopped tomato and cabbage salad.

Serves 6

2 C dried chickpeas, soaked overnight
1 C buckwheat groats (kasha)
3 cloves garlic
2 eggs
handful of fresh parsley
2 tsp sea salt

¼ tsp cayenne pepper
2 tsp cumin powder
1 tsp dried oregano
extra virgin olive oil (EVOO),
** or macadamia or peanut oil**
** for frying (about ½-inch in pan)**

Using the steel blade of a food processor, blend ingredients until they resemble fine breadcrumbs. If batter will not hold together when pressed between fingers, mix in water, 1 Tbsp at a time, until it will. Allow to stand for ½ hour.

Heat oil in fry pan. Make balls the size of walnuts. Drop into sizzling oil with a slotted spoon. Be careful not to cause the oil to splash. Stir falafel around a few times and fry them to a deep brown.

Serve immediately inside pita with fixings, with toothpicks as an appetizer or as a side to a meat entrée. They can be the entrée themselves surrounded by salads and topped with a tahini sauce. Just remember that falafel should be eaten piping hot!

Note: Want to make a tahini sauce? Blend ¼ C tahini, ¼ C lemon juice, ½ C water, 2 cloves garlic and 1 tsp salt. Simple as that.

*Can you bake falafel instead of frying? Yes. It won't be as crunchy or luscious, but the flavors will still be there. Baking instead of frying will keep your stove top clean and save calories. (Still, when I take the time to make falafel balls, I want them fried.) How to bake? Preheat oven to 400 degrees. Make balls and arrange in rows on oiled cookie sheet so they're not touching. Spray with a little oil. Bake 30-40 minutes until golden.

Bulgur and Amaranth Pilaf

I introduced this dish at a cooking class in my home some years ago. Amaranth is perfect for people on a strict gluten-free diet, for diabetics, for vegetarians and for people who are trying to eat a heart-healthy diet or just seeking a more balanced diet.

Amaranth has been grown and harvested for more than 8,000 years. The Aztecs called amaranth a "super food." Amaranth was fed to runners and warriors because it provided energy and was believed to improve athletic performance. The crop was regarded so highly that each year bushels of amaranth were presented to their leader, Montezuma. Because the crop figured so prominently in Aztec culture and religious ceremonies, the conquering armies of Cortez burned the fields to the ground.

As European crops replaced indigenous ones, amaranth slowly fell out of use. Twenty years ago, the "ancient crop with a future" enjoyed a renaissance when the National Academy of Sciences recommended amaranth as one of 20 foods to be re-introduced into the American diet.

This is quick, easy and a nutritious change of pace.

Serves 4

2 Tbsp extra virgin olive oil (EVOO) or ghee
1 onion, chopped, about 2 C
4 cloves garlic, minced
¾ C coarse red bulgur
¼ C amaranth
1 C diced tomatoes (put liquid in measuring cup)

½ C oil-cured olives, pitted
½ C currants or chopped dates
1 Tbsp cinnamon
1 tsp black pepper
1 tsp sea salt
2 Tbsp EVOO or ghee

Gently warm 2 Tbsp EVOO or ghee in a skillet. Add onion and sauté about 5 minutes. Add garlic and sauté until it is golden. Stir in bulgur and amaranth so they are coated with oil. Add tomatoes (save liquid and add water to that to make 2¼ C liquid). Add the 2¼ C liquid to bulgur together with olives, currants or dates, cinnamon, black pepper and salt. Bring mixture to a boil, cover, lower heat and simmer for 25 minutes, or until all moisture is absorbed.

Uncover skillet and drizzle on remaining EVOO or ghee. Or not. Your choice. I like the good fats! Serve together with a nice green salad for a complete meal.

CHINESE FORBIDDEN BLACK RICE

A version of this appeared in our March 2002 store newsletter.

What's the difference between brown rice, white rice and Chinese Forbidden Black Rice? White rice is whole-grain, brown rice that has been milled so there's no bran. White rice is therefore mainly carbohydrate without B vitamins, minerals, fiber and other nutrients found in the bran of whole-grain, brown rice. Chinese Forbidden Black Rice is whole grain. It's brown rice with all the good stuff, only it's black.

The story about Chinese Forbidden Black Rice is full of intrigue. Eating it was forbidden to all but the Emperor of China and his immediate family. If you were caught with this rice, it was off with your head!

Serves 6

2 Tbsp extra virgin olive oil (EVOO)
2 Tbsp minced garlic
1 C Chinese Forbidden Black Rice
1 tsp sea salt
1 tsp black pepper
**1½ C marinated artichoke hearts
  (save liquid)**

up to 3 C water
2 C frozen peas and carrots
**1 bunch fresh spinach, torn into
  bite-sized pieces, about 6 C**
1 tsp dried thyme
1 C shelled pistachios (optional)

Gently warm EVOO in a large skillet. Add garlic, rice, salt and pepper to skillet. Stir for 1-2 minutes, or until garlic is aromatic and rice is well-coated with oil.

Into a measuring cup, put the liquid from the marinated artichoke hearts. Top off with water to reach 3 C and then add to skillet. Bring mixture to a boil, cover pot, lower heat and then simmer for 1 hour. (Depending upon the weather and how tightly your pot lid fits, you may need to add a little more water towards the end.)

Uncover pot. Add artichoke hearts, frozen peas and carrots, spinach and thyme. Gently toss everything together in the skillet. Cover and let stand 5-10 minutes so peas and carrots get hot and spinach wilts. Spoon onto plates. Garnish with pistachio nuts.

Note: Adding nuts to any grain makes a complete protein.

Corn and Millet Pudding

This is another recipe from Amanda, which she introduced in a 2008 cooking class.

"Millet isn't just for birds," says Amanda. "This tiny, yummy whole grain is tasty in this adaptation of an American Thanksgiving favorite. You cook the millet ahead of time, and then stir it up with sautéed onion and seasonings. A custard is made with a couple of organic eggs and a can of corn, juice and all. Feel free to use fresh corn with a ½ C of milk if you are feeling decadent. And if you happen to make this in the summer."

Serves 6

3 C water
1 Tbsp sea salt
1 C millet
¼ C Earth Balance spread
1 onion, chopped, about 2 C
1 tsp fresh sage, chopped
1 tsp fresh thyme leaves
2½ tsp sea salt
1 tsp black pepper

Bake at 325 degrees in a 9x13 baking dish

1 tsp garlic, minced
1 15-oz can Eden brand corn,
   with juice, about 2 C corn
2 eggs
1 Tbsp fresh parsley, chopped
pea greens as garnish (optional)
   dressed with salad dressing
mache as garnish (optional)
chives for sprinkling on top

Bring the water to a boil. Add salt and millet. Turn heat down, cover pot and simmer for 30 minutes.

Preheat oven to 325 degrees.

Melt Earth Balance spread in a sauté pan. Add onion, sage, thyme, salt and black pepper. Sauté on low for about 7 minutes until the onion becomes sweet and translucent. Stir in the garlic and sauté 30 seconds more. Remove sauté pan from heat and stir in the cooked millet.

Dump the whole can of corn, juice and all, into a big bowl. Whisk in eggs, add millet/onion mixture and fresh parsley. Pour into 9x13 baking dish. Cover baking dish and put into oven. Bake for 40 minutes. Remove from oven and slice to serve. Garnish with dressed pea greens or plain mache and a few chives sprinkled on top.

Note: This dish can be made ahead (without the garnishes) because it reheats well. Simply reheat and then garnish. Serve.

Couscous with Roasted Vegetables and Pistachios

Boychik and girlchik, we have shelled pistachios in our nut refrigerator. You do not need to shell them yourself. By the by, did you know that pistachios have 20 grams of protein per 4 oz? They also are high in vitamin A and contain more iron than any other nut. If you're anemic, try a handful of pistachios daily. This kind of iron won't upset your tummy.

I always store my nuts and seeds in the freezer, and then they can keep forever.

Serves 8
½ C extra virgin olive oil (EVOO)
6 C cubed sweet potatoes or 6 C
   peeled, seeded, butternut squash
3 zucchini, halved and sliced on
   diagonal
2 red onions, peeled, cut into 6
   wedges each
½ tsp ground allspice
½ tsp cinnamon
1 tsp sea salt
1 tsp black pepper

Bake at 400 degrees
2 C boiling water
2 tsp grated orange rind
2 C French couscous
¼ C EVOO
1 can Eden chickpeas, about 2 C
   cooked, drained well
½ C shelled pistachio nuts
3 Tbsp fresh parsley, chopped
black pepper grinding (optional)

Preheat oven to 400 degrees.

Place EVOO into a large roasting or baking pan (I have a speckled black, round, enamel paella pan that I love to use for dishes like this). Add vegetables, spices, and salt and pepper.

Toss so vegetables are well-coated with everything (hands are the best tool for this). Spread vegetables in a single layer in the pan and roast in oven for 1 hour.

In the meantime, in a large mixing bowl, pour boiling water over orange rind and couscous and let stand about 20 minutes, or until the water is completely absorbed by the grain. Add remaining ¼ C EVOO and chickpeas to couscous. Toss.

Take vegetables out of oven. Add ½ of the roasted vegetables to the couscous and toss gently. Taste and adjust seasoning. Spoon onto individual plates or onto a serving platter. Make an indentation in the center of the couscous and spoon remaining roasted vegetables into the well. Garnish everything with pistachios and parsley. You might want a few grindings of black pepper too.

DENISE'S LENTIL LOAF

"This dish pleases my whole family," says Denise. "I served it recently with gravy, mashed potatoes and green beans. My daughter asked if we could have this on Thanksgiving instead of turkey. Next time, I'll add cranberry sauce."

Lentils are to India as meatloaf is to America—the quintessential comfort food. And here you have a loaf that uses lentils, which makes this a double-dip comfort food.

Serves 6
½ C extra virgin olive oil (EVOO)
1 onion, minced, about 2 C
2 beaten eggs
2 C evaporated milk
1 C mashed cooked lentils (Eden's canned lentils are also okay)

Bake at 350 degrees in 8x8 glass or loaf pan
1½ C crushed seasoned stuffing mix
2 tsp vegetable broth powder
½ C chopped walnuts (optional)
Road's End Organics golden gravy mix (optional)

Preheat oven to 350 degrees. Grease a glass 8x8 square or loaf pan.

In a small skillet, gently warm EVOO. Sauté onion in oil. Place sautéed onion in a large mixing bowl and add eggs, evaporated milk, cooked lentils, stuffing mix and broth powder. Include walnuts if you like. Mix everything thoroughly and pour into the pan.

Bake lentil loaf approximately 1 hour.

Remove from oven and let lentil loaf sit for about 5 minutes. Then unmold onto a platter. (Denise says this unmolds easily.) Serve plain or with vegetarian gravy. Invite Denise's daughter, Camilla, over for dinner...

GRANMISTO DI FUNGHI WITH CANNELLINI BEANS, BASIL AND SUN-DRIED TOMATOES

Our March 2008 newsletter featured this dish. Chickpeas, aka garbanzo beans, originate in the Middle East and the Mediterranean. Today everyone everywhere eats them. Why is that, aside from the fact they taste good? Well, they're high in soluble fiber, which helps lower cholesterol and decreases insulin requirements for people with diabetes. They contain protein, calcium and iron (isn't that a surprise?). You get nutrition and de-li-tion—all for a fair price, even if you don't cook the beans yourself.

Serves 4

¼ C extra virgin olive oil (EVOO)
2 chopped onions, about 4 C
4 cloves garlic, pressed
1 can Eden cannellini beans, with ½ C liquid, or 2 C cooked
4 C asiago brand mixed frozen mushrooms
4 C coarse-chopped kale
2 C sliced cabbage

½ C marinated sun-dried tomatoes, halved
1 Tbsp dried basil
1 Tbsp fennel seeds
1 Tbsp black pepper
1 tsp sea salt
3 Tbsp lemon juice

In a large skillet, gently warm EVOO. Add onions and sauté 5 minutes. Add garlic and sauté 1-2 minutes. Then add remaining ingredients (except lemon juice) with ½ C liquid from beans, or ½ C water. Mix everything well, then cover pot and simmer for 20-30 minutes. Turn off heat, uncover pot and add lemon. Taste and adjust for seasoning.

Note: You can serve this dish garnished with any number of things. Some add-ins that I have used are crumbled Mt. Vikos feta cheese, pine nuts, cashews, steamed shrimp, Wolfe Neck Farms meatballs or a sprinkling of Pecorino romano. Once again, it's completely up to you!

JANET'S TLT
(TEMPEH, LETTUCE AND TOMATO)

This is a fun, tasty sandwich, a vegetarian version of the classic BLT. Instead of bacon, it's made with Fakin' Bacon, a smoky tempeh product made by Lightlife. What is tempeh? It's a food made by fermenting soy beans with a starter culture (often rice).

As soon as these tempeh strips start to sizzle in the frying pan, people in the store flock back to the kitchen to ask what smells so good. The smell is as delicious as the flavor—hearty, smoky, meaty and satisfying.

A few omnivorous staff members say they like these tempeh strips better than real bacon, and these sandwiches often sell out before we finish making them!

Makes 3 sandwiches

2 Tbsp extra virgin olive oil (EVOO)
1 6-oz pkg Fakin' Bacon (9 strips)
6 slices whole-grain bread*
3 Tbsp Vegenaise brand non-mayo spread

raw minced garlic (optional)
6 leaves romaine lettuce
2 small to medium tomatoes
balsamic vinegar (optional)

Gently heat EVOO in a frying pan. When oil is hot, add the tempeh strips and cook until golden brown on each side. Drain the strips on a paper-towel-covered cookie sheet and allow them to cool.

Lay out bread (toasting is optional). Spread Vegenaise on each slice. (Garlic lovers may want to add a bit of minced garlic to the spread.)

Wash and dry lettuce. Wash and slice tomatoes thin. If it's not tomato season, it's nice to add a bit of balsamic vinegar to flavor your winter tomatoes.

Assemble the sandwiches, using lettuce, tomato and three strips of the Fakin' Bacon per sandwich. Cut in half and enjoy!

*Janet chose the seeded bread from The Baker because the slices are nice and large, but any whole-grain bread is fine.

Japanese-Style Lentils with Bok Choy

Lentils are green, brown, black, blue, yellow, red and orange. In this country, the green and brown are the most economical. They also seem to have the nuttiest flavor. All lentils are nutrient dense, help lower cholesterol, promote heart health and give us energy. Their fiber stabilizes blood sugar. What's not to like? Eat 'em and enjoy!

Serves 4

1 C green or brown lentils
2 C water
½ C toasted sesame oil
1 onion, diced, about 2 C
4 stalks celery, sliced, about 4 C
2 C mushrooms (I like shiitakes), sliced
6 cloves garlic, minced
1 can Eden navy beans, about 2 C cooked

1 Tbsp tamari (soy sauce)
1 tsp sea salt
1 tsp marjoram
½ tsp nutmeg
1 tsp ginger powder
4 C bok choy greens, cut into ribbons

Put lentils and water into a small saucepan and bring water to a boil. Lower heat, cover pot and simmer for about 20 minutes.

In the meantime, in a large skillet, gently warm toasted sesame oil. Sauté onion, celery and mushrooms until they begin to brown. Then add garlic and beans together with tamari, salt, marjoram, nutmeg and ginger. Simmer together for 5 minutes.

Lentils should have absorbed all the water in the saucepan. If they haven't but are tooth tender at the end of the 20 minutes, drain. Add lentils to skillet. Stir and allow to cook another 5 minutes.

While the lentils are cooking with the rest of the ingredients, cut bok choy into ribbons. Dish out lentil stir-fry and put a cup of shredded bok choy onto the top of each plate.

Note: If you don't like raw bok choy, simply add to the skillet during the last minute of cooking so the bok choy softens slightly before dishing out. Try it raw at least once in your life.

Jim's Kidney Bean Empanadas

Jim says, "I've been making this recipe for years. It's great winter or summer, and my wife and I, and my book group (five hungry men), love my empanadas. The combo of organic grains, beans and vegetables satisfies. Which beans to use? Eden beans are cooked with kombu, which makes them more digestible, and Eden doesn't use bisphenol-A to line their cans. Lin's Farm tahini is made from whole sesame seeds so you get a lot of calcium. For the pie crust (I first discovered this basic pie crust recipe in 1976), add water to the dough until it reaches earlobe consistency. The result: a great pie crust and a pair of sticky, doughy ears."

Whenever it says "I" in the recipe below, that's Jim.

Serves 12-14

2 medium carrots, diced, about 4 C
1 large parsnip, diced, about 2 C
1 medium onion, chopped, about 2 C
2 Tbsp extra virgin olive oil (EVOO)
2 cans Eden kidney beans, drained, about 4 C
2-3 Tbsp tamari (soy sauce)

Bake at 350 degrees

2 C whole-wheat pastry flour
½ tsp sea salt
½ C Earth Balance spread
½ C tahini
10 Tbsp cold water
grated cheese (optional)

Prepare veggies. Gently warm EVOO in a large skillet. Add the vegetables and sauté them slowly to bring out their sweetness. When veggies are tender, about 10 minutes, add drained kidney beans and 2-3 Tbsp (to taste) tamari. Let simmer while you make the crust.

Mix the whole-wheat flour and salt and cut in the Earth Balance and tahini. Mix well by hand. Add approximately 10 Tbsp water and knead well. Adjust by feel (earlobes if necessary) to get good elasticity. Roll out the dough. You can either roll out the entire batch or divide batch in ½ and do ½ at a time. I roll it between two sheets of wax paper to make it easier to handle.

Preheat oven to 350 degrees.

Cut into circles about 4¾-inch in diameter. (I use an upturned jar to make the circles.) Remainders can be re-formed and re-rolled until all dough is used up. Spoon about 3 Tbsp of filling onto each circle and fold over into a crescent. I've never added cheese, but if you're not a vegan, that would be delicious! Press empanadas closed with your finger and thumb. Press with a fork to make a decorative edge. Lay empanadas onto shallow, greased pan (or 2). Put in oven and bake for about 25 minutes, or until empanadas are nicely brown.

Jocelyn's Saffron-Cashew-Pistachio Rice

Jocelyn says, "This vegan and gluten-free rice dish is a perfect cold dish on a hot day. I make a big batch when there's a hot spell coming and keep it in the fridge. And on a cold night, it serves as a hearty, sweet side dish that will surprise your taste buds..."

Serves 4-6

2 C brown rice (or your favorite rice)
4½ C water
¼ C MimiCreme (unsweetened cashew milk) or other unsweetened nut milk
¼ C agave nectar or maple syrup
1 Tbsp cinnamon

pinch cayenne pepper
1 tsp dried saffron
½ C unsalted cashews
½ C pistachios
½ C raisins

Put rice and water in pot. Bring water to a boil. Turn down flame, cover pot and let rice simmer on low for 30-40 minutes. Water will be mostly absorbed and rice will be al dente.

While rice is cooking, mix nut milk, sweetener, cinnamon, cayenne and saffron in a small pot. You may have to add a little water to make sure ingredients are dissolved and well mixed. Stir in nuts and raisins. Set mixture aside.

When rice is al dente, add nut and raisin mixture. Gently stir. Simmer everything another 5 minutes. Serve hot or cold, depending upon the time of year and your preference!

KASHA WITH WILD MUSHROOMS

Kasha, or buckwheat, is rich in B vitamins which nourish our adrenals. Kasha is not only great survival food, but it's hearty and filling too. Studies have shown that people who ate buckwheat after the Chernobyl incident fared much better than people who didn't eat buckwheat afterward. It is said that buckwheat pulls excess radiation out of the body.

You can eat this on its own or use it to accompany chicken or fish.

Serves 6

½ C extra virgin olive oil (EVOO)*
2 C kasha (toasted buckwheat groats)
2 C fresh sliced mushrooms (any kind)
2 oz dried mushrooms

1 tsp sea salt
1 tsp black pepper
4 C boiling water

In a skillet with a cover, gently warm EVOO. Stir in kasha and mushrooms so everything is nicely coated. Mix in salt and pepper and pour boiling water into skillet carefully. Stir to disperse ingredients and then cover skillet. Turn heat down to low and simmer for 10 minutes. Turn off heat and let pot sit another 10 minutes. Taste to adjust seasoning. Enjoy.

If you prefer, use butter or Ghee instead of EVOO. You can even use coconut oil. Really.

MEXICAN QUINOA WITH PEPITAS

From a 2006 cooking class I taught in my home. You'll note the same seasonings for this quinoa dish as used in the "Quinoa with Pine Nuts and Apricots" that appeared in our first cookbook. I like the combination, and it works in so many different ways!

Pumpkin seeds and their oil have lots of zinc. Zinc heals wounds and has been shown to be effective in the treatment of prostate problems.

Pumpkin seed oil is sensitive to heat. Don't use it to sauté or fry.

Serves 6

2 C water
1 C yellow quinoa
¼ C red quinoa
½ C pumpkin seed oil
2 Tbsp ground cumin
1 tsp coriander
⅓ C lemon or lime juice

1 tsp each salt and black pepper
1 C roasted pumpkin seeds
1 can Eden black beans, rinsed, or
    about 2 C cooked
½ C pitted green olives
½ C minced red onion
chopped parsley or cilantro, as
    garnish

Bring water to a boil. Add yellow and red quinoa, cover pot, lower heat and simmer for 10 minutes. Remove pot from burner and let it sit covered another 20 minutes, or until water is all absorbed. Then dump grain out into a large mixing bowl. Using a rubber spatula, fluff quinoa every few minutes to allow heat to escape.

When quinoa has cooled and is almost room temp, add remaining ingredients. Toss while humming "Torreadora, don't spit on the floor'a…" Taste and adjust seasoning. Garnish with chopped parsley or cilantro. Serve with an "Ole!"

Moroccan Millet Stew with White Beans

A variation of this appeared in our February 2008 store newsletter. It's an aromatic, satisfying vegetarian stew—a bean mixture served over a whole grain (millet in this case).

Millet is one of those under-utilized grains that are alkalizing, easy on the digestive system and somewhat foreign to us but tasty. Millet is worth getting to know.

Are there too many ingredients in this recipe? Not really. There are lots of spices, but I bet you have most of them in your kitchen.

Serves 4

¼ C extra virgin olive oil (EVOO)
1 onion, chopped, about 2 C
6 cloves garlic, minced
2 tsp paprika
1 tsp sea salt
1 tsp black pepper
1 tsp ground cumin
1 tsp turmeric powder
1 tsp ground ginger
2 tsp crushed red pepper flakes
2 C diced tomatoes, with juice
1 carrot, diced, about 2 C
2 zucchini, halved and sliced, about 3 C

1 C Eden navy beans, about 2 C cooked
2 Tbsp lemon juice
2 Tbsp EVOO
1 onion, chopped, about 2 C
1 tsp sea salt
½ tsp turmeric powder
1 tsp cinnamon
4 C water
2 C millet
½ C raisins or currants
1 bunch cilantro, chopped
lemon wedges

Stew: Gently warm EVOO in a large saucepan and sauté onion until soft, about 5 minutes. Add garlic and stir another minute. Mix in spices, diced tomatoes, carrot and zucchini. Bring to a boil. Turn flame to lowest, cover pot and simmer 20 minutes. Add navy beans and lemon. Set bean stew aside.

Grain: In a pot with a tight-fitting lid, gently warm the next 2 Tbsp EVOO. Add onion and sauté together with salt, turmeric and cinnamon. Add water and millet to pot together with raisins or currants. Bring to a boil, turn flame to lowest, cover pot and simmer until grain has absorbed all the liquid, about 45 minutes.

Spoon grain onto serving platter, or onto individual plates. Form well in center of grain. Spoon bean stew into well. Sprinkle with cilantro. Garnish each plate with a lemon wedge.

PILAF WITH CHESTNUTS AND YAMS

This recipe, which ran in our November 2002 newsletter, is good anytime it's cold and dark outside. Back then I wrote, "It's Thanksgiving, and guess who's coming to dinner? Uncle Ed, who has to eat turkey or it's not Thanksgiving, and Aunt Gertrude, who says, 'Don't worry about me, I brought kale in Tupperware!'"

So how do you please everybody? How do you marry tradition with belief systems, eccentricities and dietary restrictions? How do you make everyone comfortable and still make it a celebration?

And I factor in another concern—how do I create a feast that will keep those I love healthy?

You might try the following recipe, which is fast and easy to make. My mother, Beatrice, would omit the apricots and prunes because the only thing she liked sweet were desserts.

Serves 8-12 as a side dish (You can halve the recipe, and it works fine too.)

¼ C extra virgin olive oil (EVOO)	4 C peeled chestnuts*
3 C brown basmati rice	6 C yams, 1-inch diced
6 C boiling water	1 C dried apricots
2 saffron threads	1 C dried pitted prunes
1½ tsp sea salt	minced parsley for garnish
1½ tsp black pepper	minced chives for garnish

Gently warm EVOO in a pot with a tight-fitting cover. Add rice and stir to coat. Add boiling water, saffron and salt and pepper. Stir gently to combine. Put chestnuts in pot on top of rice together with diced yams, and apricots and prunes. Don't mix. The rice needs to stay on the bottom so it can absorb water and become tender.

Lower heat, cover pot and simmer for close to an hour. Check after 45 minutes and add 1 more C of water if needed. After another 15 minutes, test chestnuts and yams to make sure they are tooth-tender. They should be, but if not, cover pot and let steam another 10 minutes or so.

Turn pilaf into bowl and let it rest for 10 minutes. Then toss gently with rubber spatula so ingredients are mixed. Taste and adjust seasoning. Garnish if you like.

*Of course you can peel your own chestnuts, but I use dried ones that I first boil in water for 10 minutes, or I buy frozen peeled chestnuts or use ones that come in jars. The choice is yours!

POSOLE

"Posole" appeared in our November 2006 newsletter. Never heard of posole? Historians think it originated with the storage of corn in damp limestone caves by the pre-Columbian Anasazi. Today posole is made when kernels of corn are soaked in lime water, then hulled and dried.

Posole is used for soup or stew and generally combined with pork (or other meat), chili and other seasonings and often served with chopped lettuce, radishes, onions and fresh cilantro. You might want to add a pinch of saffron to this dish, which gives posole a lovely golden color and a wonderful aromatic flavor. It is traditionally served on Christmas Eve to celebrate life's blessings.

You can make posole in advance because it actually tastes better a day or two later.

Serves 8 as a side dish

1½ C Los Chileros brand posole
1 tsp sea salt
2 Tbsp chili powder or posole spice blend
1 can Eden diced tomatoes, about 2 C
4 cloves garlic, diced
1 onion, chopped, about 2 C
2 bay leaves
1 tsp dried coriander

choose either 1 pkg Tofurky sausages, Fakin' Bacon, 2 lb cubed meat or 1 pkg duck, turkey or regular bacon
1 can Eden pinto beans, about 2 C cooked
2 Tbsp fresh lime juice
2 tsp chopped cilantro (optional)
sides, see below (optional)

Put posole into non-reactive pan such as enamel or stainless steel and cover with water. Soak overnight. Add salt to water and boil posole 2 hours (I covered my pot). Add remaining ingredients except lime juice, cilantro and sides.* Cover and simmer on low heat for another hour. You can stir occasionally, but it's not necessary.

Taste and adjust seasoning. Squeeze lime juice on top and garnish with cilantro. Serve nice and hot.

Note: Serve with sides like chopped lettuce, sliced radishes, chopped red onion and more fresh cilantro. This is comfort food. It's nice and chewy too!

If you're using Tofurky, you might want to wait and add that the last 5 minutes so the sausages stay flavorful and tender.

SHIITAKE PUNJABI CHHOLE

This recipe ran in our September 2006 newsletter: Remember when we gave away Aurora Creations seasoning mixes? Well, I've discovered they're not only easy to use, but different and versatile! And while I like making my own flavor combos, where on earth would I find "amchur" or "ajawaya?" So I keep a few Aurora packets on hand for that last minute "What do I make for dinner tonight?"

Shiitakes provide protein (18%) and they have natural antiviral and immune-boosting properties, help lower cholesterol and regulate blood pressure. Lentinan, an immunostimulant derived from shiitakes, has been used to treat cancer, AIDS, diabetes, and chronic fatigue syndrome, with impressive results.

I made this without any of the protein add-ins the first time, and it was great simply that way, but you may want to dress your chhole up or modify it for someone in your family who has to have meat—therefore the variations. It's completely up to you!

Serves 2 as a main course, 4 if used as a side

¼ C extra virgin olive oil (EVOO), coconut butter, ghee or butter
1 red onion, sliced or diced, about 2 C
1 pkg Aurora Punjabi chhole spice
1 can Eden chickpeas, about 2 C cooked, mostly drained
2 C sliced shiitakes (or other mushrooms)

MIX-INS (OPTIONAL)
1 C toasted cashews
8 oz sliced steak or chicken
8 oz shrimp or scallops
1 C shredded radicchio, garnish
½ C minced cilantro, garnish
½ C sliced scallions, garnish

In a large skillet, gently warm EVOO or the butter. Sauté the onion about 3 minutes. Stir in spices until warm and aromatic, about 1 minute. Then add chickpeas and shiitake mushrooms. If you chose to mix in meat or seafood, add that now. Stir chhole over high heat for a few minutes. If you're using shrimp, for instance, those will turn pink.

Remove skillet from flame. You're ready now to dish out and serve. Garnish with radicchio, cilantro and scallions. Isn't the crunch and color wondrous?

Note: This dish is wonderful alongside steamed spinach or green beans. Nice with a side of yogurt. Good spooned over steamed basmati rice or quinoa.

Simple Four Grain Pilaf

Grains are comfort food just like pasta and potatoes, except whole grains have more fiber, vitamins and minerals than grains that are processed and then "enriched."

You can make this on an evening that's cold and dark and use it to accompany chicken or meat. You can serve it without those and sprinkle toasted nuts on top. You can toss with tempeh or add beans or melt cheese on top.

A staple in Biblical times, millet was also considered a sacred food by the Chinese. It has significant amounts of iron, lecithin and choline, which helps keep cholesterol in check. I like millet best in combination with other grains.

Buckwheat is not a member of the wheat family and is not even a true grain, but it is especially rich in potassium and the B vitamins. Buckwheat is said to help strengthen capillaries, build blood and help adjust the acid/alkaline balance.

Serves 8

2 Tbsp extra virgin olive oil (EVOO)
   or ghee
1 C hulled barley
2 C brown rice (your favorite kind)
1 C buckwheat groats (kasha)
½ C millet

10-12 C boiling water or
   vegetable broth
1 tsp sea salt
1 tsp black pepper
¼ C EVOO or ghee (optional)

In a large pan with a tight-fitting lid, gently warm the 2 Tbsp EVOO. Add grains and stir to coat. Add 10 C boiling water or vegetable broth and salt and pepper. Stir once, cover pot, lower heat and simmer about 45 minutes. (I move pot partially off heat so the grains really do slow cook.)

If grains absorb all the water and need a little more* (depends upon your pot, the weather and how chewy or tender you like your grains), add remaining water, cover pot again and continue to simmer. Once cooked, feel free to add the additional EVOO or ghee.

Serve hot. This grain pilaf reheats beautifully during the week too.

Note: Does this go well with curry sauce? Ooh la la, yes! Also wonderful tossed with pesto or tapenade.

One way to tell if all the water has been absorbed is that holes appear in the top surface of the grains.

WILD RICE AND PURPLE POTATO PANCAKES

This recipe appeared in our November 2007 newsletter. Wild rice is expensive, but is special and perfect for holidays. Wild rice is not a grain like other rices, but a seed. Go figure! Just like buckwheat is not a grain, but a fruit… Wild rice kernels are unpolished so you get every drop of nutrient this seed provides, and the flavor is nutty with a nice chewy texture. Wild rice gives us copper, fiber, folate, magnesium, niacin, phosphorus, vitamin B6 and zinc!

A reason to use organic: I heard Dr. Green of the Dr. Green's Rx website speak at Natural Products Expo East and he said, "Potatoes are consistently on the list of most pesticide-contaminated vegetables. In recent USDA testing, the Environmental Working Group found 81% of potatoes still contained pesticides *after* being washed and peeled. The average potato had the highest total amount of pesticides of all of the 43 fruits and vegetables tested."

Serves 4

1 C water, boiling	**1 onion, chopped, about 2 C**
⅓ C wild rice	**1 tsp sea salt**
1½ lb purple potatoes*	**1 tsp black pepper**
2 Tbsp extra virgin olive oil (EVOO),	**2 eggs**
or macadamia or grapeseed oil	**additional oil for frying**

Put wild rice into boiling water. Cover pot and simmer for an hour. If any water remains, drain it, but don't pour down the drain. Either drink liquid or save for soups.

In the meantime while rice is cooking, steam unpeeled potatoes until easily pierced by a knife. Drink or reserve this liquid as well. Mash potatoes with a fork in a bowl. Add cooked rice.

Place 2 Tbsp EVOO in a medium pan and sauté onion until soft. Add to the bowl with rice and potato together with salt and pepper and eggs. Mix lightly with fork; don't smush with spoon. In same sauté pan, add just enough EVOO to cover the bottom. Over medium heat, warm EVOO and then spoon potato mixture by Tbsp into the hot pan. Fry for 4 minutes. Flip. Repeat on second side.

Serve hot, warm or at room temperature. (You can cook a day ahead and reheat on serving platter in a 350 degree oven for 10 minutes.)

Note: Would you like to bake wild rice and potato cakes? Pat the potato mixture into 2 greased pie plates, brush generously with EVOO and bake at 350 degrees for 40 minutes, or until lightly browned around the edges. Cut into wedges, just like for pie, and serve. Are you serving these for Chanukah? Serve with applesauce and sour cream.

*No purple potatoes? Russets are fine.

Poultry and a Little Meat

I'm not a vegetarian. I eat organic meat. I do not eat factory-farmed, commercially grown meat from animals that are crowded into pens or feedlots and kept "healthy" with antibiotics. I do not eat animals that are fattened up with growth hormones.

For me, the important thing is to eat meat from animals that are humanely treated, whose owners respect nature and all her cycles. Not only is this the way things should be, but the meat tastes better and is better for me too.

Historically, we have only used seafood and poultry in the store, no red meat. The reason for that isn't entirely clear. If we say we were trying not to offend vegetarians, why did we use seafood and poultry?

However, we've pretty much continued on that path, which makes even less sense today, because so many more people are eating meat, red or otherwise, and the grass-fed, pastured "movement" seems to be gaining more converts each day. People I know who were vegetarians for years and years, now eat meat.

What does make sense is that we've chosen that path for our kitchen in the store because it's a small kitchen and as it is, we can't seem to get to all the recipes we want to make. If we were to add another category, red meat, oy carumba.

So, here's a chapter which emphasizes poultry but gives a nod, with a few recipes, to other meats.

Calzones with Potato and Sausage

Making calzones seems like a lot of work, but if you have little hands at home, many hands make light work; and this is fun. I know you won't make this everyday, but this is here for when you're in the mood…

Serves 6

DOUGH
1½ tsp baking yeast
1 C lukewarm water
1 tsp honey
¼ C extra virgin olive oil (EVOO)
3 C whole wheat flour
1 tsp sea salt

Bake at 450 degrees

FILLING
4 potatoes, diced, about 6 C
6 Tbsp extra virgin olive oil (EVOO)
2 onions, finely chopped, about 4 C
6 cloves garlic, finely minced
1 tsp black pepper
8 oz sausage of your choice, real or
   veggie, chicken, lamb or pork

Sprinkle yeast over warm water and honey. Stir to dissolve. Let mixture stand 5 minutes, or until yeast is foamy. Stir in EVOO.

Whirl flour and salt together using the steel blade of a food processor. With the machine running, pour yeast mixture through the feed tube.

Process until dough is smooth and cleans the sides of the workbowl (about 30 seconds). Add more water, a tsp at a time if dough will not form a ball, or more flour if dough seems sticky. (Dough will be somewhat sticky until after the first rise.) "Knead" with processor 15-20 seconds.

Place dough in a bowl. Cover with plastic wrap or shower cap and let rise until doubled in bulk, about 30 minutes.

Prepare filling while dough rises.

To prepare filling: Cook potatoes until soft, about 10-15 minutes, in a small pot, using just enough water to cover them. Drain and mash with a potato masher or wooden spoon.

Gently warm EVOO in a skillet and sauté onions and garlic until onions are translucent, about 5 minutes. Add mixture to potatoes together with black pepper.

Slice sausage into ¼-inch rounds.

Preheat oven to 450 degrees.

Punch down risen dough. Divide into 6 pieces and using a rolling pin, roll out into rounds that are ¼-inch thick. Place ⅙th the potato filling onto one end of each calzone, divide turkey sausage into 6 piles and place each 1 in turn atop the potato filling. Fold empty side over and pinch edges together to seal filling. Prick calzone so steam can escape.

Bake on an oiled tray for 15-20 minutes, or until crisp and lightly browned.

Note: Variation that doesn't have sausage at all? Of course there are many. One I especially like is ½ C pine nuts, 1 C raisins and 1 tsp allspice mashed into potato filling instead of the sausage. Or just mash 2 C pesto into the potatoes.

CHICKEN WITH GINGER CILANTRO PESTO

When I was growing up, I'd never heard of cilantro. Now I love it madly and dearly. It's said to protect us against salmonella, as well as helping us digest food more easily. Cilantro is also said to cure upset stomachs. Wouldn't you know that it's also a good source of magnesium and is rich in plant nutrients and flavonoids?

You'll like it here combined with ginger, which also has a long tradition of health and healing.

Serves 4

1 C fresh cilantro
1 C scallions
¼ C walnuts
1 Tbsp chopped fresh ginger (leave peel on)
4 cloves garlic
¼ tsp cayenne pepper

Broil chicken at 425 degrees

1 tsp sea salt
1 tsp black pepper
¼ C extra virgin olive oil (EVOO)
4-6 boneless chicken breasts, or thighs with skin and bones (my favorite)

Preheat broiler to high.

Combine first 8 ingredients in a food processor and blend using the steel blade until nuts are finely chopped. Add the EVOO and process until well-blended. You have pesto!

Place chicken on a broiler pan, or your favorite pan that can take the high heat of a broiler. (My favorite pan for broiling, roasting or baking is my speckled, black-and-white enamel paella pan.)

Place chicken in the oven and broil for 20 minutes, or until juice runs clean when you poke chicken with a knife. Top chicken with pesto and broil another 5 minutes. Serve alongside a baked potato and some steamed carrots and peas. Simple. Delicious.

CINDY'S MUSHROOM SMOTHERED CHICKEN BREASTS

Cindy says, "One evening I decided I was bored with baked chicken, or chicken done on the grill. I had mushrooms on hand, which my husband, Tom, and I often sauté as an accompaniment to just about everything, or which I might put over rice. Lo and behold, I mixed the chicken and mushrooms together and ended up with a quick, moist and delicious meal! While it simmered I was able to run around and do other things…"

4-6 servings

4-6 boneless, skinless chicken breasts
2 Tbsp extra virgin olive oil (EVOO)
1 lb white, brown or portobella
   mushrooms, washed and sliced
1 onion, thinly sliced, about 2 C

1 tsp sea salt
1 tsp black pepper
2-4 sprays Bragg's Liquid Aminos*
3 Tbsp water

Wash and pat dry the chicken breasts, then gently warm EVOO in a skillet. Sauté chicken over medium heat until lightly browned (about 5 minutes each side).

While chicken is sautéing, wash and slice mushrooms. Slice onion.

Remove chicken from skillet and add the mushrooms and onion to the pan. Sauté them over low heat until mushrooms are slightly brown and the onion is translucent, about 10 minutes. Remove mushrooms and onion from the skillet.

Place the sautéed chicken back in the skillet and season with salt and pepper. Spoon mushrooms and onion over chicken. Spray with Bragg's Liquid Aminos and then add water around the edges of the pan. Cover and simmer over low heat for approximately 25-30 minutes.

Note: Cindy says she serves this over a white basmati and wild rice blend, or brown rice. Accompany with a green organic vegetable or a mixed green salad. Dinner is served, she says.

Bragg's Liquid Aminos is an old-time product that is made from fermented soybeans and water. It tastes salty. Some spas suggest the use of Bragg's as a pick-me-up for the mid-afternoon slump. One can add some Bragg's to a cup of hot water and sip contentedly.

DANIEL'S CHOLLENT

Daniel says, "Chollent is a traditional Jewish slow-cooked, bean-barley stew for Saturday afternoons. You put it up before the start of the Jewish Sabbath (Friday at sundown) and it cooks slowly until around lunch the next day. This way, observant Jews can still enjoy a hot Sabbath lunch without violating the biblical prohibition against cooking on the Sabbath. That being said…this stew is good anytime. The proportions below are what I use, but the fun of chollent is that you can adjust it to your liking. I consider this recipe as a potpourri, because your house will smell amazing for about 12 hours while the chollent is cooking."

Most people think that chollent is an Eastern European, or Ashkenazi, Jewish dish. Not necessarily true. It's also a traditional dish made by Jews who lived in warmer climes.

Ashkenazi cooking is "heavy" or "fatty" because Jews living in Eastern Europe often faced poverty, extreme cold and grueling physical labor. Consequently, their food needed to contain as much fat as possible. This chollent is more like versions made by Jews from Spain, Portugal and other Mediterranean countries (the Sephardim). This Sephardic version of chollent is made with barley, meat and root vegetables.

Serves 8

2 large onions, chopped, about 4 C
3 C white beans (or red if you prefer),
2 C barley
2 lb flanken*, brisket or chuck roast,
   boneless; if using a roast with a
    bone, increase the amount of meat
10 cloves garlic, chopped coarsely
a few peppercorns

Made in a large crockpot

2 bay leaves
1 tsp dried thyme
4 red potatoes, cut into quarters
2 parsnips, cut into chunks, about 6 C
1 tsp sea salt
1 tsp black pepper
1 32-oz jar marinara sauce (optional)
hot sauce (optional)

Daniel makes his chollent in a crockpot. I make mine in the oven, and I think meat slow-roasted in the oven is beyond compare as far as flavor and appearance. So bear with us both!

Crockpot chollent: Spray the inside and top of crock pot with Spectrum spray to help with clean-up later. Start layering chollent by spreading onions in pot first. Then layer with beans, next barley and then the meat. Cover meat with garlic, herbs, potatoes and parsnips.

If you're using marinara sauce, pour over potatoes and parsnips. Rinse the jar out with a little water and shake it/stir it so as to get the last of the sauce out of the jar.

Pour this over the potatoes as well. The idea is to cover potatoes with as much liquid as you can without having it spill over as it cooks. Wait a bit for the water to seep in. Then add more if needed. Add hot sauce if you like things spicy.

To make in crockpot: Plug in and cook on low. Daniel says he always turns the pot on right before he lights the Sabbath candles, which means it cooks a few hours longer in the winter and a few hours less in the spring/summer. It seems to come out fine either way. And the same holds true for chollent baked in the oven.

To slow-roast in the oven: Assemble chollent in layers as above in a large, heavy casserole with a tight-fitting lid, put into a 200 degree oven and then slow-roast overnight.

Note from Debra: I follow another tradition, which is to include a smoked beef bone or marrow bone and whole, raw eggs in their shell in the chollent. How do you use the eggs? Wash the eggs and then carefully slip the raw unshelled eggs under chollent mix. They slow-cook with the mixture. When I'm ready to serve, I dig them out and shell them, and serve them in quarters as a first course. My grandmother used to accompany chollent with an assortment of good pickles and sauerkraut.

A cut of meat taken from the short ribs of beef.

DEBBIE MCCORMACK'S TURKEY CHILI & CORNBREAD BAKE

Debbie says, "This is a nice gluten-free dish. I used to feed this recipe to my children when they were small. They always enjoyed it, never leaving a crumb on their plate. Even today, with my kids all in their 30's, I still serve it, and they still eat it up every time we get together."

Serves 6-8

Bake at 350 degrees

- ⅓ C extra virgin olive oil (EVOO)
- ½ onion, chopped, about 1 C
- ½ red bell pepper, diced, about 1 C
- ½ green bell pepper, diced, about 1 C
- 1 tsp sea salt
- 1 tsp black pepper
- 1 pinch garlic powder
- 1 lb ground turkey
- ½ C water
- 1 tsp ground cumin
- 1 tsp chili powder
- 1 pinch cayenne pepper
- 1 Tbsp Worcestershire sauce
- 2 Tbsp ketchup
- 1 Tbsp molasses
- 1 Tbsp coconut sugar
- ½ can Eden navy beans, 1 C cooked
- ½ can Eden pinto beans, 1 C cooked
- 1 C shredded gouda
- yogurt or sour cream (optional)

In a saucepan, gently warm EVOO. Add onion and peppers together with salt, pepper and garlic powder. Sauté until onion is soft, about 5 minutes. Stir in ground turkey and brown the meat. Drain off excess fat. Turn heat to medium low. Add ½ C water and stir. Add spices and Worcestershire sauce and stir some more. Add ketchup, molasses and sugar. Simmer for 15 minutes. Drain beans and add to the meat. Stir and simmer another 10 minutes. Turn off flame, cover pot and set aside.

Preheat oven to 350 degrees.

To make cornbread: Use a gluten-free corn bread mix, and prepare according to directions. Grease a 12x8-inch glass or metal non-stick pan with corn oil. Pour ½ the batter into the pan, spreading evenly with a rubber spatula. Drop spoonfuls of chili on top so they're close together. Spread carefully with spatula so chili covers the batter to 1 inch from the edge of the pan. Pour remaining batter on top and spread to the edges of pan. Sprinkle with shredded Gouda.

Bake 30-35 minutes.

Note: Debbie says you can use more cheese on top when you remove the dish from the oven. Or use sour cream or plain yogurt to garnish individual servings.

DIJON CHICKEN WITH HERBES DE PROVENCE

This appeared in our June 2007 newsletter. This is one of my favorite chicken dishes, but you can easily translate this into a vegetarian entrée by using tofu instead of chicken.

Herbes de Provence originated in southern France and includes herbs found in the region: rosemary, basil, marjoram, thyme, sage, savory, tarragon, bay, fennel and lavender. There are variations on the theme, but any mixture called *Herbes de Provence* that you have will do just fine here.

The mixture of garlic, mustard and all those wonderful herbs and spices makes this simply divine.

Serve 6

12 garlic cloves*, chopped
1 Tbsp Herbes de Provence
1 tsp ground rosemary
4 Tbsp Dijon mustard

Roast at 425 degrees

2 tsp sea salt
2 tsp ground black pepper
½ C extra-virgin olive oil (EVOO)
4 lb chicken thighs with skin and bone

In a little bowl, whisk marinade together. Put chicken in roasting pan and spoon marinade over. Mix everything so chicken is well-coated, tops and bottoms! I use my hands because it reminds me of childhood and making mud pies. Hands also work better than any tool.

Let chicken marinate in the refrigerator at least 2 hours, or covered overnight. In a hurry? Let chicken marinate at room temp for an hour.

Preheat oven to 425 degrees.

Roast chicken until the skin is brown and crispy, about 30-45 minutes (every oven is different—I look for crispy skin). If you're worried that the chicken might not be cooked sufficiently, prick chicken with a knife. If the juice runs clear, chicken is fully cooked.

Note: If using tofu, cut into ½-inch slices and place in shallow baking pan. Using ½ marinade, brush slices. Flip tofu slices over and use remaining marinade to brush this second side. Bake for about 15 minutes.

*I know this seems like a lot of garlic, but believe me it's worth it! Worried about garlic breath? Use a little liquid chlorophyll in your water in the morning. Liquid chlorophyll takes care of any problem because it's an internal deodorizer, and works even better than simply chewing on a sprig of parsley.

Dinner with a Friend

This appeared in our March 2009 newsletter. There I said, "Recently I invited a friend to dinner. I was delayed at the store and got home literally five minutes before she arrived at my house, and we were heading out to something that evening, so time was of the essence! Well, dinner was on the table in 30 minutes and my friend kept saying, 'I can't believe you made dinner that quickly.' Roasting the chicken is why it took that long, and it occurred to me many people bring home 'fast food' because they don't think they can make good food fast. Here's the dinner I made that evening. Nothing extraordinary, but yummy, colorful and healthy too."

Dinner for 2

4 chicken thighs (Eberly's* organic is the best!)
Spike seasoning (sprinkle with gay abandon)
2 C water
1 tsp sea salt
1 C roasted buckwheat groats

Roast chicken at 450 degrees

2 large carrots, sliced, about 4 C
2 small zucchini, sliced, about 4 C
1 bunch Swiss chard, chopped, about 6 C
1-2 Tbsp coconut oil (optional)

Preheat oven to 450 degrees.

Put Eberly's thighs in a pie plate or a shallow roasting dish. Sprinkle liberally with Spike. Pop chicken into oven and roast 20-25 minutes or until skin is brown and crispy.

In a small pot with tight-fitting lid, bring 2 C water to a boil. Add tsp sea salt (rich in minerals). Bring water to a boil and then pour in buckwheat groats (otherwise known as kasha). My mother always served kasha with chicken, so that's how I love it. Turn heat down to low and cover pot. Simmer 10 minutes—that's all it takes for kasha to absorb water and be ready to eat. Turn off heat. Let kasha sit while chicken roasts. You will have kasha left over for breakfast or lunch.

Wash carrots and zucchini with a scrub brush. Halve carrots lengthwise. Slice thickly. *Don't peel. Who has time? Nor do you want to waste all those vitamins in the skin.* Put carrots in skillet and add 1 C water. Cover and turn heat to medium.

Simmer carrots while you shake chard under water and then chop into large bite-sized pieces. Slice zucchini. Add chard and zucchini to carrots. Add another C of water if necessary (depends on how tightly your lid fits). Simmer 5 minutes. You can serve veggies plain, beautifully colored and crisp-tender. Juicy. Refreshing. Easy to digest. For added richness and inner moisturizing, add a spoonful or two of coconut oil right into the pot. Stir to coat veggies.

When chicken is done (poke with a knife and press—if juice runs clear, chicken is done), dish out. Place a cup of cooked kasha next to chicken, and dress kasha with chicken broth from pan. Using a slotted spoon, fill plate with a heaping amount of those lovely, juicy vegetables. Voila!

*Here I've mentioned a chicken by brand, because this is the way the recipe appeared in our newsletter. I'm sure there are wonderful, organic chickens from other farms out there, but to this day, Eberly's is still my favorite.

FRUITED SWEET AND SOUR CHICKEN

Most sweet and sour food in this country seems to be a fusion of pseudo-Cantonese and pseudo-Polynesian food. Which means take the fattest meat you can buy and cook it with even more fat, a sickening mixture of sugared canned fruits and more sugar, some MSG, cheap soy sauce and lots of cornstarch to thicken the whole mess to a gooey, glue-like glob...

The truth is that sweet and sour doesn't have to be that way and isn't, I'm sure, in either China or Polynesia. This dish has the sweet and savory influences of Eastern Europe.

Serves 4

4 boneless, skinless chicken breasts or thighs
2 Tbsp extra virgin olive oil (EVOO)
1 tsp sea salt
1 tsp black pepper
1 tsp ground ginger
1 tsp ground cinnamon

Roast at 350 degrees

1 onion, chopped, about 2 C
1 C pitted prunes, chopped coarsely
1 C dried apricots, chopped coarsely
2 pears, halved, cored and sliced
2 apples, peeled, cored and chopped
¼ C lemon juice

Preheat oven to 350 degrees.

Toss the chicken with the EVOO and salt and pepper. Place it in a large skillet or roasting pan with a tight-fitting cover.

In a little bowl, combine the remaining ingredients. Toss to mix well, and then spoon onto and around the chicken. Cover the skillet or roasting pan and put it into the oven. Bake dish for 1 hour.

After an hour, the dish will be lovely and flavorful, but the chicken won't be brown. If that bothers you, put the uncovered skillet or roasting pan back into the oven on broil for 1-2 minutes.

GEORGIAN ROAST CHICKEN

I love savory, garlicky and spicy meats. I especially like the flavorful nature of this roast, and the fact that it uses baby eggplants, which I typically have in abundance growing in my garden each summer. As I write this, it's November in New England, and I'm about to pull the last of the summer eggplants out of my fridge to make this dish. Alas, the summer cilantro was hit by a frost some weeks ago, but I know where I can buy that!

Serves 6

½ C extra virgin olive oil (EVOO)
1 Tbsp coriander seeds
1 Tbsp dried parsley
1 tsp dried oregano
2 tsp dried tarragon
1 tsp ground fenugreek
12 cloves garlic, pressed

Roast at 425 degrees

1 tsp sea salt
1 tsp black pepper
6-10 pieces chicken with skin and bones
6 plum tomatoes, halved lengthwise
6 baby eggplants, about 3-inches long
6 small potatoes, quartered
2 Tbsp chopped cilantro for garnish

In a small bowl, make a paste by mixing the EVOO with all the spices, garlic, and salt and pepper. Rub the chicken pieces with ½ the paste and refrigerate them in a covered dish for at least 2 hours, or overnight.

When ready to roast, preheat oven to 425 degrees.

Place the chicken in the middle of a large lasagna-type pan, skin-side up.

Toss the tomatoes, eggplants and potatoes with the remaining paste. Place the coated vegetables in the roasting pan, scattering them around the chicken. Put pan in oven and check it after about 20 minutes. If vegetables look too dry, drizzle with some more EVOO. Bake for a total of about 45 minutes, or until chicken is done and potatoes and eggplants soft and tender.

Serve chicken surrounded by eggplant, tomato and potato. Garnish with cilantro.

This is very delish and very satisfying.

INDIAN CURRIED KABOBS

There's evidence that curry has been used since 1700 B.C.E. in Mesopotamia. Did curry originate in India? Most likely, but it was used in England as early as the 1300's and can be found as an ingredient in cookbooks of that time. Curry gets around!

Curry is not a single spice, but a blend of different spices, and can be mild or hot.

Serves 4

2 lb meat of your choice like chicken (boneless, skinless), beef or lamb
1 tsp cinnamon
½ tsp ground cardamom
1 tsp cumin seeds
1 tsp coriander seeds
1 tsp ground turmeric
1 tsp ginger powder

1 tsp chili powder
2 tsp sea salt
1 tsp black pepper
12 cloves garlic, pressed
4 Tbsp extra virgin olive oil (EVOO)
yogurt or kefir cheese
cilantro as garnish (optional)
toasted cashews as garnish (optional)

Cut chicken, beef or lamb into 1-inch cubes. Set aside for now.

Put spices in a heavy frying pan and stir dry over low heat until they are toasted and fragrant, about 2 minutes. Remove frying pan from heat. Add garlic, EVOO and meat to the frying pan, and mix well. Cover frying pan and refrigerate seasoned meat for at least 1 hour or overnight.

When you're ready to make the kabobs, turn grill on to high. Thread meat onto 8 skewers. Grill about 8 minutes. Turn several times.

Serve with yogurt as a sauce over seasoned rice or couscous. Garnish with cilantro and toasted cashews. Some fresh greens and roasted yams round out the meal nicely.

Lamb Shanks with Chickpeas and Beans

Lamb has always been my favorite meat, and I love the shanks even more than the leg or chops. This is the ultimate slow-cooked meat that melts off the bone.

Serves 4

½ C extra virgin olive oil (EVOO)
1 tsp Spike seasoning
1 tsp dried rosemary
1 tsp dried sage
1 tsp dried thyme
1 tsp black pepper
8 cloves garlic, pressed

Roast at 225 degrees

4 lamb shanks or 2 lb lamb stew chunks
1 can Eden chickpeas, about 2 C cooked
1 can Eden white beans, about 2 C cooked
¼ C lemon juice
1 Tbsp tomato paste
chives or scallions as garnish

In a small bowl, mix the EVOO with the herbs, spices and garlic. Place the lamb shanks (or stew meat chunks) in a large roasting pan, and pour the marinade over. Stir around so they are well-coated. Add the beans, lemon and tomato paste.

Let the mixture sit for 1 hour or overnight.

Preheat oven to 225 degrees.

Put the roasting pan into the oven and roast the lamb shanks, covered, for at least 6 hours, but all day is also fine.

Serve garnished with chives or scallions.

Lindsey's Tantalizing Turkey Meatloaf

Lindsey says, "Though it's become a staple in the deli in the store, this recipe originally came from cleaning out my refrigerator and freezer one day. Using turkey instead of beef, this is a healthier and leaner take on traditional meatloaf. In fact, you practically get all of your food groups in this one dish! Served with a side of creamy mashed potatoes, this is a hearty, comforting home-style meal."

Serves 6

- 1 green bell pepper, diced, about 2 C
- 1 red bell pepper, diced, about 2 C
- 1 onion, diced, about 2 C
- 1 C sweet, frozen corn
- 1 Tbsp garlic, minced
- 1 Tbsp black pepper
- 1 Tbsp dried oregano
- 1 jalapeño, de-seeded and de-ribbed, minced

Bake at 375 degrees in a 9-inch pie pan

- 1 C pepper jack cheese (cubed)
- 1 C whole-grain bread crumbs*
- 2 Tbsp Worcestershire sauce
- 1 Tbsp lemon juice
- 1 Tbsp extra virgin olive oil (EVOO)
- 1 Tbsp sea salt
- 1 lb ground turkey
- 1 egg

Preheat the oven to 375 degrees. Grease a 9-inch round pie pan.

Place all the ingredients except the turkey and egg into a large mixing bowl. Mix well. Add turkey and egg and mix again.

Firmly pack meatloaf into pie pan. Put into oven and bake for 45 minutes to 1 hour, or until internal temperature reaches 170 degrees. Let cool and slice into 6 pie-shaped pieces.

Of course you can use a gluten-free bread crumb mix instead.

MARTHA'S CHICKEN PIE

Martha says, "This is an adaptation of a recipe from a 1940's *Good Housekeeping* cookbook, which originally began: 'Hold roaster over flame to remove hairs. Remove pinfeathers; cut out oil sac at tail end of back.' Needless to say, I don't do this anymore.

"When we were growing up, my brothers, sister and I loved my mother's chicken pie, and several years ago, I adapted this recipe for my own family. My mom made it with one of her inimitable pie crusts; I found that a simple biscuit crust makes it a bit easier and quicker. I also use more vegetables than the original, so this can be a one pot meal. Serve with a green salad for a satisfying meal."

Serves 4-6

BISCUIT CRUST
2 C flour of your choice*
3 tsp baking powder
1 tsp sea salt
6-7 Tbsp butter
about ¾ C milk

LIQUID FILLING
4 Tbsp butter
7 Tbsp flour* (see discussion on flour)
1 C milk or light cream (not skim)

Bake at 450 degrees using a 2-qt casserole

2 C chicken broth
1 tsp sea salt
1 tsp black pepper
dash of mace or nutmeg
2-3 lb cooked, boned white meat

VEGGIES
3 C frozen veggies (Martha suggests peas, carrots, corn, green beans, or colorful veggies that won't get mushy)

To make the biscuit crust, Martha says to measure and sift the first 3 ingredients. Drop in butter, using a pastry blender to blend until mixture looks like coarse corn meal. Make a small well in center of mixture and pour in ½ C milk. Mix quickly and lightly with a fork. Then add enough milk to make the dough light and soft, but not sticky. It will cling to the fork in a ball. Stir little, to avoid making biscuits tough.

Rub a little flour into pastry board. Turn dough onto board and sprinkle with a little flour. With lightly floured hands, knead this way: Pick up side of dough farthest from you. Fold it over towards you; press palms down on fold, pushing it away lightly. Turn dough around part way; repeat process seven times, kneading very gently to avoid toughness. Remember: handle gently for a delicate crust! Refrigerate while you prepare chicken filling.

Preheat oven to 450 degrees.

Melt 4 Tbsp butter in double boiler over boiling water. Add flour. While stirring, slowly stir in milk and chicken broth. Cook until thickened, stirring frequently. Add salt, pepper and spice. (cont.)

In 2-quart casserole, place chicken pieces together with vegetables. Pour warm, liquid filling mix over chicken and vegetables. Take biscuit crust from refrigerator. Gently roll it out, and fit it to the top of the casserole like a pie crust; slice a few holes in the top to allow air to escape.

Put the casserole in the oven and bake for 30 minutes, or until top is a soft brown color. Serve warm.

Martha says she uses 2 C sifted all-purpose flour with up to ½ that as whole wheat. Since I have never used all-purpose flour, I would love to see this made with sprouted whole-grain spelt or whole wheat pastry flour. Whole wheat pastry flour is softer than whole wheat bread flour.

MARY STERLING'S TARRAGON CHICKEN

Mary says, "This was a favorite shared neighborhood recipe from my childhood. Our milk was delivered in bottles with the cream at the top. This cream was the 'top milk' used here."

Serves 8

1 cut-up chicken, bone in, skin on
1 tsp sea salt
1 tsp black pepper

Roast at 350 degrees

tarragon, fresh or dried
top milk or medium cream thinned
    with milk

Preheat oven to 350 degrees.

Place chicken in a roasting pan, skin-side up. Sprinkle with salt and pepper. Add some tarragon.

Roast chicken in oven until done, about 45-60 minutes. You'll know the chicken is done because the juice runs clear when poked with a knife, and the skin should be nice and brown.

When done, remove chicken pieces and place on a platter. Drain off excess fat from roasting pan, leaving any scrapes and juices from the chicken.

Place the roasting pan over the stove burners and gently heat juices to a bubble. Don't cook this at such a high heat that the juices or chicken pieces will burn. Add enough top milk to the pan to make enough gravy for that amount of chicken. (There's no wrong or right here, just whatever amount feels right to you in the moment!)

When gravy is warm, add more tarragon, and salt and pepper to taste. Gravy should be thin and delicate tasting.

Pour oven chicken. Serve with rice or egg noodles.

MATT'S CHICKEN WITH ALMOND CREAM SAUCE

This dish, which Matt made for us all in the store, is delicious. While I save my cream for desserts, the extra calories don't count here if you have a fast metabolism or can still run the bases!

Serves 4

SAUCE
¾ C almonds, coarsely chopped
½ C extra virgin olive oil (EVOO)
4 cloves garlic, pressed or minced
1 tsp sea salt
½ tsp dried thyme
1 C chicken stock
1 C heavy cream

2 chicken breasts, or 4 chicken thighs
2 Tbsp EVOO
1 tsp sea salt
1 tsp black pepper
pinch cayenne pepper (optional)
8 oz pasta of your choice
½ tsp dried parsley

Dry-roast chopped almonds in a skillet over a low flame for 1-2 minutes. Be careful not to burn.

In a saucepan, gently warm EVOO. Add garlic and sauté 1-2 minutes, or until garlic is aromatic and begins to brown. Add salt, thyme and chicken stock together with the toasted almonds. Bring sauce to a gentle boil, then turn down the flame and simmer 5 minutes. Remove pan from stove top and let the mixture cool.

Blend cooled sauce in a food processor or blender with a few quick on/off turns. Don't over-blend because you want some texture. Place sauce back into the saucepan and add cream. Warm to serve.

In the meantime, bring a big pot ½ full of water to a rolling boil. Add pasta and stir once. Cook until pasta is al dente and ready to eat (time depends upon the kind and shape of pasta you choose).

While pasta is cooking, gently warm 2 Tbsp EVOO in a large skillet. Add chicken pieces seasoned with salt and pepper. Brown on all sides, about 4 minutes per side.

Drain pasta and put into a warm bowl. (Alternatively, you can divide the pasta among 4 individual serving plates.) Top pasta with cooked chicken, and spoon sauce on top. Garnish with parsley.

"Dig in and enjoy!" says Matt.

Note: Want a completely different take on chicken with roasted almonds? Rub chicken with EVOO, garlic, and salt and pepper. Roast at 425 degrees about 45 minutes. Dry-roast almonds as above. At serving time, use almonds to garnish chicken. Adding a baked yam and steamed or roasted vegetables makes a colorful, complete dinner.

MIDDLE-EASTERN BURGERS

This is a favorite mixture that makes a very flavorful burger. Serve them with hummus, or just on a bun with lettuce and tomato. Mustard? Sure. These burgers sit nicely on a pilaf too, made with rice, quinoa or couscous.

Derrick Riches on *About.com* says, "The origin of the hamburger is clouded in history and controversy. In Medieval times the Tartars, a band or warriors from the plains of Central Asia would place pieces of beef under their saddles while they rode. This would tenderize the meat that would then be eaten raw. This is the legend of the origin of the modern dish, Beef Tartare, perhaps the first hamburger."

Serves 4

2 lb ground turkey, lamb or beef
1 onion, minced, about 2 C
8 cloves garlic, minced
1 tsp dried oregano
2 tsp ground cumin

1 tsp sea salt
1 tsp black pepper
1 egg
2 Tbsp rice or oat bran
2 Tbsp dried parsley

Place all ingredients in a large mixing bowl. Lightly knead everything together. Shape into 4 or 8 burgers, depending upon how large you like your burgers.

Grill or broil burgers on high for 4-5 minutes on each side.

RAGOUT OF CHICKEN WITH ORANGE AND OLIVES

A ragout is defined as a thick, well-seasoned stew made from fish, meat, poultry or game and cooked in a thick liquid. The liquid becomes the sauce. Here, the sauce is a joyful juxtaposition of tomatoes, orange and olives.

Serves 4-6

¼ C extra virgin olive oil (EVOO)
2 lb boneless, skinless chicken
2 tsp dried tarragon
2 tomatoes, diced, about 3 C
1 whole orange, juiced, about 1 C
    juice
2 Tbsp zest from orange

8 cloves garlic, minced
1 cup black olives, oil-cured, pitted
1 cup green olives, herbed, pitted
1 tsp black pepper
1 tsp sea salt
2 Tbsp parsley as garnish

Gently warm EVOO in a large skillet with a tight-fitting lid. Sauté chicken until golden brown, about 5 minutes. Stir in tarragon, tomatoes, orange juice, zest, garlic and olives. Cover and cook stew over very low heat for 1 hour, stirring occasionally.

Taste ragout. Season with more salt or pepper if you like. Sprinkle with parsley to serve.

Note: This is wonderful served over steamed quinoa or rice to soak up the juices.

Roast Chicken with Pomegranate Sauce

This has overtones of Persia. Meats prepared with pomegranates are served at special occasions in the Middle East. Typically made with duck, this dish works great with chicken and tastes even better the next day.

Serves 4

1 large chicken, about 3-4 lb, or 2-3 lb chicken pieces with skin and bones, such as thighs, legs or breasts, or any combination of these
2 Tbsp extra virgin olive oil (EVOO)
4 cloves garlic, pressed
1 tsp sea salt
1 tsp black pepper

Roast at 425 degrees

2 more Tbsp EVOO
2 red onions, chopped, about 4 C
½ C tahini
2 Tbsp pomegranate molasses
½ C water or chicken stock
1 tsp cumin
1 tsp sea salt
1 tsp black pepper

Preheat the oven to 425 degrees.

Rub chicken with EVOO, then with garlic, and salt and pepper. Put it in a rack in a baking dish and roast for about 1 hour, or until the skin is crisp and brown. If you're using chicken pieces instead of the whole chicken, place those skin side up in a shallow roasting pan and do the same.

Gently warm the second 2 Tbsp EVOO in a saucepan. Add onions and sauté about 5 minutes, or until they soften and start to brown. Add tahini, pomegranate molasses, water or chicken stock, cumin, and salt and pepper. Stir and simmer on low for 15 minutes, or until sauce thickens.

To serve, carve the chicken into pieces. Place over plain rice, bulgur or couscous. Pour sauce on top.

ROASTED SAUSAGES WITH BUTTERNUT SQUASH AND HERBS

This is from our March 2007 newsletter. It's a perfect recipe for days that are cold and often blustery. If you're able to buy peeled and diced organic butternut squash, this dish becomes a 5-minute snap to prepare for the oven! Of course you can halve, peel and cube your own squash, or substitute diced yams.

Vegetarian? Substitute a fake sausage—there are many that are pretty terrific.

The savory herbs used here provide complex tones and flavors to dishes, but also have medicinal properties valued since the beginning of time. The word sage is derived from the Latin meaning "health" or "healing powers." The ancient Greeks and Romans administered sage for everything from snakebite to promoting longevity. And rosemary? In Shakespeare's Hamlet, Ophelia says, "There's rosemary, that's for remembrance!" Rosemary's constituents have been shown to inhibit the growth of skin tumors and to provide a natural antioxidant protection against skin cancer.

Thyme is generally used in combination with other remedies as an antiseptic, and in some long-ago wars, thyme was used as a dressing for wounds.

Serves 4

6 C cubed and peeled butternut squash
1 lb sausages, cut into bite-sized pieces
12 garlic cloves
3 Tbsp extra virgin olive oil (EVOO)

Roast at 450 degrees

1 tsp dried sage
1 tsp dried thyme
1 tsp dried rosemary
1 tsp black pepper

Preheat oven to 450 degrees.

Toss everything together in a large bowl or mix carefully right in the oven-proof serving platter or shallow roasting pan. Place platter or roasting pan in oven and roast until squash is tender, about 30 minutes. Your sausage will be nicely browned too. Amazing how something so simple can taste so good! Isn't this easy?

This is very nice served alongside steamed spinach, kale, collards or broccoli. Think color!

SAFFRON CORNISH GAME HENS WITH LEMON AND GINGER

Another simple, simple poultry dish which uses a Cornish game hen. Jacques and Therese Makowsky, who came to America via Russia and France, settling after some years on a farm in Connecticut, are credited with giving us the Cornish game hen. They bred Cornish game cocks and Plymouth Rock hens. The result was a plump little bird in a single-serving size that made its debut in 1950. The usual weight of a Cornish game hen is about 1 lb.

Serves 4

4 Cornish game hens
1 C extra virgin olive oil (EVOO)
½ C lemon juice
8 cloves garlic, minced

Roast at 400 degrees

4 threads saffron
4 tsp ginger powder
2 tsp sea salt
2 tsp black pepper

Place 4 Cornish game hens in a roasting pan that has a lid.

Mix EVOO, lemon juice, garlic, saffron, ginger, and salt and pepper in a little bowl. Pour over hens and turn them several times so they are well coated. I like to use my hands so I can feel what I'm doing.

Cover the hens and refrigerate overnight.

When you're ready to cook, preheat oven to 400 degrees.

Take roasting pan out of the refrigerator. When oven is ready and hot, uncover pan and put it into the oven. Roast little hens for about 30 minutes, or until all brown and crispy.

Serve to cries of delight. Serve with wild rice and steamed spinach or bok choy.

SAVORY CHINESE CABBAGE AND CHICKEN

Leftover turkey or chicken? This is a snap to make and will have everyone asking for seconds.

If there's one word that describes chicken, it's versatile. Feel free to use the basic formula below and substitute any vegetable you have in your fridge. Do you have broccoli and asparagus instead of Chinese cabbage and bok choy? Snow peas? Green beans and spinach? They all work here.

Serves 6

¼ C toasted sesame oil
1 onion, chopped, about 2 C
4 Tbsp garlic, minced
6 C Chinese cabbage, sliced thinly
6 C boy choy, leaves and stems, sliced
6 C leftover, boneless chicken or
    turkey meat (more if you like)

1 Tbsp ginger, grated fresh or ginger
    powder
2 Tbsp tamari (soy sauce)
1 tsp red chili flakes
1 tsp sea salt
1 tsp black pepper
6 sprigs watercress

In a large skillet, gently warm toasted sesame oil. Add onion and garlic to skillet and sauté until onion begins to soften and brown, about 5 minutes. Add Chinese cabbage and bok choy. Stir to coat 1-2 minutes, and a few minutes more if you are using a "tough" vegetable like broccoli. Now add chicken or turkey, ginger, tamari, chili flakes, and salt and pepper.

Stir just long enough so everything is mixed, vegetables are tooth-tender but still have color and crunch, and the chicken or turkey is hot. Dish out and top a sprig of watercress.

Note: Do you want to add a cup or two of chickpeas to the stir-fry? Go ahead and do it! You can also serve with a simple baked potato, or over rice, egg noodles, lentils or quinoa.

Spanish Chicken a la Paella

Inspired by paella, but simpler, fewer ingredients. Saffron is the most expensive spice in the world, perhaps because it has to be harvested by hand with tweezers for a yield of 2 threads per plant! It does impart an indefinable something wonderful. Of course you could substitute a pinch of turmeric, which is called "poor man's saffron."

Serves 8

2 Tbsp extra virgin olive oil (EVOO)
1 onion, chopped, about 2 C
2 Tbsp garlic, minced
2½ C chopped red bell pepper
2 tomatoes, diced, about 3 C
1 carrot, sliced, about 2 C
1 stalk celery diced, about 2 C
6 oz Fakin' Bacon, or real bacon, diced

Bake at 350 degrees

2 C short-grain brown rice
pinch saffron, about 3-4 threads
2 tsp sea salt
1 tsp black pepper
4 C boiling water
8 pieces of chicken, with skin and bones
1-2 C marinated artichoke hearts (optional)
1 C oil-cured olives (optional)

Preheat oven to 350 degrees.

In a large skillet, gently warm EVOO and sauté onion and garlic together with pepper and tomatoes until onion softens, about 5 minutes. Add carrot and celery together with bacon (real or Fakin'). Sauté another 5 minutes, stirring once or twice.

Spoon sauce into a 9x13 or somewhat larger shallow baking pan or casserole dish. A lasagna pan would work fine too. Add rice, saffron threads and salt and pepper. Stir so rice is coated. Put pan in oven and carefully pour in boiling water. Place chicken pieces over the top and bake uncovered for 45 minutes, or until the rice has absorbed the water, the chicken is nicely browned and the dish fragrant.

Remove pan from the oven and top with artichoke hearts and olives if you like.

THAI CHICKEN NOODLE HOT POT WITH EGG

This is my version of a fondue-like dish where everyone dips things in hot broth. I like my hot-pot already assembled so I can just dig in!

Serves 4

4 oz bean thread or cellophane noodles
3 Tbsp extra virgin olive oil (EVOO)
1 Tbsp red curry paste
1 tsp turmeric
1 carrot, cut in thin sticks, about 2 C
1 zucchini, cut in thin sticks, about 2 C
1 onion, sliced, about 2 C
4 C chicken strips (boneless, skinless) cut from breasts or thighs

Bake at 400 degrees

4 C chicken broth
1 tsp ginger, minced
1 tsp lime zest
¼ C fish sauce or 2 Tbsp tamari (soy sauce)
4 eggs
½ C mung bean sprouts or snow peas
2 scallions, sliced
¼ C chopped peanuts (optional)
sprinkling of black pepper (optional)

In a medium saucepan, bring water to a boil. Add noodles, turn off the heat and let them sit for 5 minutes. Then test one. Leave for a few more minutes if still too firm, otherwise drain and run cool water over them to stop the cooking. Set drained noodles aside in a large bowl and toss with 1 Tbsp EVOO.

Gently warm the remaining 2 Tbsp EVOO in a large wok or skillet over medium-high heat. Add curry paste and turmeric and stir 1 minute. Add the noodles and stir-fry until they start to get crunchy, about 5 minutes. Add carrot, zucchini, onion and chicken. Stir fry over medium-high heat, until onion begins to soften and chicken is done, about 5 minutes.

Preheat oven to 400 degrees.

At the same time, bring chicken broth to a boil and then simmer 10 minutes with ginger, lime zest and fish sauce.

Divide the chicken and noodle stir-fry among 4 single-serving shallow soup bowls or individual casserole dishes (they must be fairly large and able to hold about 3-4 C of food). Carefully crack an egg on top, keeping the yolks intact. Cover and place in the oven.

Bake for 5-10 minutes, or just until eggs are set. To serve, divide chicken broth among the bowls, garnish with mung beans, scallions, peanuts and a sprinkling of black pepper.

Note: You can replace the noodles with 4 C cooked brown rice.

TURKISH PIZZA

Pizza doesn't have to have cheese, and you don't have to make your own dough for the crust, though you certainly can. I use the Alvarado-brand sprouted wheat pizza crust, which we've sold at the store for years, because it saves me time and because it's pretty terrific too. So do whatever floats your boat because life is too short to worry about this!

Serves 4-6

1 Alvarado-brand pizza crust
2 Tbsp extra virgin olive oil (EVOO)
2 red onions, minced, about 4 C
8 cloves garlic, minced
1 lb ground lamb or turkey
1 small plum tomato, chopped, about ½ C
2 Tbsp tomato paste

Bake at 450 degrees

2 Tbsp pine nuts
¼ C parsley, finely chopped
1 tsp paprika
1 tsp sea salt
1 tsp black pepper
1 C Pecorino romano
1 Tbsp chopped mint (optional)
lemon wedges (optional)

Preheat oven to 450 degrees.

Remove pizza crust from package and put onto lightly oiled cookie sheet with sides.

Gently warm EVOO in a large skillet. Add onions and garlic and sauté until onions begin to soften and brown slightly, about 5 minutes. Add meat, tomato, tomato paste, pine nuts, parsley, paprika, and salt and pepper. Give everything a good stir and sauté another 5 minutes.

Remove skillet from the stove top. Spoon this topping onto the pizza crust and put the cookie sheet with your pizza into the hot oven. Bake 15 minutes (the crust should be nicely browned).

Sprinkle Pecorino romano on top. Cut pizza into 6 pieces. Garnish with chopped mint and serve with lemon wedges if you so choose!

WHITE BEAN CHICKEN AND VEGETABLE CASSOULET

A cassoulet is the quintessential dish of Southwest France. It is made with pork and has a crust. This has neither. I just like the word "cassoulet." Forgive me, France…

Serves 8

2 Tbsp extra virgin olive oil (EVOO)
2½ C chopped red bell pepper
1 onion, chopped, about 2 C
1 carrot, sliced, about 2 C
2 Tbsp garlic, minced
1 yellow summer squash, sliced
2 C green beans, cut into 2-inch pieces
1 fennel bulb, sliced, about 2 C

Bake at 425 degrees

1 Tbsp ground cumin
2 tsp harissa paste, or ½ tsp red pepper flakes
3 C diced tomatoes with their juice
1 can Eden cannellini beans, about 2 C cooked
8 pieces of chicken*, with skin and bones
2 tsp Spike seasoning
½ C chopped fresh basil for garnish

Heat 2 Tbsp EVOO in a heavy pot over medium heat. Add pepper, onion, carrot and garlic and sauté until tender, about 15 minutes. Add squash, green beans, fennel, cumin and harissa paste and stir another minute. Add tomatoes with juices and bring to a boil. Reduce heat to medium and cook until mixture thickens slightly, about 10 minutes. Mix in cannellini beans and give another good stir. Transfer mixture to a 9x13 (or thereabouts) baking pan.

Preheat oven to 425 degrees.

Place chicken pieces over vegetables. Sprinkle the 2 tsp Spike seasoning over everything. Roast for 30-45 minutes, or until the chicken skin is nice and crispy. Serve garnished with chopped fresh basil.

*This would taste wonderful with a ham bone added into the cassoulet in addition to the chicken, if you do eat pork.

Seafood

Fish is the original "fast food." In general, the cooking time for fish is 10 minutes for every inch of thickness - whether you bake, poach, broil or grill. For frozen, unthawed fish, double the cooking time to 20 minutes for every inch. To test for doneness, slip the point of a sharp knife into the thickest part of the fish and pull aside. If flakes begin to separate, the fish is probably done. Remove fish from heat and let it stand 3-4 minutes to finish cooking.

Generally speaking, fish is baked in about a 400 degree oven for 10-15 minutes.

Generally speaking, fish is poached in liquid (doesn't have to be a lot and shouldn't ever cover the fish) for about 10 minutes. What liquid? Could be broth, water, juice or any kind of milk, including coconut.

Generally speaking, to broil or grill fish, marinate first; or brush with a little extra virgin olive oil before and during cooking to keep fish moist. Cook about 10-15 minutes.

When buying fresh fish, look for fish with eyes that are clear and not sunken. The body should be firm and bounce back when poked. There should be only a mild odor, or none at all. If a fish smells fishy, then it's not fresh.

When storing fish in the fridge, wrap loosely and use within a day. Store frozen fish in its original wrapping in the freezer where it will last a considerable time.

As with poultry, rinse seafood before using.

Any recipe calling for shrimp in this book means peeled shrimp without heads.

BEAN THREAD NOODLES WITH SEAFOOD AND LIME

Serves 4

2 C bean thread or cellophane
  noodles
4 Tbsp extra virgin olive oil (EVOO)
8 cloves garlic, minced
4 Tbsp fish sauce*
2 Tbsp tamari (soy sauce)
1 jalapeño pepper, seeded and minced
4 Tbsp lime juice
2 C Chinese cabbage, thin sliced

1 lb mixed seafood such as shrimp,
  clams, mussels, squid, etc.
1 C cilantro, chopped
1 C fresh basil, torn off stems
2 scallions, sliced, about 1 C
1 tsp black pepper
1 tsp sea salt
pinch of red pepper

Soak the noodles in cool water for 1 hour, or until soft. If you're in a hurry, gently boil the noodles until they're soft and transparent (about 10 minutes).

While noodles are soaking (or boiling), gently warm EVOO in a large skillet (that has a cover). Add garlic, fish sauce, tamari and jalapeño pepper. Sauté about 5 minutes, or until garlic begins to brown. Stir in lime juice and Chinese cabbage, cover skillet and simmer 5 minutes more. Add noodles to vegetables, turn off heat and allow the mixture to sit so everything becomes soft and fragrant.

Bring 3-4 C water to boil in a soup kettle. Add the seafood and boil for 1-2 minutes. Don't worry about the short cooking time. Seafood will be cooked so don't be tempted to overcook!

Drain seafood. Add to the noodle-cabbage mixture. Toss with cilantro, basil and scallions. Taste. Add more fish sauce if not salty enough. If you like it spicier, add some more black pepper or a pinch of red pepper. Serve warm or at room temperature.

Fish sauce is blended anchovies and water. If you don't have fish sauce, you can make your own by putting a few anchovies in a blender with 2 C water. Blend and store in the refrigerator where it keeps forever. Alternatively, if it's the salty taste you want in your dish, use more tamari or some extra sea salt instead.

Brazilian Seafood Stew

The word shrimp comes from the Middle English *shrimpe*, meaning "pygmy." My mother used to call my brother Daniel "shrimp" when he was little. It was a term of endearment. Perhaps he loves shrimp because of this.

While shrimp are the most popular seafood in this country today, they have been so in China since the 7th century.

Serves 6

4 Tbsp extra virgin olive oil (EVOO)
2 Tbsp lime juice
1 lb any fish fillets (tuna, haddock, cod, etc.), cut into 1-inch pieces
2 Tbsp EVOO
1 onion, chopped, about 2 C
1 green bell pepper, chopped, about 2 C
4 cloves garlic, minced

2 C chopped tomatoes
1 14-oz can unsweetened coconut milk
½ C chopped fresh cilantro
2 scallions, sliced
1½ lb uncooked medium shrimp
1 tsp sea salt
1 tsp black pepper
3 C steamed, cooked rice

Whisk 4 Tbsp EVOO and lime juice. Add fish pieces and toss to coat. Allow to stand 15 minutes.

Gently heat the next 2 Tbsp EVOO in a skillet over medium heat. Add onion, pepper and garlic. Sauté 5 minutes, or until onion is beginning to brown. Mix in tomatoes, coconut milk, half the cilantro and half the scallions. Add shrimp and the fish with its marinade. Simmer just until shrimp turn pink and fish is opaque in center, about 5 minutes. Season with salt and pepper.

You can serve one of two ways: Either transfer seafood stew to serving bowl, sprinkle with remaining cilantro and scallions, and bring to the table with a separate bowl of steamed brown rice; or divide rice among 6 individual serving plates, spoon stew over rice, then garnish each plate with remaining cilantro and scallions

In either case, if there are juices left in the pan, don't waste those! Pour over fish and shrimp. This is heavenly!

BROILED SEAFOOD WRAPPED IN CHARD LEAVES

My mother bought whole fish. Most times she asked the fish market to cut off the head, tail and fins. She buried those in the yard as fertilizer. Her gardenias didn't smell fishy, and they were the most fragrant in the whole neighborhood. Her pineapple plants rivaled any prize specimens found on any pineapple plantation in the world!

Was that the only reason Mom bought whole fish? No. Her mother, my grandma Sarah, taught her that it is easier to tell if a fish is fresh when you can look it in the eye. And a whole fish imparts more flavor to a dish than one made with just the fillets.

Today, I am guilty of using fillets. They're just easier for me to work with and to eat (no bones). I do ask for the fish head, tail and fins to bury in the vegetable garden or rose bed.

Serves 4

4 large chard leaves, long stem cut off	**2 Tbsp lemon juice**
1 Tbsp extra virgin olive oil (EVOO)	**2 Tbsp EVOO**
4 8-oz fish fillets	**1 lemon, cut in wedges**
1 tsp Spike seasoning	
1 C orange juice (the Volcano brand is best)	

Preheat broiler on high.

Place a chard leaf on the work surface with the inside of the leaf facing up. Brush with EVOO, place fish fillet along the length of the leaf, so it's parallel with the spine.* Sprinkle with Spike and then roll the leaf up lengthwise, again working parallel with the spine and fish, into a tidy parcel. Place parcel into a glass or ceramic baking pan.

Repeat this process with the remaining 3 chard leaves and 3 fish fillets. Pour the orange juice, lemon juice and last 2 Tbsp of EVOO over the chard parcels. Place pan in broiler about 5-6 inches from the flame, and broil about 5 minutes. Serve with lemon.

Note: Of course you can put just about anything you like on the fish before you roll it with the chard. I sometimes use pressed garlic, chili pepper or a favorite salsa (fruit or tomato).

* You can see why you need to put the fish parallel with the spine, because the spine cannot be rolled up easily and will crack. Lengthwise, rolling works just fine. I guess you could steam the chard first and soften the spine, but that requires another pot and another step...

BUTTERNUT SQUASH AND FISH CASSEROLE

Fish that are white contain virtually no fat and few calories, but do have plenty of protein as well as B vitamins. I like the combination of white fish with winter squash like a butternut squash. Butternut squash was so important to Native Americans that they buried them along with their dead to provide nourishment on the journey to the afterlife.

Serves 4

4 Tbsp butter or ghee
1 parsnip, diced, about 2 C
1 lb peeled and cubed butternut
    squash, about 4 C
1 onion, chopped, about 2 C
1 Tbsp tomato paste
2 tomatoes chopped, about 3 C
6 cloves garlic, minced
2 bay leaves
1 C clam juice or fish stock

2 lb mixed firm white fish fillets
    such as halibut, swordfish or
    haddock, cut into 2-inch pieces
1 tsp sea salt
1 tsp black pepper
2 Tbsp capers
1 tsp paprika
1 Tbsp lemon juice
4 Tbsp chopped fresh dill for garnish

In a large soup kettle, melt the butter over medium heat. Add the parsnip, butternut squash and onion. Sauté until the onion begins to brown, about 5 minutes. Stir in the tomato paste, chopped tomatoes, garlic and bay leaves. Sauté another 5 minutes.

Add clam juice or fish stock, and simmer another 10 minutes. Add the fish together with the salt, pepper, capers, paprika and lemon juice. Simmer, covered, until the fish is opaque, 5 minutes more.

Turn off heat and allow mixture to stand about 15 minutes. Serve garnished with dill.

COCONUT RISOTTO AND CHILI-LIME SHRIMP

What makes risotto different than other rice dishes? The rice used (there are several varieties of Italian rice suitable for risotto) stays starchy and creamy. Instead of dry, disparate grains, risotto looks almost like rice pudding. But properly cooked risotto, although creamy, has resistance or bite, unlike rice pudding. It is "al dente."

Serve risotto right away because it continues to cook in its own heat. You don't want it too dry or too soft.

Serves 4

4 C vegetable stock, water or clam juice
1 14-oz can unsweetened coconut milk
1 Tbsp coconut oil
1 onion, diced, about 2 C
1 C Arborio rice
1 tsp sea salt
1 C white wine or mirin*
1 Tbsp coconut oil
1 lb shrimp
½ Tbsp chili paste
½ C lime juice
½ C Pecorino romano
4 sprigs watercress for garnish

In a medium saucepan, gently warm the vegetable stock together with coconut milk, until the mixture is just about to boil. Turn flame to low and allow mixture to simmer.

In a large skillet over medium heat, melt 1 Tbsp coconut oil. Add onion and sauté until translucent, about 5 minutes. Add rice together with salt. Toast by stirring for 2 minutes.

To make risotto, add the white wine to the rice. Stir rice until it absorbs most of liquid. Continue by adding 1 ladle-full at a time of the stock and coconut milk mixture to the rice, stirring constantly, until the rice is just tooth-tender. This usually takes about 15-20 minutes. Remove risotto from the heat.

In another skillet, melt the 2nd 1 Tbsp coconut oil over medium heat. Add shrimp together with chili paste and lime juice. Sauté shrimp (they will turn pink). If you have any of the stock and coconut milk mixture left, add that to the shrimp.

Divide risotto among 4 individual serving plates. Sprinkle risotto with romano. In the middle of the risotto, spoon shrimp and sauce. Garnish with watercress as edible garnish.

Mirin is rice wine. It's available in just about every market nowadays.

CRABMEAT WITH MUSHROOMS AND FISH OVER POLENTA

The website www.foodtimeline.org says, "According to the *Encyclopedia Americana* [1995 edition] there are approximately 4,500 different species of crabs living on Earth…It is impossible to tell for sure who (much less where!) ate the first crabs. Food historians tell us crabs were known to ancient Greeks and Romans. How do they know? From art and literature. And historians also tell us crabs were not well liked by these ancient Mediterranean people as food."

Can you imagine anyone not licking their chops when eating this dish?

Serves 4

¼ C butter or ghee
16 large mushrooms, sliced
¼ tsp nutmeg
1 Tbsp lemon juice
½ tsp sea salt
½ tsp black pepper
1 lb fish fillet (such as flounder or sole)
2 C crabmeat
another ¼ C butter or ghee, melted (optional)

Bake at 400 degrees

POLENTA*
¼ C butter or ghee
1 onion, chopped, about 2 C
4 cloves garlic, minced
1 tsp dried oregano
1 tsp dried basil
1 tsp sea salt
1 C coarse cornmeal
3 C boiling water
½ C Pecorino romano

In a large skillet using medium heat, melt butter or ghee. Add the mushrooms and sauté about 10 minutes. The mushrooms will get "juicy" and then almost reabsorb their liquid. Stir in nutmeg, lemon, salt and pepper.

Preheat oven to 400 degrees.

Place fillets in a glass or ceramic baking dish. Cover fish with crabmeat and then sautéed mushrooms. If desired, drizzle the last ¼ C of butter or ghee over all. Bake 10 minutes.

To make the polenta: At the same time the mushrooms are sautéing, melt butter or ghee in a saucepan. Sauté onion and garlic about 5 minutes. Add herbs with salt and cornmeal, and stir to coat. Slowly pour in boiling water. Stir constantly for 15 minutes. During the last 5 minutes, add the Pecorino romano.

To serve, dish out polenta putting it on one side of the plate. Place crabmeat and fish on the other side.

Put a bowl of extra romano for sprinkling at the table in case people want. (cont.)

This dish goes beautifully with steamed broccoli or any other green vegetable.

If making your own polenta, start swhile the mushrooms are sautéing. Do you have to make your own polenta? No. I sometimes use a ready-made polenta that comes in a log shape. If that's what you're doing, simply slice the polenta into rounds and warm in a skillet with some butter, ghee or extra virgin olive oil. I do like to sprinkle it with romano.

Fillet of Fish and Potato-Veggie Sauté

We've been told for years that fish is good for us, that it feeds our brains and makes healthy hearts. But how does one balance that "fact" with concerns about contaminants such as mercury in fish? How can one eat fish knowing that the oceans are in trouble and some fish endangered?

There's no easy answer. It's all about balance, sustainability and healthy oceans. I am grateful that there are people and organizations working on the restoration and conservation of healthy ocean ecosystems.

Serves 4

1 red onion, diced, about 2 C
2 stalks celery, about 4 C
2 tomatoes, chopped, about 2 C
4 C diced eggplant
1 sweet bell pepper, diced, about 2 C
4 small yellow potatoes, quartered, about 6 C
1 tsp dried basil
1 tsp dried oregano

1 tsp dried marjoram
1 tsp dried thyme
1 tsp sea salt
4 8-oz favorite thick fish fillets
4 Tbsp extra virgin olive oil (EVOO)
2 Tbsp lemon juice
1 tsp black pepper
bunch of spinach, chard or kale
1 lemon cut into 8 wedges

Mix vegetables (except the greens) with the herbs and salt. Place in large frying pan or skillet with a cover. Arrange fish fillets over vegetables. Mix EVOO and lemon juice and pour over fish. Sprinkle with black pepper. Cover pan and simmer on low for 20 minutes.

While fish is cooking, choose a bunch of greens you like or have on hand. Wash them and chop into bite-sized pieces. Take a pot with a cover, pour in 1 C water and bring that to a boil. Add greens to the pot, lower heat, cover pot and steam tender greens for 2-3 minutes; steam hardier greens such as kale for 5 minutes.

To serve, spoon fish and vegetable stew onto ½ the plate. Fork greens on other side of the plate. Garnish with lemon wedges.

JIM'S EASY SALMON AND RICE

Jim says, "This recipe came from the mother of invention: the necessity to make dinner without the requisite enthusiasm for cooking. So what was in the refrigerator? A nice big pot of cooked brown rice from the night before, a red pepper, some parsley, a jar of Vegenaise. These were the items that caught my eye. Then I remembered I had some cans of wild-caught Alaskan salmon in the cupboard too!

"It did not take too much imagination to whip these together into a summer meal together with vegetables of two different colors. Like all my recipes, it is something I have made by feel so often now that I know quantities of ingredients are variable. The result is always fine.

"For the purpose of this book, I measured as I went along. As far as servings go, I can only say it serves one Jim and two Dianes; or 2 Jims, or 4 Dianes. It also depends on whether you serve as a meal or part of a meal."

Serves 4

5 C cooked short-grain, brown rice
2 7.5-oz cans wild salmon, drained
⅔ C Vegenaise non-mayo mayo

1 red pepper, diced, about 2 C
½ C parsley or fresh dill, chopped
½ C scallions, sliced (optional)

Cook brown rice the night before, making sure you have enough for 5 cups cooked rice when you want to make this dish. (That would be 4 C water with 2 C rice—bring water and rice to a boil, cover pot, lower heat and simmer 45 minutes. Alternatively, you can simply find the rice in the fridge, as Jim did.)

Put the cooked rice into a large bowl together with the salmon (use the bones because those are rich in calcium). Add the Vegenaise, red pepper, and parsley or dill. Toss everything together. Garnish with scallions and serve.

You have a quick, easy and nourishing dinner on a lazy summer evening.

LENTILS WITH TUNA, LEMON AND OLIVES

Wikipedia says, "Tuna are fast swimmers—they have been clocked at 70 kilometers per hour (43 mph)... Unlike most fish, which have white flesh, tuna flesh is pink to dark red, which could explain their odd nickname, 'rose of the sea.'"

Serves 2

¼ C extra virgin olive oil (EVOO), butter or ghee
8 cloves garlic, minced
1 onion, thinly sliced, about 2 C
2 Tbsp grated lemon zest
¼ C lemon juice
2 tsp capers, rinsed well
1 C pitted kalamata olives

1 C lentils
2 C boiling water
1 lb tuna steak, cut into 1-inch chunks
1 tsp black pepper
1 tsp sea salt
2 sprigs fresh watercress for garnish

In a large skillet, gently warm EVOO. Sauté garlic and onion until aromatic, about 5 minutes. Add lemon zest, lemon juice, capers and olives. Simmer this sauce on low for 5 minutes more. Turn off flame until you're ready to proceed.

In the meantime, put lentils in a small saucepan together with boiling water. Cover pot, turn down flame and cook lentils for 20 minutes, or until water is absorbed and the lentils are tooth-tender.

Add tuna chunks to the garlic lemon sauce. Turn flame on again to medium high, and cook 2-5 minutes, depending upon size and thickness of tuna.*

Spoon lentils onto 2 serving plates and top with tuna mixture. Garnish with watercress. Serve alongside steamed green beans or broccoli.

Alternatively, you could grill a tuna steak over a high heat 2 minutes per side, or sear in a greased skillet on top of the stove. Once the tuna is seared and cooled, break it into 1-inch chunks and then add to skillet with garlic and olives. Let the flavors marry while the lentils cook.

MARY'S GARLIC SHRIMP OVER LINGUINE

Mary Kadlik (since we have two wonderful Marys in the store) says, "When Applefield Farm's basil is ready to be made into pesto, I make plenty and put the pesto into ice cube trays and freeze it. Once the pesto is frozen into ice cubes, I pop them out, put them into plastic storage bags and store them in the freezer.

"For this recipe, I use two cubes. You can make your own pesto, or buy your favorite store-bought brand. When I don't make my own, I love Linabellas pestos because they're made nearby with organic everything."

Serves 2

2 Tbsp extra virgin olive oil (EVOO)
1 Tbsp garlic, minced
2 medium tomatoes
4-6 oz linguine, cooked al dente
1 Tbsp butter
12-14 large shrimp, peeled and de-veined

1 Tbsp lemon juice
1 tsp sea salt
1 tsp black pepper
2 Tbsp parsley, minced
½ C feta cheese, crumbled
2 cubes pesto*, warmed to room temp

You'll want to plan so the pasta and shrimp are ready at the same time...

Bring a large pot filled ⅔ full of water to a rolling boil.

At the same time, gently warm EVOO in a skillet and sauté the garlic and tomatoes until garlic begins to brown, about 5 minutes. Tomatoes will begin to soften as well.

Add linguine to boiling water and cook about 5-7 minutes.

Turn up heat under garlic and tomato mixture. Add the butter and then the shrimp. Cook just until shrimp turn pink, a few minutes. Do not overcook!

Sprinkle shrimp with lemon juice, salt, pepper, parsley and feta cheese.

Drain cooked linguine and put back in pot. Toss with pesto. Divide pasta between 2 plates. Serve shrimp mixture over linguine.

This is the equivalent of ¼-½ C pesto. To make pesto, blend 3 C fresh basil leaves with 1½ C pine nuts (or any kind of nut), 8 cloves peeled garlic, ¼ C grated parmesan or romano together with 1 C EVOO and some salt and pepper.

Blue Ribbon Edition

Moroccan Baked Fish with Couscous

This recipe calls for firm fish. What are some varieties in this category? Mahi-mahi, sturgeon, swordfish, tuna and marlin. Also somewhat firm and okay here are halibut, red snapper, striped bass and grouper.

Serves 4

½ C extra virgin olive oil (EVOO)
¼ C lemon juice
6 cloves garlic, pressed
1 tsp paprika
¼ tsp cayenne pepper
1 tsp ground cumin
½ tsp ground coriander
1 tsp sea salt
1 C chopped cilantro

Bake at 450 degrees in a 9x13 pan

2 lb firm fish fillets
2 C French couscous
1 tsp sea salt
1 tsp black pepper
¼ C EVOO
2 C boiling water
2 tomatoes, chopped, about 3 C
2 C arugula, torn into pieces
2 Tbsp EVOO

Blend the EVOO, lemon, garlic, paprika, cayenne, cumin, coriander, salt and cilantro in a blender or food processor. Use ½ the sauce to marinate the fish in a 9x13 glass or ceramic baking pan for 1 hour (more is fine too). Save the other ½ the sauce to pour over fish just before serving.

Preheat the oven to 450 degrees.

While the oven is preheating, mix couscous with salt, pepper and EVOO in a mixing bowl. Pour boiling water over couscous.

Put the fish-marinating pan into the oven and bake the fish uncovered for 10 minutes, or until it becomes opaque and flakes easily with a fork.

Couscous will have nicely absorbed the water. Break it up so it's crumbly.

Divide the couscous among the 4 plates and lay fish on top, or to one side of the plate. Pour remaining sauce over fish. Mix tomatoes and arugula with the last 2 Tbsp of EVOO. Place next to fish or on couscous. Serve a meal that is pretty and zesty.

POACHED FISH WITH CURRIED CRÈME FRAÎCHE

Why crème fraîche? It doesn't curdle when boiled, which makes it the ideal thickener for many sauces and soups. Here it imparts a delicacy that is divine.

Serves 4

1 C crème fraîche*
1 tsp ginger powder
1 Tbsp curry powder
1 Tbsp lemon juice
2 tomatoes, chopped, about 3 C

4 6-8 oz fish fillets, such as salmon
1 tsp sea salt
1 tsp black pepper
1 C spinach or baby bok choy, cut chiffonade (into ribbons)
¼ C chives or scallions, chopped

Put crème fraîche into skillet and mix with ginger, curry, lemon and chopped tomatoes. Mix well. Lay fish fillets over sauce. Sprinkle with salt and pepper. Gently bring crème sauce to a simmer. Cook fish in sauce for 5 minutes. Turn off flame and add spinach or bok choy to pot. Cover and let sit 5 minutes more.

Spoon fish and sauce with vegetable onto 4 individual serving plates. Pour any remaining sauce over the fish and garnish with chives or scallions. Goes nicely with any grain.

Note: To make your own crème fraîche, take a jar with a lid and mix 1 Tbsp buttermilk or ½ C sour cream into 1 C heavy whipping cream. Cover jar and shake. Let jar sit covered at room temperature for 24 hours, or until mixture is thick. You can stir once or twice during the thickening time. Crème fraîche is ready faster if your room is warm. It keeps almost forever in the refrigerator…

*Can you use yogurt instead of crème fraîche? You can if you're worried about calories, but the crème fraîche is worth the calories. Schedule an extra walk with a friend so you can indulge.

POMEGRANATE BAKED FISH

Scientists in Israel have conducted research on the health benefits of pomegranates and pomegranate juice for years, probably because they had so many pomegranates and wanted to encourage people to eat them! However, we know from their research, and the research of others, that pomegranates are rich in antioxidants. One study found that 8 oz of pomegranate juice daily for 3 months increased the amount of oxygen getting to the heart in patients with heart disease.

Serves 4

Bake at 375 degrees in a 9x13 pan

4 8-oz fish fillets (any kind) rinsed and patted dry
1 tsp sea salt
½ tsp black pepper
4 cloves garlic, pressed
2 Tbsp extra virgin olive oil (EVOO)
2 zucchini, sliced, about 4 C
1 Tbsp EVOO

1 C pomegranate concentrate or pomegranate molasses
½ red onion, chopped, about 1 C
6 cloves garlic, minced
¼ tsp dried red pepper flakes
¼ C fresh basil, chopped
¼ C cilantro, chopped (optional)
1 tsp sea salt

Preheat oven to 375 degrees.

Rub fish with salt, pepper, garlic and EVOO. Place in a 9x13 glass or ceramic baking dish.

Toss zucchini with next 1 Tbsp EVOO and put in a second baking dish.

Put both baking dishes into oven and bake for 15 minutes, or until fish is opaque and zucchini has some golden-brown edges.

In the meantime, in a small pot bring the pomegranate concentrate or pomegranate molasses to a near-boil. Stir in onion, garlic, red pepper flakes, basil, cilantro and salt. Turn off heat and let sauce sit until the fish and zucchini are ready.

Serve fish flanked by zucchini and topped with sauce. Very yummy for the tummy.

RAY'S FAVORITE BAKED FISH

Rays says, "I plagiarized this recipe from a restaurant I worked at 25 years ago. The restaurant made it with sole, but I've been making it with haddock, cod or pollock since. I like it because it's clean and clear tasting, not overpowering. It's the subtle flavors of the onion and dill that make fish prepared this way unique."

Serves 6-8

3 lb haddock, cod or pollock (boneless and skinless)
1 lemon, about ¼ C juice
1 Tbsp dried dill weed
1 onion, minced, about 2 C
1 tsp Herbamare seasoning, or more to taste

Bake at 375 degrees in a 9x13 pan

2 sticks butter, melted, 1 C
4 Tbsp fresh parsley, chopped
4 C Barbara's brand saltines, crushed
4 Tbsp water
more dill weed as garnish

Arrange fish fillets in oven-proof dish and squeeze lemon juice over them. It's important to use the lemon juice first so the other seasonings don't wash off. Sprinkle fish with dill, diced onion and Herbamare.

Preheat oven to 375 degrees.

In a separate bowl, mix ¾ of the melted butter and chopped parsley together with the crumbled crackers. Pack the cracker mix on top of seasoned fish and drizzle with remaining butter.

Add the 4 Tbsp water around the edges of the pan (not on top). Bake approximately 20 minutes, or until fish slightly flakes or begins to pull apart. Don't overcook! Serve with another sprinkling of dried dill weed.

Roasted Fish with Apricots and Onions

I like the way apricots seem to melt into onions. And I like the way the honey and lemon bring out the best in both.

Serves 2

2 lb whole fish, or 2 6-8 oz fish fillets
2 Tbsp extra virgin olive oil (EVOO)
2 Tbsp lemon juice
1 tsp sea salt
1 tsp black pepper

Bake at 425 degrees in a 9x13 baking pan

2 onions, halved and sliced, about 4 C
2 Tbsp extra virgin olive oil (EVOO)
1 C dried apricots, coarsely chopped
2 Tbsp honey
2 Tbsp lemon juice
1 tsp sea salt

Place fish in a 9x13 glass or ceramic baking dish. In a little dish, combine EVOO, lemon, salt and pepper. Rub over the whole fish. Let marinate in the fridge while you prepare the onion and apricot topping.

Preheat oven to 425 degrees

In a covered saucepan over low heat, cook onions and EVOO, stirring occasionally, until onions are very soft, about 10 minutes. Remove lid and cook onions until they are golden, about 5 minutes more. Add apricots, honey, lemon and salt. Simmer 5 minutes more.

Spoon onion-apricot mixture over fish. Put in oven and roast for 30 minutes. Onions and apricots will become an exotic crust!

Alternatively, you can roast fish for 10 minutes without the topping and serve the onion-apricot mixture spooned over the fish or served alongside. I'd go for the oven-roasted crust.

Roxanne's Seafood Pasta

Roxanne says, "I first made this recipe when my sister, Cindy, was getting married two years ago. We were having a bridal shower, and I needed to make something that would feed 60 people! The recipe below serves 6, but doubling or tripling, or in my case multiplying by 10 was a breeze…It was a big hit, and I received many requests for the recipe."

"It could also be made with chicken, instead of the fish, or if you're vegetarian, tofu substituted for the seafood works too," added Roxanne.

Serves 4-6

3 Tbsp extra virgin olive oil (EVOO)	**1 C fresh basil leaves**
1 lb scallops or shrimp, rinsed &	**1 lb baby spinach**
patted dry	**1 lb tube-shaped pasta**
6 cloves garlic	**1 C freshly grated parmesan**
2 tomatoes, chopped, about 3 C	**1 tsp black pepper (optional)**
2 C heavy cream	**1 tsp sea salt (optional)**
¼ dried crushed red pepper	

Gently warm 2 Tbsp of the EVOO in a medium-sized sauté pan. Add seafood and sauté 1-2 minutes. Remove seafood from pan and set aside on a plate.

Heat the last Tbsp EVOO in the same saucepan over medium heat. Add garlic and cook until fragrant, about 1 minute. Add tomatoes, cream and crushed red pepper. Simmer 2-3 minutes more. Stir in ½ the basil and ½ lb of spinach. Cook for an additional 1-2 minutes, and then add the seafood. Give a good stir, turn off the flame, and let everything sit so the flavors marry.

In the meantime, bring a large pot filled ⅔ full of water to a rolling boil. Add pasta to boiling water, stir and cook about 7 minutes, being sure not to overcook. Pasta should be al dente. Drain pasta but save 1 C of the cooking liquid. Return pasta to pot.

To pasta in the pot, add the sauce with the seafood, parmesan, and the remaining ½ C of basil and ½ lb of spinach. Toss everything together gently to coat. If necessary, add enough of the saved pasta water to thin the sauce. Add salt and pepper to taste.

SALMON CAKES BY ROXANNE

Roxanne says, "I first created this recipe for my daughter Olivia's christening on her first birthday. Since she was allergic to many of the meat dishes everyone else was enjoying, I made these especially for her. She has loved them ever since and is now a beautiful, healthy six-year-old!"

Makes 8 fish cakes

2 7.5-oz cans wild salmon, drained
½ C celery, finely chopped
½ C onion, finely chopped
½ C frozen corn, thawed
½ C mayonnaise
1 tsp lemon juice
½ tsp Worcestershire sauce
½ tsp paprika

1 Tbsp Dijon mustard
1 tsp sweet pickles, finely chopped
1 tsp sea salt
½ tsp black pepper
½ C Barbara's brand saltine-type crackers
1 egg, beaten
1-2 C whole-grain breadcrumbs (your favorite)
2 Tbsp extra virgin olive oil (EVOO)

Place salmon into a medium-sized bowl. Gently flake with a fork and remove any unwanted skin or small bones. Add the celery, onion and corn. Toss together and set aside.

In a small bowl, stir together the mayonnaise, lemon juice, Worcestershire sauce, paprika, mustard, pickles, and salt and pepper. Add to the salmon mixture.

Crush crackers and carefully add together with the egg to the salmon cake mix. Shape into 8 patties and coat in breadcrumbs. Chill in refrigerator for 1-2 hours.

Gently warm EVOO in a skillet or frying pan. Pan-fry the fish cakes for 3-4 minutes each side, or until golden brown. Drain on paper towels and serve with the sauce of your choice.

Note: If you would like to serve these as hors d'oeuvres, shape them into smaller fish cakes before pan-frying.

SCALLOPS WITH LENTILS AND PEAS

Lentils are such a wonderful, healthy food. They are similar to beans, but they take much less time to cook. Split peas are from the same family as lentils but because they are more mature, they take longer to cook. Here the slight firmness is a nice counterpoint to the scallops.

Serves 4

1 C lentils (brown, green or black)	12 large scallops
½ C split peas	2 Tbsp lemon juice
1 bay leaf	1 tsp dried sage
4 cloves garlic, diced	½ tsp black pepper
1 tomato, diced, about 1-2 C	1 tsp sea salt
1 2-inch piece kombu* (kelp)	12 asparagus with woody bottom
1 teaspoon sea salt	removed
4 Tbsp extra virgin olive oil (EVOO)	4 sprigs watercress
2 Tbsp EVOO	a lemon cut into 8 wedges
8 slices bacon or Fakin' Bacon	

In a medium saucepan, combine lentils with peas, bay leaf, garlic, tomato and kombu. Cover with water. Bring to a boil and then simmer lentils until tender, about 20-25 minutes. If there's any water left, drain lentils and split peas. (Split peas will be somewhat firm, and that's okay.) Stir in salt and EVOO. Taste and add a little more salt if you want. Set lentils and peas aside.

Gently warm 2 Tbsp EVOO in a large skillet and then cook bacon until crisp. Remove from skillet and set aside.

Season scallops with lemon, sage, pepper and salt. In the same frying pan, add scallops and asparagus. Cook until scallops are golden on each side and asparagus is tender but crunchy, about 5 minutes.

To serve, divide lentil-pea mixture among the 4 individual serving plates. Top each with equal amounts of scallops and asparagus. Garnish with bacon strips (if you want to crumble bacon and use it as a topping that way—that's fine too). Use watercress and lemon wedges to add color.

*Why use a piece of kombu? Kombu helps break down what we have trouble digesting in beans and peas, so when you include it here, you'll just enjoy the dish that much more, and it will feel good in your tummy.

SEAFOOD MEDLEY WITH OLIVES

Olives, which have been cultivated since prehistoric times, are grown commercially today in Spain, Italy, France, Greece, Tunisia, Morocco, Turkey, Portugal, China, Chile, Peru, Brazil, Mexico, Angola, South Africa, Uruguay, Afghanistan, Australia, New Zealand and California. Whew! Most of the 800 million olive trees under cultivation are used to make olive oil.

Olives right off the tree are inedible. They have to be treated before we can eat them. Olives can be treated with lye, or cured naturally in oil, brine or dry salt. Naturally cured is the only way to go! In addition to curing, if olives are picked before they're ripe, which most are, they also need to be allowed to ferment. This begs the question: how ever did people discover how to treat olives so we could eat them and why would anyone have taken the trouble? Boy, am I glad someone did, but human ingenuity never ceases to amaze.

Olives that are tree-ripened and then naturally cured are softer. My favorites are Graber olives. I grew up with these, and my brothers and I called them "butter olives" because they are so tender and buttery. But Graber olives have pits, and so I don't use them in dishes like this one. Rather I choose oil-cured, pitted black olives, or French pitted, green olives that are cured in saltwater mixed with herbs.

Serves 6

½ C extra virgin olive oil (EVOO)	1 tsp dried thyme
12 cloves garlic, minced	½ C lemon juice
1 lb medium shrimp	½ C pitted green olives
1 lb medium scallops	½ C pitted black olives
½ lb crab or lobster meat	1 tsp black pepper
	1 tsp sea salt

In a large skillet, gently warm EVOO. Sauté garlic for 2 minutes (it will become aromatic and start to brown). Add shrimp and scallops and stir until the shrimp turn pink, about 5 minutes. Then add crab or lobster meat, thyme, lemon juice, olives (chopped or not—it's up to you), black pepper and salt. Simmer 5 minutes more. Taste. Feel free to add more lemon if you like.

Serve with any grain, baked potato or pasta. I always like something steamed and green on the side. Plain sliced, steamed zucchini is lovely.

SHRIMP CURRY WITH BUTTERNUT SQUASH

This is a different twist on a recipe from our first cookbook, now out of print. The original recipe was called "Shrimp Curry with Potatoes."

Accompany this with steamed asparagus or spinach. You won't believe how easy this is to make! Or how good it tastes.

Serves 4

¼ C extra virgin olive oil (EVOO)
1 onion, chopped, about 2 C
4 cloves garlic, minced
1 lb peeled and cubed butternut squash, about 4 C (frozen works fine too)
1 tsp ground coriander
1 tsp curry powder

1 tsp black pepper
1 tsp sea salt
1 14-oz can unsweetened coconut milk or 2 tomatoes, diced, about 2 C
1 lb shrimp, peeled
½ C lemon juice
4 sprigs watercress for garnish

In a large pot or skillet, gently warm the EVOO. Add the onion and garlic and sauté 5 minutes. Garlic will start to brown. Add the squash together with the coriander, curry, black pepper and salt. Stir so squash and spices are coated. Then add your choice of coconut milk or tomatoes. Simmer squash about 5 minutes, then add shrimp and toss everything gently. Simmer just until shrimp have turned pink, about 5 minutes more.

To serve, add lemon into curry. Toss gently again and taste. Adjust anything that needs adjusting at this point. Do you want more pepper or salt?

Spoon out onto plates and garnish each with a watercress sprig.

Syrian Fish with Tahini

Baking fish with tahini is common all over the Middle East. I first had something like this in Jerusalem many years ago where the fish was also garnished with pomegranate seeds. I'd love to suggest that below, but peeling a pomegranate is a time-consuming project. I keep waiting for fresh, peeled pomegranates to come onto the market. Maybe soon...

Serves 4

TAHINI SAUCE *
6 cloves garlic, pressed
3 Tbsp tahini
3 Tbsp extra virgin olive oil (EVOO)
2 Tbsp lemon juice
1 Tbsp water

4 8-oz fish fillets

1 C pomegranate seeds (optional)

Bake at 375 degrees in a 9x13 pan

TOPPING
5 garlic cloves, minced
1 tsp chili pepper flakes
½ C walnuts, finely chopped
½ C pine nuts, finely chopped
1 tsp coriander
1 tsp ground cumin
2 Tbsp lemon juice
¼ C EVOO
1 tsp sea salt
½ tsp black pepper

Preheat oven to 375 degrees.

To make sauce: Blend garlic, tahini, EVOO, lemon juice and water. Cover and set aside.

To make the topping: In a little bowl, combine garlic, chili, nuts, coriander, cumin, lemon juice, EVOO, and salt and pepper. Mix well.

Place fillets in a single layer in a 9x13 glass or ceramic baking dish. Spoon topping evenly over fish, pressing it on with your fingertips. Put fish in oven and bake for 15 minutes, or until fish is opaque and topping is lightly browned.

Serve fish with tahini sauce spooned on top, or served alongside if that's your preference. If you have pomegranate seeds, sprinkle on top too.

*Alternatively, fish can be coated with tahini sauce and baked with that instead of the nut mixture topping above. So you now have 2 recipes on this page for the price of 1!

WILD RICE GOURMET FISH FEAST

Serves 8

2 C wild rice
4 C boiling water
1 tsp sea salt
1 lb bluefish fillets, cut in 8 pieces
1 lb sole fillets, cut into 8 pieces
1 lb red snapper fillets, cut into 8
  pieces
1 lb haddock fillets, cut into 8 pieces
½ C Debra's Olive Oil Vinaigrette
  (find this recipe in the "Salads"
  section)

Broil in a 9x13 baking dish

2 carrots, sliced, about 4 C
2 C peas
1 lb asparagus, cut into 4-inch pieces
2 Tbsp toasted sliced almonds
2 Tbsp fresh parsley, minced
1 lemon with peel, cut into 8
  slices and seeded
1 tsp paprika (optional)
1 tsp black pepper (optional)

Place wild rice and boiling water together with 1 tsp salt in a saucepan with a tight-fitting lid. Cover pot, lower flame and simmer rice for about 45 minutes, or until water has been absorbed and rice is tooth-tender. Turn off flame and let pot sit covered on the stove.

Place fish in a shallow 9x13 glass or ceramic baking dish. Pour marinade (Debra's Olive Oil Vinaigrette) over fish. Marinate in the refrigerator about 1 hour, turning once.

Turn oven on to broil (high). Place glass or ceramic baking dish with the fish about 5 inches from the flame. Broil fish 5 minutes, or until opaque. Don't worry about flipping fish halfway through the broiling process, because you don't need to. (If you're using frozen fish fillets, move rack farther from the flame and do turn the fish once. Add 5 minutes to the cooking time too.)

While the fish is under the broiler, place carrots in a skillet together with 2 C water. Bring water to a boil, lower flame, cover pot and simmer carrots for 5 minutes. Remove lid to skillet and add peas and asparagus. Simmer with lid on for no more than 2 minutes. You want peas and asparagus to be bright green.

At the same time, toast sliced almonds, dry, in little pan over medium heat for 1-2 minutes. Almonds will become aromatic and start to brown. Set pan to one side.

To serve, spoon wild rice onto 8 individual serving plates, then arrange the assortment of fish on the rice and place vegetables on the side of the plate. Garnish fish with almonds and parsley. Place lemon wherever you think the plate needs another pop of color. If you want to sprinkle with paprika and black pepper, now's the time to do that!

Pasta and Cheese

I know there are people who don't like pasta or cheese, and I know there are people who can't eat either because of allergies or a gluten-intolerance.

To the first group, I don't know what to say, because I love, love, love pasta, and cheese is one of my greatest temptations.

To the second group, those with allergies or a gluten-intolerance, feel free to convert any of these recipes and use ingredients you can eat. Can't have pasta made with wheat? Lucky you, because there are umpteen gluten-free pastas! Can't do dairy? There are non-cheeses (aka fake cheeses) that you can substitute for any cheese called for here.

If you don't like the fake cheeses, jazz things up with more garlic and extra virgin olive oil. Use more basil and nuts. Somehow, invent your own new, wonderful recipe.

A note here about DeBoles wheat pastas. These aren't whole grain, but to compensate for that fact, DeBoles adds Jerusalem artichoke flour. (DeBoles pastas are the only non-whole-grain product I eat. I like the taste, and can justify eating white pasta because of the addition of that Jerusalem artichoke flour.)

The Jerusalem artichoke is an edible tuber, somewhat akin to a potato, which contains a carbohydrate called "inulin." Unlike starch and most carbohydrates, inulin isn't broken down in the digestive tract, so it has only a small impact on blood sugar, and few calories to boot. Inulin is also said to feed the healthy bugs in our gut, and is classified as a type of dietary fiber that aids mineral absorption. So it has some advantages.

The Jerusalem artichoke was "discovered" growing in an American Indian vegetable garden in Cape Cod, Massachusetts in 1605 by explorer Samuel de Champlain. He thought it tasted like an artichoke (no relation), a name that he carried back with the tubers to France. But I haven't a clue why they were called "Jerusalem" artichokes.

A word about pasta sauce or tomato sauce: Use a clean sauce. For me that means one with organic ingredients, and one without sugar. Unsweetened pasta and tomato sauces are getting harder and harder to find, but they are out there. You'll be amazed at how much better your dishes taste without the added sugar...

Homogenized Plastic Mass: It's What's For Dinner

This is from Adam and appeared in our February 2009 newsletter. I've inserted it here to test you, to see if you're awake!

I'm not completely opposed to junk food. For example, the occasional leftover French fry scavenged from the plate of a dining companion, or the deep fat-fried Snickers-bar-on-a-stick at Redbone's in Davis Square, Somerville. Those, I feel, are worth it.

But for the most part, I just wonder why. I mean, really, why eat most of the crap that's out there? Having been raised on good food, I'm constantly amazed that people would crave, say, a Fenway Frank over the much-more-delicious Coleman organic hot dog. Or a white-flour-Crisco-crusted corn-syrup Cool Whip pie, over something with whole grains and actual fruit and soaring peaks of whipped cream. For the most part, natural—which is to say: "real"—just tastes better.

Nowhere is this truer than when it comes to cheese. I love cheese. I respect cheese. I write love sonnets to cheese, in all its cheesy beauty. So you can imagine how shocked and offended I was when, for the first time in my more than 30 years, my taste buds experienced the day-glo dairy mucous extrusion that's splotched over lukewarm tortilla chips & called "nachos" at a movie theater.

What is this industrial waste?

That's not a rhetorical question! What, exactly is nacho spread made of? To answer that question, here's an excerpt from the U.S. Code of Federal Regulations, Title 21: Food and Drugs.

Part 133—CHEESES AND RELATED CHEESE PRODUCTS Subpart B—Requirements for Specific Standardized Cheeses and Related Products

§ 133.179 Pasteurized process cheese spread.

(a)(1) Pasteurized process cheese spread is the food prepared by comminuting and mixing, with the aid of heat, one or more of the optional cheese ingredients prescribed in paragraph (c) of this section, with or without one or more of the optional dairy ingredients prescribed in paragraph (d) of this section, with one or more of the emulsifying agents prescribed in paragraph (e) of this section, and with or without one or more of the optional ingredients prescribed by paragraph (f) of this section, into a homogeneous plastic mass, which is spreadable at 70° F.

...then follow a few paragraphs involving advanced dairy mathematics...

(a)(6) The weight of each variety of cheese in a pasteurized process cheese spread made with two varieties of cheese is not less than 25 percent of the total weight of both, except that the weight of blue cheese, nuworld cheese, Roquefort cheese, gorgonzola cheese, or limburger cheese is not less than 10 percent of the total weight of both. The weight of each variety of cheese in a pasteurized process cheese spread made with three or more varieties of cheese is not less than 15 percent of the total weight of all, except the weight of blue cheese, nuworld...

...down a few more paragraphs, the code gets multisyllabic for us...

e) The emulsifying agents prescribed in paragraph (a) of this section are one or any mixture of two or more of the following: Monosodium phosphate, disodium phosphate, dipotassium phosphate, trisodium phosphate, sodium pentaphosphate (sodium hexametaphosphate), sodium acid pyrophosphate, tetrasodium pyrophosphate, sodium aluminum phosphate, sodium citrate, potassium citrate, calcium citrate, sodium tartrate, and sodium potassium tartrate, in such quantity that the weight of the solids of such emulsifying agent is not more than 3 percent of the weight of the pasteurized process cheese spread.

I could go on. And on. But you get the point. Do we really want to eat a food that requires three pages just to define? Anyone interested in reading the rest of the three-page definition of "Pasteurized process cheese spread" can find it on-line at http://ecfr.gpoaccess.gov.

And while you're at it, you could probably find "hot dog" on there as well. But, really, why give yourself nightmares?

Adam's Down-Home Macaroni and Cheese

Comfort food. This recipe first ran in our May 2003 newsletter. April had been cold. It was the season of our discontent in Iraq, and I was having a day of woe, feeling sad. Adam advised making something old-fashioned, something down-home and comforting like this macaroni and cheese. It hit the spot.

While Adam said this feeds 4, I'd say not everyone has his appetite. I bet you can feed 12 people with this recipe, so feel free to halve or quarter it. If you choose to make the whole thing and have leftovers, well, they freeze well.

Adam says, "Add whatever leftover vegetables or smidgens of cheese you have in your fridge. And I much prefer fresh tomatoes."

Serves 8-12

- 2 lb assorted melting cheeses like pepper jack, cheddar, havarti, mozzarella
- 16 oz pkg Bionaturae brand gobbetti
- 2 cans Eden black beans, about 4 C cooked
- 2 C canned diced tomatoes
- 4 C veggies, bite-sized pieces (like kale, zucchini)

Bake at 350 degrees

- 2 C broccoli florets (frozen is fine)
- 1 C Pecorino romano
- 1 tsp dried thyme
- 1 Tbsp dried basil
- 1 Tbsp oregano
- 1 Tbsp black pepper
- 1 tsp chili pepper flakes (optional)
- 8 cloves garlic, pressed

Preheat oven to 350 degrees.

Grate or chop cheeses with either shredding disk or the steel blade of a food processor. Cook pasta according to directions. Drain and put pasta in your largest mixing bowl. Add ⅓ of the grated cheese and all of the drained Eden beans, tomatoes, veggies, romano, herbs and spices.

Mix and put into a large casserole. Top with remaining cheese and pop into oven for about 40 minutes, or until cheese is nice and bubbly. Serve and swoon.

Note: If you can't do wheat, substitute another pasta. Or use oodles of vegetables instead.

BOWTIES WITH SHRIMP PUTTANESCA

Why do I love Pecorino romano? First and foremost because of the way it tastes. It has a heavenly sharp flavor that adds character to any dish. Secondly, because it is made from sheep's milk, which is easier to digest. And finally, I appreciate its history and the fact it is one of the oldest Italian cheeses.

Serves 4

¼ C extra virgin olive oil (EVOO)
6 cloves garlic, minced
2 red onions, chopped, about 4 C
a few anchovies (optional)
16 oz bowtie pasta
4 C diced tomatoes (plum preferred)
2 C diced zucchini or diced butternut
   squash
2 Tbsp capers

½ C pitted Kalamata olives, chopped
1 lb peeled shrimp
1 Tbsp dried basil
½ tsp dried marjoram
1 tsp dried oregano
1 tsp chili pepper flakes
1 tsp black pepper
½ C Pecorino romano (2 Tbsp per
   person)

Gently warm EVOO in a skillet. Sauté garlic and onions over medium heat until onions are translucent, about 5 minutes.

In the meantime, bring a saucepan of water to boil. Add pasta and cook until al dente, about 10 minutes.

At the same time, add tomatoes, zucchini or butternut squash, capers, olives, shrimp, herbs and pepper to skillet with garlic and onions. Simmer until the tomatoes are heated through and the shrimp have turned pink, about 5 minutes.

Drain pasta and either transfer to a large serving bowl or divide among 4 individual serving plates. Spoon sauce over pasta and sprinkle on romano. I like to bring extra pepper and romano to the table.

Note: Feel free to mash several anchovies right in the skillet while garlic and onions are sautéing. Some people love anchovies, others hate them. I'm in the love 'em category, and if I knew you were too, you bet I'd add anchovies.

CARLISLE FARMSTEAD CHEESE

There are some cheeses that should be eaten plain because they are so good.

One of those comes from our neighbors at the Carlisle Farmstead in Carlisle, the next town over.

Trish, her crew and the goats have been making cheese together since the summer of 2005. This happy group includes 6 does who are considered "both our friends and co-workers," according to Trish.

We don't always have Carlisle Farmstead cheeses because milk production may be down, or because Trish and her band may be milking fewer goats. It may also be the time of year when the moms are feeding their new baby goats!

When I am lucky enough to get a Carlisle Farmstead Cheese, dinner is simple. I allow the cheese to come to room temperature and slice it. It looks elegant on a plate with finger-food vegetables on the side. Nirvana.

My favorite cheese from the farm is "Ada's Honor," named after Ada the goat. Trish describes it this way, "Chabicou-style cheese...Its texture is smooth because the curd is carefully hand-ladled into molds. The taste is mild, but complex thanks to the exquisite milk produced by our Oberhasli does."

CHEESE RAVIOLI WITH POTATOES AND ALMONDS

If you recognize this, it's from our November 2003 newsletter. This dish provides peasant-style, energy food! Buy ground almonds, or grind your own using a blender or food processor. This dish satisfies the need when you just gotta have that starch.

Serves 6-8

1 jar 32-oz pasta sauce, your favorite
1 lb potatoes, sliced in circles
½ C ground almonds
¼ C chopped flat parsley
½ C dry white wine or cider vinegar
¼ tsp ground nutmeg

2 lb frozen cheese ravioli
¼ C extra virgin olive oil (EVOO)
grated Pecorino romano, for the
  dish and the table
steamed greens like spinach

Put pasta sauce in a pot. Add potatoes, almonds, parsley, vinegar and nutmeg. Lower heat, cover pot and simmer for 30 minutes or until potatoes are soft.

Cook ravioli in a large pot of gently boiling water. Stir occasionally to prevent from sticking. When they rise to the surface, taste to see if they are tender. When done, drain, dish the ravioli out onto plates, drizzle with olive oil and top with sauce. Garnish with a few Tbsp of romano and put the rest on the table so people can help themselves to more.

Serve with steamed greens for color and nutritional balance.

Eggplant parmesan Bake

This is my easy, lazy-man's version of eggplant parmesan. I don't like to have to clean the stove top, and I don't want to take the time to sauté the eggplant slices. I think this version tastes fresher. Try it, you'll like it.

I almost forgot to mention that while parmesan cheese is okay with me, I really, really love Pecorino romano, and I've added that here too.

Serves 4-6

1 large eggplant, sliced
1 onion, diced, about 2 C
6 garlic cloves, minced
1 stalk celery, sliced, about 1 C
1 small green pepper, diced, about 1 C
1 tsp Spike seasoning
2 Tbsp basil (fresh or dried)
1 tsp dried oregano
1 tsp chili pepper flakes

Bake at 425 degrees in a 9x13 pan

¼ C extra virgin olive oil (EVOO)
2 Tbsp grated Pecorino romano
2 Tbsp grated parmesan
32 oz or more of your favorite
    pasta sauce
1½ lb sliced or shredded cheese
    (any combination such as
    scamorze, provolone, pepper jack,
    mozzarella or fontina
basil and oregano for sprinkling

Preheat oven to 425 degrees.

In a 9x13 lasagna type pan, lay eggplant rounds. Cover eggplant with onion, garlic, celery, pepper, Spike seasoning, basil, oregano and chili pepper flakes. Pour EVOO over everything, and then sprinkle with romano and parmesan. Gently pour pasta sauce over the top, being careful not to wash the other ingredients off the eggplant.

Cover casserole with cheese and then with tin foil. Bake 45 minutes. Then remove tin foil and continue to bake another 15 minutes so cheese topping becomes nice and brown.

Note: I like to sprinkle on more basil and oregano when I take the eggplant parm out of the oven. It provides a little eye candy!

Escarole with Cannellini Beans and Lotsa' Garlic over Pasta

Escarole is a member of the endive family, and its leaves are different than chicory or curly endive—they're broader and less bitter.

Once when we were driving home to MA from NJ, we got caught in a snowstorm and stopped in a roadside restaurant. I ordered this dish and was ecstatic because it was delicious, completely unlike any other road food I'd ordered and eaten. To the best of my recollection...

Serves 4-6

1 C extra virgin olive oil (EVOO)
¼ C Tbsp butter (or more EVOO)
1 head escarole, rinsed, drained and chopped, about 16 C
½ C chopped garlic
1 can Eden cannellini beans, about 2 C cooked, with juices
1 tsp sea salt
½ tsp black pepper
½ tsp chili pepper flakes
2 Tbsp Pecorino romano
16 oz pasta of your choice
½ C EVOO
¼ C Pecorino romano

Gently warm EVOO and butter in a large skillet over medium heat. Toss in escarole, turning to coat with oil. Stir in garlic and beans with juices. Simmer until creamy, about 10 minutes. Add salt, black pepper, chili pepper flakes and romano. Toss everything together.

In the meantime, bring a pot of water to boil. Add pasta and cook until al dente, about 10 minutes. Drain pasta and toss with the additional EVOO and romano.

Divide pasta among 4-6 individual serving plates. Top with escarole and bean mixture.

Note: When I ate this at the roadside restaurant, there was so much EVOO that it dripped down my chin no matter how neatly I tried to eat. So if this is too much EVOO or butter for you, use less.

GRANDMA SARAH'S BLINTZES

No one ever believed Grandma Sarah when she said she made her blintzes without flour. She did, and I know because we used to watch her make these. We also used to save apricot or peach or nectarine pits for her. When she'd visit, she'd crack the pits and use the bitter almond inside them to flavor her filling.

These blintzes may seem like a lot of work to make, but they're really a piece of cake. It helps if you have extra little hands to assist.

Serve for breakfast or lunch drizzled with honey and accompanied by fresh berries.

Makes 14-16 blintzes

CREPES
6 eggs
¼ C water or milk
2 Tbsp butter for frying
   (more sometimes)

FILLING
1 lb soft farmer cheese*
6 Tbsp honey
dash cinnamon
4 bitter almonds**, ground
1 tsp vanilla extract

To make crepes: Beat eggs and water with a fork until foamy. Heat a 10-inch frying pan over medium heat. Add ¼ tsp butter. Turn down flame before pouring in a scant ¼ C egg batter. Quickly tilt pan to spread crepe. Patch holes in any blintz with a drop of batter. When blintz underside is lightly browned, turn onto a plate. Do not try and unfold or straighten while hot.

Dot butter in pan and start second blintz. Continue buttering, swirling batter and dumping crepes onto plate until batter is used. When crepes are cool, straighten and unfold them onto a clean plate. Cover with plastic wrap to prevent drying out until filled.

To make filling: Mash filling ingredients together in a large bowl.

To assemble blintzes: Place heaping Tbsp of filling on end of blintz nearest you. Fold in sides and roll blintz away, as for egg rolls or stuffed grape leaves. When finished filling all the blintzes, cover and refrigerate until you serve with a jar of honey. My father used to love these for breakfast!

*I imagine you could use ricotta to make these too. In that case, I'd drain the ricotta by hanging in cheese cloth over the kitchen sink faucet overnight. You want as dry a cheese as you can get to make filling.

**No bitter almonds? You can use regular almonds, or substitute a few drops of almond extract.

JIM'S COTTAGE PIE

Jim said, "Just before my mother came to visit from England, she fell and did considerable damage to her jaw and mouth. Somehow, she was still brave enough to travel at age 84. When she arrived, my wife, Diane, and I faced the challenge of providing nutritious *soft* food for her. She mentioned that on the plane they had served cottage pie, a traditional English dish, and that it had been very easy to manage, so always looking for a chance to be creative in the kitchen, I asked what goes into cottage pie and then devised my own vegetarian version. She and Diane, upon tasting it, both immediately insisted that I present it for Debra's cookbook. So here it is: a brand new take on an old world recipe."

What is Quorn? Made in the UK, it's a mycoprotein, protein made from a mushroom. It is fermented like yogurt, and the package says it contains almost as much protein as an egg, no cholesterol, twice the fiber of fresh broccoli and fewer calories than chicken breast.

Serves 4-6

6 medium potatoes, about 9 C, quartered
2 Tbsp butter or Earth Balance spread
2 small to medium carrots, about 4 C, grated
1 medium zucchini, about 2 C, grated
1 small onion, about 2 C, minced

Bake at 350 degrees

12 oz Quorn or ground beef substitute
Herbamare, or sea salt to taste
tamari (soy sauce) to taste
4 Tbsp butter or Earth Balance spread
milk or cream

Preheat oven to 350 degrees.

Cut potatoes into quarters and put into pot with 4 C water. Bring to a boil. Simmer potatoes until soft, about 10 minutes.

Meanwhile, in a second pot, melt 2 Tbsp butter or Earth Balance spread and sauté grated carrots, zucchini, minced onion and Quorn for 5 to 10 minutes. Season with Herbamare or sea salt and tamari to suit your own taste. (I'd start with about a tsp of each.)

When potatoes are soft, mash them in a bowl and add the 4 Tbsp butter or Earth Balance. Then add either milk or cream to achieve the consistency you most enjoy. (If you have your own mashed potato recipe, by all means simply use that.) Put Quorn vegetable mixture in a greased casserole dish and top with the mashed potatoes.

Bake for 30 minutes. Serve on a rustic table under a thatched roof.

Linguini with Pecorino romano and Sweet Peppers

Linguini is long, slender pasta like spaghetti, except that spaghetti is round, and linguini, flat. Can you use one instead of the other? Yes. They give a different mouth feel, but both are excellent carriers for the vegetables and other ingredients below.

Serves 4-6

½ C extra virgin olive oil (EVOO)
4 large sweet bell peppers, chopped
1 stalk celery, chopped, about 2 C
2 carrots, diced, about 4 C
1 C garlic, minced (yes, 1 CUP)

4 oz pancetta or prosciutto, diced, or
    Lightlife Fakin' Bacon (tempeh)
1 tsp black pepper
¼ C flat parsley, chopped
1 lb linguini
1 C Pecorino romano

Gently warm EVOO in a large skillet. Add peppers, celery, carrots, garlic, meat, black pepper and parsley. Sauté the sauce for 20 minutes. Your nose should be doing the watusi.

Stir a few times. Add a little water if the sauce becomes too dry.

Bring a large pot of cold water to a boil. Put pasta in the water and cook 7-10 minutes, or until pasta is al dente. Drain pasta and transfer to a large warm serving dish. Pour ¾ of the sauce over pasta and toss. You can serve one big dish at the table or divide the pasta now among 4-6 individual serving plates. Top with remaining sauce, sprinkle with romano and carry to the table.

MANICOTTI WITH THREE CHEESES

There are so many cheeses to try, and I'm no cheese expert. I can't roll their names off my tongue like fine wine. Some I like here are asiago, which has a fantastic aroma, a good quality imported provolone, fontina and Bel Paese. These melt well, as do other cheeses like cheddar, colby, jack, havarti and provolone.

Serves 10

10 oz DeBoles rice lasagna noodles
16 oz ricotta cheese (fat or no fat)
¼ C Pecorino romano
2 C grated melting cheese of your choice
2 Tbsp chopped fresh parsley
2 Tbsp dried basil
1 tsp dried oregano

Bake at 450 degrees in a 9x13 pan

1 tsp dried thyme
1 tsp black pepper
4 cloves garlic, pressed, or 1 tsp garlic
⅛ tsp ground nutmeg
2 C tomato sauce
2 C grated melting cheese of your choice once again

Preheat oven to 450 degrees.

Fill any baking dish with very hot water; lay noodles in water and let stand 10 minutes, or until softened. (Leave noodles in the water until you need them, one by one, to fill.)

In the meantime, in a large bowl, combine ricotta, romano, 2 C grated melting cheese, 1 Tbsp of the parsley (save the rest to garnish), basil, oregano, thyme, pepper, garlic and nutmeg. Mix well. Divide into 10 portions.

Spoon about ¼ C tomato sauce on bottom of the 9x13 baking pan.

On a clean work surface, place 1 sheet of lasagna noodle at a time, lengthwise. Spoon a generous ½ C cheese mixture in the center third of the noodle. Fold the flaps (the other two sides) in and then carefully place your elongated package into baking pan, seam side up.

(By now you realize we're making an improvised manicotti using lasagna noodles. Some filling may leak out while baking. It doesn't matter, does it?)

Repeat filling-and-folding until you've finished with all 10 lasagna noodle sheets. Transfer each to the pan in a single layer. Cover with remaining 1½ C tomato sauce, and then sprinkle with the last 2 C grated cheese. Cover with foil and bake 10 minutes. Remove foil and finish baking until top is browned and sauce is bubbling, about 15 minutes.

Garnish with saved parsley and serve. There will only be moans of delight from the hungry crowd.

MARY'S LAYERED CORN TORTILLAS

Mary says this recipe, which you can make in a flash, was born thanks to the mother of invention. "I just kept adding things I found in the refrigerator that I needed to use up." Her advice? Make this recipe as flexible as the tortillas themselves, and add anything your heart desires. Leave out what you don't like, add more of what you love, maybe more cheese, for example.

Food for Life (FFL) Ezekiel breads and tortillas are made from sprouted grains, which are digested more like a vegetable instead of a starch. They *are* definitely easier on the digestive system.

Makes 2 tortillas

2 FFL Ezekiel sprouted grain tortillas
2 Tbsp extra virgin olive oil (EVOO)
1 red onion, thinly sliced, about 2 C
**12 fresh shiitake mushrooms, about
  4 C**
**6-8 oz baby spinach, steamed &
  chopped**
4 oz cheddar cheese, grated

Bake at 350 degrees

4 oz pepper jack cheese, grated
1 15-oz can diced tomatoes, drained
1 C frozen corn, thawed
½ C oil-cured, pitted black olives
salsa for topping
sour cream for topping

Take tortillas out to thaw. Gently warm EVOO and sauté onions and mushrooms until onions are translucent, about 5 minutes. In a second pot, bring 1 C water to a boil. Add spinach, steam a few minutes. Drain and chop spinach. (Save water to use in soups, stews or to cook grains. Or let it cool and drink it yourself as an alkalizing pick-me-upper.)

Preheat oven to 350 degrees.

Choose a baking sheet with sides. Put tortillas on the baking sheet.

Layer 1: ½ the cheddar and pepper jack cheeses
Layer 2: onion-mushroom mixture
Layer 3: diced tomatoes
Layer 4: thawed corn
Layer 5: olives
Layer 6: baby spinach
Layer 7: remaining cheeses

Bake until hot and cheese is bubbly, about 15 minutes. To serve, fold each tortilla over like an omelet. Using a wide spatula, place on dinner plates. Top with salsa, then sour cream.

MARY'S QUORN BOLOGNESE

Mary Kadlik's husband, Don, brought some of this old-fashioned comfort food, made by Mary, to a friend at work. The friend promptly offered to pay Mary to make him more. So she now burns the midnight oil making Quorn Bolognese on the side... (No, not really.)

Serve along side steamed greens or broccoli. A tossed salad and berries or fresh pineapple for dessert make this meal complete.

Serves 4-6

¼ C extra virgin olive oil (EVOO)
1 onion, halved and sliced, about 2 C
6 cloves garlic, minced
1 Tbsp dried oregano
1 Tbsp dried basil
1 tsp dried thyme
1 tsp chili pepper flakes (optional)

Bake at 350 degrees

1 12-oz pkg Quorn grounds
1 24-oz jar favorite Puttanesca sauce
½ lb DeBoles ziti pasta
½ tsp sea salt
1 tsp black pepper
1 C grated asiago cheese,
   or 1 C Pecorino romano

Preheat oven to 350 degrees.

Gently warm EVOO in a large skillet. Sauté onion and garlic until onion is translucent, about 5 minutes. Add herbs together with Quorn grounds and Puttanesca sauce (or your favorite pasta sauce). Simmer 5 minutes or so. (Mary says to simmer for 20 minutes—I was in a hurry and 5 minutes was finito for me!)

In the meantime, cook the ziti. Bring water in a large pot to boil, add in ziti, stir once and cook for about 7 minutes, or until the pasta is tooth tender. Drain and then add them to the sauce. Stir. Taste. Adjust seasonings. Serve with the asiago or Pecorino romano.

MARY JANE'S ZUCCHINI QUICHE

Mary Jane has grown vegetables in the Hugh Cargill Community Gardens in Concord for more than 35 years. "My dear husband, Bernie, always grows way too many zucchini, so I've had to develop lots of zucchini recipes. Some have been successful; others we have given to the family pets. This quiche recipe has been the cream of the crop. I make many quiches every year, and they freeze beautifully. Lightlife Fakin' Bacon is a great vegetarian soy tempeh substitute for bacon."

Makes 1 quiche

Bake at 450 degrees first, then 350 degrees

- ¼ C whole wheat pastry flour
- 1 tsp sea salt
- ¾ tsp fresh ground pepper
- ½ C grated Swiss cheese
- 1 C grated cheddar cheese
- 1 C diced onion
- 2½ C shredded zucchini
- 5 eggs, beaten lightly
- ½ C Lightlife Fakin' Bacon, broken up
- 1 whole wheat pie shell

Preheat oven to 450 degrees.

Mix flour and salt and pepper. Stir in cheeses, onion and zucchini. Add eggs and Fakin' Bacon, stirring until well blended. Pour filling mixture into an unbaked pie shell and place in oven, immediately turning temperature down to 350 degrees.

Bake for 70-90 minutes, or until quiche is brown and firm to the touch.

Enjoy and do not feed to the family pets!

NOT-ONLY-GOAT CHEESE PIZZA

This recipe appeared in our March 2003 newsletter. You gotta love goat cheese… It's easier to digest than cow's milk, and it's higher in protein and calcium too! Can you use all goat cheese on this pizza? Yes, there are wonderful grating goat cheeses that melt like a dream. Any of those would be excellent on top of the crust. If you're not a goat cheese aficionado, and the goat cheese topping is adventure enough, stay where you are and with the suggestions below.

If you don't like one of the toppings—Jim, for instance, isn't crazy about artichoke hearts—choose another, or double up on one you especially love. Adam used to like refried beans on his pizza. Leftovers, if you're lucky to have any, travel well to school and the office.

Serves 2-6   *Bake at 425 degrees*

about 8 oz jack cheese, shredded   **1 C mushrooms, sliced**
about 8 oz mozzarella, shredded   **1 C marinated artichoke hearts**
2 Tbsp extra virgin olive oil (EVOO)   **½ C marinated tomatoes, sliced**
1 tsp black pepper   **1 C red onion, sliced**
1 tsp dried oregano   **1 Alvarado* pizza crust (or your**
2 Tbsp grated Pecorino romano   **favorite crust)**
1 C baby spinach   **1 C soft goat cheese, crumbled**

Preheat oven to 425 degrees.

If your cheese isn't shredded cheese, shred it now. The easiest way to "grate" cheese for dishes that go into the oven is to chop using the steel blade of your food processor. Put chunks of cold jack and mozzarella cheeses into machine. Using on/off turns, process until smallish pieces.

In a large bowl, place all ingredients except crust and goat cheese. Toss so everything is coated with EVOO. Hands make the best tool!

Place crust on baking sheet. Mound cheese and vegetable mixture on crust, leaving a clear ¾-inch border. Top pizza with crumbled goat cheese. Push goat cheese down and into the rest of the topping or it will roll off.

Bake pizza until topping is heated through, 20-25 minutes. Remove from oven, let sit for 5 minutes, and then place on cutting board. With a large knife, cut pizza in ½, and each ½ into 3-4 pieces.

*Alvarado pizza bread crusts are in our freezer. They are made with certified organic, sprouted wheat.

ONE-SKILLET POLENTA WITH BLACK BEANS, GREENS AND CHEESE

This is a rustic, peasant-style dish which provides lots of energy. It first ran in our October 2005 newsletter, but we use it at so many events. Yes, it's a snap to make when you use ready-made polenta. And it's lovely that there's only one pot to wash! There are variations on this theme too. In my first cooking class with kids, we put portobella mushroom caps in the skillet instead of polenta, and sliced zucchini instead of leafy greens.

This dish makes it easy to get more beans in your diet. Beans have been an important part of the human diet for thousands of years because they are satisfying and healthy. They're also good for the planet. Black turtle beans are a great source of protein and cholesterol-lowering fiber, which also prevents blood sugar levels from rising too rapidly after a meal, making these beans an especially good choice for individuals with diabetes, insulin resistance, hypoglycemia or anyone trying to loose weight. And the USDA states that black beans are one of the top 10 antioxidants right up there with blueberries!

Serves 4-6

4 Tbsp extra virgin olive oil (EVOO)
1 pkg Food Merchant polenta
1 can Eden black beans,
   or 2 C cooked
few Tbsp Pecorino romano
1 lb greens like kale, spinach, chard,
   broccoli

1 jar Eden, Mom's, or other no-sugar
   pasta sauce
1 pkg (8 oz) Applegate Farms
   sliced havarti cheese
1 tsp dried oregano
1 tsp dried thyme
1 tsp dried basil

Drizzle EVOO in a large skillet. Open roll of polenta and cut in ½" slices/rounds. Cover bottom of skillet with rounds. Open can of Eden beans with their terrific taste and fiber—Eden cooks its beans with a piece of kombu (kelp, which is seaweed) so they're easy to digest. Spoon beans evenly over polenta. Sprinkle with romano. Rinse and shake greens. Chop coarsely into bite-sized pieces and spread them in skillet. Top greens with pasta sauce and then slices of havarti. Sprinkle with herbs. Put lid on skillet and simmer 5 minutes. Serve to cries of delight with a tossed salad or sliced cucumbers and cut up tomatoes. You've served up protein, fiber and great carbs. This dish is truly energy food!

Note: Alternatively, you can make this dish in a lasagna pan and bake it covered in a preheated, 350 degree oven for 1 hour. Uncover for the last 15 minutes to brown the cheese and allow some of the liquid to evaporate.

Red Scallop Stew
with Artichoke Cheesy Toasts

This is from Adam and ran in our February 2007 newsletter. "For many of us, canned tomato soup with a grilled cheese sandwich is quintessential quick'n'easy comfort food. This recipe is a decidedly gourmet upgrade on the old favorite—just as quick, and just as easy. If the phrase 'artichoke cheesy toasts' doesn't sound especially gourmet, call them crostini alla formaggi e carciofi. (Does anyone out there speak Italian? Did I say that right?)"

Serves 4

a roughly 25-oz jar tomato sauce
½ jar of Turtledove Company lemon artichoke pesto (or your favorite pesto, about 1 C)
about 1 C extra virgin olive oil (EVOO), or melted butter

Bake at 400 degrees in a 9x13 pan

4 Food for Life Ezekiel hamburger buns (for 8 halves total)
4 C Organic Valley Italian shredded cheese blend
1½ lb scallops

Preheat oven to 400 degrees.

Empty jar of tomato sauce into a pot or large saucepan and set it to simmer.

Mix pesto with an equal amount of EVOO or melted butter, and spread 2 Tbsp over each 4 halved Food for Life Ezekiel hamburger buns (meaning 8 halves total) on a baking sheet. Sprinkle buns liberally with Organic Valley Italian cheese blend. Bake 5 minute or until the cheese is nice and melty and slightly browned.

As the sauce begins to simmer, throw in scallops and cook for about 5 minutes.

Serve a bowl of scallop tomato stew and two cheesy toasts per person, perhaps with a simple tossed salad.

Four Notes

-It's crucial to use a clean, fresh-tasting tomato sauce—top-quality tomatoes and very little else. Too rich and hearty, and it will overpower everything; too sweet and syrupy, and you've wasted good scallops on something that's going to taste like ketchup. The Dell'Amore brand is excellent here.

-Don't worry about the decadent, high-fat cheesy toasts: remember, they're paired with a stew which is low calorie and almost entirely fat-free.

-Garlic bread with melted cheese is a great substitution for the cheesy toasts.

-A vegetarian version can be made by substituting cubed yellow summer squash for the scallops.

RIBBON PASTA WITH BROCCOLI, SPINACH, PINE NUTS AND FETA

Thyme and chili peppers are said to be antibacterial—in other words, good for you. I'm giving this nugget of information in case you need a reason to justify eating this luscious dish. So make, eat, go forth and conquer.

Serves 8

16 oz pkg ribbon pasta
½ C extra virgin olive oil (EVOO)
2 Tbsp butter
4 cloves garlic, minced
1 tsp dried basil
1 tsp dried thyme
1 tsp red pepper flakes
1 C pine nuts

4 C broccoli florets
4 C baby spinach
1 C pasta sauce (your favorite)
2 C crumbed feta
2 Tbsp Pecorino romano
drizzle of balsamic vinegar
½ tsp black pepper

Bring a large pot of water to a boil. Add pasta and cook for 8-10 minutes, or until pasta is al dente. Drain, transfer to a mixing bowl and set aside.

In the meantime gently warm EVOO and butter in a large skillet over medium-high heat, stirring to blend. Stir in garlic, basil, thyme and red pepper flakes, and reduce heat to medium. Add pine nuts and sauté just until lightly browned. Add broccoli, spinach and pasta sauce; cover skillet and cook on low heat for 5 minutes, or until broccoli is tooth-tender and spinach is wilted.

Toss broccoli and spinach mixture with pasta as soon as it has been drained. Spoon out onto individual plates and top with feta, romano, a drizzle of balsamic vinegar and a sprinkling of black pepper.

RICE FETTUCCINE WITH PUMPKIN SEED OIL

Pumpkin seed (aka Pepita) oil is made from Austrian pumpkins whose seeds have no hulls. It's a lovely, dark oil which is extracted by drying, crushing and mixing the seeds with water and salt to make them more digestible, then roasting at low temperature to evaporate the water. Once dried, seeds are pressed to extract the oil. It takes 5 pounds roasted seeds, or about 35 pumpkins, to make 2 C of the oil! The oil is heat sensitive, so don't cook with it.

Kurt is the one who first made this recipe for me. He proved that sometimes simpler is better, and you can have this satisfying dish in about 5 minutes flat. He also made this recipe wheat and dairy free, which is a nice change of pace for pasta.

Serves 4

1 pound rice fettuccine　　　　　　　　**½ C pumpkin seed oil**
1 Tbsp Celtic*sea salt

Fill a large pot ½ full with water and bring to a boil. Add pasta and stir. Cook for about 7 minutes, or until pasta is tooth-tender. Rice pasta can go from being perfect and al dente to overdone and mushy in a flash. So be careful not to overcook. Drain pasta.

Put pasta in a large mixing bowl and add pumpkin seed oil and salt. Toss. Serve. This goes nicely with steamed greens too.

*I'm mentioning Celtic sea salt here, instead of just sea salt. There are many terrific natural sea salts in the world, but the Celtic sea salt was Kurt's favorite. So in deference to Kurt, that's what the recipe calls for. Can you dress other foods such as grains and vegetables with pumpkin seed oil and Celtic sea salt? Yes, of course you can.

ROASTED VEGETABLES WITH GOAT CHEESE

A Greek historian, Zenophon, wrote in 349 B.C.E. about a goat cheese called Arabian Kishk, made from coagulated goat's milk, popular then and eaten in Peloponnesus. This early cheese, one website said, is probably the cheese that David carried with him before he went into battle against Goliath. Did David's healthy diet and the fact he ate a lot of goat cheese have anything to do with his winning the battle? Hmmm.

Goat milk has the same amount of protein and vitamins C and D as cow milk; but goat milk has more vitamins A and B, and the bioflavonoid riboflavin. Goat milk is non-allergenic, and children who are fed goat milk surpass those on cow milk for weight gain, stature, skeletal mineralization and bone density. So they say, hombre.

Serves 8

3 colored peppers, halved, cut into
    2" pieces
2 zucchini, about 4 C, sliced on slant
2 yellow squash, about 4 C, sliced
    on slant
2 thin oriental eggplants, about 6 C,
    sliced
2 red onions, quartered

Roast at 450 degrees

1 head cauliflower florets, about 4 C
1 C extra virgin olive oil (EVOO)
1 Tbsp black pepper
16 oz soft goat cheese
1-2 C oil-cured, pitted olives

Preheat oven to 450 degrees.

Cut vegetables. Place in a large baking dish, and toss with EVOO and black pepper.

Roast vegetable for about 30 minutes, stirring once or twice, or until vegetables are lightly brown and tooth-tender. Allow vegetables to cool to room temperature.

To serve, spoon vegetables onto a serving platter or 8 individual serving plates. Lay goat cheese alongside vegetables on one side of plate with the olives on the other. Of course, if you want, you can top the vegetables with the goat cheese and olives.

Note: You can serve this over pasta, any grain, or rolled into a sandwich with lavosh bread. If you want to use this for an antipasto, you might want to add artichoke hearts. And, yes, these vegetables are wonderful on the 2nd or 3rd day too.

SOUTHWESTERN CHEESY DELIGHT

I'm not sure why we think dishes with cheese automatically have to go with pasta. Here's a cheesy delight that pairs with rice instead of pasta.

Serves 4-6

3 Tbsp extra virgin olive oil (EVOO)
1 C brown rice, or other whole-grain
  rice
2 C boiling water
2 Tbsp EVOO
4 cloves garlic, minced
1 onion, chopped, about 2 C
1 sweet bell pepper, chopped, about 2 C
2 stalks celery, chopped, about 3 C
2 jalapeño peppers, seeded and minced

1 C sliced mushrooms
2 C tomato sauce
2 Tbsp Pecorino romano
1 lb assorted melting cheeses such
  as cheddar, havarti, mozzarella or
  Monterey jack, shredded
1 tsp dried oregano
1 tsp dried basil

Gently warm 3 Tbsp EVOO in a skillet. Add the rice and sauté until rice is aromatic, 1-2 minutes. Add boiling water, cover pot, turn heat to low and simmer rice 40 minutes.

In the meantime, gently warm 2 Tbsp EVOO in a second large skillet with a lid. Add all the chopped vegetables and sauté 10 minutes, stirring from time to time. Then add the tomato sauce and stir. Cover skillet, turn off flame and let the vegetable stew just sit.

As soon as the rice is cooked (it will be slightly al dente), add it to large skillet with the vegetables. Mix the whole concoction together, turn the flame back on low, cover pot and simmer 5 minutes.

Finally, remove the skillet cover so you can top the rice and vegetables with romano, melting cheeses, and oregano and basil. Cover skillet and steam until cheese is melted, a couple of minutes.

Note: If you don't have a large skillet with a lid, you can spoon cooked rice and sautéed vegetables into a lasagna-type pan and mix there. Then top rice and vegetables with cheese and herbs and bake in a hot 375 degree oven until cheese melts and begins to brown. You could cover the casserole with foil and bake for 30 minutes, then uncover and bake for another 15. It's up to you.

SZECHUAN NOODLES WITH TOFU BY AMANDA

This dish is made with mung bean noodles, which are called by many names, such as cellophane noodles, shining noodles, saifun noodles and Chinese vermicelli. They are almost flavorless, readily absorb other flavors and are also gluten-free.

Amanda says, "This is a great dish to experiment with your own taste palette because there are so many flavor components: agave and mirin for sweetness, tamari for salt and "umami" (Japanese for "tasty"), and lemon juice for tartness...You can learn a lot about yourself by seasoning! Personally, I love lots of everything."

Serves 4-6

about 3 C mung bean noodles
3 Tbsp extra virgin olive oil (EVOO) or toasted sesame oil
1 tsp cumin seed
1 tsp brown mustard seed
1 tsp chili flakes
1 lb asparagus or broccoli, trimmed and chopped into bite-sized pieces
1 tsp sea salt
3 Tbsp wheat-free tamari (soy sauce)
3 Tbsp mirin

2 Tbsp agave nectar
1 Tbsp garlic, minced
1 Tbsp ginger, minced
1 Tbsp sesame oil
1 Tbsp lemon juice
1-2 tsp arrowroot, dissolved in a little water (optional)
¼ C thinly sliced red onion
1 lb extra firm tofu
1 tsp ground Szechuan peppercorns (optional)

In a medium saucepan, bring water to a boil. Add mung noodles, turn off the heat and let them sit for 5 minutes. Then test one. Leave noodles in the water for a few more minutes if still too firm, otherwise drain and run cool water over them to stop the cooking. Set drained noodles aside in a large bowl and toss with 1 Tbsp oil.

Gently warm the remaining 2 Tbsp EVOO in a pan. Add cumin and mustard seeds. When the mustard seed begins to pop, add chili flakes and chopped broccoli or asparagus. Sprinkle with salt and sauté 2 minutes before adding tamari, mirin, agave, garlic, ginger, sesame oil and lemon. Stir and remove from the heat. Taste and correct the seasoning with tamari or agave if it isn't salty or sweet enough.

If you desire a thicker sauce, turn the heat back on and whisk in a little of the dissolved arrowroot. This will thicken the sauce admirably.

Scrape the contents of the pan onto the noodles and add the raw red onion. Toss well. Using the same pan the vegetables just came out of, crumble tofu and sauté until it is dry. Combine noodles, veggies and tofu. Add ground Szechuan peppercorns. Toss and taste for seasoning, adding extra tamari if you need to.

Note: You can add or garnish with anything you like such as scallions, cilantro, peanuts, cashews or toasted pumpkin seeds. Very versatile!

TAMALES STUFFED WITH ROASTED YAMS

You saw this in our November 2003 newsletter. A word to the wise: don't try and eat the husk that holds these nifty little packages. While it's true they're high in fiber, it's not the kind you can chew, much less digest!

Makes 15 tamales

2½ lb, or about 4 C cooked yams
1 lb, or about 2-3 C diced parsnips
1 C yellow cornmeal
4 Tbsp extra virgin olive oil (EVOO)
2 tsp ground cumin
1 tsp oregano
1 tsp sea salt

Bake at 450 degrees and 350 degrees

2 eggs (optional)
2 C great melting cheese like Monterey jack, cheddar, or havarti, shredded
1 pkg Los Chileros de Nuevo Mexico husks
chopped fresh cilantro

Preheat oven to 450 degrees.

Scrub yams and parsnips. (Up to you if you want to peel yams. I don't.) Poke yams with a knife, place yams and parsnips on pan, and roast at 450 degrees for about 1 hour. While yams and parsnips roast, bring a large pot of water to a boil, separate corn husks and plop them into the pot. (You'll need ½ the package for this recipe. Save the rest.) Let husks soak 1 hour to soften.

Remove veggies from oven, place in a bowl and mash together with all ingredients (except cheese and cilantro). This will be your dough. When dough is cool, mix in cheese.

Preheat oven to 350 degrees.

Lay corn husks on counter with point side facing away from you. Use 1 large husk or 2 small ones overlapping per tamale. Put ⅓ C dough in the middle of the corn husk and flatten slightly. Fold husk around the dough to form a packet. I do this by folding up the bottom and folding in the sides and rolling pretty tightly. (If you've time and want a prettier presentation, take 1 corn husk and tear lengthwise into ribbons and tie around both ends of the tamale, which means you just fold sides in and around filling.) In either case, place folded side down in an ovenproof dish from which you can also serve. Bake at 350 degrees until tamales are hot, about 20 minutes. Let cool for 5 minutes. Garnish with cilantro. Serve, hear 'em say, "Wow!"

Note: Tamales are something different and fun. These freeze well if you want to double the recipe and freeze ½ or more. Then all you have to do is take out of freezer, thaw, steam and serve.

TEFF POLENTA SMOTHERED WITH CHEESE

Teff is an amazing little grain. Did you know that 1 pound of teff can produce up to 1 ton of grain in only 12 weeks? And did you know that 3,000 grains of teff weigh 1 gram, and 1 gram equals 0.00220462262 of a pound? This, and the fact that teff can grow in inhospitable places and under dire weather conditions such as drought, make it an important grain.

Serves 4-6

2 C water
2 Tbsp extra virgin olive oil (EVOO)
8 cloves garlic, thickly sliced
1 C coarsely chopped onions
1 tsp dried basil
1 tsp dried oregano
2 tomatoes, chopped, about 2 C

Bake at 350 degrees

⅔ C teff
1 tsp sea salt
½ C Pecorino romano
1 C grated fontina*
1 C grated Bel Paese*
1 C grated mozzarella*

Boil water in a teakettle.

Place EVOO in a 10-12-inch skillet, and gently warm it over medium heat. Add garlic and onions. Sauté, stirring occasionally, for 5 minutes, or until onions are translucent and fragrant. Stir in the basil, oregano, tomato and teff.

Turn off the heat under the skillet so mixture won't bubble out and burn you. Carefully add boiling water. Stir and add salt and romano.

Preheat oven to 350 degrees.

Turn flame on again to low, cover pot and simmer the teff polenta for 10-15 minutes, stirring once or twice, until the water's absorbed. There may be some extra liquid from the tomatoes, but as long as the teff is not crunchy, the polenta is done.

Put grated cheeses on top, cover pot and put into the oven for about 5 minutes, just long enough for cheeses to melt. Let stand about 5 minutes out of the oven and cut into wedges to serve.

*I know I've specified definite cheeses above, but feel free to use a combination of favorites, or use only one kind...

VEGGIE LOVER'S PASTA AND SAUCE BY KRISTINA

From Kristina Joyce who has been shopping in our store for years and loves to share her recipes and her artwork. She says that her husband, who is definitely not a vegetarian, eats this with gusto.

Makes sauce for 4

⅔ C extra virgin olive oil (EVOO)
1 onion, halved and sliced into wedges
4 cloves garlic, minced
1 Portobella mushroom, medium slice
1 zucchini, medium slice
1 14.5 oz can Muir Glen diced
   tomatoes

1 7-oz jar Bionaturae tomato paste
some water to thin (optional)
¼ C (or more) sunflower seeds
1 Tbsp (or more) Maine Coast brand
   Triple Blend seasoning flakes
1 8-oz box Deboles linguine

In a large skillet with a lid, gently warm EVOO over medium-high heat,

Sauté onion wedges until they begin to brown, about 5 minutes. Add garlic, mushroom and zucchini. Quickly stir-fry 2 minutes, or until vegetables are just barely tender. Then add diced tomatoes and tomato paste. Stir 1 minute. If you choose, add some water to thin (fill the empty tomato paste jar to the top with water and shake—you don't waste any tomato paste this way). Then add sunflower seeds together with a generous sprinkling of Maine Coast Triple Blend seasoning flakes. Allow pasta sauce to simmer at least 30 minutes.

In a large pot, bring water to a boil. Add DeBoles linguine and cook according to directions on package. Drain linguini, divide among 4 individual servings plates and top with sauce.

Note: Kristina says she varies this recipe by adding a grated fresh carrot, diced celery or chopped parsley. I'd suggest sprinkling Pecorino romano on top.

Zucchini Orzo Pudding

Did you know that the zucchini is a member of the cucumber and melon family? People in Central and South America have been eating zucchini for thousands of years, but the zucchini we know today is a variety of summer squash developed in Italy. Zucchini means "small squash" in Italian, and the word squash comes from the Indian skutasquash meaning "green thing eaten green." History tells us that it was Christopher Columbus who brought the zucchini seeds to the Mediterranean and Africa.

Serves 4-6

Bake at 350 degrees in a 9x13 pan

2 C water
1 lb zucchini, quartered lengthwise, thin sliced
1 C orzo pasta
2 C grated melting cheese, such as cheddar

1 egg, beaten
¼ C extra virgin olive oil (EVOO)
pinch of nutmeg
½ tsp sea salt
1 tsp black pepper

Bring water to a boil in a small saucepan. Add zucchini to boiling water, lower heat, cover pot and simmer for 5 minutes, or until zucchini is soft. Drain (but save liquid to drink or to use in breads, stews or soups).

Preheat oven to 350 degrees.

At the same time bring a large pot ½ full of water to a boil. Add orzo and cook until al dente, about 5-7 minutes. Drain pasta.

Mash zucchini in a bowl. Add 1 C cheese (save 1 C for the top), egg, orzo, EVOO, nutmeg, salt and black pepper. Mix. Spoon everything into a 9x13 baking pan, top with remaining cheese and put pan into oven.

Bake 15 minutes, or until cheese is melty and begins to brown.

Blue Ribbon Edition

Breakfast Goodies

Breakfast can be whatever you feel like. Pancakes? Sure. Whole-grain cereal? Naturally. But growing up, often as not, breakfast in our house would be something completely different. If Mom had bananas that needed to be used, we got a banana split smothered in peanut butter with strawberries, peaches and pineapple on the side. If there were leftover hamburgers (made with grass-fed, organic beef or lamb), we got those on a whole-grain bun for breakfast.

And there was the infamous "egg drink." My brother, Daniel, in his book *Silence of the Bunnies*, describes that best.

"How could a woman who was so warm and loving be transformed into Attila the Hun when it came to food? You think I exaggerate? Let's start with breakfast. One cannot mention the word in my family without two feared words coming to mind—"egg drink." That was the concoction made daily by my mother for which we could have had her hauled away for abuse. It was made with a raw egg base*, into which would be poured all sorts of healthy powders—dolomite, carob, calcium, or frankly anything that had received a favorable write-up in *Prevention Magazine*. This was then mixed together in a blender with water, or milk if the latter was starting to go bad. It produced a brown-looking drink, with a brackish head of foam. It chilled the soul to look at it, and scarred the soul to drink it.

"But mom always was looking to improve it. In fact, our liberation from egg drinks came the day she decided to add the egg shells along with the eggs, in order to increase the calcium content. Why not? It would all go through the blender. The usual decibel level at the breakfast table went off the charts, and my mother finally agreed to taste her own drink to see what all the fuss was about. She immediately pronounced it undrinkable, and asked in complete and maddening sincerity why we had never said something about it."

There is no moral to this story, but do make breakfast an adventure. Share the world of food with someone you love. Or enjoy different foods even if you're by yourself. The other morning, for instance, I had some plums and a bowl of hot cereal. Yesterday it was smoked salmon and a cucumber salad. I think I might make pancakes tomorrow. It's all okay. (cont.)

So there are no rules for breakfast as long as you don't skip it! Eating breakfast is how you fuel your engine, and when you eat a good breakfast, it starts your day off right.

*In fact, Mom coddled her eggs because she didn't believe in eating them raw. She never claimed to be Rocky...

AYURVEDIC BREAKFAST TOAST
for busy, back-to-school or work mornings...

This one appeared in our September 2004 newsletter. Adam wrote back then that research shows cinnamon lowers blood sugar by making insulin work more efficiently, and may also lower cholesterol. He wrote that the noted naturopathic doctor, Bill Mitchell, saw impressive results with his patients' cholesterol when they took ½ tsp of the powdered spice twice a day.

Turmeric is touted in Ayurveda (and elsewhere) as an antioxidant and anti-inflammatory. Ginger is said to improve circulation, and we all know ginger is the first thing we think about for nausea. Did you know it's also said to be good for nervousness? And who isn't nervous going back to school or heading to a new job?

Enjoy the ghee or coconut oil! Don't worry about these fats. According to Ayurvedic medicine they're not stored like other fats, but boost energy and endurance, support thyroid function and increase metabolism. They also are said to improve absorption of fat soluble vitamins, minerals (especially calcium and magnesium) and amino acids.

Make toast on any chilly morning. Take a minute to enjoy.

Serves 4

3 Tbsp honey or maple syrup
2 Tbsp ghee or coconut oil
1 Tbsp cinnamon

1 tsp ginger
½ tsp turmeric
4 whole wheat English muffins or 8 slices whole-grain bread

Using a fork, combine honey or maple syrup with ghee or coconut oil and all spices until well blended. (Both ghee and coconut oil can be kept at room temperature. When they are, they become soft and are easily mixed with other things.)

Slice muffins in half and toast. If you're using bread, toast those slices. Spread the spiced butter mixture on the toasted muffins or toast, and serve with another sprinkle of cinnamon and a mug of your favorite herbal tea or warm milk (of any kind).

Note: Enjoy every lip-smacking bite! You might want to serve with a glass of kefir or two soft-boiled eggs. How about with half a grapefruit or a bowl of berries?

BASIC BREAKFAST HOT CEREAL

I love hot cereal, and it's one of the easiest ways to serve and eat whole grains. Hot cereal was my favorite breakfast growing up, especially because Mom let us choose what we wanted to add or mix in to our individual bowls. Milk and honey? Butter and salt? Raisins and cream? These were some of our wonderful choices. It was only when Mom started adding in things like wheat germ to make sure we got top nutrition that hot cereal caused us to groan.

I chose the grains below because I like them, but also because they have lots of protein. Cooked amaranth contains about 20 grams of protein per cup, oats about 19 grams, quinoa has 18, and buckwheat (no relation to wheat) has 19. White rice, if you want some means of comparison, has 11 grams of protein per cooked cup.

Botanically, both buckwheat and quinoa are fruits, and all but the oats are gluten-free. If gluten is an issue for you, you can purchase gluten-free oats too.

Feel free to just use oats, or just buckwheat. Whatever grain or combination of grains that suits you!

Serves 2-4

4 C water
1 C buckwheat (kasha)
½ C quinoa
½ C rolled oats
2 Tbsp millet

2 Tbsp amaranth
1 tsp sea salt
mix-ins/toppings such as milk, honey, maple syrup, cinnamon, butter and salt, raisins, dates, coconut, sunflower seeds

In a saucepan with a tight-fitting lid, bring the water to a boil. Add grains and salt. Stir once to distribute grains. Lower heat, cover pot and move partially off the flame. Simmer cereal for 25 minutes. Remove from heat. Serve with whatever your heart desires.

Note: My mother would often combine many grains with 3 times the amount of boiling water in a crockpot or thermos overnight. Wake up and breakfast was ready.

BASIC PANCAKE FLIPS

Though the batter takes just minutes to make, I often make a double or triple batch to freeze. It's easy to make extra when you're close-by the kitchen doing other things anyway. How do you reheat pancakes? I reheat by putting a few pancakes per person on individual oven-proof plates and sousing with maple syrup (and sometimes butter too) before putting the plates into a 350 degree oven for about 5-10 minutes.

Serves 4

butter or coconut oil for greasing
6 eggs
2 C milk (any such as sour, soy, rice, oat, almond, coconut or hemp)
1 tsp vanilla or almond extract
1 C nut meal (almond, hemp, sesame, pecan, coconut, sunflower, etc.)
1 tsp cinnamon

1 C sprouted spelt flour, or any other flour such as buckwheat or millet
½ tsp sea salt
2 tsp baking powder
1 C blueberries, fresh or frozen, maple syrup, honey, agave or jam (optional)

Choose the pancake setting for your griddle and preheat. Or heat a cast-iron skillet. If using a cast iron skillet, once it's nice and hot, turn flame down to medium-low.

Grease griddle or skillet with butter or coconut oil. I like a nice big dollop of coconut oil and make sure I have my vent/exhaust fan going at the same time.

In a mixing bowl, using a fork, mix together eggs, milk and either vanilla or almond extract. Add dry ingredients and mix quickly. Not too much mixing or your pancakes will be tough!

Immediately drop batter by ¼ cupfuls onto griddle or skillet. If you choose to use blueberries, press those lightly into batter now.

Bake until bubbles form and begin to pop on the unbaked side, 1-2 minutes. Flip pancakes.

Bake until brown on the second side, another 1-2 minutes.

Serve with maple syrup, honey, agave or jam. I like mine with lots and lots of maple syrup!

Note: Want to make a blueberry sauce to pour over the pancakes? Warm 1 C of blueberries in a little pot together with 2 C of the sweetener of your choice (mine is maple syrup). Mash blueberries in sweetener and then either spoon warm sauce over the pancakes or bring to the table in a little pitcher.

BLUEBERRY AMARANTH AND TEFF BUBBLE

This comes from a 2006 cooking class. Using amaranth and teff this way was definitely a stretch, but I was trying to introduce different grains. Humor me. Try these terrific little grains.

Both amaranth and teff resist heat and drought, have no major disease problems and are among the easiest of plants to grow. Each plant produces more than 50,000 seeds, which have more protein and fiber, by far, than wheat. I'm not saying we shouldn't eat wheat, I'm only saying it's good to diversify and eat a variety of foods. And doesn't doing so make life more interesting too?

Serves 6
1 C boiling water
½ C teff
½ C amaranth
1 C maple syrup or coconut sugar
1 Tbsp lemon juice

Bake at 350 degrees
6 C blueberries*, fresh or frozen
1 tsp cinnamon
½ tsp nutmeg
pinch sea salt
pinch thyme

Preheat oven to 350 degrees.

In a small saucepan, bring the water to a boil, and then add the teff and amaranth. Cover pot, lower heat and simmer for 10 minutes, or just until water has been absorbed and grains have begun to soften. Timing, for me, seems to differ according to humidity and even the time of year. Go figure.

Mix everything together in an oven-proof baking dish. Put dish in oven and bake 1 hour, or until blueberries bubble. Remove from oven and spoon into serving bowls. Serve warm, room temperature or cold.

Note: This is great with a yogurt topping, or with a glass of milk.

*You can use any fruit that bakes well, such as apples, pears, peaches or nectarines. This dish is a great way to use up banged-up fruit. Feel free to mix fruit too, and use up an apple, a pear and some blueberries. Mixing different berries, such as blueberries, cranberries and raspberries, is a winner too. I often use a frozen mix of wild Italian berries that we have in the store.

CHRIS'S CHEEZY SOUTHWESTERN BREAKFAST BURRITO

The *Encyclopedia of American Food and Drink* by John F. Mariani says, "Burrito. A tortilla rolled and cooked on a griddle, then filled with a variety of condiments. Burritos are a Mexican-American staple. The word, from the Spanish, means 'little donkey' and first saw print in America in 1934."

Chris made this one day for us in the store. He had just discovered the Field Roast veggie apple-sage sausages, and was pleased as punch that we absolutely loved the burritos he made.

Serves 2

3 eggs
½ C milk
2 tsp ground cumin
1 tsp sea salt
1 tsp black pepper
1 Tbsp extra virgin olive oil (EVOO)
½ green pepper, chopped, about 1 C
½ onion, chopped, about 1 C

1 jalapeño pepper, seeded, sliced
1 Field Roast brand veggie apple-sage sausage, halved, sliced ¼-inch slices
2 C grated pepperjack cheese
2 whole-wheat tortillas
1 tomato, chopped, about 1 C
ripe melon slices as accompaniment

Chris says to whisk eggs, milk, cumin, salt and pepper in a bowl. Lightly oil a pan or small skillet and sauté pepper, onion and jalapeño until almost tender, about 5 minutes. Then add sausage and continue sautéing until the sausage is lightly browned.

Pour egg mixture over pepper-sausage mixture and scramble just so eggs are cooked. Add cheese and let it melt. Divide this wonderful, hot mixture between the two tortillas. Top with tomato and roll the tortillas into burritos.

Serve with slice of your favorite local organic melon.

DATE CARDAMOM MORNING DRINK

This came to us from Ric Scalzo, founder of Gaia Herbs. Gaia, formerly out in Harvard, has its fields and laboratories in North Carolina today. We stay in touch with Ric and when we sent him organic Israeli Medjool dates, he pronounced them the best he ever had and perfect for the recipe below, which builds Ojas (strength and energy in the Ayurvedic tradition).

Why did Ric choose some of the ingredients he did? Cardamom, a member of the ginger family, helps digestion. Dates are considered energy and brain food, and weight for weight contain more potassium than bananas. Dates also are high in fiber and are loaded with B vitamins (the nerve and stress vitamins). Why the rose syrup or rose water? Rose is said to be a powerful tonic for the heart. It enhances positive emotions, and intensifies the experience of happiness and bliss. What better way to start the day! Last but not least, cinnamon helps stabilize blood sugar...

Serves 2

2 C milk (almond, hemp, rice, goat, cow or any other kind that floats your boat)
24 raw almonds (soaked overnight)*
4 Medjool dates, pitted

pinch saffron
1 teaspoon cardamom
1 pinch cinnamon
2 Tbsp Purely Organic brand rose petal syrup, or use rosewater

Blend all together at high speed for several minutes and then drink as a morning energy drink.

Ric says that almonds are more easily digested and blend more easily if you remember to soak them overnight. It's not essential to soak them, he says. I use 2 Tbsp of almond butter instead of whole almonds when making this drink and that solves the problem for me!

GLUTEN-FREE MUESLI

It was Dr. Maximilian Bircher-Benner, in his sanatorium in Switzerland, who first promoted muesli in the early part of the 20th century. Dr. Bircher-Benner prescribed life modeled on the life of Swiss shepherds for his patients, because he believed shepherds led the healthiest of lives. The Bircher-Benner model included daily physical exercise and gardening, and a diet of hearty wholegrains together with nuts and seeds. No meat.

I don't believe the original muesli included dried fruit, and it was based on oats and wheat, not rice and quinoa. You can use whatever you like. If the rice flakes are too hard for you, feel free to use more gluten-free oats.

Makes 23 C, or about 15 servings

4 C rice flakes
4 C gluten-free rolled oats
4 C quinoa flakes
2 C sunflower seeds
1 C Chia or hemp seeds

2 C raisins
2 C sliced almonds
2 C dried apricots, diced, or 2 C date pieces
2 C shredded coconut or coconut fiber

Combine these ingredients and store in the freezer or in an airtight container in the refrigerator.

To serve, put about 1½ C muesli per person in a bowl. Top with any kind of milk or fruit juice. You can add some fresh fruit too.

Note: Some people like to add liquid to muesli and let it soak overnight. I don't find this necessary. Alternatively, you can use this to make a hot cereal too. Simply cover a portion with your choice of liquid and then simmer gently for 5 minutes. Eat warm.

HOMEY FARMHOUSE OMELET

Just right for the dark of winter, this appeared in our February 2004 newsletter. February is indeed dark in New England!

In this dish, shiitakes boost the immune system, eggs are good protein, and the spices warm and increase circulation. The whole house smells fragrant too. This is a real treat.

Aren't you glad eggs are back? They don't deserve a bad rap, do they? I use eggs from happy chickens that run around and hunt and peck for bugs. These eggs taste so much better and, I'm sure, are so much better for me too.

Serves 4

¼ C extra virgin olive oil (EVOO), or butter, ghee or coconut oil
2 C chopped red onion
4 C fresh shiitake mushrooms or ½ C dried shiitake pieces*
1-inch piece fresh ginger, minced
½ tsp turmeric
2 tsp garam masala or curry powder
½ tsp chili powder
1 tsp coriander
4 tomatoes, diced, about 4 C
2 Tbsp yogurt
1 tsp sea salt
1 tsp black pepper
1 Tbsp lemon juice
8 eggs
5 oz baby spinach watercress as garnish

In a large skillet, gently warm EVOO. Add onion and stir to coat. Sauté on medium heat while you coarsely chop mushrooms and mince ginger. (I use the mushroom stems, and I don't peel the ginger because the ginger I use is organic.) Add mushrooms and ginger to skillet and stir everything together. Continue to sauté about 5 minutes. Add turmeric, garam masala or curry powder, chili powder and coriander. Sniff. Nirvana!

Add in diced tomatoes, yogurt, sea salt, black pepper and lemon juice. Sauté another 5 minutes (you may need to add a little more oil). In a little bowl, beat the eggs with a fork. Pour them into the skillet and top with spinach. Cover pot and reduce heat to low. Let mixture cook about 10 minutes. Serve right away. You can garnish with watercress for an edible, peppery addition.

If using dried shiitakes, soften them by soaking in hot water for 20 minutes. Squeeze the mushrooms dry before using in omelet. Save the soaking water to drink or to add to soups.

JIM'S ALVARADO SPROUTED BAGEL BREAKFAST

Jim says, "Avocados are my weekend treat. Andrew Weil sang their praises and suggested using avocados in place of butter. That's what I've been doing for a long while with this recipe, which I enjoy because of its flexibility."

What makes sprouted wheat bagels different? When most bakeries get going in the morning, they open up a bag of flour and make something. At Alvarado Street Bakery, whole organic wheat berries are soaked in filtered water until they sprout, or actually begin to grow. The living sprouts, which make moist dough, are used, not a dry powdered flour.

Makes 4 bagel halves

2 Alvarado Street Sprouted Bagels	**few slices Organic Valley sharp**
2 Tbsp Linabella's pesto	**cheddar or muenster cheese**
1 avocado	**sliced tomato**

Jim says to cut the bagels in half and toast them. Spread about ½ Tbsp of Linabella's pesto on each half of both bagels. Take avocado and divide into 4, then spread ¼ on each bagel half.

You can eat your bagel this way or add a few slices of cheese. In either case, top with a slice of tomato.

Alternatively, you can spread the avocado on the bagel and use the pesto as a topper. You can use more or less of the pesto. You can even add another bagel for an unexpected guest because this recipe is just Jim's excuse, he says, to mix together some of his favorite foods.

Note: Jim says that Linabella's Honey Pesto is delicious. If you want to be adventurous, try their Garlic Lover's or Maple Pesto.

MIDDLE EASTERN BREAKFAST

Just to completely shake things up, here's a smorgasbord you might be served for breakfast in Israel.

Serves 2

pickled herring
smoked salmon
smoked mackerel
hard-boiled or scrambled eggs
white cheeses and labany or Greek-
   style yogurt
olives of all kinds
assorted rolls and breads
pickled beets
pickled carrots and cabbage

SALAD
2 tomatoes, chopped
2 pickling cucumbers, chopped
½ C chopped scallions or red onion
1 small sweet pepper, chopped
2 Tbsp extra virgin olive oil (EVOO)
1 Tbsp lemon juice
½ sea salt
½ tsp black pepper
watercress as garnish

Make a wonderful smorgasbord. The only thing you need to fuss with is the salad, and here's how you do that: Gently toss together tomatoes, cucumbers, scallions or red onion and pepper together with the EVOO, lemon, and salt and pepper.

Can't you just visualize the colors?

Note: You don't need to serve everything, of course, but you can put out whatever you have, and what floats your boat.

MOM'S BREAKFAST FRUIT PLATE

I mentioned this in the introduction to this section of the cookbook. I used to love this rainbow breakfast; it made me feel as if all were right with the world. And it was great fun trying to decide what to eat first. The strawberries? Pineapple? Usually I chose the banana and peanut butter first so I wouldn't be left with peanut butter stuck to the roof of my mouth.

You do have to plan ahead to make sure you have a variety of fruit on hand, and enough for everyone. But what a treat, what a breakfast! Not even the fanciest hotel serves a breakfast like this...

Per person

1 banana, peeled and cut into half, lengthwise
2 Tbsp peanut butter, or nut butter of your choice
1 C strawberries, washed and hulled
½ C blueberries, rinsed
1 C pineapple, peeled and cut
a few grapes, slice of mango or papaya
1 Medjool date

Place the banana on a plate and top with peanut butter. Yes, it's hard to spread. Sometimes peanut butter that is warm or more oily spreads more easily. Not to worry. If you can't spread it, glob it on. It will still taste terrific.

Place the rest of the fruit in order, going around the plate. You'll have red strawberries, then blue blueberries and then golden pineapple. You get the idea. Put the Medjool date wherever you want.

Note: Can you use other fruit instead? Of course! If you have black mission figs, those are wonderful. Do you prefer blackberries to blueberries? Go for it! Raspberries instead of strawberries? Be my guest.

OMELET WITH TARRAGON AND POTATOES

Another wonderful egg dish that makes a hearty breakfast. I'm going to make myself this omelet right now with the last of the potatoes I dug up in my garden last weekend!

HealthDiaries.com says, "Eggs are great for the eyes. According to one study, an egg a day may prevent macular degeneration due to the carotenoid content, specifically lutein and zeaxanthin. Both nutrients are more readily available to our bodies from eggs than from other sources. In another study, researchers found that people who eat eggs every day lower their risk of developing cataracts, also because of the lutein and zeaxanthin in eggs."

Serves 4

½ C extra virgin olive oil (EVOO), or butter, ghee or coconut oil

2 onions, coarsely chopped, about 4 C

4 potatoes*, boiled and cubed, about 6 C

6 eggs

2 tsp dried tarragon

1 tsp sea salt

1 tsp black pepper

Gently warm EVOO, butter, ghee or coconut oil in a skillet and sauté the onions until they are nice and soft, about 5 minutes. Add cubed potatoes and fry until lightly colored, about another 5 minutes.

In a small bowl, beat eggs with tarragon and salt and pepper, and pour over the potato mixture. Cook until almost set. Cover the pan with a plate and invert. Slip the omelet back into the pan to cook and brown the other side. Serve this homey omelet hot or cold.

I like Yukon gold potatoes best in this omelet, but feel free to use another variety.

PECAN CHESTNUT WAFFLES

Gluten-free by Susan Turner, who gave us this recipe that she developed for a friend. It appeared in our January 2006 newsletter. Susan says, "Chestnut flour is expensive, but worth it for the flavor. If nuts are an issue, substitute an equal volume of a combination of flours like rice, millet, corn, or oat (many celiacs do fine with oats). If you want to substitute oil for butter, feel free to do that too!"

Makes 12 waffles

1⅓ C quinoa flour
⅔ C chestnut flour
¾ C pecans, finely chopped
big pinch salt
1 tsp baking powder
¼ tsp ground cardamom
zest of 1 lemon, or ½ an orange

1 Tbsp coconut sugar
3 eggs, separated, whites beaten to
  stiff peaks
⅛ C water
1 Tbsp or more melted butter, ghee, or
  oil of your choice
1 Tbsp gluten-free vanilla*

Start heating a lightly oiled waffle iron. Choose the "browner" setting, so the griddle gets nice and hot. Mix all the dry ingredients in a good-sized bowl. Add the egg yolks, melted butter and vanilla, and stir (all the dry stuff won't mix in...just get the mixing started). Add the water in batches, stirring quickly, to make a loose-ish batter. Then, fold in the egg whites—mixing enough that there aren't great chunks of egg white, but not so much as to deflate the batter.

Cook 'em up, using about 1/3 C batter for each waffle. The hot griddle makes all the difference. You want waffles that are crisp on the outside.

Susan sent me toppings to try besides the usual straight maple syrup. Here are two. **(1) Maple cranberry compote:** Put 1 C of maple syrup in a saucepan together with ½ C fresh cranberries. Bring to a boil, reduce heat, simmer, stirring occasionally, until the cranberries burst. Ladle over waffles or pancakes. **(2) Full-fat Greek-style or sheep's milk yogurt and rose syrup:** Put two waffles on a plate, top with a generous dollop of yogurt and a drizzle of rose syrup.

Note: If you want to use this recipe to make pancakes, Susan suggests increasing the water to 1¼ C and the melted butter to 1½ Tbsp.

Singing Dog vanilla is our favorite gluten-free vanilla. It's the only one we use in our kitchen in the store.

POMEGRANATE SMOOTHIE

This delish, stress-buster breakfast contains whey protein, which according to my son, Adam, is the best protein out of a can. Protein builds muscles and prevents dieters from losing muscle. The body uses protein to make mood-regulating brain chemicals and hormones and to stabilize blood sugar. And the enzymes that digest food in the gut, neutralize toxins in the liver and fight infections are all proteins. Protein is the very stuff of life. It truly is that basic, Adam says.

Pomegranates are one of the oldest fruits known to man. There is recorded history of pomegranates as food in China around 100 B.C.E. Too bad the fruit is such a mess to eat, but the concentrate is pretty darn good too.

Borage oil is great for skin problems like eczema. Brewer's yeast (aka nutritional yeast) is the richest source of the B-vitamins—the nerve and stress vitamins.

Makes 2 generous servings

2 C water, or your favorite milk or juice

2 sliced bananas (I use ripe ones I've peeled and frozen)

2 C strawberries or blueberries

2 Tbsp pomegranate concentrate

2 Tbsp Chia seeds

¼ C or 1 scoop whey protein powder

1 Tbsp brewer's yeast (optional)

2 Tbsp flax or hemp seed oil (optional)

½ tsp borage oil (optional)

1 tsp bee pollen (optional)

drizzle fish oil (optional)

Using a blender, blend ingredients. Isn't that fast? The hardest part about this recipe is getting out the ingredients…Pour out for 2 hungry people. Drink. Make like Superman or Superwoman.

Note: Instead of whey protein powder, feel free to substitute two coddled eggs per person. Eggs are the best source of protein known to man or woman! You all know how I feel about eggs, they're great food. Remember that egg yolks contain lecithin, which is used for all kinds of things like fat metabolism and to lower bad cholesterol. Remember those studies of twins—one of whom came to this country, the other stayed home in Ireland and France. The twin who came to this country and adopted our diet developed heart disease. The twin who stayed home and ate real foods like eggs and butter as part of a balanced diet had no heart or cholesterol problems. So eggs are not the culprit!

Coddle eggs by boiling water, adding eggs to pot and counting to 30. That's all. That's what my mother used to use in her infamous egg drinks. They were infamous, not because of the eggs, but because of all the other stuff she used to add with gay abandon. (See excerpt from *Silence of the Bunnies* by brother, Daniel Stark.)

POPPY SEED RICOTTA PANCAKES

Poppy seeds, used to give a nutty flavor and texture to baked goods, are used primarily in Middle Eastern, Eastern European and Asian cuisine. Considered to be a digestive aid, poppy seeds are also rich in calcium and, like all seeds, contain goodly amounts of protein and healthy fats.

Makes about 24 pancakes

1 lb ricotta cheese
4 eggs
½ C whole wheat pastry flour or
    nut meal
2 Tbsp melted butter, ghee or oil
2 Tbsp honey, maple syrup or agave
1 Tbsp vanilla extract

2 Tbsp poppy seeds
pinch cinnamon
1 Tbsp orange or lemon zest
½ C water or orange juice
butter, coconut oil, ghee or your
    favorite oil for greasing

Choose the pancake setting for your griddle and preheat. Or heat a cast-iron skillet. If using a cast-iron skillet, once it's reached a nice, hot temperature, turn flame under it to medium-low.

Grease griddle or skillet. I like a nice big dollop of coconut oil, and I make sure I have my vent/exhaust fan going at the same time.

Mix all the ingredients together to make the batter. Drop batter by generous Tbsp onto griddle or skillet. Cook until bubbles appear in center of unflipped side of pancake, about 1-2 minutes. Flip and brown on second side another 1-2 minutes.

Serve with your favorite topping. Mine is definitely maple syrup. My father used honey.

Note: Want to make these pancakes savory instead of sweet? Simply take out all the sweet stuff and add ¼ C sliced scallions, 1 tsp dried basil and 1 tsp dried oregano. Serve with salsa and avocado.

QUINOA BREAKFAST CEREAL

Sherry Seaver shared this recipe with us some years ago. Here quinoa is prepared in the Ayurvedic tradition, with cinnamon and ghee. Quinoa is the gluten-free "supergrain" Inca warriors ate to stay healthy. Neither Sherry nor I are promising you'll have the strength of a warrior if you eat this, but you will love knowing you had some super food.

Ghee (also known as clarified butter) is a staple in Indian cooking. Ghee is simply butter that has been boiled until all the water evaporates and the milk solids cook off. The resulting product can be stored at room temperature for a year or more, is great for high heat cooking and is fine for those who can't do dairy. It's not hard to make, but I mostly buy my ghee so I don't have another thing to add to my to-do list!

Serves 2-3

1 C quinoa
2 C water or milk of any kind
1 apple, diced, about 1 C
1 Tbsp coconut flakes
1 tsp cinnamon

½ C almonds or walnuts, ground
1 Tbsp ghee
maple syrup, honey, stevia, coconut
  sugar or agave

Combine quinoa and water or milk. Bring to a boil. Add apple, coconut, cinnamon, ground nuts and ghee. Lower heat, cover pot and simmer about 15 minutes, or until liquid is absorbed. Serve with the sweetener of your choice.

Note: Try adding raisins, dates, rosewater, cardamom or whatever variation floats your boat...

RUSSIAN MILLET AND PUMPKIN PORRIDGE

Pumpkins complement millet, and when you make this dish, you'll be making a time-honored Eastern European dish. Just goes to show that food and culture are all mixed up—pumpkins, pumpkins, pumpkins everywhere. And millet is a staple in Asia, Africa, Eastern Europe and maybe, soon, here too. We get even more multicultural with this dish because we're using coconut oil from the South Pacific. This is certainly not your average breakfast, is it?

Millet is the most alkaline of grains, and it helps balance our modern Western diets that make us too acidic. Did you know that even stress makes us more acidic? So eating millet is a good thing!

Oliver Twist knew his millet, a key ingredient in gruel. He asked, "Please sir, may I have more?" Millet cooked with water as gruel was known to sustain life during difficult times. More recently, cattle fed millet versus corn were found to be healthier too.

Did you know that millet can be grown and harvested more than once a year too? It's prolific and hardy!

Serves 6

3 Tbsp coconut oil or butter
2 C peeled, diced pumpkin, fresh or frozen
1 Tbsp cinnamon
3 C milk (any kind, including coconut)

Bake at 325 degrees

1 C millet
½ tsp sea salt
2 Tbsp honey or maple syrup
½ C brown, unhulled sesame seeds

Preheat oven to 325 degrees.

On the stove top, in an ovenproof skillet or casserole dish with a tight-fitting lid, melt coconut oil or butter. Add pumpkin and cinnamon and sauté 5 minutes. Pumpkin will soften and cinnamon will become aromatic. Add milk and bring mixture to a gentle boil.

Add everything else. Stir until sweetener is dissolved. Cover pot or casserole and place in oven. Bake 30-45 minutes, or until millet has absorbed the liquid and is dry.

When you're ready to serve, fluff millet with fork. Serve with additional coconut oil or butter if that's your pleasure.

SALLY'S OMELET

Jennifer says, "Sally was my mother who taught me everything I know about love and chasing sunsets."

Eating eggs promotes healthy hair and nails. It's their high sulfur and rich B-vitamin content that does that for us. When I eat more eggs, my hair and nails grow faster!

Serves 4

3 eggs
⅓ C milk
1 tsp sea salt
1 tsp black pepper
½ C extra virgin olive oil (EVOO), or
   butter

⅓ C chopped red onion
½ C feta cheese, crumbled
½ C green olives, pitted and chopped
1 small tomato, chopped, about ½ C

Mix eggs with milk and salt and pepper.

Heat a non-stick pan or cast-iron skillet and add the EVOO or butter. Pour in egg and milk mixture. Cook over medium heat just until the bottom stops "slipping around." Add onion, and spread evenly over eggs. Do the same with the feta cheese.

When the feta has begun to melt, add the olives and tomato. As the ingredients melt and warm, fold ½ the omelet over on itself to make a half-moon. Allow that side to cook for about 30 seconds, then flip the entire omelet and let it cook on the other side while turning the flame to low. Serve warm and enjoy every bite!

Scrambled Eggs with Chard and Goat Cheese

I just made the most delicious breakfast in 5 minutes. You can expand on this theme in umpteen ways, and that's why I'm putting the recipe here. Go for it, habibi!

Grown as an edible ornamental, chard comes in red, yellow and white, all with brilliant green and purple leaves. Chard is known as the beet without the root, but is also related to quinoa (I had no idea). I relish the crunchy stems of the chard, and I love the fact it's a hardy green. As I write this in November, following a few hard frosts, my chard is still growing. I go out, snip some leaves and let the plant continue to grow.

Serves 2

10-12 leaves and stems of chard
¼ C water

2 rounds of Kunik* cheese, each
¼-inch thick
2 eggs

Quickly rinse greens under running water and then chop roughly, stems and all. Put chard in a large skillet, add water and top with Kunik cheese. Cover pot and turn heat to low. Let chard steam for 5 minutes.

When you take off the cover, the chard should be wilted and the cheese melted. Crack eggs into skillet and stir vigorously. Cover pot and let the mixture sit for another few minutes.

When you serve, you'll see that the eggs and cheese have become a wonderful creamy sauce for the chard. You'll note with amazement, that for once I didn't add any garlic or black pepper!

*Kunik cheese from Nettle Meadow in NY is a white, lovely melting cheese made form goats' milk with jersey cow cream. Their label says, "This cheese is a sumptuous concentration of the organic grains and wild herbs our goats eat everyday, including wild raspberry leaf, nettle, kelp, comfrey, garlic, barley and goldenrod."

SESAME-HEMP SEED WAFFLES

I don't know why waffles seem so exotic. They are a snap to make. Did you know that they've been around since the time of ancient Greece and Rome? And that Cornelius Swarthout got the first patent for a waffle iron in this country on August 24, 1869?

Serves 4

1½ C quinoa flakes (or oatmeal)
1½ C cornmeal
¼ C sesame seeds
¼ C hemp seeds, ground
1 tsp sea salt
1½ C water or milk of any kind

1 Tbsp extra virgin olive oil (EVOO)
   or butter or coconut oil
1 egg
2 apples, cored and sliced
1 C maple syrup
1 Tbsp cinnamon

Blend quinoa flakes, cornmeal, sesame seeds, hemp seed powder, salt, water and EVOO together with the egg.

Ladle onto a hot, greased waffle iron and follow directions. My waffle iron has a light that comes on and tells me when it's time to take the waffle out. I hope yours does too!

In the meantime, while the waffles are cooking, put apples, maple syrup and cinnamon in a little saucepan. Simmer until apples are tender and soft, about 5 minutes.

Serve waffles with apple syrup. What a treat!

WHOLE-GRAIN CEREAL, ANOTHER WAY

Here's another cereal mixture, in case you didn't like the first one. You might want to try this combination with gomasio, a sesame salt mixture. Or you can go the sweet route with honey, maple syrup, agave, coconut sugar or fresh fruit.

If you want to use milk or cream, that's fine, but try the milks made from plant sources like hemp and almond as well.

Makes 17 C dry mix

4 C oat groats*
4 C wheat or rye flakes
2 C hulled barley*

4 C toasted, hulled buckwheat (kasha)
1 C Chia seeds
2 C millet

Mix all these grains and store in the freezer. The mix will keep forever.

How to make this into hot cereal: Scoop out ½ C of the mixed grains per person. Bring 3 parts of water to a boil. So if you're making hot cereal for 2, bring 3 C of water to a boil. Add 1 C grain mixture and stir pot. Bring cereal to a boil again. Remove pot from heat. Cover and let sit overnight. In the morning simply reheat.

Or you can use my mother's method mentioned before. Put grain and boiling water into a thermos or crockpot, and your cereal will be ready to eat in the morning as well.

If this cereal is too chewy for you, substitute rolled barley flakes for hulled barley, and rolled oats for oat groats. You could also add more water the next morning and cook some more.

WILL'S APPLE CINNAMON APRICOT CRÊPES

I drove Will crazy in the kitchen one day as he was making these. He made the recipe so many times he never wanted to see another crêpe, but the results are worth the aggravation.

Serves 4

BATTER
1¼ C whole wheat pastry flour
½ C water
½ C milk
2 Tbsp butter
½ tsp nutmeg
1½ tsp cinnamon
1 tsp vanilla
½ tsp sea salt
1½ Tbsp coconut sugar
butter for sautéing

FILLING
¾ C finely grated apple (with the skin on is fine)
½ C finely chopped dried apricots

more cinnamon as garnish
more coconut sugar as garnish

Mix the batter together in a medium-sized bowl. Mix apple and apricots together in another bowl (a little one) and set aside.

Using a well-oiled crêpe pan or small, buttered frying pan, make very hot over high heat. Add fruit filling to the batter, and then use a ladle to place about ¼ C of the crêpe batter in the center of the pan. Lift the pan off the burner and tilt it in a circle to allow the batter to fully cover the bottom of the pan. Once the crêpe turns light brown, flip it and wait for about another 30 seconds before flipping crêpe onto a serving plate. Roll it up and serve with a fresh fruit or a topping of your choice.

You could simply garnish with another sprinkle of cinnamon and coconut sugar.

Will says that you will enjoy. Or else!

Little Breads and Muffins

Making bread at home does make the whole house smell wonderful. At this stage of my life (the busy part!) I mostly make breads that aren't really breads—breads that can be made quickly. My favorites? The sesame cornmeal crackers and the chestnut bread.

I make these two and the others in this section when I have company. By taking the time to bake, I'm showing how much I love friends and family.

Rules of the road if you bake:

1. Have ingredients at room temperature before mixing.

2. Liquid in which yeast is dissolved must be lukewarm, comfortable to bathe in. Yeast can be killed by temperatures that are too high or too low.

3. A tsp of sweetener activates yeast. Yeast should become foamy in 10 minutes when mixed with water and a sweetener. If not, your yeast may not be live. Or your water was too hot or too cold. Start over.

4. Store dry baking yeast in the freezer in an air-tight container. It will keep forever that way.

5. To rise, dough must be warm and kept in a draft-free location. My mother used to use a towel or shower cap to cover her bowl.

6. Greasing baking pans with lecithin keeps everything from sticking.

7. Baked goods dry out in the fridge. Store them in the freezer.

8. Slice loaves of bread before freezing. When you need fresh bread, frozen slices pull apart easily and toast beautifully.

9. Save crumbs when you slice homemade bread. Store them in a covered container in the freezer until the next time you need breadcrumbs.

10. Bake breads the amount of time specified, and then check to see if done by tapping on the bottom. Bread should sound hollow.

11. Save soured milk (milk of any kind) for use in muffins. Nothing makes muffins rise better than sour milk, and you won't taste any hint of sourness in the final product.

12. If you are planning on using wheat, you might want to substitute sprouted spelt or wheat flour instead because those "flours" are easier to digest (they are said to digest like a vegetable).

13. Remember that oven temperatures and baking times are tricky because not every oven is calibrated the same, and factors like humidity change everything too. So use your eyes, nose and fingertips to determine when's the right time for you to take that loaf of bread or cookie sheet of crackers out of the oven!

14. You can always make little, mini loaves of bread instead of fewer larger loaves. You'll have to keep an eye on these little loaves since the baking time is reduced.

15. How do you know if your bread is done baking? A fully baked loaf of bread will have an internal temperature of about 190-200 degrees. Insert a meat thermometer into the center of the loaf and check the temp. If it's not quite up to that temp, leave bread in the oven for another few minutes. It is recommended to insert the thermometer through the bottom of the loaf, not the top.

ANNE'S GLUTEN-FREE RICE BRAN MUFFINS

Anne Marple worked in our store for only a few months, but during that time found out she was gluten-intolerant. She came up with these great muffins that we still make. This recipe appeared in our June 2008 newsletter.

Teff is a grain native to Ethiopia. It's a nutritional powerhouse and is smaller than a poppy seed. If you've ever had *injere*, Ethiopian pancake-bread, you've had teff.

"In the recipe below," says Anne, "you can sub potato starch for the corn starch, but don't use potato *flour*, which is made from ground whole potatoes, rather than just their starch. If you use potato flour, your muffin will tastes like a potato, so don't say I didn't warn you!"

Makes 12 muffins

1 C sweet brown rice flour
¼ C teff flour
¼ C rice bran
¼ C tapioca flour
¼ C non-GMO corn starch
1 tsp baking soda
1½ tsp aluminum-free baking powder
½ tsp sea salt
½ tsp xanthan gum

Bake at 375 degrees.

2 tsp cinnamon
½ tsp nutmeg
½ C butter or Earth Balance spread
⅓ C coconut sugar
2 ripe bananas, peeled
2 eggs
½ tsp vanilla extract (gluten-free)
1 C raisins

Preheat oven to 375 degrees. Grease a muffin tin and set aside.

Combine dry ingredients in a bowl.

Using an electric mixer, cream butter or Earth Balance spread with coconut sugar. Add bananas, eggs and vanilla. Beat until smooth. Remove bowl from mixer and add dry ingredients together with raisins. Use hands or a spoon to lightly incorporate everything.

Scoop batter into muffin tins, filling each cup to the top. Bake 20-30 minutes, or until muffin bounces back when pressed lightly.

Note: Anne says that you can use this recipe as a template. She says to feel free to substitute any fruit you want instead of the bananas and raisins. Think cranberry-orange or blueberry-spice (add cardamom).

BARLEY BASIL BREADSTICKS

An old-fashioned, heavy and hearty breadstick, the kind that will stick to your ribs (in a good way). These go well with soup, or can be eaten for breakfast with butter and honey.

According to Anastasia Schepers in her book, *Barley: Ancient Grain, New-Found Nutrition*, barley was a staple during biblical times, eaten as porridge and in barley cakes. And, she says, "Barley was a food favored by Greek gladiators, known as 'barley eaters.'"

Makes 8 breadsticks

1 Tbsp honey
1½ C warm water
2 C sprouted spelt flour

Bake at 400 degrees

1 tsp sea salt
2 C barley flour
2 Tbsp fresh chopped basil, or 1 Tbsp dried basil

Mix honey, water, spelt flour and salt in a mixing bowl. Beat into smooth batter with wooden spoon. Let the dough stand for 10 minutes, or until the liquid has been absorbed.

Add barley flour and work into wet, somewhat sticky dough. Knead a little in the bowl, cover it and then allow it to stand for another 20 minutes.

Preheat oven to 400 degrees.

Knead in basil. Dough will be soft, but workable. Divide dough into 8 roughly equal pieces. Mold each piece into a breadstick about 7-inches long. Arrange breadsticks on a lightly floured or greased baking tray, cover and allow to sit for 20 minutes.

Bake for 15 minutes, when breadsticks will be somewhat golden. Remove from the oven and let them cool for a few minutes before enjoying their hearty chewiness. These are not your ordinary crisp or crunchy breadsticks…

Note: You'll note that I keep mentioning sprouted flour. Too bad I hadn't discovered how wonderful sprouted flours are when I was writing the dessert section, or even years ago. I grew up eating Food for Life sprouted breads, which I love until this day, so it's a wonder I didn't think to use the sprouted flours before now. Maybe they weren't available in stores? Sprouting grains to make a sprouted "flour" yields a product that digests like a vegetable instead of like a starch.

Obviously, if you don't have access to sprouted flours, use what you have and don't worry about it.

BRAIDED EGG BREAD

One could call this challah, but I don't. Challah today is synonymous with the cotton candy bread which sticks to your teeth... The challah today is what my Grandma Sarah used to call "kvetch." Here that would be defined as something without substance that you can squeeze into a small ball.

This bread is hearty and chewy. It will nourish you.

Makes 1 loaf

4 tsp baking yeast
4 strands saffron
½ C warm water
1 tsp honey or agave
3½ C sprouted whole-grain flour
1 tsp sea salt

Bake at 375 degrees

3 eggs
¼ C extra virgin olive oil (EVOO)*
¼ C honey or agave
1 Tbsp poppy seeds as garnish
1 Tbsp unhulled, brown sesame seeds as garnish

Dissolve the yeast and saffron in the warm water, and then add the honey. (I use the bowl that goes with my Kitchen Aid mixer or the workbowl of my food processor. You can choose 1 of these machines or make braided egg bread by hand.) Mix well.

Place flour and salt into a mixing bowl.

Separate yolk from 1 egg and reserve. Then add that egg white and the remaining eggs to EVOO and honey. Beat well and add to yeast mixture. (If you are using a mixer, add the 1 egg white, remaining eggs, EVOO and honey to the yeast mixture in the bowl and mix with the dough hook. If using the food processor, use the steel blade and quick on/off turns to combine the yeast mixture with the eggs and EVOO.)

No matter which way you've chosen to make this bread, now add ½ the flour to the liquid and mix. Then add remaining flour.

If making by hand, knead on a floured board for 10 minutes. Dough should be pliable, soft and slightly sticky.

If using a mixer, knead dough on slow speed with the paddle attachment or dough hook for 1 minute. Mix on medium-low speed, occasionally scraping down the bowl, for another 2 minutes, or until the dough forms a ball and starts to clean the sides of the bowl. You can add more flour or more water, 1 Tbsp at a time, as needed, until the dough is pliable, soft and slightly sticky.

If using the food processor, pulse the on/off button and knead for about 1 minute, or until the dough forms a ball and cleans the sides of the workbowl. Once again, (cont.)

you can add more flour or more water, 1 Tbsp at a time, as needed so the dough is pliable, soft and slightly sticky.

Form dough into a ball and place in an oiled bowl. Turn to coat. Cover bowl with plastic wrap or a cotton towel and let dough rise about 45 minutes, or until double in bulk. Punch down and let rise another 30 minutes.

Punch down again and divide into 3 equal pieces. Roll each piece into a ball, then into strands of equal length. Tuck all three ends together under one end, and then imagine yourself braiding someone's hair. If you don't know how to braid someone's hair, this is what you do: cross one strand from the outside over the center strand, and alternating sides until you reach the end, squeeze together the ends of the braid and tuck both ends under at the other end.

Place bread on a cookie sheet sprinkled with flour or in a greased loaf pan.

Add 1 tsp water to the reserved egg yolk, mix and brush the top and sides of the loaf using a pastry brush. (The egg yolk will make the bread shiny and keep it moist inside.) Sprinkle with poppy and sesame seeds now, before bread begins to rise again.

Preheat oven to 375 degrees.

Cover and let bread rise 1 more hour. Then bake 30 minutes, or until golden brown.

Use the same measuring cup for both the honey and oil. If you measure the oil first, and then the honey, the oil residue in the measuring cup will allow the honey to run out smoothly.

Buckwheat Parsnip Whole Wheat Bread

This is a different take on whole wheat bread. The buckwheat and parsnip make the bread a little different.

Buckwheat is high in the B vitamins. It's also as versatile as rice when you're planning meals. To cook buckwheat (or kasha, as it was called in my house), measure it just as you would rice, with 1 C dry groats to 2 C water. Bring water to a boil, add the buckwheat, give a quick stir, cover pot and then simmer for 10 minutes. It's definitely a quick cooking grain with a nutty flavor.

Makes 2 loaves

4 C whole wheat bread flour*
1 Tbsp dry yeast
2 Tbsp honey or agave
1 Tbsp sea salt

Bake at 350 degrees in 2 9x5 loaf pans

2 Tbsp extra virgin olive oil (EVOO)
1½ C hot water or vegetable stock
1 C cooked buckwheat
1 parsnip, grated, about 2 C

Using the flat paddle of your mixer, combine the flour, yeast and honey. (Yes, you can make this by hand, but it's easier on the elbow joint to use a mixer...) Let mixture stand for 5 minutes.

Add remaining ingredients and beat for several minutes until dough begins to clean the sides of the mixing bowl and forms a ball. Let dough rest another 10 minutes.

Place the dough in an oiled bowl and turn to coat. Cover and let bread rise in a warm place until almost doubled in bulk, about 1 hour.

While bread is rising, preheat oven to 350 degrees.

Turn bread onto a board. Divide in 2, shape into loaves and place into greased loaf pans.

Bake 45 minutes to 1 hour. Cover loosely with foil the last ½ hour of baking. Test bread for doneness (see #15 at the beginning of this chapter). Turn loaves out on a rack to cool.

Note: You can use any cooked grain (what leftover grain do you have in your fridge?) instead of buckwheat, and you can use any grated vegetable instead of the parsnip too.

Once again, feel free to use sprouted spelt or whole wheat flour.

CUMIN BREAD WITH CHEESE

It's hard to imagine anything not tasting good with cheese. If you're one of those people who chooses not to eat cheese, or can't eat dairy products, there are cheese alternatives you can substitute here.

Cumin is a member of the parsley family, and it has been used in food preparation and healing for more than 5000 years. The seeds are believed to help the body absorb nutrients, and they have been shown to boost the liver's ability to help us detox too.

Makes 1 loaf

Bake at 350 degrees in a 9x5 loaf pan

¾ water or vegetable stock
¼ C extra virgin olive oil (EVOO)
1 Tbsp honey or agave
3 eggs, beaten
2½ C whole wheat bread flour*
½ C cornmeal
1 Tbsp baking yeast

2 tsp sea salt
1 Tbsp ground cumin
¼ C unhulled, brown sesame seeds
6 oz Organic Valley Mexican blend
   grated cheddar, colby and jack
   cheese, or about 2 C grated cheese
cumin and sesame seeds for garnish

Using the flat paddle of your mixer, combine water with EVOO, honey and eggs. Mix in ½ the flour (including the cornmeal), all the yeast, salt, cumin, sesame seeds and cheese.

Beat several minutes. Add the remaining flour and mix until dough begins to clean the sides of the mixing bowl and forms a ball. This bread is typically a little sticky, but you can scrape it out easily with a rubber spatula.

Place dough into an oiled bowl. Turn to coat and cover. Allow to rise 1 hour.

While bread is rising, preheat oven to 350 degrees.

Shape bread into a loaf and place into greased loaf pan. Press some cumin and sesame seeds into the top of the loaf.

Bake 45 minutes. Check bread for doneness (see #15 at the beginning of this chapter). Cool on a rack.

Once again, feel free to use sprouted spelt or whole wheat flour.

JAN'S GLUTEN-FREE CHOCOLATE CHIP AND GINGER MUFFINS

Jan said, "This recipe evolved as a result of three things. First, Anne Marple created her wonderful, basic, gluten-free muffin recipe. Next, my addiction to chocolate naturally resulted in the addition of chocolate chips. Finally our worldly-wise customers suggested we add crystallized ginger to the mix. The result is one of our best-selling muffins. Enjoy!"

Makes 12 large muffins

1 C Earth Balance spread or butter
2 C coconut sugar
4 eggs
1 tsp vanilla extract (gluten-free)
2½ C or 3 bananas
2½ C sweet brown rice flour*
½ C potato flour*

Bake at 350 degrees

½ C tapioca flour*
1 tsp xanthan gum
2 tsp baking soda
3 tsp gluten-free baking powder
1 tsp sea salt
3 C chocolate chips (gluten-free)
1½ C crystallized ginger

Preheat oven to 350 degrees. Grease a muffin tin.

Blend Earth Balance and coconut sugar together with hands or in mixer. Add eggs, vanilla and mashed bananas. Blend well.

Combine flours (either 3½ cups of Gifts of Nature brand flour, or mix the brown rice, potato and tapioca flours with xanthan gum) together with baking soda, baking powder and salt. Mix together wet and dry ingredients by hand. Fold in 2 C of chocolate chips and 1 C of crystallized ginger.

Fill muffin cups almost to the top with batter. Sprinkle remaining chocolate chips and ginger on tops. Bake for 30 minutes. Test to see if muffins spring back when pushed with a finger. If using the flour blend they should be done. Otherwise turn and bake for another 5-10 minutes.

We use 3½ C of the Gifts of Nature All Purpose Flour Blend, which is gluten-free, instead of mixing the individual flours and gum above. So you can choose, buy the mix or mix your own blend by following the recipe above.

FESTIVE HOLIDAY BREAD

This is another recipe by Jim, Renaissance man and long-time store manager. "As a student of German literature in my teens, I spent a year in Freiburg, Germany, where I was introduced to a traditional Christmas delicacy called Stollen. It is definitely not a health food, so some years later I decided to try my own whole foods version. Well, I was not able to duplicate the unique quality of a traditional Stollen, but what I came up with is a festive holiday bread, which can work for any occasion. It's delicious, fruity, and the recipe is an original. Thus it is neither stolen nor Stollen!"

3 loaves

1 C raisins
¾ C chopped dried pineapple
2 Tbsp whole-wheat bread flour
1 Tbsp dried yeast
¼ C warm water
1 C milk or soymilk
½ C butter
¼ C honey

Bake at 350 degrees

1 tsp salt
½ tsp almond extract
2 eggs
4-5 C whole wheat bread flour
¾ C sliced almonds
½ tsp cinnamon
½ tsp nutmeg

In a small bowl, toss raisins and pineapple with the 2 Tbsp flour.

Mix yeast into warm water and let stand for 10 minutes.

Meanwhile, warm milk and butter in a saucepan until butter melts. Pour this warm milk mixture into a mixing bowl and add honey, salt and almond extract. Cool to lukewarm.

Beat in eggs and yeast water. Add flour, beating thoroughly until desired consistency is reached and gluten is developed. Add the dried fruits, sliced almonds and spices. Knead for 8-10 minutes.

Turn into a greased bowl, cover and set in a warm place until dough doubles in size, about 30-45 minutes.

Preheat oven to 350 degrees.

Turn dough onto a floured surface, punch down and divide into 3 loaves. Roll each loaf into an oval, or shape as you wish. Cover and place in a warm spot to rise another 30-45 minutes. Bake for 35-45 minutes. Test bread for doneness (see #15 at the beginning of this chapter).

Note: Brushing the top with butter 10 minutes before removing from oven will give a nice shiny crust.

GOURMET CORNBREAD WITH WALNUTS

Cornbread can be thrown together in a flash, and leftovers make a good breakfast or snack the next day. When it's cold and dark outside, cornbread with a bowl of bean soup makes a feast! This one ran in our January 2004 newsletter.

Yes, cornbread and other breads contain carbs. Please don't stop eating good carbs! Remember that we need a balanced diet. We need a balance of protein, fats **and** carbohydrates. Protein and fat satisfy appetite, but "good" carbohydrates, like those in whole grains, boost mood by lifting serotonin levels. Complex carbohydrates not only make us feel happy, they keep us feeling that way. (In addition, seek out the Omega 3s—there are some in walnuts—to keep mood level.)

Makes 12 servings

3 C yellow cornmeal
1½ C whole wheat pastry flour or rice flour
1 tsp ground black pepper
1½ tsp Spike seasoning
1½ tsp baking powder
¾ tsp baking soda
1 C walnuts, chopped

Bake at 400 degrees

1½ C jack or cheddar cheese, or Follow Your Heart brand soy cheese
4 eggs
2¼ C buttermilk*
1 C sun-dried tomatoes marinated in olive oil (optional)
½ C walnut or extra virgin olive oil (EVOO)

Preheat oven to 400 degrees.

Grease two 9½-inch pie plates. Combine dry ingredients in a large bowl. Grate cheese or soy cheese. In a second bowl, combine eggs, buttermilk, sun-dried tomatoes (chopped coarsely), walnut oil and cheese. Whisk to blend. Quickly stir wet ingredients into dry (don't over-mix). Divide batter between prepared pie plates.

Pop in oven and bake cornbread until top begins to brown and tester inserted into center comes out clean, about 30 minutes. Cool slightly, cut and serve.

Note: Cornbread can be prepared ahead. When ready to eat, cover with aluminum foil and reheat it covered in a 350-degree oven for 10 minutes. It's always best served warm.

You can substitute any "milk" which is sour, or which you've soured. How to make sour milk? Add one Tbsp lemon juice to "milk"—soy, rice, or the real thing. Let sit for 5 minutes. You now have sour milk!

ITALIAN CHESTNUT FLOUR BREAD

This unleavened bread made from chestnut flour is mentioned in print as far back as the 16th century in Italy when the chestnut was often referred to as a "grain that grows on a tree." Chestnuts were survival food. In the mountain regions of Italy, the nuts were used fresh during season, and then dried and ground to make flour so there would be food when it was snowy.

I don't imagine the original, peasant chestnut bread had either pine nuts or sesame seeds, but I've used them both here.

I first discovered chestnut bread when I was in college, in the 1960's...

Bake at 450 degrees

1¼ C chestnut flour*
1 tsp sea salt
1¼ C water
few Tbsp extra virgin olive oil
  (EVOO)

3 Tbsp pine nuts
½ Tbsp fresh or dried rosemary
1 Tbsp caraway seeds (optional)
1 Tbsp sesame seeds (optional)

Preheat oven to 450 degrees.

Mix flour, salt and water in a small bowl with a Tbsp of EVOO. You'll have a rather thin batter.

Oil a 12-inch pizza pan and pour the batter onto the pan, spreading it out evenly with a spoon. Top with pine nuts (or caraway or sesame seeds) and rosemary, drizzle with another Tbsp EVOO, and bake for about 20 minutes, or until the bread turns golden brown and the surface is a little crispy.

Alternatively, you can make this bread in a skillet by heating a 12-inch skillet over medium heat until a drop of water will dance on it. Add 1 Tbsp EVOO and swirl pan to distribute it. Stir the batter and then add to the skillet all at once. Top with nuts and rosemary. Cover the pan and cook for 2 minutes. Spread another 2 Tbsp of EVOO on top and cook, covered, 5 minutes more. When the bread appears dry around the edges, loosen with a spatula and then flip it over. Reduce heat to medium low and cook 5 minutes uncovered.

Put bread on a plate and allow everyone to tear off pieces.

You can make this with garbanzo bean flour instead.

KELLEY'S SURPRISE SPICED BERRY MUFFINS

Kelley says, "I know Debra sometimes made muffins for Adam's birthday at school. Years later, I faced the same problem, having to compete with chocolate concoctions and cookies, and so I was surprised and delighted that my daughter, Josie's friends, schoolmates and grandparents enjoyed these muffins instead of cake. Josie loves Surprise Spiced Berry Muffins. They are great!"

Makes 12 large muffins or 24 mini-muffins   Bake at 400 degrees

1½ C spelt, or other flour like coconut
¼ tsp sea salt
1 tsp baking powder
1 tsp cinnamon
½ tsp nutmeg
2 eggs
⅓ C coconut sugar

2 Tbsp maple syrup
1 C milk of any kind, like dairy, rice, soy, almond or hemp
¼ C coconut oil (melted so it is liquid)
1½ C raspberries, fresh or frozen
1 Tbsp maple sugar granules
½ tsp nutmeg

Preheat oven to 400 degrees. Grease muffin tin.

In a bowl, mix the flour, salt, baking powder, cinnamon and nutmeg together. In a second larger bowl, beat the eggs; add the coconut sugar, maple syrup, milk and coconut oil.

Now add dry mix to the wet, stirring until everything is blended. Fill greased muffin tins about ⅔ full. Then add berries to each muffin tin. By adding the berries now, you can make sure every muffin gets a good and fairly equal amount. Sprinkle the tops with maple sugar combined with the second ½ tsp of nutmeg.

Bake until the muffins are browned on top and a toothpick inserted in the middle comes out clean, about 25 minutes, depending on the amount of berries added.

Remove muffin pan from oven and place on a rack to cool. Tip muffins out in about 10-15 minutes. Cool completely. Serve to happy campers.

MOM'S BREAD – MADE EASIER

My mother used to make her own bread (see excerpt on the next page from *Silence of the Bunnies*, written by my brother Daniel Stark). As a child, I hated Mom's bread. As an adult, now that I make this bread into individual pancake-shaped disks, I love it!

Europeans use lots of flax seeds in their breads, so did Mom. Mom's bread has hearty, whole-grain goodness together with the nutritional punch of seeds with all their good stuff like calcium, protein, essential fatty acids. Mom's bread is really a meal in itself. Serve with nut butter, butter, cheese, jam or honey, or nibble plain.

Makes 28 flat breads

1 Tbsp molasses
⅔ C warm water
2 Tbsp baking yeast
2 C sprouted whole wheat bread flour
4 C wholegrain 7-grain cereal
⅓ C rice bran

Bake at 350 degrees

1 Tbsp sea salt
1 C flax seeds
1 C pumpkin seeds, coarsely ground
1 C whole brown sesame seeds
2 Tbsp caraway seeds
2-3 C warm water

Mix molasses, warm water and baking yeast in a bowl or large measuring cup. Stir to dissolve and let mixture stand until foamy.

Place remaining ingredients (except 2-3 C water) in a large bowl. Add yeast mixture and then gradually stir in remaining water a little at a time. Add just enough so dough will hold together.

Preheat oven to 350 degrees.

Grease baking sheet. Place ⅓ C dough per bread onto baking sheet about 3 inches apart. Flatten each slightly with the palm of the hand.

Bake about 30 minutes, or until bread is lightly browned.

If you like your bread crunchy, bake a little longer or pat them out thinner.

Note: Make a batch and freeze. You can also bake until all the moisture is gone and they are hard and crunchy. Then they travel great, and you have terrific survival food that you can gnaw on like hardtack.

Excerpt from *Silence of the Bunnies* by my younger brother Daniel Stark about our mom's bread.

"My mother approached diet with a religious fervor, and she didn't give a hoot what others might think. Which brings us to lunch, which for me was the worst meal of the day. As a teenager, I did care what others thought of me. How lucky the kids were who were allowed to purchase their lunches at school and blend in with everyone else! It was a little awkward to bring a lunch, but you could get away with it if it was cool stuff. But you were 'weird' if you showed up as I did with a large brown bag, packed with five pounds of one freakish looking thing after another.

"Bread should be flexible. Most is. My mother made her own dark brown bread, sometimes without any flour, and it did not bend. If you got it the first day or two after it was made, it crumbled into a million little pieces when you bit it. It was like a building collapsing. The sandwich infrastructure would crumble into your hands, followed by the one to two pounds of meat or other ingredients that had temporarily been placed in between the slices. After the second day, I would remember wistfully when mere teeth could put a dent in the bread. It would become so hard that you could only hope to take a bite by putting your full weight and strength into the effort. Generally this didn't work. When it did, the breakthrough would be so violent that the sandwich contents would end up exploding into the air for a respectable distance. This would never fail to impress the kids around you. For those of you who know one of Bea's children, are things starting to make sense to you now?"

MOM'S SESAME CORN CRISPS

This recipe, which appeared in our first cookbook, now out of print, is another one Mom used to make. Like the "Glowing Salad," another recipe repeated in this book, it's simply too good to let die. Sesame Corn Crisps take minutes to make and are always a hit with family and friends. Are they homey and funny looking? Yes, but one bite makes everyone a convert. And people are always so impressed that you made your own crackers!

Sesame seeds with their rich-tasting crunch, contain fibers called lignans, which are good at lowering cholesterol. Sesame seeds have lots and lots of calcium and magnesium that our body can utilize more easily than those same minerals ingested from dairy products. But use unhulled brown or black sesame seeds because both the lignans and the calcium and magnesium are found in the hulls.

Serves 4-6

1 C cornmeal (coarse preferred)
1 C unhulled sesame seeds
1 tsp sea salt

Bake at 400 degrees

2 Tbsp extra virgin olive oil (EVOO)
1 C boiling water

Preheat oven to 400 degrees.

Grease a large cookie sheet.

Place all ingredients in a bowl. Mix with a regular tablespoon. Onto cookie sheet, drop corn crisps by Tbsp close together. Flatten crisps into about 2-inch rounds, using your fingers. Don't worry about perfect symmetry. The rough hewn look is fine and homey. And don't worry if they nestle close to one another on the cookie sheet, because they won't spread.

Bake corn crisps about 20 minutes. You'll know they're done when the edges brown, when the bottoms are brown, or when you can slide them around the cookie sheet by using a finger.

Remove tray from oven and let the sesame corn crisps cool.

Serve plain, with guacamole, cheese or a simple lentil soup. They are best eaten the day they are made. Otherwise, just freeze in an air-tight container and warm when you want to use next time.

Note: I store my sesame seeds in the freezer.

MY DUMPLINGS (MATZO BALLS)

I've been making these for years for Passover. I often wonder why I don't make them more often. I'll probably keep wondering and save them for Passover, which makes them special…

Serves 8

⅓ C extra virgin olive oil (EVOO)
¼ C water or chicken or vegetable stock
4 eggs
2 Tbsp chopped chives or scallions
¼ C fresh dill, minced, or 2 Tbsp dried dill weed

1½ tsp sea salt
½ tsp black pepper
¼ tsp ginger powder
1 C matzo meal
large pot of boiling water
pinch of sea salt

Lightly mix all the ingredients (except boiling water and salt) together in a bowl. Refrigerate overnight, or at least 2 hours.

When ready to make dumplings, with dampened hands, form cold matzo meal dough into 1-inch balls.

Bring the large pot of water with the pinch of salt to a boil. Drop the matzo balls into the pot. Turn down heat so pot will do a slow boil or strong simmer. Cover and cook until matzo balls are cooked through and tender, about 1 hour. Transfer balls to shallow dish. They can be made 1 day ahead as long as you cover them and store them in the fridge. When you're ready to serve them, either put them in the soup, or steam them for 15 minutes to re-warm

No-Knead Whole-Grain Bread

When the *New York Times* ran a recipe for no-knead bread adapted from one by Jim Lahey of Sullivan Street Bakery in November 2006, people went gaga. Baking bread became do-able with excellent results according to friends and the press, *except* for those of us who bake with whole grains. The word from on high was, "Don't try this with whole-grain flours!"

Well, this recipe works great with whole-grain flours, with some additions and extra liquid, and with a modification here and there. Granted, the results aren't quite as "risen," but the bread is satisfying and chewy. Try adding herbs and the pepper for a variation on the flax-chia theme too.

Makes 1 large loaf

3 C sprouted whole wheat or spelt flour
1 tsp baking yeast
1½ tsp sea salt
¼ C ground flax or chia meal
2½ C water

Bake at 450 degrees

1 Tbsp basil (optional)
1 tsp oregano (optional)
1 tsp rosemary (optional)
1 tsp thyme (optional)
½ tsp black pepper (optional)

The *New York Times* wrote, "In a large bowl combine flour, yeast and salt. Add water [Debra's note: and ground flax or chia now. Add herbs and black pepper now, too, if you want to add those] and stir until blended. Dough will be sticky. Cover bowl with plastic wrap and let dough rest at least 12 hours, preferably about 18 at warm room temperature, about 70 degrees. [I let my dough sit for up to 24 hours.]

"Dough is ready when its surface is dotted with bubbles [whole wheat flour has to work a little harder and you won't see as many bubbles]. Lightly flour a work surface and place dough on it; sprinkle it with a little more flour and fold it over on itself once or twice. Cover loosely with plastic wrap and let rest about 15 minutes.

"Using just enough flour to keep dough from sticking to work surface or to your fingers, gently and quickly shape dough into a ball. Generously coat a cotton towel (not terry cloth) with flour, wheat bran or cornmeal; put dough seam side down on towel and dust with more flour, bran or cornmeal. Cover with another cotton towel and let rise for about 2 hours. When it is ready, dough will be more than double in size and will not readily spring back when poked with a finger.

"At least a half-hour before dough is ready, heat oven to 450 degrees.

"Put a 6-8 qt heavy, covered pot (cast iron, enamel, Pyrex or ceramic) in the oven as it heats. When dough is ready, carefully remove pot from oven. Slide your hand under towel and turn dough over into pot, seam side up; it may look like a mess, but that is O.K. Shake pan once or twice if dough is unevenly distributed; it will straighten out as it bakes. Cover with lid and bake 30 minutes, then remove lid and bake another 15-30 minutes, until loaf is beautifully browned. Cool on a rack."

NONNA BUONAIUTO'S FOCCACCIA ROSEMARY BREAD

Daniel says, "This is my great grandmother's recipe from Naples. It's very easy but creates a pretty impressive product!"

How does Daniel serve his nonna's foccaccia? Covered in chopped tomatoes and garlic for bruschetta, broken and dipped in herbed olive oil, or as great sandwich bread (especially great when served with goat cheese and veggies).

Makes 2 pizza pie plate loaves of bread

2 Tbsp baking yeast
2 C warm water
2-4 tsp honey, or other sweetener
2 tsp sea salt

Bake at 400 degrees

2-3 tsp chopped fresh rosemary or
  1 tsp dried rosemary
4+ Tbsp extra virgin olive oil (EVOO)
4-5 C bread flour

Preheat oven to 400 degrees.

Dissolve yeast in water and let stand until foamy, about 5 minutes. Add honey or other sweetener, salt, rosemary, 2 Tbsp EVOO and 2 C flour. Mix well. Stir in the remaining flour, a little at a time, until the dough becomes too thick to stir with spoon. You can then either knead the dough vigorously for about 10 minutes by hand, or use a dough hook and your mixer. In this case, knead until the dough cleans the sides of the bowl and becomes smooth and elastic.

Divide the dough into 2 balls. Stretch each, or roll or spin the dough until each ball resembles an uncooked pizza pie. Put into pizza pie pan and make little indentations with your fingertips all over the surface. Drizzle with remaining 2+Tbsp of EVOO. Bake for 25 minutes, or until browned.

Note: Daniel suggests adding chopped garlic to the dough. He says you can also make crackers by rolling out the dough so it's very thin, baking it on a cookie sheet at 425 degrees until the dough is golden brown, cool and then break into pieces.

Oatmeal Bread with Chia Seeds

Makes 2 loaves

Bake at 400 degrees in 2 9x5 loaf pans

2 Tbsp baking yeast
½ C warm water
1 tsp honey, or other sweetener
¼ C extra virgin olive oil (EVOO)
¼ C honey, or other sweetener
1 Tbsp sea salt

½ C chia seeds
1½ C boiling water
2 C rolled oats
1 C millet or teff flour*
3 C sprouted spelt or whole wheat flour

Combine the baking yeast, warm water and 1 tsp honey in a small bowl. Stir and then let stand for 5 minutes, until foamy. Stir yeast mixture until smooth.

Dough can be made one of 3 ways: 1) by using a mixer with a dough hook; 2) by using a food processor and the steel blade; or 3) by mixing the dough in the bowl with just a strong spoon. Choose one of these ways and combine the EVOO, ¼ C honey, salt, chia seeds and boiling water. Mix until everything is lukewarm. Add the yeast mixture and mix until smooth.

Gradually add the remaining ingredients, adding enough spelt or whole wheat flour so that a smooth ball forms that starts to pull away from the bowl. Place dough in a clean, oiled bowl, turning to coat completely. Cover and set in a warm place to rise until doubled in bulk. Then punch down and place on a floured board. Divide dough in half. Form into 2 loaves and place in 2 oiled loaf pans. Cover and let rise to tops of pans, about 1 hour.

Somewhere along the rising process, preheat the oven to 400 degrees.

Bake about 45 minutes to 1 hour, until bread is nicely brown and sounds hollow when you thump the side of the pan or see #15 at the beginning of this chapter.

*If you don't want to use extra flours like the millet or teff, simply add another C of sprouted flour. If you don't have sprouted flour, well, then feel free to use a whole wheat or spelt bread flour.

PUMPKIN MAPLE MUFFINS

So many of you have become addicted to these muffins, which our kitchen bakes, that we can't keep up. They are lovely indeed! For those of you who have begged for the recipe, here it is (it ran in our February 2003 newsletter). Feel free to make a batch and bring some in for us!

Note the old switcheroo again. Called "pumpkin," but these are made with sweet potatoes. Don't know why people think pumpkin is appealing and sweet potatoes are not. While both are healthy, sweet potatoes are on my top 10 list of foods to eat. They're also rated #2 by Center for Science in the Public Interest as the best vegetable to eat in terms of overall nutrient content.

Makes 12 muffins

2 C spelt or whole wheat pastry flour
1 C pumpkin seeds
¾ C coconut sugar
2½ tsp baking powder
¼ tsp baking soda
½ tsp salt
1½ tsp cinnamon
⅛ tsp cloves

Bake at 350 degrees

½ tsp nutmeg
1 C cooked sweet potato puree
⅓ C canola oil
2 eggs
¼ C water, milk, soy milk
1 C maple syrup
1½ Tbsp vanilla
2 Tbsp pumpkin seeds for garnish

Preheat oven to 350 degrees. Grease a muffin tin.

In a large bowl, mix dry ingredients (except for those last two tablespoons of pumpkin seeds, which will be used to garnish the muffins just before they go into the oven).

Mix wet ingredients (I use the food processor so it takes a second or two.) If you use the food processor, you can put in a steamed sweet potato that has not yet been pureed, because the food processor will do that for you when it's mixing all your wet ingredients.

Combine wet and dry. Don't over mix. If you used the food processor, just dump dry ingredients into wet and pulse 2 or 3 times.

Spoon batter into prepared muffin cups and sprinkle reserved seeds on top.

Bake 35-45 minutes (don't disturb while in oven). A toothpick inserted into the center of the muffin will come out clean when they're done. Muffins should also look golden brown. When they're done, remove the muffin tin to a wire rack and cool the muffins for 5 minutes before turning them out of the pan.

Blue Ribbon Edition

Sprouted Spelt Raisin Sunflower Muffins

These are great for breakfast, and they travel well in lunch boxes too. Are they easy to make? Yes. They are a one-bowl, one-spoon kind of a muffin, and leftovers freeze beautifully.

If you're worried about nut allergies, you should know that sunflower seeds are not tree nuts and, in fact, are commonly used in cooking as substitutes for tree nuts and peanuts because they provide a lot of nutritional value and are somewhat similar in taste. They are rare allergens, with only a very few cases ever reported.

Makes 12 large muffins

1½ C sprouted spelt flour
2 tsp baking powder
½ tsp sea salt
1 tsp cinnamon
¾ C honey or coconut sugar

Bake at 375 degrees

2 eggs
½ C milk (dairy or non-dairy)
¾ C oil (like macadamia or safflower)
1½ C sunflower seeds
1½ C raisins

Preheat oven to 375 degrees. Grease a muffin tin.

Mix all the dry ingredients, except sunflower seeds and raisins, in one bowl, and the wet ingredients in a second bowl. Add wet to dry ingredients and then add sunflower seeds and raisins. I like to do my mixing with a rubber spatula.

Spoon batter into muffin wells. Fill each ⅔ full. Bake muffins for 30 minutes, or until lightly brown and springy to touch. Remove tin from oven and let stand 10 minutes before turning muffins out to finish cooling on a rack.

TAHINI SWEET ROLLS

Makes 18 buns

Bake at 375 degrees

1 Tbsp baking yeast
½ C warm water
3 Tbsp honey
¼ C milk of any kind, room temp
¼ C honey
1 C tahini
1 tsp sea salt

4-5 C sprouted spelt or
   whole-wheat flour
1 C sesame tahini
1 C honey
1 C raisins or date pieces
1 Tbsp cinnamon
½ C honey

Sprinkle yeast over warm water and 3 Tbsp honey in the workbowl of a food processor. Using the steel blade, stir to dissolve with a few on/off turns. Let yeast mixture stand until foamy, about 10 minutes. Add milk, ¼ C honey, tahini and salt. Turn the machine on and off several times to mix. Add flour, 1 C at a time, to form soft dough. Knead with on/off turns until smooth and elastic, about 1 minute. Let dough rest in workbowl for 20 minutes. Punch down (be careful of the blade).

Remove dough from workbowl to an oiled bowl and turn to coat. Cover bowl with plastic wrap or a dishcloth and let dough rise until doubled in bulk, about 1 hour.

Grease enough muffin pans so you will have a total of 18 muffin wells. Punch down dough and let it rest, covered, about 10 minutes.

Roll dough out on a floured work surface to form an 18x18-inch square.

Mix 1 C tahini, 1 C honey, raisins or dates and cinnamon. Spread mixture over dough, leaving a 1-inch border on all sides. Roll dough up jelly-roll fashion to form a cylinder. Slice with a sharp knife into 18 pieces.

Place 1 tsp honey of the final ½ C honey in each muffin well. Place a sticky bun roll in each well with 1 of the cut sides facing up (which means the other cut side is facing down!) Cover with a damp cloth and let rolls rise again in a warm place until doubled in size, about 35 minutes.

While dough rises, preheat oven to 375 degrees.

When risen, bake 25 minutes. Remove tins from oven and set on racks for 10 minutes. Turn sticky buns out of tins onto a serving plate and serve warm, bottom side up, so that the honey glaze shows.

Desserts

It goes without saying that desserts (and everything we eat) taste best when we use the highest quality and freshest ingredients. That means farm-fresh eggs from happy chickens, organic heavy cream from grass-fed cows, real vanilla extract, nuts whose oils are not rancid and fruits that have wonderful aromas and look as if you just picked them off the vine or tree! And if you bake with wholegrains and real foods, you'll get layers of flavors and textures instead of just sweet or just salty. You get my drift…

Sweeteners

Why am I writing about sweeteners here? Because 90% of the sweeteners I eat and work with are in desserts I eat or prepare for others to eat. It's the same in our kitchen in the store. We use sugar in cookies, not in soups or salads.

In the early years, we used honey, rice syrup, barley malt syrup, maple syrup (always use Grade B maple syrup because it's thicker and richer) and agave in our kitchen. We also used Rapadura and Sucanat, both less refined forms of sugar-sugar with more minerals and nutrients than white sugar, Florida Crystals, turbinado sugar, brown sugar or crystallized cane juice. But we were so pleased to discover coconut sugar in 2008.

Coconut Sugar

Many of you knew I was hot to trot on the trail of coconut palm sugar when I heard it was healthy and safer for diabetics because its glycemic index was in the mid-30s). I was so pleased when I could announce we found two companies selling coconut palm sugar at Natural Products Expo East in Boston, and again when it finally arrived in bulk at our store.

Suffice it to say, our kitchen loves baking with coconut sugar and now uses it exclusively in any baked good that calls for sugar. We still use and love maple syrup, rice syrup, barley malt, honey and agave.

How is coconut palm sugar made? It's the tropical version of maple syrup. The palm flowers atop coconut palms are tapped to release juice which is then kettle-boiled over an open hearth fire until the juice thickens into a golden sugar with overtones of caramel. In Thailand, it's called "nam tan bpeep," and is similar to "jaggery" in India.

Testing done by the Food & Nutrition Research Institute found that coconut palm sugar has a glycemic index of 31-35, compared to 64 in table sugar. The comparative chemical analysis shows coconut sugar contains more nutrients than other unrefined sugars, and you'll love it in recipes. Use like regular granulated sugars.

This is what Adam wrote about coconut sugar in our October 2009 newsletter: "And now we're seeing coconut sugar in the U.S. Made from the sap of coconut flowers, this is by far my favorite sweetener. I mean, maple syrup and raw honey are both wonderful too, but they taste almost too distinctive to use in a lot of recipes. Coconut sugar, on the other hand, tastes like sugar crossed with some sort of earthy-yet-heavenly caramel. It can replace cane sugar 1:1 in recipes. And it's got a glycemic index value in the mid-30s, better than just about anything else out there."

Gluten-Free Baking

When I want to bake something gluten-free, I mostly use ground nut flour or desiccated coconut instead of any flour called for. Why? Well, I'm not happy with the gluten-free flour mixes on the market because the flours they use are refined (I'm told this will change soon), and because many of the whole-grain, gluten-free flours like buckwheat or millet make a cake or cookie too crumbly. I haven't gotten the knack of how to use those flours comfortably. Nor have I been successful using coconut fiber in lieu of flours in baking. Sometimes I get lucky and things gluten-free work out because I've added a spoonful of tapioca flour or xanthan gum—but one formula that always works? I don't have one yet.

If I'm baking for someone who has a tree-nut allergy, I use ground sunflower seeds, or sesame or hemp meal. Chestnut flour may be fine for folks with tree-nut allergies, but you have to ask. All these are nutritional power-houses.

Vanilla Extract

If you're trying to make a recipe gluten-free, make sure you use a gluten-free vanilla too. (Most extracts use a wheat alcohol in which vanilla beans are soaked, and that alcohol contains gluten.) I happen to love a brand called Singing Dog vanilla, which is gluten-free and tastes heavenly. We use Singing Dog vanilla exclusively in our store's kitchen.

Greasing Pans

There's nothing better for greasing pans than brushing on a thin film of a mixture made of ½ liquid lecithin and ½ good vegetable oil. Years ago I read this in someone's book (sure wish I could remember whose), and it's the best hint ever. Baked goods simply will not stick.

I always have a jar mixed up in my cupboard. What oil do I usually use together with the liquid lecithin? Sunflower, grapeseed, extra virgin olive, safflower, macadamia or canola oil. I keep a pastry brush that I use just for the purpose of greasing right in the jar.

If I get lazy when my jar is empty, I'll buy a Spectrum spray with lecithin and oil and use that to grease my pans. Not as economical but works great.

Sprouted Flours

We keep learning everyday. Too bad I hadn't started using sprouted flours when I typed the dessert chapter, or even years ago. Mom used to give us Food for Life Sprouted Breads when she was out of her own bread. The Food for Life Sprouted Breads always made me feel good, and I love them still today. We use their breads for many of the sandwiches we make in our kitchen in the store too. The sprouting of the grains yields "flour" that digests like a vegetable instead of like a starch. Obviously, if you don't have access to sprouted flours, use what you have.

ALEX'S FROZEN ICE CREAM PIE

Alex Gardner brought this to the store's potluck in 2009. He no sooner put it on the table then the hordes descended. Did I get a single bite? Nada. Gurnisht. As you can see, it's easy to make, but what you can't tell in the reading is how pretty it looks.

Serves 8-12

2 pts Julie's vanilla frozen yogurt or ice cream*
1 whole-wheat frozen pie shell
1½ pints fresh raspberries

cocoa nibs or chocolate pieces (optional)
Stark Sisters Granola (optional)
chocolate or butterscotch sauce

Soften two pints of frozen yogurt or ice cream. Don't melt, just soften.

Bake frozen pie crust as directed on package. Let pie crust cool, then spoon softened ice cream into shell. (If you want to mix in cocoa nibs or chocolate pieces or Stark Sisters Granola, do it now while yogurt or ice cream is nice and soft.) Smooth until full and level. A spoon or rubber spatula works fine.

Place pie in freezer on a flat surface and let ice cream freeze in crust for up to 24 hours.

Before serving, garnish with raspberries around the edge of the crust. Drizzle with chocolate or butterscotch sauce. Cut with a wet knife and serve. Guaranteed no leftovers!

* Any flavor ice cream or frozen yogurt or coconut ice cream may be used.

ALMOND FUDGE

Did you know that one-fifth an almond's weight is protein, and that its oil is said to be among the most nutritious of all nut oils?

The Romans found almonds cured upset stomachs and gastrointestinal disorders. (Their recipe? Bring 2 C of water or milk to a gentle boil. Add a few Tbsp of barley or oatmeal with 1 Tbsp of crushed almonds. Steep uncovered on low for at least 30 minutes. Eat.)

Makes about 16 fudge squares or balls

1 C raw almond butter
¼ C honey or agave
½ C cocoa or cacao powder
½ C unhulled, brown sesame seeds*

8x8 pan, or any serving plate

½ C hemp seeds*
1 Tbsp vanilla extract
½ tsp almond extract
½ tsp cinnamon

Using a wooden spoon, blend almond butter with honey until smooth. Add remaining ingredients and mix well. You really have to work this, but eventually the cocoa or cacao powder and seeds will be part of the divine whole. I use my hands to knead until everything is fudge-like.

At this point, you can either press the fudge into an 8x8 cookie pan and cut into squares, or divide batter into chunks about the size of a large walnut and roll into balls in your hands.

You can put out to eat immediately, or store in covered container in the fridge. These are good, too, for breakfast or a snack in the afternoon. Look at all the good stuff you're getting!

*You can use all sesame seeds or all hemp seeds, if you prefer. Don't want to use sesame or hemp seeds? How about cocoa nibs instead?

ALMOND BRITTLE WITH PUMPKIN SEEDS

This goes way back to our September 2002 newsletter… A study done at Loma Linda University concluded that people who ate nuts such as almonds 5 or more times a week were half as likely to have a heart attack or die of heart disease than people who rarely or never ate them. And the nut-eaters were less likely to be overweight than those who went the fat-free route. With regard to cholesterol, researchers speculate almonds reduce cholesterol due to the nut's fiber and fatty acids. In a study done in CA, people with high cholesterol ate a few handfuls of almonds a day for a period of some months. Though they ate more fat, blood cholesterol levels fell about 24 points. Harmful LDL went down; good cholesterol stayed put.

Almonds are the only nut which alkalizes the blood (all others acidify). While Ayurvedic practitioners advise soaking almonds overnight and peeling them because they believe the peel may irritate the gut, they say the almond is the healthiest of nuts, building energy throughout the body.

16 servings

2 C sliced almonds
2 C pumpkin seeds
½ C barley malt syrup or rice syrup
1 C honey

2 Tbsp blackstrap molasses
1 tsp cinnamon
½ tsp ginger powder

Grease a cookie sheet (see directions at the beginning of "Desserts").

Place almonds and pumpkin seeds into a large heavy skillet and stir on low fire a few minutes until aromatic. Don't burn! Dump them onto a tray where they can cool.

In the same skillet over a low flame, combine remaining ingredients and bring to a full, rolling boil while stirring constantly with a wooden spoon. Remove from heat, and mix in almonds and pumpkin seeds.

Spoon 16 "cookies" onto greased cookie sheet. Pat mostly flat using heel of hand.* When completely cool, remove cookies with metal spatula. Eat right away or store in fridge or freezer.

Note: This irresistible, healthy nibble is great with a cup of tea. It makes a different kind of dessert, and one to complement fresh fruit and chocolate mousse.

* *Don't press too hard as brittle may still be hot and can burn. I often dip my hand into cold water before patting flat.*

AMANDA'S COCOA BUTTER ALMOND FINANCIERS

These appeared in our December 2007 newsletter and were a big hit.

What is cocoa butter? It's the natural fat of the cacao bean from which we get the incredible stuff known as "chocolate." Cocoa butter has a melting point just below average body temperature, which is why chocolate remains solid at room temperature but melts in your mouth. Cocoa butter gives a smooth texture to confections containing chocolate, and is often used by culinary experts (ahem, now you're one).

As is often the case, science is busy catching up with folk wisdom (here with regards to almonds). So many studies these last few years talk about almonds' ability to help lower cholesterol (an Australian study found men with normal cholesterol who then ate 3 ounces of almonds a day for 3 weeks cut total cholesterol by 7% and bad/LDL cholesterol by 10%); cancer clinics around the world recommend 10 almonds per day. Almonds are nutritionally dense—one fifth an almond's weight is protein, and they are rich in absorbable calcium and antioxidant vitamin E.; they have good fat, magnesium, potassium, fiber and more. We all know the FDA takes forever to allow claims, but even they said almonds reduce the risk of heart disease! In Italy, it's a time-honored tradition for wedding hosts to give sugar-coated almonds to guests as a symbol of good health, fertility, romance, fortune and happiness.

Makes 20 little financiers (2-inch wells)   *Bake at 375 degrees*

1½ C coconut sugar
1½ C almond meal (in our nut
   refrigerator)
5 egg whites

½ tsp sea salt
6 oz cocoa butter, melted
Toasted almonds for garnish

Amanda says:

1. Blend coconut sugar and almond meal/flour.
2. Whip egg whites and salt until white are stiff. Slowly drizzle in melted cocoa butter.
3. Blend #1 and #2 and scrape into a pastry bag. Chill the dough.
4. Preheat oven to 375 degrees. Grease tiny muffin tin pan (see directions for greasing at the beginning of "Desserts").
5. Take the pastry bag and pipe out 20 little financiers. Put one toasted almond on each one.
6. Bake for 30 minutes until done. They will be risen and cute. I rest my case.

Note: A "financier" is a French pastry that typically contains ground almonds together with butter and eggs. Some believe they got their name because they were especially popular in bakeries in the financial district of Paris.

Amaranth Strawberry Pudding a la Amanda

Amanda's recipe from our joint *Light and Lively Grains for Summer* cooking class in 2008.

"Feeling iron deficient? Have some amaranth! You can make this tasty pudding with any berries you like, but I picked strawberries because it is the season. Eat it plainly, for breakfast or light lunch or enjoy this grown up version as dessert. You'll need a food processor or Vitamix to process the amaranth. If you don't have one, you can buy amaranth flour." So sayeth Amanda.

Serves 16

1 C amaranth seeds
4 C apple juice
1 lemon, zest only
1 qt strawberries, hulled and sliced
½ C honey or agave

¼ C sliced almonds, toasted
1 C heavy cream, whipped, or
   2 C Greek yogurt
fresh mint for garnish

Grease a cookie sheet. (See directions at the beginning of "Desserts").

Pulse the amaranth a few times in the food processor to grind it. Place in a pan with the apple juice and lemon zest; bring to a boil and lower flame. Cover pan and simmer for 10-15 minutes. Turn off flame and let pot sit while you prepare strawberries.

Rinse, hull and slice strawberries. Place in a mixing bowl. Add agave or honey and give a good stir. Let them sit. This is macerating!

Pour amaranth mixture out of pan into a large bowl. Fold in the strawberry mixture and spread in a large serving dish or distribute into individual serving bowls.

Chill slightly, or completely. It is good warm or cold. Top with sliced almonds and whipped cream or Greek yogurt. Garnish with mint sprigs.

APPLE CHOCOLATE BAKLAVA

You'll recognize this from our November 2004 newsletter. It's great for entertaining because you can make ahead, and it doesn't require refrigeration. Note that The Fillo Factory fillo dough has no yeast and no hydrogenated fats, and it comes as spelt or whole wheat. It's also non-dairy, but that's not an issue because, well, look at all the butter we use in this recipe!

Note that Ah!Laska chocolate syrup and Tropical Source chocolate chips are dairy-free too, but I chose them because they taste great, not because they happen to be non-dairy. Tropical Source chocolate chips were named #1 by *Cook's Illustrated*!

Makes 18 large pieces

2 C Tropical Source chocolate chips
6 C apples, peeled and diced
2 Tbsp cinnamon
1 tsp ground cardamom
⅔ C unsalted butter or ghee*

Bake at 375 degrees in a 9x13 baking pan

1 C almond meal
1 lb pkg The Fillo Factory fillo
1 C honey
Ah!Laska chocolate syrup

Preheat oven to 375 degrees. Clear a working surface so you've enough room for the unfolded fillo leaves and the 9x13 pan side by side. (Read the instructions on the package of fillo dough. Don't unwrap before you're ready to put the baklava together.)

In a bowl, combine chocolate chips, apples, cinnamon and cardamom. Melt butter or ghee in a flameproof measuring C or saucepan. Have almond meal ready and on hand.

Take fillo out of package. Using a pastry brush, coat the pan with butter. Lay 1 fillo sheet folded in half crosswise on the pan, brush with butter and sprinkle with almond meal (it doesn't have to be even or all over—just a quick grab with fingers and let fly over dough). Repeat the whole process 3 times. Spread ½ the chocolate-apple mixture evenly over the top, leaving ¼ inch uncovered on all 4 edges. Layer 4 more doubled sheets of fillo, buttering and sprinkling almond meal on each layer. Cover with apple mixture and layer on remaining fillo sheets as before. Brush top with butter.

With a sharp knife, make 2 lengthwise cuts and 5 crosswise cuts so you have 18 rectangular pieces. Bake for 35-40 minutes. While baklava is still hot, cut all way through the scoring. Drizzle honey in cuts. Make an avant-garde design with Ah!Laska chocolate syrup. Done!

Serve when you want at room temperature.

You can use a non-hydrogenated margarine, or one of my favorite oils, macadamia nut oil, instead of butter or ghee.

APPLE PIE WITH A CHERRY BLUSH

What's Thanksgiving without pie? This recipe ran in our November 2001 store newsletter.

Though we claim them for our own, both apples and cherries originated in the Middle East. High in fiber, apples are said to reduce cholesterol and help us detox. Food writer Jean Carper says they also have mild antibacterial, antiviral, anti-inflammatory and estrogenic activity. Cherries are a well-known remedy for gout, arthritis and rheumatism. Rich in iron, cherries are often used to treat anemia. And, as if that's not enough, cherries are also said to prevent tooth decay by stopping plaque formation.

Makes 1 pie, but can easily be doubled
1 unbaked 9-inch whole wheat pie crust
6 C peeled, sliced apples
1½ C fresh or frozen pitted cherries
2 Tbsp tapioca flour*
½ C maple syrup
¼ tsp sea salt

Bake at 350 degrees
1 Tbsp lemon juice
1 Tbsp cinnamon
½ tsp ground nutmeg
½ tsp ground allspice
½ tsp ground cloves

Preheat oven to 350 degrees. Place piecrust onto a cookie sheet with sides so it's easier to put pie in oven, and so any drips while the pie bakes won't mess up your oven

In a large mixing bowl, place all remaining ingredients. Toss with a rubber spatula so everything is nicely coated. Spoon filling into crust which will be full, indeedy! Your pie will look like a mountain—higher in the middle. Carry cookie sheet with pie to oven and put in.

Bake 1½ hours, or until crust begins to brown and apples are soft. Remove cookie sheet from the oven and place on a wire rack so pie can cool. Serve pie warm, room temperature or cold. Feel free to serve with whipped cream, ice cream or crunchy granola on top.

Note: Yes, you can use a top crust. I don't because I like to see the fruit and because it's easier this way. No crimping and sealing for me!

*Tapioca is made from cassava roots. It thickens like cornstarch or arrowroot but without making liquids opaque. Used in gluten-free recipes, it holds things together.

Ayurvedic Pecan Brownies

We found a recipe in *The Ayurvedic Cookbook* by Morningstar, and kept monkeying around with it until April 2003, when we ran this in our newsletter. Whenever these are being made, we all are in seventh heaven!

Makes 12 large cookies

2 C ghee (clarified butter)
4 C coconut sugar
1½ C pecan halves, coarsely chopped
4 eggs

Bake at 350 degrees in a 9x13 pan

2 Tbsp vanilla extract
3 C whole wheat pastry flour
2 Tbsp baking powder
1 tsp sea salt

Preheat oven to 350 degrees. Grease a 9x13 pan (see directions at the beginning of "Desserts").

Warm ghee in a pan over low heat. Stir in coconut sugar. Sugar will get moist, but won't melt.

Chop pecans and put aside.

Using an electric mixer, beat eggs, vanilla and ghee mixture for about 4 minutes. Take bowl off mixer stand and put aside.

In a second bowl, mix together flour, baking powder and salt. Add dry mixture to wet, mixing with a spatula until it is all combined thoroughly. Add pecans.

Spoon batter into pan and bake on top level of oven. Turn pan after 15 minutes, and set timer for another 30 minutes. Check your brownies after 30 minutes. The cookies should be just pulling away from the edges of the pan, and a knife inserted in the center should come out clean.

Depending on weather and oven, these cookies may take another 5-10 minutes before they're ready to come out. (Our oven at the store, for instance, is very slow. It's old and the calibration never seems to hold. Your oven may cook much faster, so watch these cookies!)

BLUEBERRY TOFU CHEESECAKE BY JIM

"This is one of those recipes I have been making for years without writing it down," said Jim. "But for this cookbook, I kept track of my every move. The secret ingredient is the tahini, which gives a certain mouth feel (fat content) so the tofu has a cheesecake consistency. When I mentioned this to Debra, she exclaimed, 'My mother used to use tahini in her tofu cheesecake too!'

"For the topping, use what's organic and seasonal. Blueberries, raspberries or frozen cherries are easy because they go straight into the saucepan, whereas peaches have to be sliced. Use a gluten-free graham cracker if you want to make this gluten-free."

Serves 8

7½ oz graham crackers
1 stick Earth Balance spread or butter
1 lb silken tofu
½ C tahini
¼ C lemon juice
¼ C maple or agave syrup

Bake at 350 degrees

2 C blueberries, or other fruit
¼ C fruit juice like pomegranate
2 more Tbsp maple or agave syrup
1 generous Tbsp kudzu
1 Tbsp cold water

Preheat oven to 350 degrees.

Blend graham crackers in blender a few at a time and empty into a large mixing bowl. Add Earth Balance and then mix thoroughly by hand. Press into a 9-inch pie plate. If you prefer a pre-made graham cracker shell, use that instead.

Clean out the mixing bowl and mash in the tofu. Add tahini, lemon juice and syrup. Scoop the filling into the shell and place in the oven for about 40 minutes.

While the cheesecake is baking, put blueberries into a saucepan with the fruit juice (I think pomegranate juice is delicious here). Add the extra syrup, and bring mixture to a boil.

While the blueberries are on the stove, take a heaping Tbsp of kudzu and stir it in 1 Tbsp of cold water. It is important that this be done in cold water or you will have a lumpy mess. When fruit is boiled, stir in kudzu and then simmer for 10 minutes.

Allow fruit to cool. Remove cheesecake from oven when pie shell just starts to turn brown and the tofu is slightly golden. Top with fruit. If you don't want it to overflow the shell, you may have a little left over. Refrigerate cheesecake for at least 2 hours before serving. Leftovers keep a few days in the refrigerator.

CHOCOLATE GINGER BARK

I spotted a recipe in an old issue of *Bon Appetit* called "Chocolate Anise Bark," which sounded heavenly. Had fun playing around with it and ended up with this variation, which I love, and which ran in a store newsletter years ago. *Bon Appetit* says of their bark, "Nibble yourself, or wrap it as a gift." Amen to that! We still make it all the time in our kitchen, and, of course, we use only organic chocolate, organic spices and organic nuts and dried fruit.

Want a reason to eat pistachios? Love them but don't know how to defend your passion? Still afraid of good fat? Well, four ounces of pistachios have 140 mg of absorbable calcium, 750 mg of potassium, 20 grams of protein and 14 grams of iron.

Makes enough for 12 people

1 tsp ground cardamom
½ C dried cherries, coarsely chopped
½ C crystallized ginger*, coarsely chopped

½ C roasted, shelled pistachio nuts (we sell them in our nut case)
2 C bittersweet chocolate chips

Brush a baking sheet with a mixture of oil and liquid lecithin. (Check the how-to at the beginning of this chapter.)

In a bowl, combine cardamom, cherries, ginger and pistachios. In a second bowl, melt chocolate. (I do it by placing my bowl in a saucepan of barely simmering water, stirring occasionally, until chocolate is melty and smooth. Some in our kitchen use the microwave to melt chocolate.)

Into the melted chocolate, stir half of the dried fruit mixture and spoon the bark onto center of the greased baking sheet. Using a rubber spatula, quickly spread chocolate mixture into a rough 10x6-inch rectangle. Sprinkle with remaining fruit and nut mixture. Press this into chocolate lightly to help adhere. Chill until firm, about 30 minutes. Break bark into pieces. Try and eat just one piece!

*If you use the "bakers' cut" ginger you don't have to chop as this is already nicely diced.

Chocolate Raspberry Teff Pie

Again from a cooking class. Tinier than poppy seeds, ivory and brown teff are power house, sweet tasting grains unlike any other. Brown teff has a subtle hazelnut, almost chocolate-like flavor and a moist texture. Ivory teff is milder than the brown. An 8-ounce serving of teff yields 32% of the USRDA for calcium and 80% for iron. While not quite a complete protein, a 2-ounce serving of teff has 7 grams of protein, equal to an extra large egg.

In all grains, nutrients are mostly in the germ and bran (which is why white flours have little nutritional value and things are added back to make them "nutritious").

Since teff is so small and the germ and the bran make up virtually the whole grain, it is almost impossible to refine. You get all that good stuff, and teff is also gluten-free.

Serves 12

CRUST
1 C teff flour
1 C almond meal (or other nut or
   seed meal)
½ tsp cinnamon
¼ tsp salt
¼ C macadamia nut (or other) oil
½ C honey, agave, or maple syrup

Bake at 375 degrees

FILLING
2 C chocolate chips*
2 C dried apricots, chopped
   or 2 C fresh berries
chocolate for drizzling

Preheat oven to 375 degrees. In a bowl, blend together the crust ingredients. Without rolling or refrigerating, press dough with your fingers into a pie plate. You can crimp the sides of the crust or not, or use a fork to press up into interesting ridges. Prick bottom of crust with a fork. Put in oven and bake for 10 minutes.

Remove the crust from the oven, spoon in chocolate chips and pop pie back in oven for 5 minutes. Take out and using a heat-proof rubber spatula, smear chocolate into a smooth, melty-mass so it covers the bottom of the pie crust. Garnish with anything you like, like the apricots mentioned above, or fresh berries. There's no wrong or right way here. Drizzle chocolate sauce over berries.

Note: This pie is more like a cookie topped with a layer of chocolate and fruit, not a pie in the traditional sense.

*Once again, Tropical Source chocolate chips are my current favorite. We keep tasting and I'm sure there are other organic chocolate chips coming down the pike that are as good as Tropical Source. Just make sure you use organic chocolate...

CRANBERRY OAT CRUNCH

This is an easy dessert to make for your holiday table! Isn't that a relief? What's more, this makes a terrific breakfast dish served together with yogurt, kefir or milk (of any kind). This appeared in our November 2005 newsletter, and we have made it every Thanksgiving since then. We keep making it for as long as our supply of fresh organic cranberries lasts, which typically means we are able to make it through the New Year.

Why eat cranberries? Studies show cranberries have anticancer properties, inhibit growth of food-borne pathogens and contain antibacterial properties to aid in the prevention of urinary tract infections.

Recent studies show that oats, despite the small amount of gluten they contain, may be well-tolerated by people who can't eat gluten-containing foods. A double blind, multi-center study involving 8 clinics treating 116 children randomly assigned to receive the standard gluten-free diet, or a gluten-free diet with oats, showed after a year that children in both groups were well: the mucosal lining of the small bowel had healed and the immune system, reactive in celiac patients, had returned to normal. Which means oats may be fine for your celiac!

Serves 12-16

4 lb cranberries
2 C honey
3 C rolled oats
1½ C whole wheat pastry flour

Bake at 350 degree in a 9x13 pans

3 C coconut sugar
1½ C macadamia nut oil*
3 Tbsp cinnamon

In a large skillet, stir DRY cranberries in a pot until they pop. Yes, stir them dry! A minute or so after cranberries have popped, turn off flame, add honey and let cranberries sit while preparing oat mixture.

Preheat oven to 350 degrees. In a large mixing bowl, combine oats, pastry flour, coconut sugar, macadamia nut oil and cinnamon until everything is crumbly. I use my hands because it feels good.

Grease pan with an extra Tbsp-full of macadamia nut oil. Spread ⅓ the oat mixture in bottom of the pan, cover with cranberry mixture, top with remaining oat mixture.

Bake 45 minutes.

You can use another oil instead of macadamia nut oil (olive or peanut), but macadamia nut oil has a delicate flavor and is not harmed by heat. It's a heart-healthy oil great for sautéing or baking.

DEBRA'S NATURAL GOURMET RICE PUDDING

This recipe was adapted dramatically from one we found in the *Nasoya Tofu Cookbook* in 1999, and we've been making our variation all these years. This recipe first ran in our August 2004 newsletter.

It's simply a favorite in our store because it's easy to make, good as a dessert or for breakfast, satisfying and loved in winter or summer.

Serves 12
3½ C water
2 C sweet brown rice, uncooked
2 lb silken or soft tofu
¾ C honey
5 eggs
2 Tbsp lemon juice

Bake at 350 degrees in a 9x13 pan
¼ C canola oil
1 tsp sea salt
2 tsp cinnamon
1 tsp ground nutmeg
2 C milk (soy, rice, almond, hemp)
1 C Thompson organic raisins

Preheat oven to 350 degrees. Put a 9x13 pan on the counter ready and waiting!

In a large pot, place 3½ cups water together with rice. Stir once and bring to a boil. Cover and simmer rice for 30 minutes. Remove pot from stove and let it sit covered for 20 minutes. Muy importante!

Using a blender or food processor, blend all ingredients except rice and raisins (you may need to do this in more than 1 batch). Once smooth, pour batter into the 9x13 pan. Add rice and stir in. Sprinkle raisins over and stir in lightly with a fork.

Put pan in oven and bake for about 90 minutes. Pudding will firm up once it's removed from the oven and as it cools, so don't overbake. Ta dah. That's all there is to it.

GINGERBREAD WITH PEAR AND MOLASSES

This recipe originally appeared in our October 2003 newsletter. A good pear means fall has arrived. And even if spring was late and summer was short, there's something so lovely about fall and pears that you find yourself not really minding at all.

Do pears only taste good? Nope. Pears are said to be a natural laxative because they have a high insoluble fiber content. They're also said to be helpful when dealing with arthritis and gout, and with chronic gall bladder disorders.

We know blackstrap molasses is rich in iron. We know ginger not only promotes good digestion, strengthens circulation and warms extremities, but also helps alleviate nausea. This cake and a good cuppa oughta do ya.

Of course you can top with caramel ice cream or organic heavy cream whipped to soft peaks with a splash of vanilla. Add more ginger if you like. You can eat plain and it's heaven too.

Serves 12
4 C whole wheat pastry flour
2 C coconut sugar
2 Tbsp ginger powder
1 Tbsp cinnamon
1 tsp sea salt
1 Tbsp baking soda

Bake at 350 degrees in a 9x13 pan
1 C blackstrap molasses
1 C macadamia nut oil*
4 eggs
1 C milk, any kind, dairy or
   non-dairy
1 Tbsp lemon juice
4 pears, any kind, peeled, diced

Preheat oven to 350 degrees. Grease a 9x13 pan (see directions at the beginning of "Desserts").

In a large mixing bowl, combine dry ingredients. In a second bowl, mix wet ingredients. Prepare pears. Pour wet into dry, and stir just until combined. Don't over mix. Fold in pears.

Spoon batter into pan and bake for 35-45 minutes, or until knife inserted in center of cake comes out clean. Remove cake pan from oven and place on a wire rack.

Cool. Cut into 12 large pieces and serve. Once again, you can serve with ice cream or whipped cream, but plain is divine, or plain with some raspberries on the side as garnish.

I like to use macadamia nut oil in baking, but you can use sunflower, safflower, canola, olive, or whatever oil you like to use in baked goods.

GRAPEFRUIT PARFAIT WITH BERRIES

In 2006 Emily of Pure Food & Wine restaurant in Manhattan conducted a dessert class in my kitchen in Concord. What a thrill to have her visit! I fell in love with this recipe in particular, and adapted it slightly. You saw my tip of the hat to Emily and this adaptation in our August 2006 newsletter.

If you own a Vitamix, this takes minutes. If you don't have one, follow the more traditional way to make this dessert below.

This is refreshing, light and great for anyone with blood sugar issues. Agave, with its low glycemic index, is the sweetener here. Notice agar too. Agar is made with a variety of sea vegetables that have thickening properties. Seaweed fills you up and also acts as a decontaminator. Healthy stuff.

Serves 6 (12 oz) martini glass or wine glass servings

1¼ C grapefruit juice from fresh fruit
¾ C agave
1 C water
2 Tbsp agar powder or flakes*

1 C raspberries or halved strawberries
1 C blueberries
6 mint sprigs (optional)

Blend in a Vitamix all the ingredients in the first column until mixture is warm, about 5 minutes. Let cool to room temp in a bowl and then refrigerate until firm, at least 3 hours, or overnight.

Alternatively, place 1st column ingredients* in a saucepan and bring to a boil, stirring occasionally. Reduce heat and simmer 2-3 minutes. Turn off heat, cool to room temperature and then refrigerate until firm, at least 3 hours, or overnight.

Into each of 6 wine or martini glasses, put ¼ C chilled grapefruit "custard," then a Tbsp of raspberries, then the same of blueberries. Cover with another ¼ C custard followed by the same amount of raspberries and blueberries. Garnish with a mint sprig.

Note: Emily made this with lime. I love it with grapefruit juice instead but have also used blood oranges instead of grapefruit. Works best when juice is fresh-squeezed. Bottled juice doesn't "gel" as well, but if that's what you use, know that the taste is great either way.

Emily used kiwi, but visually kiwi didn't work for me, and berries are great for those with blood sugar issues too.

Don't forget to check out the Pure Food & Wine cookbook *Raw Food, Real World!*

Note that agar powder works better here than flakes in the non-Vitamix, traditional method.

HOLLAND HONEY CAKE

This was adapted from a Moosewood Restaurant recipe some years ago. The Moosewood Restaurant has given us wonderful cookbooks that have become Bibles to many of us, but this is how we make it in our kitchen. We always use only whole-grain flour, and we always use way more cinnamon and spice than called for by other bakers. We use only honey as the sweetener. I am always amazed at honey cakes that call themselves honey cakes but are made with sugar and a small wave of honey. Makes no sense to me!

Makes a bundt or tube pan or 4 mini-loaves   *Bake at 350 degrees*

¾ C good vegetable oil like sunflower
2½ C honey (1 lb)*
3 eggs
3 C whole wheat pastry flour
½ tsp baking powder
½ tsp baking soda

2 Tbsp cinnamon
1 tsp ground allspice
½ tsp ground cloves
1 tsp ground ginger
1 C black coffee, cooled

Preheat oven to 350 degrees. Lightly grease tube pan, bundt pan, or 4 mini-loaf pans (see directions at the beginning of "Desserts").

Cream oil and honey with an electric mixer until thick and light-colored. Beat in eggs 1 at a time. In a 2nd bowl, mix all the dry ingredients together and then add to honey mixture together with coffee. Mix well.

Pour the batter into the prepared pans and bake for 50-60 minutes, or until cake pulls away from the sides of the pan and a knife inserted in the center comes out clean. Cool the cake in the pan on a rack for 15 minutes. Invert onto a serving plate.

Cake is moist and dense and falls somewhat. Honey cake will actually taste better if it has a chance to sit overnight, covered, so all the spices permeate and the flavor have a chance to meld.

*Choose your favorite honey for this cake. Some honeys have a strong flavor, and if that's what you like, use one of those. Clover and orange blossom are typically mild in flavor, but I like using whichever honey is local and seasonal. The bees fly hither and yon to all kinds of plants, and as a result that honey has a more complex bouquet.

JAN'S BANANA CREAM PIE

"What can you make if you have too many ripe bananas and are a bit tired of banana bread?" asks Jan. "This is as yummy a cream pie as I've ever tasted, and it took care of all those bananas!"

Serves 8   *Bake at 350 degrees*

1 9-inch whole-wheat pie shell, baked   3 egg yolks, beaten
¾ C coconut sugar   2 Tbsp butter (or non-dairy
⅓ C cornstarch   substitute)
¼ tsp sea salt   1¼ tsp vanilla extract
2 C milk (dairy or non-dairy)   4 ripe bananas, sliced

Bake pie shell according to directions on package.

Preheat oven to 350 degrees for pie.

In a saucepan, combine the sugar, cornstarch and salt. Add milk gradually while stirring gently. Cook milk mixture over medium heat, stirring constantly until the mixture is bubbly. Keep stirring and cook for about 2 more minutes, and then remove saucepan from stove.

Remove a small amount of the hot mixture and stir into beaten egg yolks (save egg whites to add to scrambled eggs that night for dinner or add them to pancakes in the morning). Add the egg-mixture back into the saucepan and return pan to stove top. Cook for 2 more minutes, stirring constantly. Remove pan from stove and stir in butter and vanilla. This is your pudding mixture.

Slice bananas into the cooled pie shell. Top with pudding mixture.

Bake for 12-15 minutes. Once you've removed pie from oven, cool and then chill in the fridge for an hour. Easy to make and easy to love this dessert...

JIM'S BETTER-THAN-TRADITIONAL ENGLISH CHRISTMAS PUDDING

Serves 8

1 cup whole wheat pastry flour
1 tsp baking powder
1 ½ tsp cinnamon
⅓ tsp ground cloves
⅓ tsp ground ginger
⅓ tsp ground nutmeg
1 C coconut oil
2 ½ C dry breadcrumbs

grated rind & juice of one lemon
1 ¼ C coconut sugar
¾ C chopped pecans
2 ¼ C raisins
1 ½ C date pieces
1 ½ C chopped figs
1 ½ C apple juice
1 ½ cups milk or soy milk

Jim says, "Mix first 6 (dry) ingredients. Add coconut oil, bread crumbs, lemon rind (save the juice for later), sugar, nuts and fruits. Mix thoroughly. Make a well and add lemon juice (yes, now!), apple juice or cider, and milk. Mix thoroughly. Cover with cloth and store overnight in refrigerator.

"On the following day, stir and moisten if necessary (I never have). Fill well-greased pudding basin to within 1 inch of the top, cover with pleated greaseproof paper (wax paper), and tie tightly (I use a rubber band). Place on a trivet (small wire rack) in a large covered pot or pressure cooker of boiling water. The water should come ½ to ¾ of the way up the pudding basin. Steam for 4 hours (3 if you use a pressure cooker), checking and refilling water level as necessary. *I burned this pudding twice by failing to do so.*

"I have served this both right away and a few days later, in which case I just wrap it in greaseproof paper and refrigerate it, then re-steam it for 45 minutes before serving. My favorite accompaniment is plain cream, organic of course, poured over it. Then I close my eyes and think of England."

A CHILD'S CHRISTMAS IN ENGLAND

By Jim Leahy from his book, Living in Concord.

One Christmas was so much like another in those years..." *A Child's Christmas in Wales* by Dylan Thomas has become a fond tradition for me in the 27 years I have lived in Concord, attempting for myself to recall the lost world of a receding childhood romanticized by selective memory and an ever-present love for the family that we once were. My father, grandparents, uncles, aunts, "alas no longer whinnying with us," live on in remembrance of Christmases past.

In the 1950's and 60's we spent Christmas every year at my grandparents. They had founded a small club on the outskirts of Oxford. Temple Farm Country Club they called it. The oldest part of the building dated back to the 12th century, and during the reformation it had served as a secret monastery.

Every year family and friends gathered to celebrate at their table. My two brothers and I looked forward to the Christmas presents, some surprises, others secrets which Granddad had been unable to keep despite Gran's admonitions. While the adults indulged in a little Christmas spirit at the bar, we waited for uncles and aunts, some by blood, some simply by deference and familiarity, to shower us with gifts. Amidst the fulfilled hope of toys and the disappointment of socks, we absorbed the atmosphere of the season.

If we had stayed over Christmas Eve we were still sleepy from the excitement of having been up until midnight to receive the first gifts from our grandparents. We slept upstairs in a guest room, wondering whether we would hear the gray lady who haunted the hallways, or if anyone would see the coach full of headless monkeys that came up the driveway after midnight, and if the driver looked at you, you would die within the year.

Christmas dinner started at two o'clock after the regular patrons left the premises to the inner circle of relatives and friends. Sitting around the table with our gaily colored paper hats, after reading the jokes and inspecting the tiny toys from our pulled crackers, trying to get the miniature ball into the miniature cup to which it was attached by a string, we ate our way through all the yuletide fare, which was topped by Christmas Pudding.

It is the Christmas Pudding tradition which has stayed with me. A few years ago I decided to revive that tradition and looked up a Christmas Pudding recipe. Not surprisingly it was full of things I now foreswear. Sugar, white flour, lard, ale, liquor. "Well, I bet one can make it with entirely healthy ingredients," I said to myself.

Fifteen years later I have enjoyed many years of serving this recipe to family and friends, who have all delighted in this flavor of old England. All have wondered at the fragrance and flavor. I'm sure the recipe has undergone many changes. I never follow it exactly, but it always comes out perfectly.

Maple Almond Frangipane

This is a flourless nut cake. You'll love it for dessert or breakfast if there are leftovers! Use a thick, rich maple syrup like Butternut Mt. Farms' grade B. Grade B always has a more pronounced maple flavor than grade A, which is why that's what we use in Stark Sisters Granola and in our kitchen too.

Don't be afraid of eggs! Do you remember those studies done on twins, one of whom stayed home in Ireland, Scotland or France, and ate eggs, and the other twin who avoided them like the plague after coming to America? Guess which twin had heart problems and who got fat while eating fat-free? Oy carumba.

Eggs are a whole food with phosphatides to balance cholesterol. The main ingredient in egg yolks is lecithin, which doctors prescribe to help combat LDL. One study published in *Arteriosclerosis, Thrombosis and Vascular Biology*, showed men were able to consume two eggs per day without significantly raising their blood cholesterol levels.

Serves 12   *Bake at 350 degrees*
Use a 10-11-inch quiche dish, or any interesting shaped dish with 1½ inch sides

3 C almonds, roasted   **1 apple, peeled and thinly sliced**
6 eggs   **(optional)**
⅛ tsp almond extract   **1 C apricot jam (optional)**
1½ C maple syrup   **¼ C maple syrup (optional)**

Preheat oven to 350 degrees.

Using the steel blade of a food processor, grind nuts using quick on/off turns. Don't let machine run because you'll end up with almond butter! Add eggs, almond extract and maple syrup. Process a few seconds until blended. Consistency won't be smooth, but your frangipane will have character and interest!

Pour batter into dish. Put into oven and bake frangipane until a sharp knife inserted into cake comes out clean, about 45-60 minutes (damp weather lengthens baking time). Remove pan from oven and place onto rack to cool.

I like this cake plain, as it comes out of the oven, but if you want a fancier presentation or topping, combine apple, apricot jam and additional maple syrup in a small pot. Over low heat, stir until apples are slightly softened. Spoon on top and serve this way.

MAPLE-BAKED APPLES WITH WILD BERRIES

There's nothing like an old-fashioned baked apple served for dessert to warm the cockles of your heart. Whenever I make these for company, they're a hit. People ask to take leftovers home!

If you have banged-up, bruised apples, use those. No one will ever know once they're baked, I promise. (I often bring home all the apples we can't sell that no one else on staff wants to take home, make a huge, lasagna pan full of maple-baked apples and happily have leftovers for breakfast with my oatmeal.)

Serves 8

8 apples like Pink Ladies, Granny Smith or Braeburn, keeping peel on
1 C grade B maple syrup
2 Tbsp cinnamon

Bake at 350 degrees

1-2 C berries*
1 C boiling water
another C maple syrup (optional)

Preheat oven to 350 degrees. Rinse apples. Do not peel them. Create a small well in the center of each by cutting out the stem and core and leaving the bottom intact. I use a grapefruit knife to do this, and it works like a charm. Fast and easy.

Transfer apples to a baking dish. You want them to stand up and fit fairly snugly. If I'm making these for company, I put them in a decorative pie plate or an interesting oven-proof dish. Normally I use a stainless steel frying pan that can go into the oven.

Mix maple syrup, cinnamon and berries in a little bowl. Spoon maple syrup mixture into each apple well. If there's leftover, pour over apples. It's fine and dandy that much ends up in baking dish around apples. (At this point, if you want your apples really maple-y, drizzle over the extra maple syrup.) Add boiling water to bottom of pan, put dish in oven and bake 45 minutes to an hour, until apples are tender.

Serve warm or at room temperature. Serve alongside ice cream or whipped cream if desired. Plain is wonderful too.

Note: Most recipes for baked apples ask for butter and ask that you cover the dish with foil. I prefer my baked apples without butter and haven't found the need for foil.

*I like to use mixed berries, and we sell a wonderful, frozen wild berry mix from Italy, which is easy. When I can get local organic berries, I use wild blueberries. The berries add color to the apples, but you can also leave them out entirely and still have a scrumptious dessert.

Maple Banana Cream

Bananas, as we all know, are rich in potassium, which helps the body's circulatory system deliver oxygen to the brain and helps maintain a regular heartbeat. But did you know that bananas are rich in tryptophan (also found in turkey), which helps us relax and feel happy? Eat a banana and see if you feel happier!

I read online that Alexander the Great tasted his first banana in India in 327 B.C.E. (Who took notes, I wonder?) Arab conquerors brought the banana back to the Middle East and then took them to Africa. It wasn't until 1502 that the Portuguese started the first banana plantations in the Caribbean and Central America.

Serves 4

4 ripe bananas
1 C orange juice (blood orange is my favorite)
1 C maple syrup

2 C heavy whipping cream
fruit for topping like mango slices or fresh berries (optional)

Blend bananas with orange juice and maple syrup until very smooth.

Using a mixer, beat heavy cream until stiff peaks form. Fold blended fruit puree into whipped cream then spoon into pretty parfait glasses or water goblets. Cover with plastic wrap and chill until time to serve. When you're ready to serve, top with fresh tropical fruit like mango slices, or sprinkle some blueberries or raspberries on top too.

This is a simple but delish dessert that can be made 2 days ahead.

Mexican Brownies with Chili Pepper

These are to die for and appeared in our December 2005 newsletter. Moist and chocolate-y. Mexican cuisine is known for its combinations of chocolate and chili peppers with a dash of cinnamon. Try it and you'll agree there's a depth and complexity of flavor which makes these not-your-mother's-brownies!

For those of you who love carob, of course you can substitute. For those of you who can't do wheat, I imagine there's enough "glue" in this recipe to use quinoa or rice flour instead of wheat. But note that there is oat flour on those dates if you can't do oat flour...

Makes 16 large brownies

Bake at 350 degrees and use a 9x13 pan

- 1 C boiling water
- 1 C cocoa powder
- 1 Tbsp instant coffee or coffee substitute
- 2 C date pieces in oat flour (buy these ready)
- 1 C butter, ghee or macadamia nut oil
- 2 C whole wheat pastry flour
- 2 tsp baking powder

- ½ tsp sea salt
- 1 Tbsp chili pepper powder
- 2 C dried fruit (see below)
- 2 tsp cinnamon
- 4 eggs
- 2 C coconut sugar
- 2 Tbsp vanilla extract
- 2 C chocolate chips

Preheat oven to 350 degrees. Grease a 9x13 pan (see directions at the beginning of "Desserts").

In a large bowl, combine boiling water, cocoa powder, coffee, dates and butter. Stir until cocoa is dissolved.

In a second bowl, mix flour with baking powder, salt, pepper and your favorite combination of dried fruit (such as chopped apricots, crystallized ginger, currants, pineapple dices, cranberries, golden raisins or dried cherries) and cinnamon. If you're in a hurry, use dried fruits that come in small pieces or are already diced.

Stir eggs, coconut sugar and vanilla into cocoa mixture. Now add dry ingredients and incorporate quickly. Don't over-mix. Stir in chocolate chips.

Spoon batter into prepared pan. Bake until firm around the edges and just set in the center, about 25 minutes. Cool slightly and then cut into squares. Good with a glass of milk, almond, soy or rice milk too. Good with whipped cream, ice cream and fresh berries like raspberries or blueberries.

PEACH CRUMBLE WITH MARZIPAN

Peaches, nectarines, apricots or blueberries—any of these or a combination of any and all of these make a delicious crumble. If you use butter in the topping, you'll have a softer crust, one that is more homogenous. I liked the crunchy, nubby non-butter crust too. If you prefer to save calories so you can slather butter on toast, try the crumble without butter. Marzipan—sweetened, ground almonds—is divine. Yes, we have organic marzipan!

Did you know that almonds are said to relieve stagnant energy in the body and to make you smarter because they are so nutrient-rich?

Enjoy this summer dessert!

Serves 8

CRUMBLE
½ C whole wheat pastry flour*
1 pkg Biastramondo marzipan
¼ C maple syrup
2 Tbsp butter, cubed (optional)
¼ C sliced almonds (with the skin is fine)

Bake at 350 degrees

FILLING
5-6 C halved, pitted, sliced peaches
¼ C maple syrup
⅓ C rolled oats
1 tsp almond extract

Preheat oven to 350 degrees.

Using the steel blade and several quick on/off turns of the food processor, blend flour, marzipan and maple syrup (and butter, if using). Crumble should resemble coarse crumbs. Transfer crumble to bowl and mix in sliced almonds.

In a large bowl, toss filling ingredients together. (I like to use a rubber spatula to mix.) Spoon filling into a pie plate or ovenproof dish. Cover with crumble topping. Bake until filling bubbles and top is golden brown, about 40 minutes. Cool 10 minutes. Can be made the day before. Serve cold or at room temperature.

*Or other whole-grain flour such as spelt or rye.

PEACHES WITH BLACKBERRY SAUCE

From a summer cooking class in 2006. Blackberries (known as bramble berries in England) have lots of pectin, which forms a gel in our digestive systems and slows down the absorption of sugars into the bloodstream, thus stabilizing blood sugar levels. The literature says that blackberries also help lower blood cholesterol by binding with fats and cholesterol to eliminate them from the body. They're said to be a blood builder and blood cleanser (so they make the complexion more beautiful).

Berries are the best fruits for diabetics. Agave has a low glycemic index and a neutral flavor, so it's easy to work with here too.

Serves 4

1 C blackberries
¼ C agave
juice of ½ lime

¼ C water
6 peaches, sliced

Blend blackberries with agave, lime juice and water. Strain into a cup. Arrange sliced peaches on individual dessert plates and pour blackberry sauce over.

Want an even simpler dessert? Put whole blackberries and sliced peaches on little dessert plates. Drizzle agave and lime juice over fruit. Forget about the water. The heck with making a sauce.

Very few calories but lots of fiber...

PINEAPPLE AMBROSIA BY JIM

Jim's ambrosia is a nice transition to spring, and this recipe appeared in our April 2004 newsletter. Pears are still flavorful and abundant, but we're already yearning for summer fruit. But the organic pineapples we get are extraordinary, and dried cherries have more iron and minerals than their fresh counterparts. And dried cherries are easier to use than fresh because they're already pitted... They taste great and help conditions like arthritis and gout.

Jim says he served this to his book group and they were wowed. He and Diane think it tastes as if it has liqueur, but it doesn't. The pear, pineapple and cherry marriage was made in heaven.

Serves 4-6

2 Tbsp butter
3 Anjou pears, quartered, cored and sliced
½ C dried cherries
3 C (about) fresh pineapple, peeled, cubed*

Bake at 400 degrees

⅔ C apple juice
2 Tbsp coconut sugar
½ tsp lemon extract or flavor

Preheat oven to 400 degrees. Melt butter and put aside. Cut up fruit and place in a medium-size Pyrex dish, or any nice baking dish. In a small bowl, whisk the apple juice, coconut sugar, and lemon extract or flavor together with the melted butter.

Pour apple juice mixture immediately over cut fruit in Pyrex dish. Cover dish with foil and place in oven for 15 minutes.

After 15 minutes remove cover and bake for a further 30-40 minutes.

Spoon fruit into bowls and serve with your favorite accompaniment. Jim says he really likes stirring in Seven Stars Vanilla yogurt, but sour cream or Julies Ice Cream (vanilla or caramel) are also luscious.

*Don't know how to cut a pineapple? Twist off crown. Using a sharp knife, cut pineapple in half lengthwise, then into quarters. Trim ends and cut out core. Cut off peel and slice in bite-size pieces.

POT DE CRÈME

This is a 5-minute dessert to make, which can also be used as a custardy filling between two layers of cake or to fill a pie shell or tartlet shells. It can be simply served as suggested below.

Over the years, I transitioned from carob to chocolate, and over the years I decided to use the whole egg because using both the white and yolk made the mousse lighter and healthier. Why waste anything, I thought. I'm convinced the boiling cream kills any pathogens that might be in my wonderful, organic eggs anyhow!

Like all things chocolate, I use only organic chocolate chips because commercially-grown chocolate is a crop that is heavily sprayed, and organic also means fair-trade and shade-grown. Non-organic coffee and cacao are typically grown in the sun. That means the canopy of greenery that controls pests and weeds naturally is destroyed. When this canopy is destroyed, the use of pesticides becomes almost necessary. Another example of man getting in the way of nature...

Serves 6

2 C bittersweet chocolate chips   **6 eggs**
2 C heavy cream   **2 Tbsp vanilla extract**

Place chocolate chips in food processor or blender.

In a small pot, gently bring cream to a boil. With the processor motor running, slowly pour cream through the feed tube. Add eggs and vanilla. Whirl about 30 seconds.

Pour pot de crème into 6 pot de crème pots or 6 pretty liqueur glasses. Cover each. Refrigerate for several hours or overnight before serving. Of course you can also pour mousse into a glass bowl, but this way you have no chance to "dictate" portion control. There are people who will try to eat their weight in mousse!

Note: Pot de crème can also be used as a decadent frosting to camouflage a cake that isn't perfect.

POT DE CRÈME A LA COCONUT MILK

Please read the recipe on the previous page first. That recipe started out as the rich carob mousse from our first cookbook, now out of print. Here it is now, not only streamlined but dairy-free to boot. Yes, one can make another variation without any eggs, but I just don't like that as well. I know people use silken tofu instead of eggs, but that isn't my cup of tea!

Serves 6

2 C dairy-free chocolate chips
**2 C full-fat, unsweetened coconut
  milk**

6 eggs
2 Tbsp vanilla extract

Place chocolate chips in food processor or blender.

In a small pot, gently bring coconut milk to a boil. With the processor motor running, slowly pour coconut milk through the feed tube. Add eggs and vanilla. Whirl another 30 seconds.

Pour pot de crème into six pot de crème pots or pretty liqueur glasses. Cover each. Refrigerate for several hours or overnight before serving. Alternatively, you can pour pot de crème into a glass serving bowl.

PUMPKIN CHEESECAKE BY JAN

"Light and perfect for autumn!" says Jan.

Serves 12

1⅓ lb cream cheese
⅔ lb sour cream
⅔ C honey or coconut sugar
4 eggs
1 Tbsp vanilla extract
2 C pumpkin puree

Bake at 350 in a 9-inch cheesecake pan

CRUST
2 C favorite ginger snap cookies
1 Tbsp butter
1 Tbsp water

Let all ingredients come to room temperature.

Grease one 9-inch cheesecake pan (with removable bottom). Place cheesecake pan on cookie sheet.

Preheat oven to 350 degrees.

Prepare crust by pulverizing ginger snaps in a food processor (use steel blade). Add butter and water and mix with a few on/off turns of the processor. Press this crust mixture firmly into the greased pan to form a solid crust. Set aside.

Using the same steel blade of your food processor, blend all the remaining ingredients, except the pumpkin puree, until cheese mixture is smooth and no pieces of cream cheese remain. Pour batter into cake pan that is now lined with your crust.

Using a knife, gently swirl in pureed pumpkin until batter has a pretty curvy design, but cake and pumpkin puree are not fully mixed. Put cake into oven and bake 1 hour.

Cheesecake continues to cook a little when removed from the oven, so don't over-bake. Sometimes a cheesecake is done when the surface shows a slight crack. If you check after an hour, you should be safe. Remove cake from oven and cool completely. When the cake is cool, cover and keep in the refrigerator. Like any cheesecake, this tastes best the next day…

RAW MACAROONS BY STACY

This recipe was given to us some years ago by Stacy Mahoney, who still stops in and says "Hi!"

Serves 6

1 C Medjool dates
1 C dried Turkish apricots
4¼ C water

4 C dried shredded coconut*
4 Tbsp cocoa powder (optional)
1 C more dried shredded coconut

Pit the dates. Put into 2-quart container with apricots and water. Soak overnight.

Blend the 4 C coconut in food processor until "liquefied." Transfer to medium stainless bowl.

Drain fruit (save ¼ C of soaking water and drink the rest). Blend fruit and the saved soaking water for 1 minute, or until you have a fairly smooth "batter." Some chunks are fine.

Add blended fruit to coconut and mix by hand until texture is even. If you want raw chocolate macaroons, add the cocoa powder now.

Use a 2-ounce (small) ice cream scoop to portion batter into balls. Scrape the scoop against the side of the bowl to firmly pack. Using the last cup of coconut, put into a separate bowl. Gently coat each ball with coconut.

Since apricots and dates expand with soaking, double check the amount of coconut you'll actually need. The rule of thumb is to use 1 part soaked fruit mixture to 2 parts dried coconut.

Sephardic Nut Cookies

Good for Chanukah, good for Christmas, good for New Years and good anytime! No flour and lots of good fats from nuts. When these are in the oven, the whole house smells heavenly. My mother used to form these into crescent-shaped half moons, but I also think she made them with the addition of a pound of butter!

Makes 2 dozen cookies

1½ C pecan meal
½ C almond meal
1 Tbsp ground cinnamon
1 tsp ground cloves
Grated rind of 1 orange

Bake at 325 degrees

½ C coconut sugar
2 eggs
2 Tbsp vanilla extract
1 C coconut sugar for rolling

Preheat oven to 325 degrees. Lightly grease baking sheet (see directions at the beginning of "Desserts").

Mix all ingredients, except the extra coconut sugar, in a large bowl with a spoon. Take about a walnut-size piece of dough and roll into a ball in your hands. Dip in extra coconut sugar and roll lightly into a short cigar. Round into a half-moon, or not—you can shape these as you like. You can even just leave as somewhat flat buttons on your cookie sheet, press a thumb in the center and put the extra sugar there.

Whatever shape you choose, place each cookie on the prepared cookie sheet and bake for 20 minutes, or until cookies are golden brown. Remove from oven and cool slightly.

If you're not going to serve when cool, place in airtight container and store in the refrigerator or freezer.

SIMPLEST DESSERT EVER

This is a repeat of one of my favorite desserts (to complement something sinful!) from our first cookbook, now out of print. Check out the variation on this theme down below.

What I like about this dessert is that it makes no mess in the kitchen and it's quick, easy, fat-free and nutrient-rich. Leftovers can be used for breakfast with a steaming bowl of hot cereal.

Use only unsulfured, untreated dried fruit (no bright orange apricots, for instance), and no raisins sprayed with mineral oil. All our dried fruit is unsulfured and untreated. It goes without saying that every recipe in this book uses unsulfured, untreated dried fruit! Organic whenever you can too.

Serves 8-10

2 C dried Turkish apricots
2 C dried peaches
½ C crystallized ginger

2 C dried cherries
2 C pitted prunes
2 cinnamon sticks

Put dried fruit in a large pot. Cover with water by several inches. (Add more water during cooking if necessary.) Throw cinnamon sticks in pot. Bring water to boil. Turn off heat. Cover pot. Cool. Refrigerate overnight. By the next morning, the liquid in the pot will be rich-tasting and thick. The flavors will be wonderful.

I love to serve this in a pretty water goblet. A dollop of whipped cream or a sprinkle of fresh raspberries makes it look very pretty. Of course you can put a splash of something alcoholic in the glass too. Brandy?

Variation: Do you have any fresh fruit like plums that have gotten too soft for eating? Simply put about 12 C of whole fruit in pot with cinnamon (in this case I like to use 2 Tbsp powdered cinnamon) and 1 C honey. Cover with water as above. Bring water to a gentle boil and then immediately turn off heat. Cover pot. Cool. Refrigerate overnight. Eat as dessert or for breakfast. Really, really wonderful.

Strawberries with Whipped Cream

From a summer cooking class in 2005. Berries are cleansing, and they make heavy meals sit more comfortably in the stomach. They contain both soluble and insoluble fiber, and the fiber helps balance the simple sugars they contain.

Buy organic when you can. Why? Strawberries are heavily sprayed and their porous nature allows them to absorb pesticides and herbicides easily, which means you and yours get those right along with any non-organic berries you buy. I've read that allergic reactions to strawberries may actually be allergic reactions to the pesticides and herbicides.

Serves 4

2 qt strawberries, hulled and halved
2 C heavy whipping cream

1 Tbsp vanilla extract
½ C honey or sweetener of your choice

Rinse and prepare strawberries. Using an electric mixer, whip heavy cream with the vanilla. When soft peaks form, drizzle the honey or your favorite sweetener into mixing bowl as machine continues to beat. Stop when your cream is stiffly whipped (or not, if you like your whipped cream soft).

Put berries in pretty glasses and top with a dollop of the whipped cream.

You will have whipped cream left over. Can you make ½ the recipe? I suppose so, but my mother used to make the larger batch and then freeze dollops on a cookie sheet. When they were individually frozen, she would place them into a plastic bag and store in the freezer to top an impromptu dessert.

Note: Did you know strawberries clean teeth? Do you want to prevent tartar from settling on the teeth? Cut a strawberry, rub onto teeth and gums and leave on 45 minutes. Rinse with warm water.

Here's a recipe for a strawberry mouthwash: Press ripe berries through a strainer. Add ¼ C honey per C of berry juice and bring to a boil. Simmer just a few seconds. Cool. Add 1½ C water and ¼ C thyme tea and 4 drops peppermint oil. Gargle and rinse mouth. Kills all kinds of infections and tastes sweet. You'll taste fruity and minty all at the same time too.

TAPIOCA CHOCOLATE PUDDING BY AMANDA

Amanda started making this old-fashioned, light, comfort food in our kitchen, and many of you asked for the recipe, which ran in our August 2008 newsletter.

Tapioca is made from the cassava root, which grows well in poor soil, is resistant to drought and can live without fertilization—so the cassava root is a godsend in hot climates. It's a staple crop in Asia and Africa, where its roots produce more food per energy unit of land than any other staple crop! Nutritionally, cassava is often compared to potatoes, but with twice the fiber and much more potassium.

Business Mexico reported that agave (yes, the same plant used to make tequila) may help with weight loss and lowering cholesterol. "The structure of agave contains, among other things, substances known as fructans. Fructans reduce cholesterol and alter the absorption of fat in the intestine, at least in animals." Agave's health benefits disappear as the plant is distilled into alcohol, they go on to say, so it's better to get your agave in pudding… And agave is a sweetener tolerated by diabetics.

Serves 4-6

1 C small grain tapioca (not quick-cooking)
3 C full-fat coconut milk (2 cans)
1½ C water

½ C agave
pinch sea salt
up to 1 C Dutch-processed cocoa*

Cook all ingredients except cocoa in a double boiler for 1½-2 hours, stirring frequently with a large whisk. When the grains have expanded and the pudding has thickened and the texture is silky soft, remove from heat.

Then, Amanda says, "Stir in as much organic Dutch-processed cocoa as your chocolate desire can sustain! I use as much as a full C!"

*Don't want chocolate? Add several tablespoons of vanilla extract instead.

THE BEST COOKIE EVER

Variations on This Theme on the Next Page...

The Walnut Surprise cookies in my first cookbook were the first cookie my brothers and I learned to make when growing up in Orlando, Florida, and they're still a favorite. If I had to choose one cookie recipe to use over and over, this would be it.

Never mind the fancy desserts, these unprepossessing "best" cookies are delicious and always a hit. No matter what flavor you choose to make them, it's the basic formula that works so well. I love the fact that no matter which variation, all it takes is a bowl, a wooden spoon and a strong arm. Check out some other cookies made with this formula on the next page.

How to present these cookies? They look fine and dandy and better than ever when patted into a pie plate, baked and then cut into pie-shaped wedges. Wedges look different and more interesting when compared to other cookies. You can serve with chocolate mousse and fresh berries, fresh pineapple or ice cream, or serve plain with a cup of tea.

Serves 8-12   *Bake at 350 degrees and use a pie plate or 8x8 pan*

1 C coconut sugar   **½ C whole wheat pastry flour**
1 egg   **¼ tsp sea salt**
2 Tbsp vanilla extract   **1 C walnuts, coarsely chopped**

Preheat oven to 350 degrees. Grease the pie plate or 8x8 brownie pan (see directions at the beginning of "Desserts").

In a small bowl, beat together the sugar, egg and vanilla with a wooden spoon until "liquidy." Mix in flour and salt. Add walnuts and mix well. Batter will be sticky and hard to mix. Good exercise for flabby arms! Spoon batter into pie plate or pan. Pat out (easier to do with wet hands).

Bake cookies in preheated oven for 20 minutes, or until lightly brown and edges slightly pull away from the sides of the pie plate. Remove pie plate from oven and place on cooling rack for 10 minutes. While cookies are still warm, cut into pie wedges. Cut while still warm or you won't be able to cut at all. (These cookies are best eaten the day they are made, but they freeze beautifully.)

This is the note that ran in our December 2003 store newsletter: "When I want to make the recipe gluten-free, I substitute almond meal, pecan meal, or any ground nut flour for the whole wheat pastry flour. I've made them gluten-free, too, by using desiccated coconut instead of flour. If I need to bake something nut-free, well, it's easy to substitute currants or date pieces for the walnuts."

THE BEST COOKIE EVER AS ALMOND WALNUT BARS

Serves 8-12

1 C coconut sugar
1 egg
2 Tbsp vanilla extract

Bake at 350 degrees

1 C almond meal
¼ tsp sea salt
1 C walnuts

Directions as before, one bowl and one spoon. Easy as pie to get into oven. Gluten-free.

THE BEST COOKIE EVER AS COCONUT DREAM BARS

Serves 8-12

1 C coconut sugar
1 egg
2 Tbsp vanilla extract

Bake at 350 degrees

1 C desiccated coconut
¼ tsp sea salt
1 C chocolate chips

Directions as before, one bowl and one spoon. Easy as pie to get into oven. Gluten-free.

THE BEST COOKIE EVER AS PISTACHIO COCOA BROWNIES

Serves 8-12

1 C coconut sugar
1 egg
2 Tbsp vanilla extract

Bake at 350 degrees

1 C shelled pistachios, coarse chopped
¼ tsp sea salt
1 C cocoa powder

Directions as before, one bowl and one spoon. Easy as pie to get into oven. Gluten-free.

THE BEST COOKIE EVER AS SESAME DATE BARS

Serves 8-12

1 C coconut sugar
1 egg
2 Tbsp vanilla extract

Bake at 350 degrees

1 C unhulled, brown sesame seeds
¼ tsp sea salt
1 C dates, chopped

Directions as before, one bowl and one spoon. Easy as pie to get into oven. Gluten-free.

You can see that the basic formula lends itself to infinite variations. Each works and each is delectable. I've used so many variations, my head spins. Another favorite was ginger and currants with ground hazelnuts as the flour… Another was desiccated coconut with diced pineapple.

TOM'S CRIMSON PIE

Tom wrote, "This recipe is based on one my wife found in a magazine when we had our own catering business and cafe. With her 6th sense of what recipes will be really good, she recognized a winner. We tweaked it so it suited our taste and sold hundreds over the years. It was a favorite at Thanksgiving and Christmas parties. The orange with the peel is what gives the pie that extra special something. This is still my favorite pie ever. Serve it warm with vanilla ice cream and you'll become a fan too!"

Makes 1 pie

2 Mother's brand whole-wheat pie shells
½ orange, seedless
3 C fresh cranberries
3½ C frozen blueberries

Bake at 350 degrees

3 Tbsp cornstarch
¾ C maple syrup
1 Tbsp sweet butter
1 egg + 1 Tbsp water

Remove the pie shells from the freezer and allow to thaw. One will be used for top of the pie and one for the bottom.

Using the steel blade of a food processor, chop orange with its peel and all, into small chunks. Put the chopped orange into a soup pot. Coarsely chop cranberries in the food processor and add to the same pot together with the blueberries. Cook all the fruit over medium flame.

Meanwhile, whisk the cornstarch in the maple syrup until smooth. Add to the soup pot. Add butter too. Bring fruit to a gentle boil, stirring often because the bottom can burn easily. Cook until filling is thickened and then cool mixture in the refrigerator.

Preheat oven to 350 degrees.

Make sure pie shells are thawed and the filling is cool. Fill bottom crust with pie filling. Gently remove what will be the top crust from its tin, flip over onto filled bottom crust and crimp edges. Brush with the egg and water mixture.

Bake pie for about 30 minutes, or until crust is nicely browned. Allow pie to cool out of oven on rack. Serve to cries of rapture.

Note from Debra: I always like to put my pies onto a cookie sheet with sides so that if the filling bubbles over, I don't have the whole oven to clean up. And the cookie sheet makes carrying the pie to the oven and taking it out easier as well.

Ultimate Chocolate Chip Bars

Way back when, Geoff brought us a version of this recipe from *Natural Health* magazine. We played around with it and finally came up with this, which we've been making for years now. We shared it with you in our October 2006 newsletter.

Can these bars be gluten-free?* You bet! In fact, our kitchen has figured out how to make most of our treats gluten-free for birthdays, holidays, family get-togethers, or Random Nights of Indulgence.

Makes 16 bars

3 C rolled oats*
2 C whole wheat pastry flour*
1 tsp sea salt
½ tsp baking soda
2 C sliced almonds

Bake at 375 degrees and use 9x13 pan

2 C chocolate chips
1 C canola or other oil
1 C maple syrup
4 tsp vanilla extract

Preheat oven to 375 degrees. Grease the baking pan (see directions at the beginning of "Desserts").

In a large bowl, mix all the ingredients together. Spoon into the pan and flatten using your hands. (It's a lot less sticky if you wet your hands first!)

Bake cookies for 25 minutes, or until lightly browned. Remove pan from the oven and place on a wire rack so cookies can cool slightly. Cut into 16 bars. Eat with joy.

Feel free to use your favorite gluten-free baking mix instead of whole wheat pastry flour. Feel free to use a nut meal. With regard to oats, recent studies seem to indicate that moderate amounts of oats in an otherwise gluten-free diet do no harm (and there are gluten-free oats, which are grown and processed in fields and facilities where there is no cross-contamination). You can also use quinoa or rice flakes instead of oats.

Upside-Down Cake with Apples and Ginger

Another gluten-free experiment, which you can serve to everyone and have them all sighing with contentment. You can make this cake dairy-free by substituting something for the butter, and use a gluten-free baking mix (if you must!) for the nut flour. If you do use a gluten-free baking mix, leave out the tapioca flour, baking powder and salt.

Makes a 9-10" round cake pan

¼ C butter, melted
¼ C maple syrup
4 Tbsp baker's crystallized ginger
4 Tbsp currants or raisins
2 large apples, peeled, cored, sliced
1 Tbsp lemon juice
½ C nut or seed flour
2 Tbsp tapioca flour
1 tsp baking powder

Bake at 400 degrees

pinch sea salt
2 tsp cinnamon
1 tsp ground allspice
½ tsp ground nutmeg
½ tsp ground cloves
2 eggs
¼ C maple syrup
1 tsp vanilla extract

Preheat oven to 400 degrees.

Pour melted butter into cake pan. Add maple syrup and swirl. Sprinkle ginger and currants evenly over bottom. Toss apples with lemon. Arrange apple slices over currants.

In another bowl, mix nut or seed flour, tapioca flour, baking powder, salt and spices.

With electric mixer, beat eggs with maple syrup and vanilla for 3-5 minutes until thick and creamy. Add flour and spice mixture. Beat for a few seconds, just to incorporate into egg mixture. Pour batter over apples slices and bake cake in middle of preheated oven for 20-25 minutes or until sharp knife poked in the center of the cake comes out clean.

Let cake cool in pan for about 30 minutes. Run knife around outside edges and put cake plate over pan. Turn pan upside down and your upside-down apple cake will be seated properly and nicely on your cake plate! Serve warm with whipped cream or at room temperature with a cup of Rooibos tea!

Beauty Beauts

There are so many beauty secrets, but this chapter just has a few beauts for posterity.

BEATRICE STARK'S HAIR GROWER

This really worked for Mom. She claimed it would work for anyone, as long as the hair follicles weren't dead. How on earth did she come up with this? I believe that when her hair started falling out like crazy due to stress, she called Redkin Laboratories and spoke to someone who suggested she might want to try something old-fashioned like this remedy.

I do remember her using it while we lived in Orlando, Florida, and I know that her hair did grow back curly and thick. The curls lasted about a year, and then her natural wave came back instead.

1 pt vodka (cheapest kind is fine)
1 oz apple cider vinegar

2 Tbsp cayenne pepper (aka capsaicin)
1 oz aloe vera

Mom said, "Place the vinegar, cayenne and aloe in the vodka. Shake daily for 3 weeks. The mixture is then ready to use.

"Dispense some of mixture into a squirt bottle, and then squirt 10-18 drops on any bald spots. MAKE SURE NOT TO GET ANY IN YOUR EYES. Rub vigorously. It will burn and feel as though blood is running down the face, but it will gradually ease off. May be left on hair all day.

"The cayenne pepper stimulates the cells, the vinegar gives the right acid/alkaline balance, and the aloe heals and conditions the cells. The vodka drives it all in.

"DMSO would probably work in place of vodka, but the odor might be offensive.

"Results (new hair sprouting) show after 6 weeks."

BORAGE FACE & BODY BUTTER

The winds blow cold in February, and this face and body butter soothes, protects and moisturizes dry, chapped skin. Look familiar? Aren't you smart!? I ran this recipe in 1997 and still get requests for it. So for those of you who don't save our newsletters in loose-leaf notebooks, here it is again. (Thanks to everyone who does save our newsletters. Makes us feel that we are part of your life and library!)

Makes a few cups

GROUP 1
¾ C oil (your choice, but my favorite is borage with a splash of oils like jojoba, argan, sesame, almond)
⅓ C coconut oil or cocoa butter
1 tsp liquid lanolin (optional)
½ oz beeswax (essential)

GROUP 2
⅔ C rosewater
⅓ C other liquid like aloe vera or raw apple cider vinegar
few drops essential oils*
few drops vitamin E oil
dollop of royal jelly or raw honey

Melt **GROUP 1** over low heat. I have a large oven-proof measuring cup which goes right onto my burner. You can use a small pot or double boiler pot. Leave melted mixture in measuring cup or pot. Cool to room temperature, about 5 minutes. Oils will become thick, creamy and semi-solid.

Place **GROUP 2** in a blender and blend at highest speed. Drizzle (just like making mayonnaise) GROUP 1 into center vortex. Pour slowly until there is no more GROUP 1 in measuring cup or pot, and blender makes a spluttering or coughing sound. At that point, you'll have a beautiful, thick cream just like magic—the same magic that happens when you make homemade mayo!

Using a rubber spatula, spoon face and body cream into small glass jars. The blender will be tough to clean out. Use hands. Over next several days, lavish the cream over face and bod. Enjoy how it feels when it soaks in. Your skin will thank you!

Note: If you use the apple cider vinegar, you'll smell it, but it dissipates quickly and is great for skin. If you choose honey or royal jelly, don't use more than a dollop or you'll be a little sticky, and the bees will follow you around like love-sick puppies…

We love essential oils! Some enliven, some relax. Open our store testers and sniff. Discover which scents make you feel good…. I like to combine lavender, ylang ylang, clary sage, geranium, rosewood. Few drops of rose, if budget allows. All these oils are said to make skin glow. They calm and warm the heart. Geranium is said to be especially good for mature skin.

BORAGE OIL

This appeared in our June 2009 newsletter about borage oil.

Why am I hot to trot on borage oil (take a look at all the little bottles of borage oil in the fridge next to the flax seed oils)? Because this primarily omega-6 essential fatty acid is the richest source of Gamma-Linolenic Acid (GLA), which is said to be omega-3s' healing partner (fish oil is probably the best source of omega-3s). We've been hearing tons about fish oil the last few years, and more lately about vitamin D, but did you know that when you take these with borage oil, the synergistic effect of the three together yields greater benefits for things like inflammation than when any of the three are taken alone?

Borage oil became part of my regimen some years ago to combat psoriasis and eczema. It was a godsend! I went from never having heard of borage oil to being its drum-beater in our store. Studies I read said that a therapeutic dose for psoriasis and eczema appears to be between 275 and 345 milligrams daily, or about ½ tsp.

And, yes, I took borage oil by itself when I started taking it 15 years ago. I added fish oil and vitamin D as I kept reading Adam's articles and hearing more and more in the press. I just read an article that summarized current research indicating that taking 1,000 iu vitamin D and 1,000-2,000 mg fish oil *with* borage oil enhances the benefits of all three with regard to psoriasis and eczema, as well as benefits mentioned below.

Jack Challem, a nutrition writer, says that the Danish Olympic team uses fish oil and GLA to treat inflammatory overuse injuries among athletes. The regimen, approximately 600-700 mg of each fatty acid enables athletes to keep training as they heal. Mr. Challem also reports that GLA supplements have been shown to significantly reduce symptoms of rheumatoid arthritis. Studies at the U of MA, Worcester, found 1.4 and 2.8 grams of GLA daily led to a 25% to 45% reduction in symptoms—that's a lot of borage oil, about 2 teaspoons on the lower side. (This study didn't say what would happen if people took less borage oil, but took it with fish oil and vitamin D.)

With regard to obesity and these good fats, Mr. Challem reported that being overweight suggests disturbed fat metabolism. Trans-fats seem to promote weight gain, and good fats like GLA appear to help people *keep* weight off. In a small study, people who lost weight received either GLA or placebo. Those who took GLA for a year regained 4 pounds. In contrast, people taking placebos regained 17 pounds.

Taking borage oil works for my skin. I take ½ tsp daily, which means the little 4 ounce bottle yields 48 days' worth. Yes, I take 2,000 mg of fish oil and 2,000 iu of vitamin D now too.

LOVELY SKIN WITH AYURVEDIC MASSAGE

The skin, which is our largest organ, breathes, repairs itself and rids our body of toxins.

Ayurvedic practitioners believe a daily oil massage not only slows and prevents genetic breakdown and disease, but that it activates the lymphatic system whose job it is to filter blood plasma, deliver nutrients to cells and carry away cellular debris. A daily oil massage, they believe, harmonizes mind and body. In fact, scientists have discovered that skin is the richest source of both hormones and immune cells. Touching the skin encourages hormones like serotonin to calm mind and emotions.

Unlike blood which moves because the heart pumps, lymph depends upon muscular contractions such as those generated by exercise or massage.

Oils, such as an unrefined sesame oil, which is most often recommended—or coconut, almond, grapeseed, avocado and olive oil, to name a few—have antioxidant, antibacterial and anti-inflammatory properties. They can penetrate skin easily.

(If you choose sesame oil, cure by heating slowly and carefully just to the boiling point, and then cool. Curing is said to make the oil more therapeutic.)

Always use unrefined oils, organic when possible.

To give yourself an oil massage, allow 30 minutes (15 minutes for the massage and 15 minutes to allow the oil to penetrate). If you're in a mad dash, do the massage in 5 minutes, or just put a drop of oil on the top of your head, stroke down the rest of your body and hop, carefully (since oil is slippery), into the shower.

It's more important to do a little massage every day instead of a whole lot of massage once in a blue moon!

Messy? Is there tea in China? But you can get into the habit, and even 5 minutes a day will confer health benefits, and skin becomes soft and lovely. Don't worry if family members laugh like hyenas. Be dignified and just do it.

I have designated an old towel to stand on while massaging. The Ayurvedic Center in Lancaster says that towels need to be washed with baking soda and detergent so they don't become a fire hazard (all that oil). Since oil can clog drains, use a biodegradable drain cleaner like Bio-Kleen, or put 1 C baking soda followed by 2 C white vinegar down your drain. Follow that (either the Bio-Kleen or baking soda and vinegar combination) with some boiling water at least an hour later. (cont.)

How to do a daily oil massage

1. Keep some oil in a little squeeze-top plastic container. Use warm oil (warm by running hot water over the jar). You'll need about ⅛ to ¼ C each time. Add oil to hand or directly onto skin. According to Ms. Raichur of the book *Absolute Beauty*, use more oil for dry skin, less for sensitive, and even less for oily skin. According to the folks at Healing Essence Center above the store—dry brush massage first, and then use sesame oil. This double treatment normalizes skin imbalances.

2. Use the palm, the flat of the hand (fingers and thumb together). You don't have to knead deeply. Moderate pressure over the body and light pressure over the stomach and heart does the trick.

3. Use circular motions over rounded areas like joints and the head. Use straight strokes up and down over straight areas like limbs between joints.

4. Since the head is considered most important, spend the majority of your time there. Put oil into palm and place hand on top of head. Massage vigorously with circular motion. Do same on side of head and all over. Don't forget ear lobes. This feels good!

5. On hands and feet, stroke upward only

6. On neck and face, stroke upward or sideways.

Note: Make sure you sip plenty of warm/hot water or herbal tea to help the body remove toxins loosened by the massage. I've been told that age spots can be made to disappear in 4-6 months with daily oil massage. Interesting!

Leftovers

This section has recipes and musings that don't seem to fit elsewhere. They are not, however, afterthoughts, so don't skip this section!

Ayurvedic Chutney

Chutneys are condiments used to add pizzazz, and this is one I've made for years after having eaten something very similar at an Ayurvedic spa.

By the by, coconut doesn't deserve the bad rap it's gotten. It's rich in medium chain triglycerides (MCTs), which help the body burn bad fat and produce energy.

Makes about 1½ C

1 C unsweetened desiccated coconut
1 C water
4 Tbsp cilantro, chopped
1 2-inch piece of ginger, unpeeled
2 tsp sea salt

1 Tbsp ghee
1 tsp whole cumin seeds
1 tsp brown mustard seeds
¼ tsp asafoetida
¼ tsp cayenne pepper

Soak coconut in water until water has been pretty much absorbed, about 1 hour.

Place soaked coconut in blender with cilantro, ginger and salt. Blend. Use rubber spatula as needed to move mixture toward blade.

In a small pan, gently warm ghee. Add spices and stir for 1 minute or until seeds pop.

Add spice mix to blender. Blend a few seconds.

Note: You can serve this chutney with just about anything. I particularly like it with quinoa or millet.

Blue Ribbon Edition

BAY SEASONING-MIX

We made zucchini "crab cakes" in the store and mixed up our own take on Bay Seasoning mix. (The cakes were scrumptious, but made from someone else's recipe we found on-line, so I can't include it here.) When you make this bay seasoning, just store the mix in an airtight container so you'll have it on hand when you want a terrific seasoning to top just about anything.

This seasoning, I kid you not, made the zucchini fritters taste as if those zucchini came from the sea and walked out on little crab legs.

Makes about ¼ C

1 Tbsp ground bay leaves
2 tsp celery seed
2 tsp dry mustard powder
1 tsp black pepper
½ tsp ground nutmeg
¼ tsp ground allspice

½ tsp ginger powder
1 tsp paprika
½ tsp chili pepper flakes
¼ tsp ground mace
¼ tsp ground cardamom
1 tsp sea salt

Combine all ingredients and mix thoroughly. Store in an airtight container in a cool place. Can anything be simpler? (Please get your spices from bulk bins like ours because those spices are fresher, much less expensive, and you can scoop out how much or how little you want.)

Note: Feel free to multiply the recipe and make it times 4, for instance, so you have a cup's worth. That's what we did in our kitchen.

BEAUTIFUL BABY NIGHT SNACK TO EAT DURING PREGNANCY

I enjoyed this every night while I was pregnant with Adam because I was determined to eat as much *good stuff* and great nutrition so he would be born beautiful and healthy. He was a beautiful baby!

This dish provides fiber, protein, essential fatty acids and minerals like calcium and magnesium. Because of the fiber, sip red raspberry tea while you eat this. (Fiber needs warm liquid to work properly.) Red raspberry tea is the tea recommended for all women during pregnancy.

Makes 6 C

1 C raw shelled sunflower seeds	1 C raw wheat germ
1 C unhulled brown sesame seeds	1 C oat, rice or wheat bran
1 C cocoa or carob powder	1 Tbsp honey* each time you eat this

Mix all the dry ingredients. Store in a couple of wide-mouth glass jars or plastic containers and keep in the freezer.

Each night, spoon 2-3 Tbsp-fuls into a little dish and add about 1 Tbsp honey. Mush around with your spoon until all the dry ingredients are clumpy and somewhat held together with the honey. Eat and enjoy this snack and treasure the warmth of the tea cup or mug held between your hands at the same time. It becomes a lovely evening ritual.

Note: You can add any "superfood" such as chia or hemp seeds. Give a pinch of cinnamon a try too.

Note: I can't leave this page without recommending my brother David Stark's DVD, *BabyBabyOhBaby*. This DVD has changed lives. It's a Lamaze-recommended resource and is even being used at the Mother Theresa Center in Rwanda.

BabyBabyOhBaby is for moms and dads, and any other member of the family who wants to bond with that new bundle of joy. I wish I'd been able to watch this and learn how to touch and massage my baby. My advice? Get it and watch it before your beautiful babe is born! (Yes, there is also a Spanish version.)

*If you don't want to use honey, use maple syrup, agave or molasses.

CRANBERRY BLUEBERRY POMEGRANATE SAUCE

So many variations. So easy! Keeps for weeks in the fridge. I like to store in old glass peanut butter jars. Goes with more than turkey...

This sauce contains three fruits that are all at the top of the ORAC chart. ORAC is a method of measuring antioxidant capacities in biological samples. A positive link has been established between foods rich in antioxidants, high on the ORAC chart, and health. People who eat foods rich in antioxidants have extra ammunition to quench the free radicals that make our bodies age prematurely.

Makes about 10 cups

4 C cranberries, fresh or frozen
2 C blueberries, fresh or frozen
2 C pomegranate juice, or ½ C
   pomegranate concentrate

1 C honey or agave
1 Tbsp cinnamon
1 Tbsp orange zest

Put everything in a large saucepan and bring to a gentle, almost boil. Lower heat and simmer for 5 minutes, or until cranberries pop.

Remove from heat, cool to room temperature and then store in fridge. Serve cold with everything.

Note: This even makes a great mix-in with yogurt or oatmeal.

CRANBERRY CHUTNEY

This cranberry dish (a little of dis, a little of dat) is great alongside a bird, great on sandwiches, or anytime you want something a little sweet-tart.

Use organic cranberries if you can because commercially grown cranberries are heavily sprayed. I buy lots of organic cranberries in season and freeze them. That way I can enjoy them year-round.

What do cranberries do for us? Sally Fallon in *Nourishing Traditions* says that as early as the year 1860, medical science recognized cranberries as useful in the treatment of urinary tract infections and kidney problems. They also contain an anti-cancer compound called ellagic acid. And they're uniquely New England!

Makes about 6 C

2 Tbsp extra virgin olive oil (EVOO)
1 onion, diced, about 2 C
6 cloves garlic, minced
4 C cranberries, fresh or frozen
½ C dried apricots, diced, or dried currants
½ C honey, agave or maple syrup
1½ pear, papaya or mango juice

¼ C balsamic vinegar
1½ tsp sea salt
1½ tsp black pepper
½ tsp ground allspice
1 tsp cinnamon
1 tsp ginger powder
2 whole cloves

Gently warm EVOO in a large skillet. Add onion and sauté until translucent, about 5 minutes. Add garlic and stir another 2 minutes. Add cranberries, apricots (or currants), honey, juice, balsamic vinegar, salt, pepper and spices. Bring to a gentle boil over a medium flame. Lower flame and simmer until thickened, about 30 minutes.

Cool and then refrigerate. Eat whenever you want to with anything you want.

Note: This recipe keeps for weeks and weeks in the fridge.

CRUNCHY TOASTED CHICKPEAS AND PISTACHIOS

A most satisfying trail mix. Try it, you'll like it! The variations on this theme are endless...

I've made this snacking mix a little spicy because I like spice, and also because cayenne pepper increases circulation, which is a good thing.

Worried about the fat in nuts? Nuts like pistachios, as part of a balanced diet, don't make you fat and can lower blood pressure.

This mix contains fiber, protein and good fat, so enjoy guilt-free!

Makes about 2½ C

2 cans Eden chickpeas, about 4 C cooked
¼ C extra virgin olive oil (EVOO)
1 tsp coarse Celtic sea salt

Roast at 400 degrees

1 tsp black pepper
½ tsp cayenne pepper
1 C shelled pistachios

Preheat oven to 400 degrees.

Drain chickpeas and toss in bowl with next 4 ingredients. Spoon mixture on to a rimmed baking pan.

Bake until chickpeas are golden and crisp, stirring from time to time, about 20 minutes.

Remove pan from oven. Stir in pistachios. Cool and serve.

If you and yours don't consume on the spot, I'll be a monkey's uncle....

CURRIED EGG SALAD SANDWICHES

I didn't know that the word "curry" was adopted by the British from an Indian word that meant a fish stew with tamarind and curry leaves. What is clear is that the word as we use it here, today, means something completely different than the original, and the word "curry" as we know it, has no meaning in India. Nonetheless, enjoy.

Serves 6

12 hard-boiled eggs, peeled and
   halved
¼ C chopped dates, or use currants
1 scallion, sliced
½ C mayo, or un-mayo of your choice
1 Tbsp curry powder

1 small cucumber, peeled and diced,
   about 1 C
1 tsp Spike seasoning
12 slices wonderful whole-grain bread
6 pieces of romaine lettuce

Mix all the ingredients except the bread and lettuce together. You'll want to make sure eggs are mashed and that everything is well-incorporated.

Cover and chill for about 30 minutes.

Toast bread and then divide the egg salad among 6 toast slices. Top each of the 6 sandwiches with a piece of romaine lettuce, then another piece of toast. Put the sandwiches out for 6 hungry souls. I can hear their moans of contentment now.

DEBRA'S FAMOUS COLD REMEDY

Each one of my cookbooks has had this recipe because it works! Adam says that I used to torture him with it when he was too little to appreciate its effectiveness. My brother Daniel Stark took it on a bike trip to Nova Scotia and said it saved his vacation. Brother David Stark said he'd rather die than have something this spicy.

If your throat hurts too much to swallow, this will act like balm.

Enough for the whole family

1 C raw honey
1 Tbsp cayenne pepper

1-2 Tbsp prepared horseradish

Place the honey in a glass jar. Add the remaining ingredients and stir well, until liquidy.

Store until you feel something coming on, or have a sore throat. Take a $\frac{1}{16}$ teaspoon dose, which is just a tiny dot. Take the medicine off the spoon using your teeth, not your lips or tongue (you don't want to burn them). Take as needed. (Sometimes it helps having this beside the bed in case you wake up in the middle of the night with a sore throat.)

How does this work? Honey coats the throat, cayenne warms it and stops the hurt. And we all know horseradish opens blocked nasal passages. So stop laughing and mix some up today.

Note: Over the years I've gotten more creative and sometimes add ginger juice or finely minced fresh ginger. I used to think that I had to store this in the fridge, but because honey is a natural preservative, I now keep my jar of Debra's Famous Cold Remedy in the cupboard.

FAMOUS ROASTED RED ONIONS

Amanda says, "I learned how to make these really simple onions from a James Beard award-winning chef! But they're so easy, anyone can make them at home. These roasted onions keep well in the fridge in a covered container, and they're excellent to have on hand to spice up a bowl of plain grains or a boring burger. Roasted onions are even great on salad."

Makes about 3½ cups.

3 red onions, about 6 C
¼ C agave
¼ C red wine vinegar
¼ C extra virgin olive oil (EVOO)

Roast at 375 degrees

1 tsp sea salt
1 tsp black pepper
sprig of fresh thyme

Peel onions and then slice each into 6 fat rounds, first discarding the end. (Each slice should be about a pinky-finger thick.) Whisk agave and red wine vinegar. Pour over onion slices, being careful to keep them intact. Allow onion rounds to marinate for a few minutes.

Preheat oven to 375 degrees.

Oil a baking sheet with some (about 2 Tbsp) of the EVOO. Sprinkle with ½ tsp salt and ½ tsp pepper. Line up the onion slices on the baking sheet. Sprinkle the slices with the remaining ½ tsp salt and ½ tsp pepper. Crumble thyme between your fingers and sprinkle over onions too.

Drizzle the remaining EVOO on top of the onion slices so they are well-coated. Roast onions for about 30 minutes, turning once if you feel so inclined!

FIG AND DATE SESAME JAM

Figs and dates were eaten daily back in the days of ancient Greece because they were seen as a remedy for all ailments. The Roman writer Pliny believed figs increased strength and held off wrinkles! Did you know, too, that figs are high in fiber and minerals like calcium, potassium and iron? In addition, they contain an enzyme which helps with digestion.

Years ago I read that figs and dates help smokers quit smoking, but I don't personally know anyone who's put that to the test. If you give it a try, report back to me!

Makes about 3½ cups.

1 C honey or molasses
½ C water
2 C dried figs, any kind or assorted
   varieties
1 C pitted dates, or date pieces in oat
   flour

4 Tbsp lemon zest
2 Tbsp lemon juice
1/2 tsp cinnamon
½ C unhulled brown sesame seeds

Simmer honey and water in a heavy saucepan until honey melts. Stir in figs, dates, lemon zest and lemon juice together with cinnamon.

On low heat, simmer uncovered, stirring occasionally, until thick and soft, about 1 hour. Remove from heat and add in sesame seeds.

FOOD THAT IS BLACK

This column (and recipe) by Adam appeared in our September 2008 newsletter. I'm repeating it here because it's an interesting and fun read. Good recipe too!

"A few months ago, I came across a news item claiming that the newest food trend in Japan is black food: black sesame seeds, black rice, black vinegar, black soybeans, etc.

Well, that piqued my interest. I mean, don't get me wrong: I hear about a different food trend every week, and I tend to ignore most of them (Microgreens, anyone? Cod liver oil-infused potato chips? How about a nice bottle of micro-cluster water suffused with color energy and Universal Love Vibrations?) Black food may or may not be an actual trend in Japan—I don't know; I've never been there—but at least this one would make sense.

Generally speaking, the more darkly colored a plant food is—the better it's able to stain our clothing—the better it is for us. There's a reason for this. Plants produce pigments to protect themselves from environmental damage, especially oxidation . In other words, plant pigments are antioxidants—broadly protective not just of the plants that create them, but of the animals that eat them. Plant pigments protect and strengthen the blood vessels, brain, liver, kidneys and cell membranes.

So we see that red wine is healthier than white wine. Black beans are healthier than white. Purple corn is healthier than yellow. Bilberries (which have dark flesh) are healthier than blueberries (with pale flesh inside). Black rice bran lowers cholesterol better than bran from brown rice; black soybeans have a similar advantage over yellow. Both Ayurveda (the ancient medical system of India) and traditional Chinese medicine place special value on black foods.

Mostly you can use black ingredients as you'd use their lighter-colored cousins. They tend to have a deeper, stronger, more complex flavor (think, for example, of red wine versus white; or dark beer versus an India Pale Ale). Personally, I love using China Forbidden black rice to plate brightly colored foods (salmon and asparagus; scallops with sautéed yellow and red peppers). And I adore Black Beluga lentils, so named because they glisten and shine like beluga caviar.

Here's a recipe that's quick, easy, satisfying—equally good hot, right from stove top; or cold, three days later."

---

[1] *Actually, scientists have shown that plants grown under harsher environmental conditions tend to be healthier for us to eat. The idea is that plants, in protecting themselves from harsh conditions (excessive sunlight especially), respond by producing higher levels of these antioxidant pigments.*

Serves 4

1 lb meat, poultry or veggie sausage (the Field Roast brand is especially good)

cooking fat (only necessary if using veggie "meat")

2 red onions, chopped, about 4 C

2 C chopped veggies, such as celery, spinach, carrots, and/or chard (optional)

¼ C dried porcini mushrooms, chopped (optional)

2 C black Beluga lentils

2 Tbsp rubbed sage

5 C water or stock

1-2 Tbsp tomato paste

1 tsp sea salt

1 tsp black pepper

In a large skillet, brown sausage, breaking up or cutting into bite-sized pieces. If you're using a very low-fat product, or veggie "meat," add a little oil. Add the onions and optional veggies and cook until onions are translucent, about 5 minutes.

Add the lentils, sage and liquid. Cover and simmer at lowest heat until cooked, about 40 minutes.

Stir in tomato paste to taste. Add salt and pepper. Taste and adjust seasoning.

Serve with some crusty whole-grain bread, maybe, says Adam.

Gourmet Charoses

This Passover recipe makes a nice addition to any special dinner. A friend told me she served it with her Easter ham. So on matzo or with ham, it's all good. We live in a crazy, mixed up world…

Of charoses, there are many versions. It's supposed to symbolize the mortar used by slaves in building pyramids in Eygpt. Eating charoses is supposed to remind us that not everyone is free to live (or eat) as they choose.

My eclectic, unorthodox version of charoses started because I didn't like the look or taste of the traditional version, which contains apples, walnuts, cinnamon and wine. You be the judge and tell me if this doesn't rock your boat.

Makes about 6 C

1 C dried cherries
4 apples, peeled and diced
½ C Turkish apricots, diced
½ C date pieces in oat flour
½ C pine nuts (walnuts are traditional)

3 Tbsp crystallized ginger
¼ tsp ground cardamom
1 tsp cinnamon
½ C lemon juice
1 C mango juice

Put all the ingredients in a saucepan. Simmer over low heat until most of the liquid is absorbed by the fruit, about 15 minutes.

Cool. Serve immediately or store in fridge or even the freezer. (I've been known to store for months in the freezer until I have a culinary emergency.)

Note: I change this a little each time I make it, depending on what I have in my refrigerator. And sometimes I don't cook the apples; but most times I do.

HARISSA (MOROCCAN CHILE-GARLIC PASTE)

If I lived in Morocco, I'd make this with a mortar and pestle. Since I don't live in Morocco, I've been making this in a blender or food processor for many moons. Actually more than 480 moons, since a former college roommate shared with me her recipe for this fiery hot chili sauce. We used to put it inside pita with falafel and chopped veggies.

Harissa is not only a condiment, but can be used as an ingredient in other dishes. I love it with rice, beans, millet, grilled poultry or fish.

Makes about ⅔ C

8-10 dried hot chilies
¼ C extra virgin olive oil (EVOO)
8 cloves garlic
½ tsp sea salt

1 tsp ground coriander
1 tsp ground caraway
1 tsp ground cumin
2 Tbsp water (optional)

Stem and seed chilies. Break into pieces, rinse under cold water and then let stand 5 minutes. Do not pat dry. (When handling chiles, be careful not to rub your eyes. Wash hands each time you finish working with them.)

Using the steel blade of a food processor, blend the chilies together with EVOO, garlic, salt, coriander, caraway and cumin. Stop the processor when the harissa still has some texture.

Only add water if needed to move the sauce under the blades.

Note: Harissa will keep in the fridge for a week. You can spoon into ice cube trays and freeze. Pop harissa cubes into a plastic sandwich baggie and store in the freezer.

JIM'S TOFU WITH MISO/TAHINI SAUCE

Jim says, "Thirty years ago there was a macrobiotic restaurant in Boston called the Seventh Inn. One entrée I had there was served with a miso tahini sauce (made with the traditional red miso). I liked the idea, but found it too salty for my taste. Not long afterwards, I was introduced to sweet white miso, in which rice is combined with soy to add starch that then breaks down during the fermentation, and creates a smooth sweet/salty paste. I immediately saw the potential for using miso/tahini as a kind of vegan cheese sauce. After all, it has many of the qualities I enjoy in cheese—a little salt, a little fat, a little sweet—appealing to our basic atavistic dietary desires!"

Jim suggests serving this dish over brown rice and alongside steamed green and orange vegetables. Kale and carrots are his usual choice.

Makes 2 C, enough to serve 4-6 with tofu

SAUCE
⅔ C sweet white miso
¾ C water
⅔ C tahini

Bake at 350 degrees in an 8x8 pan

TOFU MIXTURE
½ C extra virgin olive oil (EVOO)
1 onion, sliced, about 2 C
2 lb firm or extra firm tofu
fresh parsley sprigs as garnish

To make the sauce: Spoon miso into a large measuring cup and add ¼ C of the water. Stir until smooth. Now stir in tahini so that you have a thick sauce. Thin by stirring in the remaining ½ C water. Set the sauce aside while you prepare the rest of the dish.

To make the tofu mixture: Gently warm ¼ C EVOO in a skillet. Add onion and sauté 5 minutes, or until translucent. Slice the tofu into ¼-inch, or slightly thicker, sheets.

Preheat oven to 350 degrees.

Using the remainder of EVOO, oil an 8x8 2-inch deep Pyrex dish or baking pan. Layer tofu slices so that they overlap slightly. Cover with the sautéed onions, and then pour the sauce over the entire dish so everything is well-coated. Cover dish with a lid or tinfoil, and bake for 1-1¼ hours, or until topping is golden and slightly brown at the edges. Serve garnished with parsley.

Note: This sauce is, of course, a vegan recipe in its own right and could be used to make vegan cauliflower cheese ("Delicious!" Jim says). Jim wonders how it would work in macaroni and cheese, but hasn't tried that.

KEVIN'S RED WINE SAUCE

Kevin says, "The first time I made this sauce, I really didn't have a plan. I had learned some basics over the years about making a good sauce, where else but from the movie *Goodfellas*, and also from Molto Mario on the *Food Network*.

"Every time I make my sauce, it turns differently because I add 1 or 2 extra ingredients I feel like adding. The first time I made it, I threw in chopped clementines, which added a citrus zing. Sometimes I add hot sauce and/or chopped habanero peppers. It all depends on what I'm feeling when I'm making it.

"Regardless of whatever extra ingredients I add, the red wine always gives the sauce a nice burgundy color, and gives it a very nice flavor (enough to make up for the fact that I never add sugar or salt)."

Makes 6 C

½ C extra virgin olive oil (EVOO)
3-5 cloves garlic, finely chopped
½ C red onion, finely chopped
1 carrot, chopped, about 2 C
1 vine-ripened tomato, chopped, about 1 ½ C
fresh basil, leaves torn off stems
hot sauce (optional)
olives (optional)
peppers of all kinds (optional)

2 cans Italian peeled tomatoes, seeded with thumbs to reduce bitterness
10 oz red wine
garlic powder to taste
onion powder to taste
fresh cracked pepper to taste
oregano to taste

Gently warm EVOO in a skillet. Add garlic, onion and carrot. Sauté about 5 minutes. Add chopped ripe tomato and lots of basil. Sauté another 5 minutes. Then take out your horn and start to play jazz, Kevin says, with extra ingredients of your choice. Mix it up each time so each batch of sauce is an original. You want each batch to be unique!

Lower heat, add canned tomatoes that you've seeded, and then add wine, garlic powder, onion powder, black pepper and oregano. Simmer sauce for 3-6 hours. Stir occasionally. Taste at the end and go "Wow!"

Note: Kevin says that this sauce is excellent with fried eggplant. His recipe for fried eggplant is to cut the eggplant into ¼ inch slices, dip them in flour, then in whisked egg and then in bread crumbs. Fry in a pan with EVOO. Melt fresh buffalo mozzarella cheese on top!

KURT'S PECAN PESTO

Kurt Hackler worked in the store for years. He had a crazy sense of humor and called this his "weed-wacker pesto."

Who woulda' thunk any pesto that is vegan could taste this good (talk about a politically incorrect statement on my part!)? Not I, for sure. But I love this pesto as much as any I've made with Pecorino romano.

According to Kurt, Adam asked our Gaia Herbs representative what his #1 choice was for the herb most critical for overall health. The answer was "Basil!"

Pecans in this recipe add healthy fat, and the garlic does so many wonderful things for us that I am, on this page, speechless.

If a raw extra virgin olive oil like Bariani is used, this pesto is also a raw recipe.

Makes about 6 C

½ C raw pecans
2-4 cloves garlic
4 oz basil leaves removed from stems
   (about 2 Applefield Farms bunches,
   or 4-6 C)

⅔ C extra virgin olive oil (EVOO)
½ tsp Celtic fine sea salt
pinch of cayenne (optional)

Using the steel blade of a food processor, blend the ingredients, starting with the pecans and garlic. Once they are chopped fine, add basil, EVOO, salt and cayenne (if using).

Stop when pesto is the consistency you like. I like mine somewhat coarse.

Use as topping for pasta, chicken, shrimp, tofu, or as a dip for all kinds of stuff. The possibilities are endless. This makes a great appetizer with tomatoes, celery or other veggies. It works in sandwiches too. One of my favorite ways to use this pesto is as a topping for slices of polenta which I then pop into a 375 degree oven, heat for 10 minutes and then serve as a great, simple gourmet appetizer.

Kurt says to make pesto in big batches so you can freeze it for later use. "Giant quantities," he says, "can be made in a 5-gallon pail with a (clean) weed-wacker. Be sure to divide into small portions before freezing."

Note: Try making this with different oils too. Kurt suggests using a bit of Austrian pumpkin seed oil for a unique taste.

Mary Jane's Lavender Mayo

Mary Jane says, "I grow lavender in my garden, but because it's not particularly hardy to our zone, I dig it up and bring it in for the winter, treating it as a houseplant. In addition to making potpourri, I have come to think of lavender as an edible plant too. This recipe is a favorite—so very easy and great in a sandwich or as a dip."

Makes 1½-2 cups

1½ tsp fresh lavender blossoms, or ½ tsp dried lavender

12 oz soft tofu

1 small clove of garlic

1 tsp extra virgin olive oil (EVOO)

3-4 Tbsp water

1 Tbsp white vinegar

½ tsp kosher salt

Using a mortar and pestle, crush lavender to release its essence. In a blender or small food processor, combine crushed lavender with the remaining ingredients, and process until smooth. Cover and refrigerate for up to 5 days.

Mary Jane says, "We always use this up pretty fast since it does not keep well, but it tastes so wonderful you'll find umpteen uses for lavender mayo!"

PINK STEVIA LEMONADE

Thanks to Adam, we've been enjoying this recipe for some years now. You can too!

If you don't know, stevia is a South American herb that tastes much sweeter than sugar. The good thing is that stevia doesn't affect blood sugar, is safe for diabetics and contains virtually no calories. An 8-oz cup of Pink Stevia Lemonade yields roughly 3 calories. You can live it up, baby!

Adam wrote, "Hibiscus is a beautiful flower and makes a pretty tea and lemonade, but does it have any health benefits? There are consistent scientific studies that show hibiscus helps with hypertension and liver disorders. One study, published in 2004 in the journal *Phytomedicine* (2004;11:375–82), concluded that 'people suffering from hypertension can lower their blood pressure significantly by drinking hibiscus tea daily. The study included 70 people—½ of whom drank 16-oz of hibiscus tea before breakfast daily, or ingested 25 mg of an antihypertensive medication (*captopril*) twice daily. After one month, the hibiscus tea drinkers' diastolic blood pressure was reduced at least 10 points in 79% of the participants; blood pressure in the medicated group was reduced at least 10 points in some 84% of the participants - a statistically insignificant difference.' And, hibiscus tea is caffeine-free, rich in vitamin C and known to act as a natural body refrigerant in North Africa. All the more reason to enjoy in the summertime."

Makes 1 gallon

2 Celebration Herbal hibiscus tea bags
¾ C lemon juice (I use organic bottled)

1 tsp pure stevia extract
water to make 1 gallon total

Pour about 8 C boiling water over hibiscus tea bags. Steep at least 5 minutes. Add ¾ C lemon juice and 1 tsp pure stevia extract powder. Add water to make one gallon total. Chill.

You'll love both taste and color.

Variation #1: Replace hibiscus with your favorite fruit or berry tea bags (elderberry, perhaps?)
Variation #2: Use fizzy mineral water instead of water.
Variation #3: Roughly double stevia and lemon to make popsicles.

ROSY BEET RELISH

Beets have a wonderful way of normalizing the acid/alkaline balance, which in itself is a wonderful thing. When I was growing up, we ate beets because they make strong red blood cells.

I find them easy to grow in the garden, and I especially like beets in my garden because the bunny rabbits leave them alone. They look gorgeous with their dark, bright green tops!

Makes 8 C

3 lb beets, scrubbed and trimmed, about 6 C
2 red onions, peeled and diced, about 4 C
2 C honey or agave
3 Tbsp prepared horseradish

2 Tbsp pickling spices
2 C apple cider vinegar
1 tsp sea salt

Grate beets, skin and all, using the shredding disk of a food processor. (You can grate by hand, but it will take forever and your hands will blush from the rosy, red beets.)

Combine everything in a large saucepan. Mix well, cover and bring to a slow boil over medium heat. Then remove cover, lower flame to low, and simmer mixture until it thickens slightly and onions are soft, about 15 minutes.

Allow relish to cool and then spoon into glass jars to store in the refrigerator. This relish keeps for a few weeks.

Rosy Beet Relish the Raw Way

More beets. Beet remains have been found in excavated Egyptian pyramids, and charred beets were found in a Neolithic site in the Netherlands.

Makes 4 C

1½ lb beets, scrubbed and trimmed, 3 C
1 C red onion, peeled and diced
1 scallion, sliced, about ½ C
½ C lemon juice

2 Tbsp extra virgin olive oil (EVOO)
½ tsp allspice
1 tsp dill weed
1 tsp sea salt

Grate beets, skin and all, using the shredding disk of a food processor. (As before, you can grate by hand, but it will take forever and your hands will be red from the beets.)

Combine everything in a salad mixing bowl. Taste and adjust seasoning. Serve with just about anything from meats to cheeses to grain dishes and even tempeh!

Note: This raw beet relish is best the day it is made, but will last in the fridge for a few days.

SAFFRON GASTRIQUE WITH STEEL-CUT OATS

This yummy treat is from Amanda. Lucky you.

Wikipedia.com says that gastrique is a thick sauce produced by a reduction of vinegar or wine, sugar, and usually fruit. "It is often served over meat or seafood to add a fruit flavor to the dish."

Serves 2

4 C boiling water
1 C steel-cut oats
1 Tbsp coconut oil
1 tsp sea salt
½ C honey

½ C apple cider vinegar
1 pinch saffron threads
1 C diced fruit (optional—Amanda
likes bananas, mango or apple)

Bring water to a boil in a teakettle.

In a separate saucepan, toast the oats in the coconut oil, and then sprinkle with salt. When oats smell nutty and fragrant, pour the 4 C boiling water over them. Stir. The oats will start to thicken in about 1 minute. Turn heat to low and simmer oats for 30 minutes, stirring occasionally, only if you must, says Amanda.

To make the gastrique: In another pan, add the honey, vinegar and saffron. Slowly warm the mixture, stirring until honey becomes liquidy and saffron dissolves. Then cook on low for about 10 minutes to allow all the flavors to meld. Remove gastrique from heat and allow to cool.

If you're using fruit, dice now. To serve, spoon oatmeal in bowls, top with fruit and then drizzle gastrique over all.

Note: Gastrique keeps indefinitely in the fridge and is great on any sweet breakfast. For the more adventurous, try it on shrimp, lobster or even baked sweet potatoes.

SEASIDE SALAD DRESSING

Anne Shubert gave me this recipe years ago, which we ran in our June 2006 newsletter. So here's a zesty way to dress salad greens or shredded cabbage, carrots, radish and summer squash. Anne says to douse anything you like with this dressing, it's that good and that good for you!

Seaweed has always been a staple in the diet of people who live near the sea (okay, not so much for those of us who live in the Western Hemisphere...). According to Seibin and Teruko Arasaki, authors of *Vegetables from the Sea*, "All of the minerals required by human beings, including calcium, sodium, magnesium, potassium, iodine, iron and zinc, are present in sufficient amounts. In addition, there are many trace elements in seaweeds."

The calcium from seaweed is receiving a lot of attention these days, and as a supplement in tablet form is said to be the best usable calcium we can take.

Makes about 1½ C

⅔ C extra virgin olive oil (EVOO)
⅓ C raw apple cider vinegar
2 Tbsp tamari (soy sauce)
1 tsp kelp powder
1 tsp nori powder

1 tsp dulse powder
1 tsp umeboshi plum paste
1 or more tsp fresh ginger, chopped
1 or more tsp garlic, minced
1 tsp black or white pepper

Anne says to simply blend everything. For an instant salad, she uses her food processor to grate/shred any and all veggies, and then douses them with the dressing.

Note: We're not used to seaweed, but those sea veggies are so nutrient rich it's worth cultivating a taste for them. You don't have to use all three (kelp, nori and dulse). You can use what you have handy. And since you're blending, feel free to use a piece of dried kelp, or a part of a nori sheet. Same with dulse—break off a piece of the dried seaweed itself.

WHITE WINE HERB VINEGAR

In September 2006, Mary Kadlik and I went to the New Age Health Spa where we fell in love with the herbed vinegars made by their head gardener. He showed us how to simply put an assortment of herbs into Colavita white wine vinegar, then top the bottles with pour-ers. The process took 5 minutes, and he sold those bottles of beautiful herbed vinegar for *mucho dinero*. Want to make your own? Here's a basic recipe.

Makes about 6 C

1 17-oz bottle Colavita white wine vinegar
2 peeled, halved garlic cloves
1 branch fresh tarragon
1 sprig fresh thyme

2 sprigs fresh oregano
1 small stalk sweet basil
6 black peppercorns or 1 hot red pepper
6 raspberries* (frozen is fine)

Push everything into Colavita white wine vinegar (you may need to take some vinegar out so it won't overflow!). Push in herbs stems first, as if you were planting trees!

Don't worry if raspberries float initially.

Replace bottle cover with a pour-er (or not, if you don't care to use one).

Set aside for 2 weeks to steep.

Note: The vinegar has a shelf life of at least 1 year. Of course you can feel free to use different herbs.

* *Raspberries impart color and a touch of sweetness, and they are a nice counterpoint to pepper.*

RECIPES BY CHAPTER

Appetizers

Alyssa's Salmon Gravlax, 2

Baked Beets or Artichoke Hearts á la Orange, 3

Buckwheat Blinis with Mushroom Caviar by Amanda, 4

Chunky Chickpea and Spinach Appetizer with Roasted Peppers, 5

Coconut Oil Popcorn, 6

Donna's Kale-Avocado-Date Roll-Up, 7

Eggplant Cilantro Spread, 8

Greek Yogurt with Za'atar, 9

Guacamole with Lots of Garlic, 10

Kelley's Baked Kale Chips, 11

Marinated Mushrooms with Blue Cheese, 12

Mary's Fig and Goat Cheese Appetizer, 13

Mom's Stuffed Shrimp, 14

My Favorite Crudité Platter, 15

Pickled Vegetables for Finger Dipping, 16

Pumpkin Seed Tomatillo Dip, 17

Seviche by Alyssa, 18

Shiitake Mushrooms with Garlic, 19

String Beans and Eggs by Beatrice, 20

Stuffed Eggs with Watercress, 21

Tom's Shiitake Sushi, 22

Soups

Aaron's Peanut Soup, 24

Anasazi Pepita Potato Soup, 25

Ayurvedic Gingery Dal, 26

Butterbean and Green Bean Soup, 27

Catalan Tomato Soup, 28

Cold Beet and Potato Soup with Lemon and Crème Fraîche, 29

Garlicky Mexican Cheese Soup, 30

Georgian Red Lentil Soup, 31

Immune Boosting Soup, 32

Grandma's Mushroom Barley Soup, 34

Italian Plum and Blueberry Soup, 35

Kenyon's Calcium Soup with Beef Bones, 36

Mediterranean Cannellini and Lentil Soup, 37

Middle Eastern Cold Yogurt or Kefir Soup, 38

Moroccan Lentil Vegetable Soup, 39

Salads

Vegetables

Seafood

Little Breads and Muffins

Desktop

INDEX

CPSIA information can be obtained
at www.ICGtesting.com
Printed in the USA
FFOW02n0211101114
8594FF